CORNELIUS VAN TIL

An Analysis of His Thought

CORNELIUS VAN TIL

An Analysis of His Thought

JOHN M. FRAME

P&R
PUBLISHING
P.O. BOX 817 • PHILLIPSBURG • NEW JERSEY 08865-0817

Printed in the United States of America

Library of Congress Cataloging-in-Publication Data

Frame, John M., 1939–
Cornelius Van Til : an analysis of his thought / John M. Frame.
p. cm.
"Volume in celebration of Cornelius Van Til's one hundreth birthday, May 3, 1995"—
Includes bibliographical references and index.
ISBN 0-87552-245-9 (pbk.).—ISBN 0-87552-220-3 (cloth)
1. Van Til, Cornelius, 1895–1987. 2. Apologetics—History—20th century. 3. Presbyterian Church—Doctrines—History—20th century. 4. Reformed Church—Doctrines—History—20th century. 5. Theology, Doctrinal—History—20th century. I. Van Til, Cornelius, 1895–1987. II. Title.
BX9225.V37F74 1995
230'.51'092—dc20 95-34407

Contents

Preface

I submit this volume in celebration of Cornelius Van Til's one hundredth birthday, May 3, 1995. I trust that God will use it to draw public attention to this important thinker, to correct misunderstandings about him, and to help the Christian church make better use of his legacy.

This book is not a popularization or an introduction, but a serious, critical, analytical study. Nevertheless, I hope that it will be helpful to the work of introducing and popularizing Van Til's thought. One of the tasks I have set for myself is the job of translating and explaining Van Til's daunting terminology. I shall not avoid the use of philosophical and technical terms here, but when I do use them, I shall seek to explain them (both Van Til's and mine) in a way that will be understandable to most people who are capable of college-level study.

Some may find it helpful to read the last chapter first, for therein I summarize my conclusions and indicate the overall thrust of the book's argument.

This is not the last word on Van Til. I hope herein to further a genuine dialogue on his work, a dialogue that has heretofore been hindered by misinformation and poorly reasoned arguments for and against him. I am trying to go more deeply into Van Til's thought than have either his traditional friends or foes. If I have not succeeded, I pray that this book will provoke one or more successful alternative accounts with the same ambitions.

My thanks to those who have helped me in this study. Van Til's own teaching, of course, has been deeply formative, not only on the matters discussed here, but in all areas of my thought and life. I am also grateful for opportunities to interact with many colleagues, students, and others who are knowledgeable in Van Tillian matters: the names of Greg Bahnsen, Ed Clowney, Bill Edgar, John Gerstner, Jim Jordan, Scott Oliphint, Vern Poythress, Norman Shepherd, and Robert Strimple especially stand out in my mind. Thanks especially to Steve Hays, for a very thorough and brilliant critique of the first draft of this book, one from which I have profited in many ways, though I take full responsibility for the contents of the final version. My thanks also to Jim Scott for his editorial work. As to published sources, my bibliography and footnotes will indicate the great extent of my dependence on other thinkers.

My prayer is that God will use this volume to bring to his church a deeper obedience to his revealed Word, particularly in matters of the intellect, and to the world a more powerful presentation of Jesus Christ and him crucified.

Abbreviations of Frequently Cited Titles

For publication information, see the bibliography. Titles are by Van Til unless otherwise indicated.

AGG	*Apologetics to the Glory of God,* by John M. Frame
C67	*The Confession of 1967*
CA	*Christian Apologetics*
CB	*Christianity and Barthianism*
CC	*Christianity in Conflict*
CFC	*The Case for Calvinism*
CGG	*Common Grace and the Gospel*
CI	*Christianity and Idealism*
CJ	*Christ and the Jews*
CMT	*Christianity in Modern Theology*
CTETH	*Christian Theistic Ethics*
CTEV	*Christian-Theistic Evidences*
CTK	*A Christian Theory of Knowledge*
DCC	*The Defense of Christianity and My Credo*
DF1	*The Defense of the Faith* (original edition)
DF2	*The Defense of the Faith* (revised 1963 edition)
DKG	*The Doctrine of the Knowledge of God,* by John M. Frame

ECE *Essays on Christian Education*
GD *Is God Dead?*
GDT *The Great Debate Today*
GH *The God of Hope*
HDRA *Herman Dooyeweerd and Reformed Apologetics*
ICG *The Intellectual Challenge of the Gospel*
IST *An Introduction to Systematic Theology*
IW "Introduction" to Warfield, *The Inspiration and Authority of the Bible*
JA *Jerusalem and Athens,* edited by E. R. Geehan
NH *The New Hermeneutic*
NM *The New Modernism*
NRC *Notes on Roman Catholicism*
NS "Nature and Scripture," in *The Infallible Word,* edited by Ned B. Stonehouse and Paul Woolley
NST *The New Synthesis Theology of the Netherlands*
PDS *The Protestant Doctrine of Scripture*
PR *Psychology of Religion*
RP *The Reformed Pastor and Modern Thought*
SCE *A Survey of Christian Epistemology*
SG *The Sovereignty of Grace*
TG *The Triumph of Grace*
TJD *The Theology of James Daane*
VTDF *Van Til: Defender of the Faith,* by William White, Jr.
VTT *Van Til: The Theologian,* by John Frame
WIB *Why I Believe in God*
WSA *Who Do You Say That I Am?*
WTJ *Westminster Theological Journal*

PART ONE

Introductory Considerations

CHAPTER ONE

Starting Point

It is an enormous privilege for me to be able to write about Cornelius Van Til, who has been, after Scripture, the major theological influence upon me, and who is, in my estimation, the most important Christian thinker of the twentieth century. I have been criticized for using such superlatives to describe Van Til, but I intend to use them again, and to defend that use, in the present volume. In any case, and especially now, around the one hundredth anniversary of his birth (May 3, 1995), he should have a tribute—but also more than a tribute.

What I would offer him on this occasion is something that was in rare supply during his lifetime: sympathetic, comprehensive, critical analysis. To be sure, many have written articles and books on Van Til's work, and many of these are useful. But none of them, in my estimation, combines sympathy, comprehensiveness, and critical analysis.

SYMPATHY

Sympathy, of course, has abounded. There are a number of books and articles about Van Til that express agreement with his point of view. Many of these are excellent as introductions, popularizations, or paraphrases. Rousas J. Rushdoony's *By What Standard?*[1] presents Van

[1]Philadelphia: Presbyterian and Reformed, 1959.

Til's thought more systematically than Van Til himself ever did. George Marston's *The Voice of Authority*[2] presents Van Til's basic assertions very simply, but accurately. Richard Pratt's *Every Thought Captive*[3] skillfully presents Van Til's apologetic as a witnessing guide for young people.[4]

These sympathetic books (and the same could be said for many sympathetic articles) rarely take note of possible criticisms of Van Til, except insofar as they reproduce, often in Van Til's own terminology, his replies to objections. That very terminology is itself often problematic, and so this method is usually inadequate to deal with the difficulties. Furthermore, these authors themselves are not at all critical of Van Til. To say that is not to disparage their books and articles. They were written for purposes other than critical analysis, and for those purposes they are valuable.

Debunkers

However, Van Til has not missed the opportunity to receive negative criticism. The first book-length treatment of him was James Daane's *A Theology of Grace*,[5] which was a rather strange attempt to debunk Van Til's book *Common Grace*.[6] "Debunk" is the right word: Daane believes that Van Til's book is entirely wrongheaded. Others, though greatly differing with Daane as to their specific criticisms, have also taken the debunking route: Buswell, Montgomery, Pinnock, Robbins, Crampton. The book *Classical Apologetics*, by John Gerstner, R. C. Sproul, and Arthur Lindsley, is in a somewhat different category. It does show some genuine affection for Van Til; indeed, the book is dedicated to him. But the authors are quite convinced that Van Til's distinctive ideas are entirely wrong, and, in trying to show that, they present his ideas very misleadingly. Thus, I list them, too, among the debunkers.[7]

---

[2]Philadelphia: Presbyterian and Reformed, 1960; reprint, Vallecito, Calif.: Ross House Books, 1978.

[3]Phillipsburg, N.J.: Presbyterian and Reformed, 1979.

[4]I am less enthusiastic about Jim S. Halsey's *For a Time Such as This* (Nutley, N.J.: Presbyterian and Reformed, 1976), which tends to oversimplify and dogmatize, and which recommends most highly the weakest elements of Van Til's thought.

[5]Grand Rapids: Eerdmans, 1954.

[6]For my critique of Daane, see chap. 16. I shall discuss other critics of Van Til in later portions of this volume.

[7]Grand Rapids: Zondervan, 1984. My review of this book is reproduced as appendix A in this volume.

G. C. Berkouwer, too, although he had a somewhat gentler approach than the previously mentioned writers, was essentially a debunker.[8] Berkouwer never studied Van Til with the carefulness and precision that he gave to others (notably Barth), and therefore, in my estimation, he never understood much of what Van Til was all about. Although he never made the point in so many words, it would seem that he regarded the differences between Van Til and himself merely as symptoms of Van Til's scholarly incompetence.

Some of these debunkers, particularly Montgomery, Berkouwer, and *Classical Apologetics,* raise good questions, but their antipathy to Van Til's ideas prevents them, in my opinion, from presenting an accurate picture of his thought. Therefore, they are unable to deal with their own good questions in an illuminating way.

Analysis

Neither the sympathetic disciples not the debunkers present much valuable *analysis* of Van Til's thought. Analysis is the process by which a thinker's ideas are carefully scrutinized in detail and in depth to produce understanding of that thinker beyond the surface level. Analysis of Van Til would seek to develop more precise definitions of his terms and more explicit logical formulations of his arguments than he himself provides. It might also seek to evaluate carefully the consistency, rational adequacy, and, above all, the scriptural character of his ideas, recommending improvement (in statement or concept) where that appears necessary (in that sense I speak of "critical" analysis).

An anti–Van Tillian can do this up to a point, but, I am convinced, really incisive analysis of Van Til requires some level of commitment to his fundamental vision. Frankly, the debunkers always seem to miss the obvious. At least the sympathetic accounts take accurate note of the obvious. But sympathy alone is not sufficient for critical analysis, which seeks to advance beyond the obvious.

There have been some examples of sympathetic analysis in the Van Til literature. Thom Notaro's *Van Til and the Use of Evidence*[9] is not critical, but it is certainly analytical, in that it greatly clarifies cer-

[8]See the appendix on Van Til in Berkouwer's *The Triumph of Grace in the Theology of Karl Barth* (Grand Rapids: Eerdmans, 1956), 384–93, and his "The Authority of Scripture (A Responsible Confession)," in JA, 197–203.

[9]Phillipsburg, N.J.: Presbyterian and Reformed, 1980.

tain matters in Van Til that are widely misunderstood. The articles in *Foundations of Christian Scholarship,* edited by Gary North (Vallecito, Calif.: Ross House, 1976), similarly, do not find fault with Van Til (with the exception of my article), but they do illuminate Van Til's thinking and apply it to areas of life and thought that Van Til himself did not address. The same can be said of many other writings from advocates of the Christian reconstruction movement.

I have tried to engage in sympathetic (and therefore constructive) *critical* analysis of Van Til in my *Van Til: The Theologian* and more recently in "Cornelius Van Til"[10] and *Apologetics to the Glory of God.* The only other examples known to me are the articles by Gilbert B. Weaver[11] and Gordon R. Lewis[12] in *Jerusalem and Athens* and the book *Dominion and Common Grace* by Gary North.[13] Writers of the Dooyeweerdian school have also attempted this sort of interaction with Van Til,[14] but I find their critique extremely implausible, and therefore not illuminating.

Piecemeal Analysis

In my view, the kind of analysis that is most needed is that which takes Van Til's system apart, bit by bit, looking at its individual elements and evaluating them both individually and in the context of the whole. Van Til's writings may give the impression that this kind of analysis cannot be done, that no element of the system can be analyzed apart from the whole. Van Til himself regularly talks about his apologetic proving Christian theism "as a unit." The pedagogy of his writing style is to throw a great many ideas at the reader all at once,

---

[10]In Walter Elwell, ed., *Handbook of Evangelical Theologians* (Grand Rapids: Baker, 1993), 156–67.

[11]"Man: Analogue of God," in JA, 321–27.

[12]"Van Til and Carnell—Part I," in JA, 349–61.

[13]Tyler, Tex.: Institute for Christian Economics, 1987. I would commend this volume with some reservations, although I have some conflict of interest in doing so. The book is dedicated to me—with, to be sure, a good amount of tongue in cheek. More on that in a moment. I do not, however, recommend another book by North, *Westminster's Confession: The Abandonment of Van Til's Legacy* (Tyler, Tex.: Institute for Christian Economics, 1991), which I consider extremely confused.

[14]See, for example, in JA, Robert D. Knudsen, "Progressive and Regressive Tendencies in Christian Apologetics," 275–98, and Dooyeweerd, "Cornelius Van Til and the Transcendental Critique of Theoretical Thought," 74–89.

not pausing very long to explain any one of them. He emphasizes constantly that no part of the system can be understood or affirmed apart from the rest.

Van Til's interpreters tend to think, therefore, that one must either accept or reject his thought *in toto,* that one cannot pick and choose among its elements. This has contributed to the polarization in Van Tillian scholarship between adulators and debunkers. How can there be any middle way, anything other than total acceptance or total rejection, if the system is wired together as tightly as it appears to be?

The compacting of everything together in Van Til's thought has also made it hard for students to learn his system with any good level of understanding. For they have not received any systematic, progressive instruction that would insure that they understand proposition A before progressing to proposition B.

There can be no doubt that Van Til's thought forms a system. There is a high level of mutual dependence among its assertions. Nevertheless, Van Til himself resisted the extreme view of idealist philosophy that one must know the whole of something before one can know any of its parts. On Van Til's own view, there is in the created world an equal ultimacy of both universal and particular, and both whole and part, because there is an equal ultimacy of one and many in the ontological Trinity.

Despite the impression that Van Til's thought is a seamless robe, it seems to me not only possible, but also highly desirable, to look at its parts separately. I propose to do that in this volume. Of course, in doing so, we must guard the equal ultimacy of part and whole; we must constantly ask how each part affects the others and affects the totality. But with that caveat in mind, I propose to take Van Til's system apart, piece by piece, analyzing and evaluating each assertion in itself and in its relation to the whole.

My conclusion will be that, after all, Van Til's system is not a seamless robe. It is possible and necessary to accept some parts of it and to reject others. In my view, the most important parts of Van Til's system are biblical and should be maintained in any future apologetic. But some of his formulations are confusing and not biblically warranted. In my view, these are less central to Van Til's system. I grant, however, that opinions may differ as to what is most important. Indeed, my opinion on that matter may be different from Van Til's own. But, of course, opinions as to what is most important may themselves be of little importance.

Comprehensiveness

As I have pointed out, sympathetic, critical analysis of Van Til has been quite rare. And what there has been, as in the titles listed above by Weaver, Lewis, North, and Frame, has not been comprehensive, but rather has been limited to one or more specific matters. The present volume, then, is, to my knowledge, the first attempt to analyze all the basic elements of Van Til's thought from a sympathetic, yet critical, perspective. Certainly it is not exhaustive, nor is it any sort of ultimate or final statement. But it is important for us to get started on the task of developing a comprehensive understanding, evaluation, and application of Van Til's work, and I hope that this book will make a contribution to that end.

It is best that analysis be both piecemeal and comprehensive, thus maintaining the equal ultimacy of whole and part.

Criticism and Movement Leaders

But why do we need a *critical* analysis of Van Til? The answer to that question may be obvious to some, as it is to me. But to those within the Van Tillian "movement," the campaign to reform apologetics and the rest of human life according to Van Til's principles, the answer may not be so clear.

The movement mentality is different from the scholarly mentality, generally speaking. I was reminded of that when I first read Gary North's dedication in *Dominion and Common Grace,* addressed to me. The inscription reads:

This book is dedicated to

John Frame

an uncommonly gracious man,
who will no doubt conclude that
portions of this book are good,
other portions are questionable,
but the topic warrants further study.

First, my thanks to Gary for the kind words, and for the enjoyable irony. His prophecy is right on target, as is his characterization of my approach to issues.[15] In *Westminster's Confession,* he comments:

> Frame likes some aspects of theonomy, but he doesn't like others. *Sic et non* John strikes again! In the words of one professor at Covenant Seminary: "There have been three approaches to apologetics at Westminster Seminary. Van Til said that everyone else was wrong. Frame thinks that there are some correct things in everyone's system and some incorrect things. Poythress thinks that everyone is correct, from a certain point of view."[16]

North is a movement leader, the movement in his case being "theonomy" or "Christian reconstruction," and he has a typical movement mentality. Everyone, he thinks, should be either for him or against him, either hot or cold. Those who accept some of his ideas, but not others, are fence-sitters, lukewarm, wishy-washy. Jesus, of course, was a movement leader in this sense. He demanded wholehearted discipleship and condemned those who put their hand to the plow and looked back (Luke 9:62). Luther and Calvin had much of this spirit, since they perceived loyalty to the Reformation as a demand of Christian discipleship, nothing less. No doubt North feels the same way about theonomy.

But I tend to look at theonomy as a mixed blessing to the church, not as a movement that requires of me, on the authority of Christ, a wholehearted commitment. I look at theonomy in a more typically academic way, as a Christian scholar, seeking to separate wheat from chaff. Hence, I tend to be amazed that anyone should actually criticize me for liking some things and not liking other things. Is that not the essence of the theological task, to sort out the good and the bad? Does North seriously expect me to like everything about his movement? The fact is that the reconstructionists themselves, including North, do not like everything about their movement, for they are deeply divided on a number of issues.

Now there was always a kind of duality in Van Til: he was both a serious theological-philosophical scholar and a movement leader. That

---

[15]In correspondence I had said this sort of thing about a number of his ideas.

[16]Pp. 202–3. See also p. 242, n. 23. Of course, the comments about Van Til and Poythress should be taken with much more than a grain of salt. *Sic et Non* ("Yes and No") was a book by Peter Abelard that simply listed theological questions and arguments for each of the opposing answers to those questions.

duality has not been entirely unique in the history of thought: among Christian thinkers, consider Luther, Calvin, Kuyper, and Machen; on the non-Christian side, consider Marx, Freud, Darwin, Wittgenstein, and the contemporary gurus of political correctness and New Age thought.

But that duality in a thinker creates a certain tension among his followers and critics: do they treat him as a thinker or as a movement leader? Usually, we treat the two types of people rather differently. A thinker is subject to criticism from other thinkers. In the case of Cicero, or Irenaeus, or B. B. Warfield, or C. S. Lewis (to name some who are not generally regarded today as movement leaders), we take what we think is good and reject what we think is bad. But movement leaders, like Gary North, are different. Criticism of the leader can be regarded as disloyalty to the movement. Those outside the movement are not supposed to say anything good about the leader, while those in the movement are not supposed to say anything bad. The leader's ideas must be defended, even when such defense requires extreme mental gyrations.

The fact that most literature about Van Til is either wholly uncritical or wholly critical shows that most writers have looked at him more as a movement leader than as a serious scholar. There are exceptions: some on both sides have wrestled with his thought in a disciplined way. But that has not been typical.

I overstate the matter somewhat, but not by much. The authority of the leader of an intellectual movement (to say nothing of political movements like fascism and communism) can sometimes reach cultic proportions. Thomas Kuhn, in his *The Structure of Scientific Revolutions,*[17] comments on parallels between religious movements and followers of scientific "paradigms." He argues that such paradigms establish "communities" in which adherence to certain formulations becomes a credential of scientific competence, so that one cannot seriously question the theory and remain a member in good standing of the scientific community. Has not Darwinism in our day achieved a cult status, particularly in the educational community?

Now Van Til was—and still is, through his writings—the leader of a movement in theology, philosophy, and apologetics. I write as a committed member of that movement. I am not ashamed at its existence. I honestly wish that everyone would be converted to Van Til's

[17]Chicago: University of Chicago Press, 1962.

basic principles, for such conversion is to nothing other than consistent Christianity. Were everyone a Van Tillian at heart, our society would be vastly transformed, and that for the better. If there is justification for movements in politics, economics, science, or philosophy, then there is certainly far more justification for a movement seeking Van Tillian reformation of all of life. And it is not wrong for that movement to adopt informally some general criteria for membership in good standing. None of this implies, of course, that Van Til was right about everything.

That having been said, we do Van Til (and other Christian theologians) an injustice when we carry the movement mentality too far. For one thing, he was much more than the leader of a movement. He was also a thinker of extraordinary insight. Treating him as a kind of "guru" stifles open discussion of the issues he raises, and that impoverishes all of us, whether we are inside or outside the movement. And if, as members of the movement, we want to make the best possible use of Van Til's ideas, we must be able to distinguish what is best and what is worst in his formulations.

More important, it is significant that the great leaders of God's people in Scripture were never beyond criticism, except when they were divinely inspired. And even prophecy had to be tested to make sure that it agreed with past revelation (Deut. 18:21–22; Acts 17:11; 1 Cor. 14:37). "Test everything," says the apostle Paul (1 Thess. 5:21). Van Til himself has taught us that no theologian is exempt from such testing. Influenced as he was by such Reformed theological giants as B. B. Warfield, Abraham Kuyper, and Herman Bavinck, Van Til nevertheless sought to warn us against elements in their thinking that he deemed unscriptural.

Would Van Til have been pleased to see us evaluating his thought on the basis of Scripture, seeking to come to a position more fully scriptural than even his own? I believe he would have. He was not, of course, a highly self-critical person. When others offered him suggestions for improving his formulations, he did not often receive such suggestions gladly. Indeed, he had a tendency to react to criticism by reading the critic out of the movement: the critic was not to be heeded, because he presupposed Scholastic, Arminian, or Kantian premises, and that was all that needed to be said!

Still, I think that Van Til, like his disciples, felt somewhat the paradox of his being both a scholar and a movement leader. The authoritarianism of the general who leads his troops into intellectual warfare is not easily reconciled with the flexibility and self-critical attitude of the ideal scholar. Sometimes it seemed as though Van Til insulated himself against any kind of serious criticism.[18] But at other times, perhaps at another level of his consciousness, he certainly desired more constructive criticism, more of the "iron sharpening iron" of Proverbs 27:17, the "multitude of counselors" of Proverbs 11:14; 15:22; 24:6. Notice, for example:

1. In his advanced seminars, he tended to prod to greater participation those students whom he thought would raise challenging questions. I was one of those students.

2. He said to me at one point that his distinctive views on apologetics should not be made a test of orthodoxy in the churches. To be sure, it is arguable that he did make some of them into a test of orthodoxy during the controversy over Gordon H. Clark. Nevertheless, his comment indicates that, at least later in his life, he did believe there was room for critical discussion of his ideas among Reformed people.

3. Although he sought the support of others, he was privately a bit scornful of the "adulation" that he received from some of his disciples.

4. Although he trained his students to use his slogans and illustrations, he nevertheless hoped for more from them. He announced that students who merely echoed his slogans without exhibiting individual thought would get C's on their papers, while students who disagreed with him, but displayed careful scholarship and intelligent analysis, would receive higher grades.

5. My 1976 paper, *Van Til: The Theologian,* called for "constructive critical analysis" of Van Til.[19] He did not take offense at that; indeed, he arranged to have the paper published in booklet form.

6. In 1979 I published a review of William White's "authorized biography," *Van Til: Defender of the Faith.*[20] I noted some good things about the book, but I felt duty-bound as a reviewer also to point out that it contained some historical errors and presented a very confused picture of Van Til's thought. *Sic et non* John strikes again! I concluded with the following exhortation:

---

[18]See my discussion in chap. 2 about Van Til's isolation from the mainstream of theological debate.

[19]P. 5, n. 10.

[20]*WTJ* 42 (fall 1979): 198–203.

> But after one reads a book like this, one becomes more impressed with our *need* for a serious critical history of Van Til and his time. A serious historian would not have allowed so many unclarities and other problems to creep into the discussion. And he would have raised more hard questions. White's Van Til does almost nothing wrong (White does say he was "wrong to think of quitting school," 30), almost never even makes an unwise judgment. All his major problems were someone else's fault. There is a spirit of adulation here which detracts from the credibility of the book, even seen as a mere memoir. Whatever happened to biblical realism—the stories of Abraham, David, Paul? But that uncritical atmosphere is hard to escape in the memoir *genre*. Even Stonehouse's book on Machen, a far more scholarly and careful book than White's, breathes too much a spirit of filial piety. So far as I know, no one within the Westminster movement has actually taken a hard, tough-minded, historical look at that movement, at least in print. Why? Are we afraid of what we might find? . . . The book fails . . . as a serious *analysis* of Van Til's life and thought and it has many detailed failings. A revolutionary thinker like Van Til deserves a better tribute than this, I think—one which demands more of writer and reader, one which radically forces us to examine our most basic assumptions, even about Van Til. He has never asked less of himself, thank God.[21]

It was good to get that off my chest! But I confess that after it was published I did worry about what Van Til would think of me. After all, the book was his "authorized biography," and White was a good friend of his, who had never been enthusiastic about my teaching of apologetics.

White, by the way, was the most extreme of the movement-minded Van Tillians. His opinion of me is on record in an exchange of letters with me in *Journey Magazine*.[22] In this exchange he accused me of violating my ordination vows—not because I had contradicted

[21]P. 203.

[22]March–April 1988, 9–11; May–June 1988, 13; July–October 1988, 45–46; January–February 1989, 14–15, 22–23.

Scripture or any Reformed confession, and not even because I had uttered some disagreement with Van Til. Rather, White gave me this strong reproof because I had contradicted his assessment of how we should apply Van Til's insights to current issues. White's charge against me is found in his letter in the issue of May–June 1988. He thought that Van Til's thought forbade us to learn from non-Christians, or even from non-Reformed Christians. I disagreed—and I will defend my position in chapter 15 of this volume. White also objected to the fact that I had advocated proclaiming and teaching the Reformed faith without using traditional Reformed terminology. Had Van Til been living at the time, I believe he would have sided with me against White on that precise point. But White thought otherwise, and he asserted that I had broken my ordination vow because I differed with the positions he attributed to Van Til. White is in heaven now and knows better, I am sure. But his comments in these letters remain behind as extraordinary examples of a quite irrational movement mentality. Naturally, then, I was a bit fearful as to how Van Til would respond to the situation.

I was therefore as relieved as surprised when I received in California a letter from Van Til praising the review. I was even more surprised when I learned, after his death, that he had asked Grace Mullens at the Westminster Seminary library to place in his archive the *Journal* issue containing my review. His note to her included the following:

> But if you *really* want to know why I am so insistent that you put this issue of the W. T. J. in my archives look at page 198. What a model I am; John H. [*sic*] Frame turns honest actually, believe it or not, some serious flaws in his teacher i.e. C. V. T. But in general it is flattering—and does C. V. T. *love* it.[23]

I am not sure what he meant by the "serious flaws," since none are actually mentioned in the article, and other elements of the note (written by him at age 85, some years after he had ceased writing for publication) are not entirely perspicuous. But it does suggest to me that he was in essential agreement with my call for "constructive critical analysis" of his work.

---

[23]Emphasis his.

A Testimony

Some believe that personal reflections are out of place in academic scholarship. I have broken that rule already in this volume and will break it again. Certainly if there is any truth at all in presuppositionalism, it is important for a writer, especially a critical analyst, to let his readers know where he is coming from.

Van Til was raised and educated entirely among Reformed Christians until his doctoral program. Unlike him, I was converted to Christianity around age thirteen through the ministry of a church that, though confessionally Reformed, was only broadly evangelical in its working theology. And I am a product of secular education, except for my three years at Westminster Seminary from 1961 to 1964.

As a college student, I struggled with the usual intellectual issues, trying to relate my faith especially to the philosophical disciplines. I was helped somewhat by the traditional evidential apologists: Arthur Pierson's *Many Infallible Proofs,* Wilbur Smith's *Therefore, Stand,* John Gerstner's *Reasons for Faith.* During this time, I also learned much from John Gerstner himself, who spoke often at youth conferences in the Pittsburgh area. He strongly influenced my theology in a Reformed direction. But it was C. S. Lewis's writings that first enabled me to see that there were deep worldview differences, philosophical differences, between Christians and non-Christians.

Then I began to hear about Van Til. In college I was a member of a campus Christian group called the Princeton Evangelical Fellowship. The PEF members were mostly dispensational in theology and somewhat anti-intellectual; they were not happy with my choice of philosophy as a major. But they were also quite in awe of certain Reformed writers: Warfield, Machen, Van Til. I read some Warfield and a lot of Machen (*Christianity and Liberalism* set me on a lifetime course of sharp opposition to theological liberalism in all its forms). And it was Van Til who set me on a clear course through the philosophical waters. I used his approach in my term papers and senior thesis, somewhat to the bewilderment of my professors; they had, I am sure, never seen anything like that before. I was amazed to find that the same Bible that presents the message of salvation also presents a distinctive philosophy, including metaphysics, epistemology, and ethics, one which alone makes sense of human life. Van Til's work encouraged me to take an offensive, rather than merely defensive, stance against non-Christian thought.

Studying with Van Til at Westminster was a wonderful, mind-expanding experience. Van Til's erudition in the philosophical and theological literature exceeded that of any of my professors at Princeton, as did the depth of his penetrating analysis. He was simply the most profound scholar I had ever known, and his very presence refuted claims that secularism was the only intelligent option. And he was not only the most profound scholar I had known, but also one of the most distinctively Christian—refuting the dictum that the more scholarly a Christian is, the more he compromises his faith.

Communication between Van Til and myself was not always easy. His philosophical vocabulary was that of idealism; mine was that of Anglo-American language analysis. He was steeped in Reformed, especially Dutch Reformed, literature and tradition; I was not. Once I served as a waiter at a dinner for scholars at the church across from the seminary. I brought some food to a table where Van Til was seated with some other men. He turned away from his conversation, looked directly at me, and said, out of the blue, "From now on, I'm going to speak only Dutch to you; then you'll learn it!" I suspect he believed that nobody could do really profound theology in the Reformed tradition without mastering that "language of the angels." Some years later, I did acquire some reading knowledge of Dutch, but never to the extent that he had perhaps hoped.

Van Til equated the Reformed creeds very closely with the teaching of Scripture and was very suspicious of any terminology or ideas that came from outside the Reformed tradition. I was, and am, more ecumenical in spirit.[24] He seemed to find his greatest delight in the doctrines that are distinctive to the Reformed faith; I, on the other hand, take my greatest delight in those doctrines which all Christians share (as defined by the Nicene-Constantinopolitan Creed of 381), although I also treasure the distinctively Reformed doctrines as the most biblically consistent way of formulating and elaborating those teachings. Van Til tended to put the worst possible construction on the statements of non-Reformed writers; I tend to give them more of the benefit of the doubt. In my view, Van Til was something of a Reformed chauvinist; in his view, I was too friendly to broad evangelicalism. Van Til never actually said that God had given all the truth to one theological tradition, but that seemed to be his working assumption. It was not, and still is not, mine.

---

[24]See my *Evangelical Reunion* (Grand Rapids: Baker, 1991).

Van Til was not good at answering my questions, particularly questions asking for precise definitions, syllogistic formulations of arguments, and the like. He tended to avoid those questions, preferring to reiterate his oft-stated positions at length. I learned quickly that in order to profit from Van Til's teaching, a student had to let him set the agenda. If readers of this book want to know whether I, as Van Til's student and colleague, asked him the sorts of questions I ask in this book, the answer is: yes, I did, but he was not able, in my opinion, to respond adequately to them.

And, of course, there was the problem of relating to Van Til as a movement leader. I am not a movement person. Although I understand the need for reformation in the church at various times, and therefore the need for reformation movements, I must balance this against Paul's condemnation of party spirit in 1 Corinthians. As I suggested earlier, I am not ashamed to be part of the Van Tillian movement, but I resist the extreme development of a movement mentality in those circles.

Van Til's classes, however, were as much movement boot camps as they were graduate courses. Students who asked too many hard questions were sometimes (prematurely in my opinion) dismissed as Arminian or worse. I was never much interested in playing this game. So my term papers for Van Til's courses were somewhat lacking in the usual Van Tillian sloganizing. I used my own vocabulary and developed ideas in my own way. They were Van Tillian in content, for the most part, but they did not sound much like Van Til, and they sometimes raised serious questions about his formulations. He was, for some years, a bit suspicious of me on that account. When I returned to Westminster to teach, it was not at his initiative or in his department, but at the initiative of Professor Norman Shepherd to teach systematic theology. Nevertheless, Van Til invited me to teach Th.M.-level courses in apologetics on the subject of analytic philosophy. Nor was I Van Til's choice to teach the introductory apologetics course when he retired from it in 1972; Harvie Conn succeeded him in that responsibility. But when Conn dropped his apologetics teaching in 1975 to concentrate on missions, Van Til had no objection to my teaching the course.

So on I went, somewhat at the edge of his circle. As I indicated earlier, he later commended me in various ways, but we were not personally close friends.

I came into conflict with some of the more extreme "movement

Van Tillians," such as Jim Halsey[25] and William White.[26] The "movement Van Tillians" were personally closer to Van Til than I was, but by that time Van Til was in his eighties and nineties and somewhat above the battle. He encouraged both them and me on various occasions.

I have decided to be open with my readers about all of this. There are different kinds of Van Tillians, and not all of them will like this book. But I do still believe that the movement itself will benefit more from embracing a critical-analytical approach than from excluding it. And thus I proclaim myself a loyal Van Tillian, although I reject the view that Van Til's ideas should have confessional[27] or deuterocanonical status.

More importantly, my ultimate allegiance, like Van Til's, is to the Christ of Scripture. Not to scholarly canons of respectability, but to God's rules for thought. Not to any human tradition or movement, but to God's Word. Not to any human means of self-salvation, but to the grace of God in Christ. As with Van Til, these commitments place me in opposition to all the idols that people put in God's place, notably the idol of human intellectual, metaphysical, or moral autonomy. This is the ultimate presupposition of my heart and thought.

---

[25]Note some of my comments about Halsey in DKG.

[26]In the review mentioned above.

[27]The "Recommended Curriculum for Ministerial Preparation in the Orthodox Presbyterian Church" (in *The Book of Church Order*) includes "the school of Van Tilian presuppositionalism as the most biblically faithful expression of Reformed apologetics."

CHAPTER TWO

Van Til's Life and Character[1]

Cornelius Van Til was born on May 3, 1895, in Grootegast, Holland, the sixth son of Ite Van Til, a dairy farmer, and his wife, Klazina.[2] At the age of ten he moved with his family to Highland, Indiana. He picked up English quickly, and most would testify that he spoke thereafter without an accent, although he always retained a nuance common to the midwestern Dutch immigrant communities.

The first of his family to receive a formal higher education, he began in 1914 to attend the Calvin Preparatory School in Grand Rapids, Michigan, where he remained to study at Calvin College and (for one year) at Calvin Theological Seminary. These institutions were all schools of Van Til's denomination, the Christian Reformed Church, which was made up mostly of Dutch immigrants like himself. But after his first year of seminary, Van Til transferred to Princeton Theological Seminary. In those days, Princeton was an orthodox Calvinistic school, as was Calvin, and there was much mutual respect between the two; but Princeton's roots were in Ameri-

[1]Most of the following is adapted from my "Cornelius Van Til" in Walter Elwell, ed., *Handbook of Evangelical Theologians* (Grand Rapids: Baker, 1993). It is used by permission.

[2]The biographical information here is (except for some items of personal knowledge) taken from VTDF.

can Presbyterianism, rather than in the Dutch Reformed tradition represented by Calvin.

Van Til was also admitted to Princeton University[3] as a graduate student of philosophy, and he was awarded a doctorate in philosophy after completing his seminary work. In 1925 he completed a Th.M. at the seminary. The following September he married his childhood sweetheart, Rena Klooster, and in 1927 he completed his Ph.D.

Influences

At Calvin, Van Til studied with Louis Berkhof, Samuel Volbeda, and others who led him to a rich appreciation of the Dutch Reformed tradition. He appreciated especially Abraham Kuyper (1837–1920), an incredibly brilliant and productive Christian leader, who founded the Free University of Amsterdam, edited a daily newspaper, led a Christian political party (serving briefly as prime minister of the Netherlands), all the while teaching a vivid and vigorous Reformed theology creatively applied to many disciplines usually considered "secular." His great message was: Christ is Lord over all areas of human life; every thought and every discipline must be brought captive to his rule.[4]

In systematic theology more narrowly understood, Van Til's chief resource was Herman Bavinck, a contemporary and colleague of Kuyper, who produced a monumental four-volume work in dogmatics.[5]

At Princeton, Van Til became a close friend of Geerhardus Vos, a professor at the seminary, like himself a Dutch immigrant who had left Grand Rapids for Princeton. Vos brought to Princeton the discipline of biblical theology, which sought to understand Scripture as a history of redemption. Vos's field, therefore, was rather far removed from Van Til's eventual area of specialization. Indeed, Van Til was later to endure the criticism that his work was insufficiently exegeti-

---

[3]Princeton University and Princeton Seminary have always been separate institutions.

[4]See Kuyper's *Principles of Sacred Theology* (Grand Rapids: Eerdmans, 1954), and especially his *Lectures on Calvinism* (Grand Rapids: Eerdmans, 1970).

[5]Most of it has not been translated into English, but *The Doctrine of God,* trans. and ed. William Hendriksen (Grand Rapids: Baker, 1977) represents most of vol. 2.

cal. But one can easily find places in Van Til's writings where he seems to be trying to be like Vos, building a biblical-theological base for his apologetics.[6] Van Til's preaching and much of his classroom teaching also contained a great deal of biblical theology: he would trace our epistemological predicament, for example, from the Garden of Eden to the judgments of Revelation.[7]

Van Til arrived in Princeton too late to study with B. B. Warfield, arguably the greatest theological scholar America has produced, who had died in 1921. But Warfield's name was legendary during Van Til's student days, and Van Til respected him deeply, as well as Warfield's predecessor, the great Princeton theologian of the previous century, Charles Hodge.

Van Til was also influenced by various philosophical thinkers and movements. At Calvin his most famous teacher was W. Henry Jellema, who was once described by Paul Weiss, a well-known non-Christian philosopher, as "the best teacher of philosophy in the United States." Jellema himself had studied with the Harvard idealist Josiah Royce, and he may therefore have motivated Van Til to study idealism at Princeton. Van Til's doctoral thesis advisor at Princeton University was A. A. Bowman, whose sympathies were also with idealism and the developing "personalist" movement. As did James Orr, with whose writings Van Til's apologetics shows some affinity, Van Til made liberal use of the idealist philosophical vocabulary ("concrete universal," "one and many," "absolute system," "eternal novelty," "limiting concept," "logic" [as a general term for "methodology"], the contrast between "implication" and "linear inference,"[8] and even "presupposition"). Nonetheless, Van Til always insisted that he rejected the substantive content of idealism, which identified the Creator with the creature and made both of them subject to one another within an impersonal universal structure.[9]

Clearly, the most important philosophical influences on Van Til, like the theological influences on him, were, unlike idealism, distinc-

---

[6]See especially CGG and CTETH.

[7]He had a special affection for the book of Revelation. He preached through it during his early pastorate, and after he had retired from active teaching and scholarship, he spent many of his hours preparing sermons on it.

[8]Van Til rarely spoke, as did the idealists, of "linear inference," preferring to distinguish "implication" from "deductivism" or "logical penetration." Yet the contrast certainly brings the idealist language to mind.

[9]For his critique of idealism, see especially CI and SCE.

tively Christian. Kuyper himself urged that all human thought be governed by a Christian worldview derived from Scripture. To Kuyper, this worldview was antithetical to every secular ideology, whether that be philosophical, theological, political, economic, aesthetic, or whatever. Some of Kuyper's disciples sought to bring that Christian worldview to bear on politics, some on education, some on journalism, and so on. Naturally, some sought to express it in philosophy as well. Thus, in the 1920s Herman Dooyeweerd, D. Th. Vollenhoven, and others in the Netherlands founded a philosophical school of thought called the Philosophy of the Idea of Law.[10] Van Til says that he had already developed his approach independently before his contact with the Dutch philosophy.[11] Certainly there are many similarities, but there are also important differences. At any rate, Van Til wrote favorably about their early work, and they, in turn, named him as an editor of their journal, *Philosophia Reformata*. Although Van Til later became critical of this group,[12] he was always aware of the developments among them. Surely, then, at least in a broad sense, we must describe the Dooyeweerdian school as one significant influence on Van Til's thought, at least after the mid-1930s.

Career

After his graduation in 1927, Van Til spent one year as pastor of a Christian Reformed Church in Spring Lake, Michigan, a work he deeply enjoyed. He took a leave of absence from that pastorate to teach apologetics at Princeton Seminary during the academic year 1928–29. The seminary offered him the chair of apologetics (in effect, a full professorship) at the end of that period, but he turned down the offer and returned to Spring Lake. He was strongly inclined to remain in the pastorate, and he did not wish to cooperate in the reorganization of Princeton Seminary mandated that spring by the General Assembly of the Presbyterian Church, U.S.A., which controlled the institution. That reorganization was intended to purge the seminary's historic stand for orthodox Calvinism and make it more

[10]It is also known as the Philosophy of the Cosmonomic Idea, the Amsterdam philosophy, Dooyeweerdianism, reformational philosophy, etc.

[11]SCE, iii.

[12]I discuss Van Til's criticisms of the movement in chap. 27 of this book.

representative of "all the points of view found in the church." Those points of view included those of 1,300 or so ministers who in 1924 had signed the notorious Auburn Affirmation, which declared such doctrines as biblical inspiration, the virgin birth of Christ, his substitutionary atonement, his bodily resurrection, and his literal second coming to be humanly formulated "theories" and not required beliefs for ministerial candidates.

However, there were those in the Presbyterian Church, U.S.A., who fought against the growing unbelief in the denomination and in the church at large. The most notable of these was J. Gresham Machen, a professor of New Testament at Princeton Seminary. Van Til did not study under Machen, but knew him well and admired his scholarship, his ability to articulate the truth, and his stand for orthodox doctrine.[13] Machen must be added to our earlier list of men who influenced Van Til, for most everything Van Til wrote and taught reflected the Machen themes: Christian orthodoxy is indispensable to a Christian profession; there is a great gulf, a religious antithesis, between orthodox Christianity and its liberal opponents. The great doctrines of the faith are not human inventions, but the teachings of God himself to us in his Word. You cannot claim to be a Christian while rejecting the teachings of Christ in Scripture. Indeed, Van Til went one step beyond Machen, seeking to show (as we shall see) that orthodox Christian doctrine is, in one sense, necessary for all human rational thought and conduct.

In response to the General Assembly's reorganization of Princeton Seminary, Machen, together with other seminary faculty members (Robert D. Wilson and Oswald T. Allis), determined to start a new seminary, independent of Assembly control, which could continue to give students orthodox instruction in the tradition of Warfield, Vos, and Hodge. Younger men were added to the faculty (R. B. Kuiper, Ned Stonehouse, Allen MacRae, and Paul Woolley), and Machen was eager to obtain Van Til's services in the area of apologetics. Van Til was enormously reluctant to leave Spring Lake, but after much correspondence and personal visits by Allis, Stonehouse, and Machen himself, Van Til, several days before the opening exercises, accepted the offer. Westminster Theological Seminary opened its

[13]Machen's *Christianity and Liberalism* (New York: Macmillan, 1923; reprint, Grand Rapids: Eerdmans, 1946) is still, in my judgment, the best argument that orthodox doctrine is indispensable to a Christian profession.

doors in Philadelphia in the fall of 1929, and Van Til remained on the faculty until his retirement in 1972. From then until around 1979, he taught there on an occasional and part-time basis.

In 1936 Machen and others were suspended from the ministry of the Presbyterian Church, U.S.A., for their unwillingness to resign from an independent missions board that Machen had organized. The independent board represented conservative dissatisfaction with the official missions board, which tolerated liberal (Auburn Affirmation–style) teaching among its missionaries. Machen and others did not accept this church discipline; among other irregularities, the ecclesiastical court had not permitted him to make a scriptural case for his conduct. Rather, Machen and other ministers totaling 130 founded a new denomination, originally called the Presbyterian Church of America,[14] but later forced to change its name under legal threat. Eventually, the body named itself the Orthodox Presbyterian Church. In sympathy with Machen, Van Til transferred his membership from the Christian Reformed Church to the Orthodox Presbyterian Church, where he remained until his death in 1987.

Machen died of pneumonia in 1937. Van Til, Stonehouse, Murray, and Woolley became full professors at the seminary and sought to hold the work together without Machen's leadership. In 1937 there was also a split within the Presbyterian Church of America. Some ministers and churches left to form the Bible Presbyterian Church. A corresponding division occurred at the seminary, in which Professor Allen MacRae and a group of students left to begin Faith Theological Seminary in Philadelphia. The controversy was over dispensationalism, "Christian liberty" (the legitimacy of the Christian's use of alcoholic beverages), and the vague feeling among the departing members that the new movement was becoming too Dutch, that it was losing its roots in American Presbyterianism. Van Til remained with the Presbyterian Church of America and with Westminster. The church and the seminary went through much difficulty and controversy (see chap. 8 on the Clark controversy). Nevertheless, they have both endured to the present, by God's grace.

As it turned out, Machen was an excellent judge of theological talent. The young professors developed reputations as outstanding scholars and teachers, even among many who strongly disagreed

[14]This should not be confused with the Presbyterian Church *in* America, which was founded in 1973 and which still bears that name.

with their theology. As for Van Til, nobody could question his credentials or his enormous expertise in philosophy, theology, and apologetics.

PUBLICATIONS

Van Til's first major work, *The New Modernism: An Appraisal of the Theology of Barth and Brunner,* appeared in 1946.[15] This was followed by *Common Grace*[16] the following year. *The Defense of the Faith* was issued in 1955, the first complete public presentation of his distinctive apologetic system (incorporating much of his basic unpublished syllabus, "Apologetics"), with answers to his critics. After he taught at Calvin Seminary for one semester in 1952, a number of articles attacking his positions appeared in the *Calvin Forum.* In 1954 James Daane, a Christian Reformed minister, wrote a whole volume critical of Van Til, *A Theology of Grace.* Earlier, J. Oliver Buswell had written a very negative review of Van Til's *Common Grace* in his publication, *The Bible Today.* Van Til addressed both Buswell and the Daane–*Calvin Forum* group in the original edition of *The Defense of the Faith.* In 1963 the book was released again in an abridged form, leaving out most of the debate between Van Til and his critics.

In 1964 Van Til published his second major critique of Barth, *Christianity and Barthianism.* (The title is intentionally reminiscent of Machen's *Christianity and Liberalism.*)

A Christian Theory of Knowledge appeared in 1969, a somewhat expanded version of the syllabus of the same name, incorporating some of the debate between Van Til and his critics left out of the second edition of *The Defense of the Faith.* In the late 1960s and the 1970s, Van Til seems to have lost much of his reserve about publishing. A great many books came out in rapid succession, including: *The Confession of 1967, Is God Dead? The Sovereignty of Grace, Christ and the Jews, The God of Hope, The Reformed Pastor and Modern Thought, The New Hermeneutic, The New Synthesis Theology in the Netherlands,* and so on. These books applied Van Til's insights to many current theological issues, but did not add anything substantial to his theological and

[15]All of Van Til's books were published by Presbyterian and Reformed Publishing Company.

[16]More recently published as the first section of CGG.

apologetic concepts. See the bibliography for brief statements about the content or value of these books.

Of the books still considered unpublished syllabi, the most important are *Christian Apologetics, Introduction to Systematic Theology, Christian-Theistic Evidences,* and *Christian Theistic Ethics.* His earliest syllabus, which dates back to 1929 in its original form, was reissued in the 1970s as *A Survey of Christian Epistemology*—still an "unpublished syllabus."

Of his many booklets, one deserves special notice, *Why I Believe in God.*[17] This is perhaps the only writing of Van Til's actually directed toward an unbeliever.

Van Til also published a great many articles and reviews. A complete bibliography of his works up until 1971 can be found in *Jerusalem and Athens,* edited by E. R. Geehan.

If you would like to get a good introduction to Van Til's own writings, begin with "My Credo,"[18] which includes Van Til's own six-page outline of his position, and the booklet *Why I Believe in God,* which shows how he would use his apologetics in an actual encounter with an unbeliever. Then look at the main book-length expositions of his general position. In my judgment, the most basic of these are *Christian Apologetics,*[19] *Introduction to Systematic Theology,* and *A Christian Theory of Knowledge.* Van Til's "Introduction" to B. B. Warfield's *Inspiration and Authority of the Bible*[20] is also an excellent and relatively brief overview of his thought. The next step is to investigate some of his ideas on more specific matters, by reading in his *Christian-Theistic Evidences, Christian Theistic Ethics,* and *Common Grace and the Gospel.* Then read in *Jerusalem and Athens* to get Van Til's interactions with his critics. The most interesting responses to Van Til in that volume are, as I suggested earlier, those of Gilbert Weaver, Gordon Lewis, and John Warwick Montgomery. The rest of Van Til's writings deal mainly with specific thinkers and topics; peruse them according to your own interests. Van Til's most impressive scholarship deals with the theol-

---

[17]Philadelphia: Committee on Christian Education, Orthodox Presbyterian Church, n.d.

[18]Found in JA, RP, and DCC.

[19]Or, alternatively, DF1 or DF2. These are expanded versions of CA. CA is more concise, with fewer illustrations and digressions.

[20]Philadelphia: Presbyterian and Reformed, 1948; reprint, Grand Rapids: Baker, 1960.

ogy of Karl Barth and can be found in *The New Modernism, Christianity and Barthianism,* and in a number of booklets.

PERSONALITY

Van Til was gracious and charming in person. Some perceived this as a paradox, since his writings often dealt so harshly with his opponents. He could spend as much time with simple people as with brilliant intellectuals. He would regularly visit sick friends in hospitals and minister to others in the hospital rooms, engaging them in conversation and prayer. He was generous with his time and resources—often being willing to preach in small, struggling churches and nursing homes, often sending out syllabi at his own expense to correspondents. When people from outside the seminary visited his class, he often simplified his lecture greatly for their benefit.

Van Til had a sometimes wild sense of humor, as did Machen. Here are a few examples:

1. He sometimes threw chalk at students whom he perceived to be naughty for one reason or another.

2. Jake Eppinga reports that Van Til used to offer sticks of licorice to students and friends. Eppinga hitchhiked to Philadelphia to attend Westminster, and providentially Van Til himself picked him up to drive him the last ten miles. Van Til invited him to dinner, and afterward they had licorice together. After a while, Van Til stuck out his tongue and asked Eppinga how black it was.

3. Walter Stoll, custodian of the grounds and buildings, would occasionally sneak into Van Til's classroom before class began and draw a circle on the board. Van Til took that as a challenge, for he always taught that a Christian worldview should be represented by *two* circles (for Creator and creature), clearly distinct from one another, with the larger one (representing God) on top. *One* circle alone referred to the non-Christian worldview, in which man and God (if he exists) are on the same level, part of one reality. So Van Til would mockingly grab Stoll by the neck and make him draw a second circle.

4. I recall sitting in a car with Van Til and some other people, listening to him do a hilarious impression of Frank Fontaine's "Crazy Guggenheim" from the *Jackie Gleason Show*.

5. Occasionally, when the bell rang to end class, Van Til would stop his lecture in mid-sentence.

6. He liked to mention that the name Van Til in Dutch has the same meaning as DuPont in French ("from the bridge"). He said that one day he would visit the DuPonts in Delaware to get his share of the family fortune.

7. He regularly satirized the pretensions of unbelief: "Nobody knows what is true, but of course you are wrong and I am right." The unbeliever, he said, is like a child slapping her daddy while she is supported by his lap. He is like a thief who walks into a private home, ignores all the signs that the property belongs to its owner, and proceeds to carry off the merchandise, later protesting that he did not realize it belonged to somebody else.

8. He enjoyed mocking the pretensions of liberal theologians, especially Germans. Friedrich Schleiermacher was known as "Freddy" in Van Til's lecture, after he wrote out the theologian's name in longhand across two blackboards. One of his exams consisted entirely of an analysis of *Anknüpfungspunkt* (point of contact). He merely walked into class and wrote the word in long letters from one end of the long blackboard to the other. He imitated the liberal theologian fudging on his unorthodoxy: "I'm just saying the same thing as the tradition *mit ein bißchen andern Worten* [in slightly different words]."

9. He was not above ethnic humor, sometimes even at the expense of his own Dutch countrymen. One joke: "A Dutchman is the only one who can buy from a Jew, sell to a Scot, and still make a profit."

Van Til was an amazingly productive scholar, as is evident from the sheer number of his publications and the high quality of thought exhibited in them. Yet he was not ungenerous with his time. He preached often in the churches, spent hours talking to students—often on long walks around and around Machen Hall on the Westminster campus—and was regularly available to speak on college campuses. Once he preached on Wall Street in New York—in the open air. In his later years, he often agreed to preach at services in nursing homes, without reimbursement, and with an audience that was inattentive at best.

He also spent much time on class work. When I was his student, there were two required apologetics courses in the first year, two semester hours apiece. For each of those courses, Van Til assigned two term papers. When a student asked how long they should be, Van Til casually replied, "Oh, longer than anything you've ever written before." The scuttlebutt was that a paper would not be considered for the highest grades unless it was at least fifty pages long, though Van Til reassured us that he had once given an A to an eight-page essay; I am told that the average paper was around thirty-five pages. The rumor was that Van Til graded papers by weight, specifically by throwing them down the stairs to see how far down they would fall.[21]

Students often wondered whether Van Til actually read the papers. Several times students put a note like this halfway through their papers: "Dear Dr. Van Til: If you have read this far, I will treat you to an ice cream soda." Van Til regularly took them up on these proposals. Indeed, many student papers received extensive written comments. But consider this: there were regularly thirty or so students in class, each writing two thirty-five-page papers. That totals 1,050 pages, more or less, that he had to read—plus at least one mid-term and one final exam. And that was for only one course. Truly, we students considered Van Til a glutton for punishment.

His habits of hard work were perhaps remnants of his life in the Dutch-American farming community where he grew up. He could, I think, have been happy as a farmer. Once he confided to me that "I am not a scholar by temperament." He loved the out-of-doors, and his long walks and gardening may have helped to keep him healthy into his nineties. But he did choose the discipline of theological scholarship. And those habits of long days and hard work certainly rendered fruitful his scholarly efforts, as they might have brought forth literal fruit from the soil.

Teaching Style

Van Til never took long to impress his students with the brilliance of his mind and his encyclopedic knowledge of philosophy and theology.

As to his communication skills, perhaps the jury is still out. His preaching was very eloquent and challenging; in some ways, how-

[21]As a student, I mocked those rumors by making my first paper 125 pages (including a few sections, acknowledged of course, from my college senior thesis); my other papers were exactly fifty pages, though I fudged a bit on the last one: there were forty-nine pages of text; I added a blank page and numbered it fifty. My 125-page term paper got people talking, and I may have that to thank for my eventual teaching position at Westminster.

ever, his preaching was better than his teaching. His teaching method was to assign his students reading in some basic written lectures of his ("unpublished syllabi"[22]) and in the writings of others, and then to conduct class mostly by discussion, punctuated by ad hoc lectures on various topics that came up. The discussion proceeded very fast, it seemed, considering that many of the students had no philosophical (and little theological) background. Van Til would write names and concepts on the board, usually just the first few letters of each word; at times the pace was dizzying. He rarely defined his concepts precisely. When students asked for definitions and tried to reduce his arguments to logical sequence, Van Til usually resisted. What he preferred in such cases was to back up and start over, using essentially the same language he had used before. He seemed to think that regular saturation in his ideas would cause them to enter the students' minds by a kind of osmosis.

Brighter students often found it difficult to engage him in a real give-and-take discussion. Van Til encouraged questions in class, but he tended to answer them in long monologues that often did not engage the specific questions. I asked him once what I thought was a fairly simple technical point, which I expected him to answer in about fifteen seconds. He replied, "To answer that, we must go back to the Garden of Eden." He did, and proceeded from Genesis to Revelation and from Thales to Existentialism. Eventually I forgot my question entirely.

Van Til had ways of intimidating questioners. He overwhelmed them with erudition, for one thing. For another, he often took on a kind of preaching mode, in which every intellectual issue became a matter of loyalty to the Scriptures and the Reformed standards, and any deviation became a concession to non-Christian thought. Van Til did not require students to agree with him. Many non–Van Tillian students got good grades. But Van Til always seemed to be doing his best to make them feel guilty. This was Van Til the movement leader.

---

[22]This "unpublished" business was something of a joke among the students. The books were, in fact, available to all; they were sold by mail-order companies and in bookstores, and Van Til himself was most generous in sending them out to people who asked him questions. We students quoted them freely in our term papers, without any objection from our teacher. Still, Van Til was rather modest about these syllabi—perhaps being aware of his limitations as a writer—and he insisted on labeling them "unpublished."

These difficulties in his pedagogy were partly responsible, I think, for the fact that Van Til found few candidates to succeed him. Many Westminster students graduated as enthusiastic Van Tillians, but among them were few serious scholars and thinkers. The more serious scholars among his students, like John Gerstner, Edward J. Carnell, and, in my seminary class, Donal Nilsson, tended to move away from Van Til's position.

Van Til did have a great knack for illustrations and slogans—reducing complex ideas to homely, familiar dimensions. Reminiscent of his love for farming, he told stories to his classes about chickens and cows. And from carpentry: the unbeliever's mind is like a buzz saw that works very efficiently but in the wrong direction.[23] Or: the unbeliever, trying to make sense of the universe on the basis of chance, is like a man made of water trying to climb out of the water on a ladder made of water.[24] The unbeliever is prejudiced about everything, like a man with yellow glasses cemented to his face; and "all is yellow to the jaundiced eye."[25] His attempt to understand the world is like someone trying to put beads on a string with no holes in the beads.[26] His concepts of "law" and "regularity" attempt hopelessly to find rational connections between events of pure chance, like a "turnpike in the sky."[27] The Arminian apologist, Mr. Grey, is like a dentist who only wants to remove *part* of the tooth decay.[28]

Students tended to latch on to these illustrations and short formulations (such as "the point of contact is deep within the natural man"[29]) and would begin to *feel* that they had understood Van Til. Unfortunately, that understanding too often was rudimentary at best and erroneous at worst. Van Til himself was quite aware that there is only so much that one can learn by slogans and illustrations; eventually there must be a role for careful analysis. (As mentioned earlier, he told us that term papers that merely repeated his slogans and illustrations without careful thought would be graded as a C.) But teaching such analysis was not Van Til's gift. As a result, even today there are many—both friends and enemies of Van Til's ideas—who, when chal-

[23]DF2, 74.
[24]Ibid., 102.
[25]Ibid., 77, 231.
[26]DF2, 17.
[27]RP, 116.
[28]Ibid., 36.
[29]Ibid., 94.

lenged, turn out to have extremely confused notions of what he actually taught.[30]

Thus, perhaps his reluctance to publish was not without basis. His books and syllabi contain some of the same problems: bold, exciting summaries, illustrations, and exhortation, but often inadequate definition, analysis, and argument. Colin Brown comments in his *Philosophy and the Christian Faith*[31] that Van Til "spends a good deal of time reiterating points without really explaining them." In my mind, this does not detract from the depth or quality of his thought. Kant, Hegel, and Heidegger are far worse than Van Til in this respect. The profundity is there, but the reader must exercise some effort and some patience to understand it. But modern readers are not patient, and these difficulties certainly detract from the overall impact of his work.[32]

It is also the case that a number of Van Til's books and syllabi spend a great deal of time quoting various sources, with only the briefest analysis and evaluation. This is especially true of *Christ and the Jews, Christianity in Conflict, Notes on Roman Catholicism,* and *The Triumph of Grace. A Survey of Christian Epistemology,* however, has full arguments and citations for his critiques of Scholasticism, idealism, and other movements. There is some justification for his "quote books." Sometimes, Van Til wanted to share with his students works by people like Richard Kroner or Etienne Gilson whose views he thought interesting or important. Rather than making his students read these texts in detail, he supplied summaries by way of quotations and paraphrases. If his students wanted more elaborate critiques of these writers, they could look up other books where Van Til took up the subjects at greater length.

Then there are problems with Van Til's way of organizing his ideas. These are delightfully described by Gary North:

> [Van Til's] books are always filled with brilliant insights, but it is very difficult to remember where any single insight appeared.

---

[30]Most all the published criticism of Van Til, in my estimation, is in this category. See the references to the "debunkers" in chap. 1. For misunderstandings by Van Til's friends, note my references in chap. 1 to Halsey and White.

[31](Downers Grove, Ill.: InterVarsity Press, 1968), 249.

[32]This is the first of John Robbins's criticisms in his booklet *Cornelius Van Til: The Man and the Myth* (Jefferson, Md.: Trinity Foundation, 1986). In my view, this criticism, though it contains some truth, says more about Robbins's impatience and his ignorance of philosophical literature than it says about Van Til.

They are scattered like loose diamonds throughout his writings, but they never seem to fit in any particular slot. Any given insight might just as well be in any of his books—or all of them. . . . He makes good use of them, too; he repeats the same ones in many of his books. "No use throwing this away after only one time; it's almost like new. I'll use it again!" The man is clearly Dutch.

His most effective critical arguments sound the same in every book. Randomly pick up a coverless Van Til book, and start reading; you may not be sure from the development of the arguments just what the book is about, or who it is intended to refute. His books all wind up talking about the same three dozen themes. (Or is it four dozen?) Just keep reading. You will probably find his favorite Greeks: Plato, who struggled unsuccessfully to reconcile Parmenides and Heraclitus. . . . Kant's name will be there, too, but only in a four-page string of quotations from a book written in 1916 or 1932 by a scholar you never heard of. . . . You will learn about univocal and equivocal reasoning. Rationalism will be doing endless battle with irrationalism. The one will be smothering the many, whenever the many aren't overwhelming the one. . . .

Watch for his analogies. Rationalism and irrationalism will be taking in each other's washing for a living. There will be a chain of being lying around somewhere, probably right next to the infinitely long cord that the beads with no holes are supposed to decorate. . . .

What memorable analogies! But where did I read the one about the ladder of water rising out of the water to the water above? Which bad argument of which philosopher did that one blow away?

What we need is a 5-inch laser disk hooked to a Sony . . . scratch that . . . a Philips (Dutch) laser disk player with a microchip, with all his works on the disk, plus a computer program that will search every phrase and pull the one we want onto the screen in three seconds. The technology exists; the market for his works doesn't. Sad.[33]

---

[33]Gary North, *Dominion and Common Grace* (Tyler, Tex.: Institute for Christian Economics [Dominion Press], 1987), 10–12. The latest word, however, is that by late

The present book will not be an adequate substitute for North's laser disk. I will not be able to exhaustively catalogue every analogy and argument. But I will indicate in my footnotes some of the best sources in Van Til's writings for investigating major topics: divine sovereignty, the problem of the one and the many, the noetic effects of sin, and so on.

I shall also try to capsulize, chapter by chapter, his main ideas on various topics. Although the broad outlines of Van Til's thought are quite clear, the problems mentioned by North make it very difficult to pin down precisely what Van Til believes on a given specific topic. Look up a section supposedly devoted to, say, analogical reasoning, and you will have to wade through the Roman Catholic view of this, Parmenides' view of that, Barth's employment of Kantian dialectic, the one and the many, the traditional apologetic, and so on. Van Til likes to throw everything at the reader all at once. All in all, you may have to read each section several times to understand what Van Til says specifically about analogical reasoning. In this book I intend to break Van Til's thought down to its individual elements and deal with each in some detail, one at a time. That will facilitate understanding, analysis, and evaluation.

These sorts of eccentricities endeared Van Til to his students, but they did and still do cause difficulties for his students and readers. They do amount to deficiencies in his communication skills. To an extent, they are simply reflections of his personality; but they are also due, to some extent, to his *isolation.*

ISOLATION

Van Til was always something of an outsider in the theological, philosophical, and apologetic discussions of his day. For one thing, he was at heart a Dutchman forced by divinely ordained circumstances to work in a non-Dutch, American environment that was, in many ways, uncongenial to him.[34] For another thing, he was a Machenite: unlike

1995 Van Til's works will be available on CD-ROM. Write to Mr. Eric H. Sigward, 35-34 84th St., #A4, Jackson Heights, NY 11372.

[34]Cf. White's comments (VTDF, 37) about the "columnization" of Dutch culture, in which every religious group had its own schools, political party, newspaper, churches, and constituency. In such a situation, one group becomes isolated from another.

some evangelicals, who seem to want very much to be part of a dialogue with the "mainstream" liberal theologians of the day, Van Til from the beginning set himself radically over against theological liberalism and, indeed, against neo-orthodoxy. In fact, he set himself so sharply against these movements that his stance toward them was one of confrontation, not at all one of dialogue.

His first published book was *The New Modernism,* which deflated the hopes of evangelicals that Karl Barth might be on their side. Van Til argued that Barth and Brunner were, in doctrine, though not in terminology, as liberal as the liberals whom Machen had fought during his lifetime; they did not represent some sort of renewal of orthodoxy. "Barth simply does not believe the Christ of the Scripture at all," he said.[35] Recent interpretations of Barth and Brunner have tended to reinforce Van Til's warnings, though few interpreters have used language as sharp as his. At the time, however, his position appeared to be radical, and it had the effect of shutting him out from the general theological dialogue concerning Barth.[36] Other evangelical and Reformed writers, to say nothing of liberals and neo-orthodox, tended to be much more moderate and positive in their evaluations of Barth, and therefore were highly negative toward Van Til. I have spoken with a number of theologians who know Van Til only from this early book, and who (unwisely, I think) view its extreme position as a reason for ignoring everything else he has to say. We shall look more closely at Van Til's critique of Barth in chapter 26.

Van Til's radicalism extended beyond the liberal and neo-orthodox. He also regularly said harshly negative things about Roman Catholic theology, Arminianism, and even "less consistent Calvinism." He often spoke about the "isolation" of the Reformed faith over against the rest of the theological world.[37] Indeed, he saw his apologetic system as something sharply opposed to the traditional apologetics practiced by both Roman Catholics and Protestants (including Reformed) for many hundreds of years. Whether he was right or wrong in this, the result was more isolation. He was not in dialogue

---

[35]CTK, 229.

[36]Note, e.g., G. C. Berkouwer's comments on Van Til in *The Triumph of Grace in the Theology of Karl Barth* (Grand Rapids: Eerdmans, 1956), 384–93.

[37]He often affirmed the comment of Berkouwer, in his early *Het Probleem der Schriftkritiek* (Kampen: J. H. Kok, 1938), that the Reformed view of Scripture is "isolated" from all other views. See PDS, 37, and JA, 9.

with these other types of theology; he confronted them. It was not a relationship in which the parties could learn from one another; rather, it was a fight to the finish. Van Til never quite denied that he could learn something from, say, an Arminian, but he never allowed himself to be placed in a position where that would be possible.

Van Til's language, too, contributed to his isolation. Unlike many popular apologists, he used many technical philosophical and theological expressions, often inadequately defined and analyzed, and even his homely illustrations could not compensate for his daunting style. Beyond this, even his philosophical vocabulary was not easily understood by other philosophers. Van Til's philosophical background was idealist, and increasingly during his career the philosophical climate turned away from idealism. In America, the newer movements were various forms of language analysis, which took great pride in its clarity, its sharp definitions, its minute analysis of individual propositions—skills that were not Van Til's. And Van Til's theological language was often very technical as well. Although he could preach the gospel very simply to children and to the childlike, he often preferred in his teaching to focus upon the more difficult areas of theological debate. He was not, like C. S. Lewis, a defender of "mere Christianity." He intended to defend the entire Reformed faith down to the smallest detail.

Van Til's isolation was also ecclesiastical: he spent his life in a tiny denomination, the Orthodox Presbyterian Church, where there was no one competent to discuss philosophy on his level (except, perhaps, Gordon H. Clark for a time, but the presence of Clark meant more confrontation, not dialogue[38]). Even on the Westminster faculty, there was no one who could really engage Van Til in discussion, on Van Til's own level. He was the only teacher of apologetics there until Robert Knudsen joined the faculty in the late 1950s, but by then Van Til's position was quite firmly established.

Some thinkers are challenged by editors of journals and books: if the scholar wants to publish, he has to submit to the editor's criticisms, sometimes even to the criticisms of referees in the author's field who are assigned to judge the worthiness of the work. Van Til never had that sort of challenge, either. Most all of his papers were published (with little if any challenge) by the seminary's in-house *Westminster Theological Journal,* and his books were published almost

---

[38] I shall discuss the "Clark controversy" in some detail in chap. 8.

routinely by Presbyterian and Reformed Publishing Company. More accountability might have forced Van Til to adopt a clearer style of communication, but that was not to be. This arrangement may have been necessary, granted the hostility of the "mainstream" to Van Til's (and, more generally, Westminster's) radical Christian approach, but such insulation from criticism entailed further isolation.

Such isolation may sometimes be necessary for the free development of important and controversial theological ideas. However, it creates obvious difficulties. For one thing, such an isolated thinker loses opportunities to influence theology and the church at large. Thus, Van Til is still not taken seriously by many people who ought, in my view, to be very interested in what he is saying (e.g., the "new Reformed epistemology" movement of Plantinga and Wolterstorff).

Also, as a result of his isolation, Van Til was not effectively challenged during his career to define his terms, to explain the theological structure of his arguments, or to examine his ambiguities. That kind of analysis, as I argued in chapter 1, falls to us.

CHAPTER THREE

Van Til's Place in History

Consolidator of the Machen Reformation

Protestants look back to the great Reformation of the sixteenth century to establish their distinctive identity within the larger Christian church. But there have been other periods, too, in which analogous reformations of the church have taken place. I believe that the fourth-century controversy, during which, through much conflict, the doctrine of the Trinity was firmly established, was in important ways analogous to the later Reformation of Luther and Calvin. Athanasius, the champion of Nicene Trinitarianism, was much like Luther in his courageous, steadfast proclamation of fundamental biblical truths against apparently overwhelming odds.

Other reformations have been more local and on a smaller scale, sometimes less successful in attracting numbers of adherents, but nevertheless of great importance for those involved. The revival of Reformed thought and life in the Netherlands in the nineteenth century, first in the movement leading to the *Afscheiding* under the leadership of Hendrik De Cock and others, then in the events leading to the birth of the Gereformeerde Kerken under Abraham Kuyper, was certainly a reformation of this sort, one still vitally important to Reformed believers in that tradition. On a smaller scale, but of great significance to confessional American Presbyterians, was the protest of J. Gresham Machen in the 1920s and 1930s against the liberalism of the Presbyterian Church, U.S.A. It was that reformation that established the distinctive identity of Westminster Theological Seminary and the Orthodox Presbyterian Church, and that deeply influenced all those American Presbyterians who were concerned to maintain the heritage of the Westminster Standards.

Reformations tend to go through three stages, which may be roughly, but not sharply, distinguished: confrontation, consolidation, and continuation.[1] In the first stage, reformers armed with biblical truth confront a crisis in the church. In the second stage, the insights of the reformers are used as a basis for a thorough rethinking of Christian theology and life. In the third stage, the church seeks to appropriate these insights and apply them to changing situations.

In the Trinitarian development, Athanasius's struggle *contra mundum* represents the confrontation stage; Augustine represents consolidation, and the period since his time represents continuation. (All reformations, if successful, "continue" into the present.) In the sixteenth century, Luther represents confrontation, Calvin consolidation. In the nineteenth-century Dutch reformation, De Cock tends to be more on the side of confrontation, Kuyper of consolidation.[2]

With these categories before us, we may begin to identify the historical role played by Cornelius Van Til by naming him the chief consolidator of the Machen reformation. There is much more to be said than that, but we may profitably begin at this point. Machen's

---

[1]Those interested in the triadic system developed in my DKG may see here a pattern of situational, normative, and existential perspectives, respectively; or should "situational" and "normative" be reversed? It is also interesting to compare this pattern to certain sequences of events in Scripture: generally, (1) divine act, (2) covenant making (or renewal), and (3) period of application (including anticipation of future divine acts). The Creation, the Exodus, the Atonement, and the lesser events recalling and foreshadowing these major events can be analyzed in these terms. The divine act is either symbolically (as in Creation) or actually (as in redemption) a confrontation between God and some opposition to his lordship.

[2]The case can be made that when the Kuyperian reformation is looked at apart from the history of the *Afscheiding*, Kuyper may be seen as the confrontation stage, followed by a consolidation phase under Bavinck, Vollenhoven, and Dooyeweerd. I tend to be less sympathetic to Vollenhoven and Dooyeweerd than to other "consolidators" down through Christian history, yet I do not deny that the historical dynamics provide some justification for this interpretation. My categories are flexible enough to allow one leader to serve as confronter from one perspective and consolidator from another. All of us play multiple roles in history.

mentality and gifts were much like those of Athanasius, Luther, and De Cock. He was highly intelligent and scholarly, but more concerned with defending basic biblical truths than with the comprehensive and detailed elaboration of Reformed theology. He was eloquent, persistent, courageous, and single-minded. No matter what rebuke he suffered, he never backed away from his positions on the issues, and he was willing to take, as it became necessary, the drastic step of breaking fellowship with others in the church.

While Van Til shared many of these qualities, his mentality and gifts were, on the whole, more like those of Augustine, Calvin, and Kuyper, than like Athanasius, Luther, De Cock, and Machen. For all the strong words of his writings, Van Til tended to avoid ecclesiastical controversy. Except for the Clark case, which seems to have been spearheaded more by zealous students of Van Til than by Van Til himself (although he supported them), he was not the focal point of any church battles. I have no doubt that he was sincere in his reluctance to move from the pastorate into a teaching position. And his strong words were more often than not cloaked in a highly technical vocabulary. Thus, although he was a strong defender of the truth, he was rarely in the midst of the battle. Of course, one major reason for that was that his particular ecclesiastical fellowships (before 1936, the Christian Reformed Church; afterward, the Orthodox Presbyterian Church), during the time of his membership in them, were not caught up in debates over the very substance of the gospel. But that very situation is more characteristic of the consolidator than of the confronter. The consolidator typically is one who is sufficiently removed from the fiery heat of battle to spend time thinking through in great depth the theological implications of the reform.[3]

It was that service that Van Til ably performed for the Machen movement. Machen's fundamental reformational insight was that orthodox Christianity and theological liberalism are not two differing Christian theological positions, as are Calvinism and Lutheranism, but rather are two different religions, radically opposed to one another. For Machen, liberalism was not Christian at all, but was fundamentally opposed to Christianity as Christianity is defined in Scripture and history.[4] Machen saw their relationship as an "antithesis." They cannot be synthesized; we can only choose one or the other.

---

[3]Recall my comments on Van Til's isolation in chap. 2.

[4]See Machen, *Christianity and Liberalism* (New York: Macmillan, 1923).

In this respect, Machen did not simply repeat the traditional opposition to liberalism of the old Princeton Seminary faculty of which he was a member. He made a significant advance beyond them in his analysis. Greg Bahnsen, in his excellent and perceptive comparison between Van Til and Machen, points out that for Machen "the battle with modernism was more than 'polemical theology' against an exegetically weak or inconsistent school of evangelical Christianity. It was *apologetics* with unbelief."[5] Bahnsen goes on to argue persuasively that, "in short, because Machen moved away from the old Princeton conception of apologetics in a presuppositional direction, Van Til could applaud and support his historical defense of the faith, even as Machen could appreciate and approve of the developments in methodology and philosophical defense by Van Til."[6]

Van Til (with more than a nod to Kuyper) applied Machen's "antithetical" thinking to neo-orthodoxy[7] and other theological movements.

Indeed, in some respects Van Til's entire apologetic may be seen as a rethinking of the nature and implications of "antithesis." Like Machen's liberals, Van Til's "natural man" is an apostate. He knows the truth, but rebels against it and directly opposes it. Nevertheless, as Machen's liberals remained in the church and comforted themselves and others by using traditional Christian language, Van Til's unregenerate live on "borrowed capital," able to avoid utter nihilism only by the inconsistency of acknowledging some elements of God's revelation.

Van Til applied the concept of antithesis not only to unbelief in general and to the more recent variations of liberal theology, but also to the historic divisions within the Christian church. The problem with Roman Catholicism, Lutheranism, Arminianism, and even "less consistent Calvinism," is that they compromise with unbelief, understood as the antithesis to true Christianity. Compromise, of course, is

---

[5]Bahnsen, "Machen, Van Til, and the Apologetical Tradition of the OPC," in *Pressing Toward the Mark*, ed. Charles G. Dennison and Richard C. Gamble (Philadelphia: Committee for the Historian of the Orthodox Presbyterian Church, 1986), 259.

[6]Ibid., 262–63.

[7]The title of his *Christianity and Barthianism* (Philadelphia: Presbyterian and Reformed, 1962) intentionally reflects that of Machen's *Christianity and Liberalism*. Compare his earlier work, *The New Modernism* (Philadelphia: Presbyterian and Reformed, 1946), the title of which also indicates its Machenite thesis.

different from capitulation, and Van Til recognized that. In *Jerusalem and Athens*, he charges John Warwick Montgomery, a Lutheran who opposes Van Til's apologetic, with "straddling the fence."[8] Nevertheless, he often uses the language of antithesis ("great gulf" language) to describe not only unbelief as such, but also those Christians who are not in his estimation fully Reformed. Consider these remarkable words describing Stuart Hackett, an Arminian critical of Van Til's apologetic:

> Indeed, the issues between us are total. There are no "fundamentals" in common between us. . . . Hackett's Christian faith and my Christian faith, which we both desire non-Christians to accept, are radically different. They are different not only in their *content* but also in the very *method* of their construction.[9]

There is some unclarity here. Van Til denies any common fundamentals between himself and Hackett, and he says that their faiths are radically different. Yet he acknowledges a commonness in their "desire" for the non-Christian to accept their faith. Does that mean that Van Til has a desire for the non-Christian to accept the Christian faith, while Hackett desires the non-Christian to accept something "radically different" from Christian faith? That would be like saying "Christians and Muslims are radically opposed, but they are alike in their zeal to win others." Or is Van Til here granting commonness between Hackett's and his own version of Christian faith, despite the "radical difference" between these versions? I believe the second interpretation is more accurate; certainly, it is more charitable and attributes to Van Til a more tenable position. But it is rather peculiar to say that two people have the "same" faith, even though their respective faiths differ "radically." And, in any case, the rhetoric here is rather extreme to use of someone with the same faith; the expression of solidarity, if it exists at all, is very subtle indeed.

I think that, in the above example, Van Til got carried away with his own rhetoric of antithesis. But that sort of thing is not uncommon in Van Til's writings, and it indicates something of the passion with which Van Til promoted the concept of antithesis as a key to

---

[8]Reply to Montgomery's "Once upon an a Priori . . ." in JA, 403.

[9]JA, 15–16 (emphasis his).

apologetics and even to the prosecution of differences between Christians.

And it gets still broader. To Van Til, antithesis is not only a means of criticizing others, but also a key to the very formulation of Christian truth. As the consolidator of the Machen reformation, Van Til rethinks the whole system of Christian theology and reformulates it with the concept of antithesis in view. He does that by showing that Christian theology is a *system* of truth, that its elements are so profoundly interrelated that to deny one doctrine is implicitly to deny the whole.[10] This demonstration, if successful, leaves us with a choice between his system and rank unbelief, with a great gulf in between. Any attempt to cross that gulf, to mediate between those two positions, is doomed from the start, being logically incoherent and spiritually bankrupt. Hence, Van Til's theological formulations, like his apologetic, reinforce the Machenite antithesis.

Understanding Van Til as the consolidator of the Machen reformation helps us to understand better the role his thinking plays in many Reformed circles today. Of course, not every Reformed Christian identifies himself or herself with the Machen movement, and of those who do, not all are sympathetic with Van Til. But among those who see themselves as sympathetic to Van Til, there are some who attribute to his thought a status just short of (if not identical to) confessional authority: recall my discussion of the "movement Van Tillians" in chapter 1. If Van Til is essentially the Kuyperian-Machenite philosopher of antithesis, we can understand why he is often treated merely as a movement leader, even though he is so much more than that.

Importance

I must now comment on the nature of the "more." Here comes my superlative: Van Til is perhaps the most important Christian thinker since Calvin. That statement (coming from a not uncritical disciple) may seem extreme. But to understand it, let me make a comparison between Van Til and the secular philosopher Immanuel Kant (1724–1804).

---

[10]I have documented and explored Van Til's concept of a theological system in VTT and will return to that discussion in chap. 13 of this volume.

Although Kant professed a kind of theism and an admiration for Jesus, he was clearly far from orthodox Christianity. Indeed, his major book on religion, *Religion Within the Limits of Reason Alone,* has as its chief theme the thesis that the human mind can never and must never subject itself to any authority beyond itself. In other words, to Kant, the human mind must be autonomous, subject only to its own law. Kant radically rejected the idea of authoritative revelation from God (either in nature or in Scripture) and asserted, perhaps more clearly than ever before (although this had always been the view of secular philosophers), the autonomy of the human mind. The human mind, that means, is to be its own supreme authority, its own criterion of truth and right.

In his other works, Kant argued that what makes our experience intelligible is largely, perhaps entirely, the work of our own minds. We do not know what the world is really like, we know only how it appears to us, and how it appears to us is largely what we make it to be. Thus, the mind of man not only is its own ultimate authority, but also replaces God as the intelligent planner and creator of the experienced universe. And, to Kant, the human mind is also the author of its own moral standards.

Kant saw, of course, that none of this could be proved in the usual sense of proof. He adopted what he called the "transcendental method," which seeks to determine the necessary preconditions or *presuppositions* of rationality. He reached his conclusions concerning human autonomy not by proving them by the usual philosophical methods, but by showing our need to presuppose them.[11] Kant's philosophy, therefore, does not merely assert or assume human autonomy, as did many previous philosophies; it explicitly *presupposes* human autonomy. It adopts human autonomy as the root idea to which every other idea must conform. That is what makes Kant unique and vastly important: he taught secular man where his epistemology must begin, his inescapable starting point for all possible reflection.

So Kant is widely regarded as the most important philosopher of the modern period. He showed "modern man," secular, would-be

[11]I question to some extent the standard view, held by Van Til and most everybody else, that "transcendental" reasoning is radically different from more traditional kinds of reasoning. See chap. 23 on this subject. Still, there are differences between transcendental and nontranscendental forms of proof, and Kant himself believed that the differences were quite radical.

autonomous man, what he would have to presuppose about knowledge and the world in order to be consistent with his presumed autonomy. In other words, Kant made the modern secular man "epistemologically self-conscious." If modern man is not to bow to God, he must bow before himself; to that extent at least, he must be a Kantian.

If Kant taught the world of secular unbelief the essentials of its own (until then, subconscious) theory of knowledge ("epistemology"), Van Til did the same for the Christian. As Kant said that we must avoid any trace of the attitude of bowing before an external authority, so Van Til taught that the only way to find truth at all is to bow before God's authoritative Scripture. As Kant presented his view transcendentally, as the inescapable ultimate presupposition of human thought, so Van Til made and defended transcendentally the same claim for the revelation of God: that God's Word is the only presupposition that does not destroy the intelligibility of human thought.

Because of Van Til, we can at last define the essential philosophical differences between the Christian and the non-Christian worldviews. If Kant's achievement makes him the most important secular philosopher of modern times, should we not say that Van Til's achievement makes him the most important Christian thinker of modern times?

Some may object that others have done the same thing as well as or better than Van Til. A case could be made for Dooyeweerd, for instance, whose philosophy is certainly much more elaborate and comprehensive than Van Til's, useful in many respects, and, like Van Til's, critical of the "pretended autonomy of theoretical thought." But precisely at the crucial point, the point of thinking and living by God's authority, Dooyeweerd, though well-intentioned, lapses into unclarity. He rejects biblical inerrancy, makes man's "supratemporal heart" the locus of some kind of nonverbal starting point for thought, says confusing things about the use of the Bible and its place in developing Christian understandings of the world, and says things that suggest the possibility of epistemological neutrality.[12]

A case could also be made for Gordon H. Clark ("America's Augustine," according to his disciple, John Robbins). Clark developed a

---

[12]See his *In the Twilight of Western Thought* (Nutley, N.J.: Craig, 1968). Note Van Til's critiques in CC, JA, and HDRA, which we shall consider in chap. 27. H. G. Stoker, another impressive thinker in the Dooyeweerd circle, compares Van Til's "level of depth" favorably to Dooyeweerd's in JA, 37.

more detailed critique of secular philosophy than did Van Til, and he did it with more clarity and more obviously logical cogency. Yet Clark gave to Aristotle's logic the same authority as Scripture, he took an unbiblically skeptical position on human sense experience, and he often oversimplified important theological issues (in my opinion!) such as the relationship between divine sovereignty and human responsibility and the problem of evil.[13] Unlike Van Til, he took the term *presupposition* to refer to a hypothesis that could not be ultimately proved, but which could be progressively verified by logical analysis. This indicates some unclarity in Clark's mind as to what the ultimate standard of proof really is. If the ultimate standard is God's revelation, then the presuppositions of the Christian faith not only are provable, but also are the criteria by which all other proofs are to be measured.

I would not advance this parallel between Van Til and Kant if Van Til's thought were on a level of sophistication far below that of the German philosopher. I do believe, however, that students of philosophy who give Van Til's work a careful examination will find the sheer intellectual quality, subtlety, and penetration of his work not one bit inferior. Indeed, Van Til's intellectual caliber reinforces the comparison.

To say that Van Til is the most important Christian thinker of our time is not to say that he is the most comprehensive thinker, or the clearest, or the most persuasive. Certainly it is not to say (as some of his more fanatical followers assume) that he is beyond criticism. Nor is it to say that he has had a greater impact on present-day Christian thought than anybody else; indeed, his isolation continues, and his influence remains relatively small. It is, rather, to say that he has made the Christian community aware of its only appropriate epistemology, thus laying a necessary foundation that ought to be the basis for all subsequent Christian reflection.

[13]We shall take a closer look at Clark in chap. 8.

PART TWO

The Metaphysics of Knowledge

CHAPTER FOUR

God: Self-contained Fullness and Absolute Personality

We shall now begin to look at Van Til's thought systematically. On my analysis, his most significant insights can be divided into four general categories: the metaphysics of knowledge, the ethics of knowledge, the argument for Christianity, and the critique of unbelief (including both the thought of unbelievers and the influence of unbelieving thought upon Christian theology). Van Til himself never outlined his system this way, so far as I know, but I do think that these categories cover most of what he had to say and provide a logical ordering of his thoughts. In Part Two, "The Metaphysics of Knowledge," I will discuss Van Til's view of the basic nature of human knowledge within a Christian worldview. Part Three, "The Ethics of Knowledge," will deal with the effects of the Fall upon our knowledge. Part Four, "The Argument for Christianity," will show how, on Van Til's view, a believer should argue and defend the gospel to an unbeliever in the light of the metaphysics and ethics of knowledge: apologetics as proof and defense, to use the categories of my *Apologetics to the Glory of God*. Finally, Part Five, "Van Til as Critic," will discuss Van Til's *offensive* apologetics, his critical analysis of unbelieving systems and of the influence of unbelief upon Christian theology. After I have expounded his thought under these headings,

I shall conclude with a look at Van Til's "legacy" (the developments of his thought among the second- and third-generation Van Tillians) and a summary of my conclusions.

Van Til often discussed relationships among metaphysics, epistemology, and ethics, three traditional philosophical disciplines. Metaphysics, roughly synonymous with ontology, describes in broad terms the nature of reality and deals with questions about the general structure of the world: the relations of unity and diversity, personality and impersonality, God and man, infinitude and finitude, time and eternity, the visible and the invisible. Ethics deals with norms for personal behavior, ways of determining those norms, and ways of applying them to behavior. Epistemology, or the theory of knowledge, discusses how we can know truth, including truth in metaphysics and ethics.

The three disciplines are closely related to one another. Metaphysics must account for ethical norms as part of the overall structure of reality, and for the possibility of knowledge within that structure. Epistemology must presuppose some elements of metaphysics, and it must understand the ethical norms to which the human quest for knowledge is itself subject. And ethics presupposes metaphysics and epistemology, because it must deal with behavior in the real world, and it must defend the knowability of the norms it proposes for behavior.

Thus, we cannot discuss metaphysics, epistemology, and ethics in complete isolation from one another. On the other hand, Van Til insists that we maintain a distinction between them. This is important, especially when we are talking about the nature of sin and redemption. It is an error to say that sin and redemption are metaphysical, for that would mean that our salvation is a salvation from finitude, i.e., that in salvation we become God. Rather, sin and redemption are exclusively ethical: we have sinned, and the work of Christ brings forgiveness and takes us to heaven. But even in heaven we remain finite, subject to God's lordship.[1]

Since we must begin somewhere, we shall begin our discussion of Van Til's thought with his "metaphysics of knowledge," a concept in which metaphysics and epistemology are drawn together. The broad strokes of my discussion here will be made more precise in later chapters where we focus more on ethical matters.

[1]IST, 253–57; cf. DF1, 160-62.

Van Til's first class syllabus was originally entitled "The Metaphysics of Apologetics."[2] "Metaphysics" in this context refers to the biblical worldview, namely, the relation between Creator and creature. Thus, he was concerned from the earliest days of his career to discuss human knowledge and Christian apologetics in relation to the biblical worldview.

In my opinion, his account of the metaphysics of knowledge merits superlative commendation. It is profoundly biblical and intellectually penetrating, and it provides substantial clarification of the fundamental nature of human thought. I am critical of Van Til in other areas, but in this one I am almost as close to him as the most slavish movement–Van Tillian. However, even in this area there is some need to clarify, explain, and defend Van Til's statements beyond his own efforts to do so. And I do have a few minor criticisms of his formulations, especially in the way he opposes his views to those of others.

Van Til wrote, "Now the basic structure of my thought is very simple,"[3] and in essence it is. Van Til's starting point is the historic doctrine of creation: God is the Creator; the world is his creation. Over and over again in class he would draw two circles on the blackboard: a large circle representing God and a smaller circle below it representing the creation. The two were connected by lines representing providence and revelation, but Van Til emphasized the distinctness of the two circles from one another. He insisted that Christianity has a "two-circle" worldview, as opposed to secular thought, which has only "one-circle" thinking. Nonbiblical thought makes all reality equal: if there is a God, he is equal to the world. But for Christianity, God is the sovereign Creator and Lord; the world is in no sense equal to him. That is, in essence, the "simple structure" of Van Til's thought.

God, the Self-contained Fullness

Evidently, then, our first priority in trying to understand Van Til's metaphysics of knowledge is to explore his doctrine of God. On the first page of his *Introduction to Systematic Theology*, he says, "Funda-

---

[2]More recently it was retitled *A Survey of Christian Epistemology*.

[3]DF1, 23.

mental to everything orthodox is the presupposition of the antecedent self-existence of God and of his infallible revelation of himself to man in the Bible."[4] "Self-existence," sometimes called aseity, refers to the fact "that God is in no sense correlative to or dependent upon anything besides his own being. God is the source of his own being, or rather the term source cannot be applied to God. God is *absolute*. He is sufficient unto himself."[5] Often Van Til summarizes this concept by referring to the "self-contained God."

He quotes favorably a passage from Bavinck to the effect that all the other virtues of God are included in his aseity.[6] Thus, when Van Til goes on to discuss God's immutability, he bases that doctrine upon the divine aseity: "Naturally God does not and cannot change since there is nothing besides his own eternal Being upon which he depends (Mal. 3:6; James 1:7)."[7] Since God's immutability is based upon his "self-contained fullness," it is quite opposite to the immutability of Aristotle's unmoved mover, an abstract thought thinking itself.[8]

Notice how he moves here from "self-contained" to "self-contained *fullness*." That is important. All would-be comprehensive metaphysical systems include something that is "self-contained." It may be an uncaused cause, an ultimate physical particle, an abstract unity in reality, an abstract form, or perhaps pure chance or randomness. The basis for such assertions lies either in an extrapolation from finite reality (the "way of eminence") or in a negation of the finite in an attempt thereby to reach infinity (the "way of negation"). Extrapolation or eminence, carried out in the usual philosophical way, leads to a "self-contained" being that is merely an enlargement of the finite universe; negation leads to a being that is self-contained simply because it has no positive qualities. Extrapolation leads to no God at all, but only a larger universe; negation leads to emptiness. Neither leads to the "fullness" of the biblical God. Both lead to "one-circle" thinking, rather than "two-circle" thinking.

Van Til does not deny the legitimacy of extrapolations and negations as such. But he objects to the way in which these have typically been carried out in the history of philosophy and theology. With

---

[4]IST, 1.
[5]DF2, 9.
[6]IST, 206.
[7]DF2, 9.
[8]IST, 210.

regard to infinity, he says, "We are again compelled to describe this attribute chiefly by way of negation."[9] He adds, however, "But it is again of utmost significance that we use the way of negation correctly."[10] The incorrect way is "abstract," which is to

> simply take the notions of time and of space, and subtract such characteristics as succession or continuity from them in order to reach the notions of eternity and omnipresence. But when we follow this advice we land at the opposite pole from that of the fullness of the being of God. We then come to pure emptiness.
>
> Accordingly, we need the indescribable fullness of the being of God as the presupposition of our notions of time and space. Then we subtract from these notions the limitations that pertain to them by virtue of the fact that they are created by God. If we do this, we walk theistically on the way of negation. The way of negation is then, at the same time, the way of affirmation. God then appears so full and rich in his being that we cannot even make negations with respect to him without the presupposition of the fullness of his being.[11]

Even in his basic discussion of God's nature, the matter of presuppositions comes into play! How hard it is to discuss one element of Van Til's thought without discussing all the rest! But, for now, I wish to focus on Van Til's basic concept of God as self-contained fullness.

Van Til also relates God's attribute of unity to his self-contained fullness. Theologians traditionally distinguish God's unity of singularity (that there is only one God) from his unity of simplicity (that he is not made up of parts or aspects that are intelligible in themselves, apart from the divine being as a whole). To Van Til, the one implies the other: "We have in the case of God absolute numerical identity and, therefore, internal qualitative sufficiency."[12] If there is only one God, then there is nothing "in" him that is independent of him. God's goodness, for example, is not something in his mind to which he brings

---

[9]Ibid., 211.
[10]Ibid.
[11]Ibid., 211–12.
[12]Ibid., 215.

himself into conformity. If it were, that goodness, an abstract quality, would be a second deity coordinate with God himself. Thus, denial of God's unity of simplicity violates God's unity of singularity.

In another sense, however, on this supposition, there would still be one god, though not the God of Scripture. For abstract goodness would be more ultimate than God is; it alone would be authentic deity. And if the true deity were an abstract principle, then the true deity would be impersonal rather than personal.

On the contrary, says Van Til, God's goodness is everything that he is. All his attributes, similarly, refer[13] to his self-contained fullness.

In summary, the nature of God is so rich and full that we could never come to know it on the basis of either eminence or negation taken by themselves. However, if God reveals himself, then we can presuppose that revelation in our extrapolations and negations. For he tells us in that revelation that he is the Creator and we are creatures, and he tells us much about how Creator and creature differ from one another. What we must do first is humbly accept that knowledge from his hands. Our doctrines of the divine attributes will simply be repetition, explanation, and application of what God has told us.

But application, of course, involves relating the teachings of Scripture to the realities of our experience. In the case of divine immutability and infinity, it is important to ask how these are related to space and time. Scripture says little specifically or in general about space and time; much of what we learn about these things comes from "natural revelation," God's revelation of himself in nature and history. But when our analysis of space and time presupposes the truth of Scripture, we can draw useful conclusions about how God transcends them, yet is also immanent in them.

Thus, divine revelation enables us to use extrapolation and negation in a fruitful way. In any case, it is only by revelation that we can avoid believing in an "empty" god, one that is only a projection of ourselves, if indeed he is anything at all.

In this manner Van Til discusses all the incommunicable attributes of God:[14] aseity, immutability, infinity, and unity. All of these

[13]From different perspectives!

[14]Incommunicable attributes, traditionally, are those that are unique to God; communicable attributes are divine attributes that can also be predicated of finite people or things. The distinction breaks down, because all of God's attributes are unique to

must be understood to pertain to God's self-contained fullness, on the basis of his revelation.[15]

The same thing is true of the communicable attributes. God's "spirituality" is not "some vague generic concept of spirituality of which God is one particular instance and man another. God is the absolute Spirit. He is the self-contained Spirit. He does not need materiality over against himself to individuate himself. He is the self-individuated Spirit."[16]

With regard to God's omniscience, his knowledge and his being are "coterminous."[17] He knows himself and his plan for the world exhaustively; therefore, there is nothing within him or outside him that is independent of him. Like all his attributes, his knowledge is self-dependent, or, as Van Til sometimes describes it, "analytical."[18] His knowledge is never dependent on anything outside himself. Otherwise, he would not be self-contained fullness.[19]

Goodness is God himself. If that were not so, he would be seeking goals outside himself.[20] Holiness is "God's absolute eternal moral

---

him, and because the creation images all his attributes in some faint way. Van Til understood the limitations of this classification, as have most Reformed theologians; like them, however, he continued to use it.

[15]You can see how Van Til's apologetic concerns press us far beyond the usual theological formulations of the divine attributes. This and other examples of his theological thinking led me to argue in VTT that Van Til is not only an apologist, but also a theologian of first importance. Additional examples of Van Til's theological creativity are noted elsewhere in this volume.

[16]IST, 233.

[17]Ibid., 234.

[18]Ibid., 236; cf. p. 8; CA, 6. For a discussion of the controversy between Van Til and Knudsen concerning this term, see JA, 275–305, and HDRA, 1:1–24. In my view, Knudsen's critique amounts to a fairly elementary misunderstanding of a term that Van Til defines quite adequately. I shall discuss the larger question of Van Til's "rationalism" at later points, especially chap. 27.

[19]This is not to say that God's knowledge of the world is knowledge of himself *simpliciter*. God's knowledge is not mere introspection; he knows himself, and he also knows what takes place in the temporal world. This point is important; otherwise, we are pressed toward pantheism. The world is genuinely other than God, and God knows it as something different from himself. Nevertheless, even in knowing the world in its otherness, God knows something that he has exhaustively interpreted prior to its existence, because he has, exhaustively, made that world what it is. Van Til does not himself make this point, but he does not deny it either, and we should recognize it as a legitimate qualification of his emphasis.

[20]IST, 238. We should make another qualifying point parallel to the one made in the preceding note: God seeks the goodness of his creatures. This does not detract

purity."[21] Righteousness is "the internal self-consistency of the divine being."[22] His will "wills himself as his own end"[23] and is "the source of all substance and power in the created universe."[24] God's secret or decretive will includes everything that comes to pass, including sin and evil.[25]

There are mysteries in all of this. How can a good God will the existence of evil? How can God's acts in the world express his eternal nature, yet be free? Van Til does not claim to have solved the difficulties.[26] But, having emphasized the self-contained fullness that is essential to God, he has made it quite understandable why we should expect to encounter such mysteries.

God, the Absolute Personality

Van Til summarizes his doctrine of God in terms of "self-contained fullness." Another Van Tillian summary of this doctrine is that God is "absolute personality."[27] Both words in the phrase are important. Some non-Christian systems (as the polytheistic religions and modern philosophical "personalisms") posit personal gods of one kind or another, but those gods are not absolute in the sense of being self-contained. Other non-Christian systems accept absolute realities of various kinds, but those absolutes are not personal. Only in biblical teaching are absoluteness and personality combined in the Supreme Being.

Van Til's "personalism" is not widely noted in the literature about him, but it is nonetheless an important theme in his thought, and it has been important since his earliest writing. In the following passage, he employs personalistic categories to defend the doctrine of Adam's representative headship of the human race:

---

from his self-containment; rather, it presupposes self-containment. Were he not self-contained, he would act to meet his own needs; self-containment frees him to meet the needs of others, to be a servant-king.

[21]Ibid., 244.

[22]Ibid., 245.

[23]Ibid., 246.

[24]Ibid., 247.

[25]Ibid., 248.

[26]Ibid., 249; see chaps. 11–13 of this book.

[27]DF2, 12, 42.

> In the Trinity there is completely personal relationship without residue. And for that reason it may be said that all man's actions are personal too. Man's surroundings are shot through with personality because all things are related to the infinitely personal God. But when we have said that the surroundings of man are really completely personalized, we have also established the fact of the representational principle. All of man's acts must be representational of the acts of God. Even the persons of the Trinity are mutually representational. They are *exhaustively* representational of one another. Because he is a creature, man must, in his thinking, his feeling and his willing, be representative of God.[28]

Therefore, "It was impossible for God to create except upon the representational plan."[29] "Every act of every finite person affects every act of every other finite person that comes after him by virtue of the one general plan of God."[30]

Van Til has often had occasion to address personalistic idealisms like those of Bowne and Brightman and "I-Thou" theologies such as those of Buber and Brunner. Such views use much personalistic rhetoric, but they reject the absolute God of historic Christian orthodoxy. Van Til argues that these views are in fact *impersonalistic,* since they make God subordinate to the impersonal principles of chance, brute fact, and abstract logic.[31] Similarly, Arminian and Lutheran theology, since they limit God's sovereignty to make room for human acts that spring from chance or creaturely autonomy, is impersonalist to that extent. On the Arminian view, "An act to be moral or immoral, must take place in a completely impersonal atmosphere."[32] Van Til also criticizes philosophical determinism for its impersonalism.[33]

Positively, Van Til cites Calvin as a true personalist. He sets forth his doctrine of man's will "boldly as the only alternative to complete impersonalism."[34] He knew that *"covenant theology furnishes the only com-*

---

[28]SCE, 78–79; cf. p. 97.

[29]Ibid., 79.

[30]Ibid.

[31]Ibid., 176–82, on Bowne; IST, 165–66, on modern liberal theologians.

[32]SCE, 87. On Lutheranism, see pp. 65–80.

[33]DF2, 62; CTETH, 35; JA, 16. Van Til is emphatic that Calvinism is not a form of philosophical determinism.

[34]Ibid., 98; cf. CTETH, 207; CFC, 23.

pletely personalistic interpretation of reality."[35] Calvin began his *Institutes* by saying that the knowledge of oneself is dependent on the knowledge of God and vice versa. His doctrine of predestination, far from being an impersonal determinism, placed man in a person-to-person relationship with God in every event of nature and history.[36]

We noted in the previous section that to deny God's self-contained fullness is to assert impersonalism. Recall particularly Van Til's argument that the denial of divine simplicity makes God subordinate to abstract qualities. Van Til finds a close relationship between divine sovereignty and the divine personality. This relationship is very illuminating. It is edifying to observe that only a personal God can be sovereign and only a sovereign God can be an absolute person. That is to say, only a personal being can make choices and carry them out, and only a sovereign God can avoid being subject, ultimately, to impersonal principles.

Van Til often brought this absolute personalism into his apologetic, especially when he compared the Reformed faith with various inauthentic personalisms, such as those mentioned above. We shall see also that his basic argument for Christianity depends on biblical personalism. To reject the personal, biblical God leaves no alternative except a world governed by impersonal fate.

In my view, a Van Tillian apologetic of the future should emphasize this principle even more than Van Til did. Some of Van Til's formulations suggest that the Van Tillian apologist is, after all, concerned mainly with abstractions: an "ultimate oneness and manyness," a "concrete universal." Abstract as these notions sound, their actual meaning is entirely personalistic; for, as we shall see in the following chapter, in Van Til's thought only a person can be a truly concrete universal, an ultimate one-and-many. But, as we build on Van Til's foundation, we should be even more explicitly personalistic.

Impersonal facts and laws cannot be ultimate, precisely because they are not personal. They cannot account for rationality, for moral value, for the causal order of the universe, or for the universal applicability of logic.

The Christian apologist should emphasize, more than Van Til did, the issue of impersonalism versus personalism. It is this issue, as

---

[35]Ibid. (emphasis his).

[36]For more references to Van Til's personalism, see CTETH, 19, 250–51; IW, 28; JA, 16; ICG, 5, 25–29; TG, 9.

we have seen, that distinguishes the Christian worldview from all others. To emphasize it gives the apologist several advantages: (1) Inquirers sometimes tell us that there is no point in investigating Christianity, for if they did that, they would also have to investigate all the other religions, philosophies, and ideologies in the history of thought—an impossible task, to be sure. We can reply that they should give special attention to Christianity, for on the crucial question of whether the universe is governed by a person or by impersonal principles, Christianity is unique. It is consistently personalistic, and all its rivals are in the opposite camp. (2) The emphasis on personalism also addresses the loneliness of modern secular people. It offers them an ultimate friendship, ultimate love, something they will never find in a non-Christian view of the world. (3) It assures them that an ultimate rationality—and (4) an ultimate justice—govern the world order. These assurances are not possible on any other basis, as we shall see.

CHAPTER FIVE

The Trinity

As we have seen, Van Til's concepts of the fullness and the personality of God are linked to the doctrine of the Trinity. His personalism depends on the fact that the persons of the Trinity are "representational" of one another. Let us, then, look more carefully at the doctrine of the Trinity that underlies Van Til's personalism and plays other important roles in his thought.

As with all his doctrinal formulations, Van Til's doctrine of the Trinity begins with an affirmation of the ancient creeds and the Reformed confessions. He lists the basic biblical texts and sketches the historical development of the doctrine.[1] In this historical survey, he emphasizes, as have Reformed theologians generally, (1) that the Trinity is ontological, not merely economic—God is both three and one in his very nature, not only in his relations to the world—and (2) that it is erroneous to assert relations of subordination (as, for example, of the Son to the Father) within the ontological Trinity.[2] He particularly emphasizes Calvin's teaching about the *autotheotes* of the Son: that the Son does not derive his being from the Father,

---

[1]IST, 220–27.

[2]In DF2, 25, he says, "It is a well-known fact that all heresies in the history of the church have in some form or other taught subordinationism. Similarly, we believe, all 'heresies' in apologetic methodology spring from some sort of subordinationism."

but is God in and of himself.[3] "Derived deity" is, of course, an oxymoron.

The Trinity and Correlativism

Then Van Til adds a distinctive twist to the historical analysis: that the heresies of Sabellianism[4] and Arianism[5] are, at root, manifestations of *correlativism.* Correlativism asserts that God and the world are dependent upon each other, contrary to the doctrine of God's self-contained fullness. Both of these heresies see God as a kind of bare unity, which cannot function without the supplementation supplied by the plurality of the world.[6]

Van Til does not explain his point very clearly; allow me to attempt an elaboration. Like the Gnostics, Neoplatonists, and (unfortunately) some of the church fathers, the Sabellians and Arians saw God as a "oneness" so far from earthly reality as to be beyond human description. Similarly, modern theologians like to say that God is "wholly other." But an utterly indescribable oneness is an abstract oneness, not a personal absolute. In that case, as I emphasized in the preceding chapter, God cannot be truly sovereign. He (or rather "it") must be relative to the world.

We can see that relativity in various ways: First, when people try to speak of the wholly other god, they must do so in human language, language about the created world. Thus, the god becomes a mere extension of the world. God's power is merely an extension of earthly power, his love is an extension of earthly love, and so on. Second, an abstract oneness, as opposed to a Trinitarian oneness, cannot be self-defined and therefore must be relative to the world. His love, for example, if it is defined at all, must be defined as a love for the world, rather than a love among divine persons, for on this view there is no true plurality of divine persons. Third, a wholly other being does not provide a basis for the rational and moral order of the world. That basis must then be found in the world itself. But then the world is ultimate, and whatever the "wholly other" is, it is relative to the world.

---

[3]IST, 227–28; SCE, 101–2; TJD, 33–38.

[4]The view that the three persons are nothing more than historically successive manifestations of the one God.

[5]The view that the Son and the Spirit are mere creatures.

[6]Ibid., 225.

This pattern of thought rules out the biblical view of God as sovereign Lord.[7]

Now orthodox Trinitarianism renounces such correlativism. On the orthodox view, God's unity is correlative only to himself, to the complexities and pluralities of his own being. The world also is a unity and a diversity, because God made it that way.

Consider love, as an attribute of God. If God is a mere unity without Trinity, then what is the object of God's eternal love? Himself? But love in the fullest biblical sense by its very nature reaches out to another, not merely to the self. The world? Then God's eternal attribute of love depends on the world; it needs the world. On a Trinitarian basis, however, God's love is both interpersonal and self-contained: God's love is the love among Father, Son, and Spirit for one another, and it is not dependent on the world.

We can see how Van Til has related, in a very profound way, the doctrines of divine aseity, personality, and the Trinity. The Trinity guards aseity, for, without it, God is relative to the world. The Trinity also guards the personality of God: he is not a blank unity, which would be impersonal. Rather, he is a unity of persons.

Three Persons and One Person

For Van Til, God is not simply a unity of persons; he is *a* person:

> It is sometimes asserted that we can prove to men that we are not asserting anything that they ought to consider irrational, inasmuch as we say that God is one in essence and three in person. We therefore claim that we have not asserted unity and trinity of exactly the same thing.
>
> Yet this is not the whole truth of the matter. We do assert that God, that is, the whole Godhead, is one person.[8]

In my VTT I called this "a very bold theological move."[9] To my knowledge, I was the first interpreter of Van Til to bring this asser-

[7]In Deuteronomy 6:4, the famous Old Testament confession of faith, the unity of God is intimately related to his lordship. He is the one Lord, whom we are to love with all our heart, permitting in ourselves no rival loyalties. One Lord means one allegiance.

[8]IST, 229.

[9]P. 14.

tion to readers' attention; had I not done so, it might have remained on the back pages of IST, relatively unnoticed. Therefore, I suppose I have to take some responsibility for the furor that my reference created. Hence the following discussion.

Gordon H. Clark criticized Van Til's assertion in a taped lecture dealing with my article. Clark's disciple, John Robbins, calls Van Til's formulation "a radically new heresy."[10] It is not clear to me what precisely Robbins objects to in this formulation.[11] What he says is that Van Til "rejects the carefully worked out doctrine of the Trinity embodied in the Westminster Confession and the Athanasian Creed as 'not the whole truth of the matter.' "[12] But that is an odd comment. In the first place, I suspect that Van Til himself would have claimed that these creeds taught his view implicitly; he certainly was not conscious of rejecting anything in them, and I do not believe that he did reject any of their Trinitarian doctrine.[13] In the second place, Robbins seems to be saying that creedal subscription requires us to believe that the creeds contain the "whole truth" about the Trinity. Since Van Til denies that they contain the whole truth, his creedal subscription is somehow defective. But since when does creedal subscription require us to believe that the creed contains the whole truth about anything? Obviously, the Athanasian Creed did not contain the whole truth, because it was supplemented by later statements such as the Westminster Confession. Nor does the Westminster Confession contain the whole truth. Only the Bible contains the whole truth of God's revelation, and even the Bible does not necessarily answer every question that we may wish to ask about the Trinity. It tells us only what God wants us to know.

The heart of Clark's and Robbins's complaint, however, has little to do with creedal subscription. Their serious point is that Van Til's

---

[10] *Cornelius Van Til: The Man and the Myth* (Jefferson, Md.: Trinity Foundation, 1986), 20.

[11] To tell the truth, I am not at all sure that Robbins understands the meaning of Van Til's proposal. He presents no analysis or paraphrase. The only thing evident is that Robbins does not like Van Til's terminology, which is to say that he does not like the *sound* of Van Til's formulation, whatever it may mean. But that sort of criticism is obscurantist in the literal sense: it hinders, rather than promotes, progress in understanding. It certainly does not deserve the attention of serious readers. I mention it only because people keep asking me questions about it.

[12] Ibid.

[13] See the discussion of Van Til's argument below.

formulation is logically contradictory: Van Til says that God is one person and three persons, and, on their view, such a formulation violates the law of noncontradiction. Now I will have more to say in later chapters about Van Til's view of logic. But if I may anticipate that discussion a bit, I would like to offer some replies to this criticism of Van Til.

1. Van Til never says that the doctrine of the Trinity is contradictory. His view of contradiction here is consistent with what he teaches elsewhere: "While we shun as poison the idea of the really contradictory we embrace with passion the idea of the *apparently* contradictory."[14] Nor does he deny the traditional view that God is one in one respect (essence) and three in another (person). His only qualification of this statement is that it "is not the whole truth of the matter." He understands his formulation to be an addition, a supplement, to the traditional one, not a denial of or replacement for it.

2. Clark and Robbins say nothing about Van Til's argument for his position.[15] Van Til is considering the implications of another statement, universally recognized as orthodox, that "each of the persons of the Godhead is co-terminous with the being of the Godhead."[16] That is to say, each of the persons is fully God, possessing all divine attributes. The persons are not parts of God, as though one could act without the others acting along with him. "God's being presents an absolute numerical identity."[17] He is one "being," not three; the three partake of one "essence."

Now the question becomes, is that one being personal or impersonal? Philosophers have sometimes said that we should distinguish between essence and individuality as follows: Fido, Rover, and Spot are three individuals with a common essence, namely the essence of "dogness" or "doghood." But "doghood" is an abstraction. You can put Fido on a leash, but you cannot so restrain doghood. Now is it legitimate to understand the Trinity (to be sure, a reality exalted far above the canine realm) according to this model? If so, the persons, Father, Son, and Spirit, would be the individuals, and the divine es-

---

[14]CGG, 9 (emphasis his).

[15]Clark once complained in correspondence with me that during the "Clark controversy" (to be discussed later in this volume), Van Til never considered Clark's arguments, but simply dismissed his statements as heterodox. Whether or not that is true, it appears that in this case the shoe is on the other foot.

[16]IST, 229.

[17]Ibid.

sence, God, would be an abstraction. But of course this model is entirely inadequate for the Trinity. God is not an abstraction. Nor is he a mere society of three gods, united by common abstract properties.

What is he, then? As we indicated earlier, Van Til's answer is that God is an "absolute person." Abstractions are impersonal. God is a concrete, personal reality. Our world is ruled by a person, not an abstract principle. As Van Til says, when God identified himself to us in revelation, "there was no universal being of which he was a particular instance."[18] If the three persons (individually and collectively) exhaust the divine essence (are "co-terminous" with it), then the divine essence itself must be personal. And if God is an absolute person, and he is one, there must be a sense in which he is one person.

It cannot be overlooked that Scripture speaks regularly about God acting personally (thinking, choosing, speaking, judging, saving), without ascribing that activity to one particular person of the Trinity. When the one God acts, he acts personally. Someone may argue that in these instances the Bible is speaking imprecisely, but such a hypothesis must bear a substantial burden of proof. And even if these references are applied to one or another of the divine persons, orthodox Trinitarian theology (Augustinian *circumincessio*) affirms that when one person acts, the others are acting too. The Son is in the Father, the Father is in the Son, the Spirit is in both the Father and the Son, and both of them are in the Spirit. Therefore, every act of God is a personal act involving all three persons acting in unity.

I do believe that when Van Til's argument is seriously considered, his formulation will not sound so outlandish. Indeed, I believe that the argument is cogent and that the formulation is true. It is also traditional, for it is clearly implied by the doctrine that the divine persons each contain the fullness of God.

3. How, then, do we relate the "one person" to the "three persons"? Van Til asserts that "this is a mystery that is beyond our comprehension."[19] Indeed! But he does not say that the two assertions are contradictory. Are they in fact contradictory? That may seem obvious, but in fact it is not necessarily the case. Anybody who has stud-

[18]Ibid., 232. Certainly God and the world may both be said to "be," and thus to "partake of being." But Van Til's point is that this is not to say that the basic nature of the universe is abstract ("being") and that God and man are mere variants of that abstract quality.

[19]Ibid., 230.

ied logic knows that something can be both A and not-A if the two A's have different senses. In this case, God can clearly be both one person and not-one person, if the meaning of "person" changes somewhat between the two uses.

The traditional language, "one in essence, three in person" (which, again, Van Til does not reject), brings out more clearly, of course, that the oneness and the threeness are in different respects. But the formulation "one person and three persons" does not deny that difference of respect. It is simply an alternative formulation that makes a point somewhat different from the point of the traditional language.

4. How is the word *person* used in different senses or respects? Obviously, there is some difference between the sense of "person" applied to the oneness of God and the sense applied to the three members of the Trinity. Van Til would agree, for example, with the creedal statements that the Father is the begetter, the Son is begotten, and the Spirit is the one who proceeds; the whole Godhead is neither begetter, begotten, nor proceeder. But neither Van Til nor I would claim to be able to state, precisely and exhaustively, the difference between God's essence and the individual persons of the Godhead. Doubtless the Clarkite critics of Van Til will find this a damaging admission, for they insist that all theological statements be perfectly precise. Never mind that Scripture itself often fails to be precise about the mysteries of the faith.[20]

But the creedal tradition, too, fails to give a "precise" account of the relations between God's "essence" and his "persons." The Greek term *ousia,* which was used to designate God's essence, was not, in the Greek language, precisely differentiated from *hypostasis,* the term used for the three persons. The choice of these terms was to some extent arbitrary. The church fathers needed a term to designate God's unity, and they chose *ousia.* They needed a term for God's plurality, and they chose *hypostasis.* But there was nothing about either term that uniquely fitted it for its particular task, over against the other. In-

[20]On an orthodox view, Scripture is always *true,* but it is not always maximally *precise.* That is an important point when we consider, e.g., biblical uses of round numbers, phenomenal language ("The sun rose"), etc. These are not errors, but they are certainly imprecise. Nor does Scripture give us a precise or comprehensive account of the eternal relations between Father, Son, Holy Spirit, and the divine essence.

deed, the church fathers might have reversed them ("one *hypostasis,* three *ousiai*") without loss. The Latin church in the West spoke of one *substantia,* but *substantia* is by etymology and use more interchangeable with *hypostasis* than with *ousia.* In English, we can translate both *hypostasis* and *substantia* as "substance." On that account, we can see that in effect the Greeks spoke of God as "three substances" and the Latins of "one substance." Doubtless these choices of terms caused some misunderstanding. But, from our vantage point, we cannot regard either formulation as unorthodox.

But if it is orthodox to say with the Greeks that God is three substances and with the Latins that he is one substance, then it is also orthodox to say that God is one substance and three substances—recognizing, of course, the disadvantages of such an apparently contradictory choice of terms. And if it is orthodox to say that God is one substance and three substances, it is also orthodox to say that God is one person and three persons.

The formulation "one person and three persons" is also valuable in curbing human intellectual pride. The fact is that we do not have precise definitions of "person" or "essence" or "substance." We cannot say precisely or exhaustively how *ousia* in God differs from *hypostasis,* or *prosopon,* or, for that matter, *substantia* or *persona.* "Cotermeneity," "mutual exhaustiveness," and "simplicity"[21] are very difficult concepts to comprehend. We can paint these relationships in broad strokes, seeking to summarize what Scripture says and trying to go no further than Scripture goes. But we are not equipped by revelation to dissect the Trinity or to perform any quasi-scientific, minute analysis of it. Scripture tells us that God is one, that the three are fully God, and that they enter into various personal relationships with one another. From these teachings we may draw implications and applications, up to a point.[22] But there is a point at which our reason must admit its weakness and simply bow before God's majesty.

On the basis of Scripture, we can say that God's nature and revelation are noncontradictory. That is a "good and necessary consequence" drawn from the truth and faithfulness of God. But Scripture does not promise that we will always be able to *demonstrate* the consis-

[21]I take these as roughly equivalent terms.

[22]Drawing implications and applications, what the Westminster Confession calls "good and necessary consequences" (I, 6), is not going "beyond" Scripture.

tency of biblical teaching, apart from the general consideration of God's truth and faithfulness. We may not always be able to show how two concepts can logically coexist. There may well be times when our inability to specify exhaustively the precise senses of terms we use will result in unresolved apparent contradictions. But why not? We walk by faith, not by sight.

The Problem of the One and the Many

Another distinctively Van Tillian contribution to our thinking about the Trinity is his use of the doctrine in connection with the "one-and-many problem." Most generally, the problem is man's quest "to find unity in the midst of the plurality of things."[23] More specifically:

> The *many* must be brought into contact with one another. But how do we know that they can be brought into contact with one another? How do we know that the many do not simply exist as unrelated particulars? The answer given is that in such a case we should know nothing of them; they would be abstracted from the body of knowledge that we have; they would be *abstract* particulars. On the other hand, how is it possible that we should obtain a unity that does not destroy the particulars? We seem to get our unity by generalizing, by abstracting from the particulars in order to include them into larger unities. If we keep up this process of generalization till we exclude all particulars, granted they can all be excluded, have we not stripped these particulars of their particularity? Have we then obtained anything but an *abstract* universal?[24]

Again, let me try to put Van Til's point into different and perhaps clearer language. After we are born, we gradually learn to organize rationally the "buzzing, blooming confusion" (William James) of our sense experience. A child learns to distinguish himself from his mother, to distinguish one object from another. His mind is organizing sensations into groups, each group representing a thing, an ob-

[23]DF2, 24.

[24]Ibid., 25–26.

ject of knowledge. He is coming to know objects by understanding their relationships with other objects. Fido would be one such object. With additional experience and education, we learn to organize these groups into larger groups. Eventually, we learn that Fido, Rover, Spot, and others themselves form a group that we call "dog." That represents an advance in learning, for it means that we recognize significant similarities among these animals and differences between them and other types of animals. Indeed, when we learn that Fido is a dog, it seems that we are learning his essence, what he really is. Then we learn that dogs can be grouped into still larger classes: canines, mammals, living beings, beings, being. This process is called "abstraction." Each of these steps may be seen as going deeper into the reality, the essence of things. Philosophizing about "being as such" seems to be the consummation of human knowledge.

On the other hand, the process of abstraction also brings cognitive loss. Fido, after all, is more than just a dog. He is two feet high, black and white, trained to roll over, partial to taking walks and playing ball. None of those qualities is included in the definition of "dog," for the concept "dog" covers some animals that have those qualities and some animals that do not. Thus, every step on the abstraction ladder is a step toward emptiness. The highest abstraction, "being," covers everything. But it includes nothing specific. As Hegel pointed out, "being," as a general or abstract term, is indistinguishable from "nothing." It might seem that we gain a very profound level of knowledge when we find "being" as the essence of all things. But actually, to say that Fido is a "being" is to say almost nothing about him.

So we might try, as some philosophers have, the opposite process: going *down* the abstraction ladder, from general to particular. We understand "being" by enumerating and describing the "beings." We similarly proceed to the living beings, mammals, and dogs. Even Fido may seem like something of an abstraction. For arguably our concept of Fido is put together from many experiences and memories.[25] We never see all of Fido at one time: once we see his profile,

[25]The emphasis here on experience will sound "empiricist" to some. However, I do not regard experience as pure sensation without any rational mental activity. There is no knowledge of human sense-data without a rational appropriation of them. In any case, the description here of the cognitive process is not intended as a description of my own epistemology, but only as a description of a common way of formulating the process of human knowledge.

another time his face, another time his backside. We never see his liver or kidneys, unless we observe him under veterinary surgery; yet, from other learning experiences, we know they are in him. Those who wish to gain knowledge by moving from abstract to concrete will want to reduce knowledge to its smallest constituents. What are the elements that go into our concept of Fido? They are a warm "licking" sensation on our right hand (rather, many momentary ones, strung together by our mind), a visual impression of whiteness with a black patch, etc.

As we move down the abstraction ladder in this way, it seems again that we are learning about essences. When we reduce our experience of Fido to its elements, it seems, we are learning what he "really is." In moving up the abstraction ladder, we sought to define objects by examining their relationships to one another. In moving down, we seek to define relationships by examining the objects related.

Or are we fooling ourselves? For we never experience any of these "elements," momentary sensations or whatever, outside of a broader context. We never actually *experience* a momentary impression of whiteness; we experience larger complexes of meaning, like Fido himself. When we speak of momentary impressions, we are *analyzing* experience into what might be plausible constituents, as the scientist analyzes ordinary things into molecules, atoms, and subatomic particles. But we have never *seen* momentary sense impressions any more than the scientist has actually seen his subatomic particles. Momentary sense impressions are actually *abstractions* from the total reality. In this way, we can see the implausibility of suggesting that Fido is "really" a set of sensations or impressions, glued together, as it were, by the mind.

And as we move down the abstraction ladder, there is also a loss of content, as there was when we tried to move in the other direction. Let us imagine that we could trace the elements of the elements of the elements to the point where we could discover some ultimate element of human experience, as scientists have sought for ultimate particles in the physical universe. Let us call that element "ultimate matter," for it would be much the same as Aristotle's "prime matter." What would it be? If it were identifiable, describable, like Fido, then it would be subject to further analysis and would not be the ultimate constituent of experience. Evidently, then, if it were really ultimate, nothing could be said about it. To put the point differently: it could have no qualities, because it would be the bearer of all qualities. But even to say that is to say something about it. So it seems that the very notion of an ultimate component to experience is self-contradictory (as was, indeed, Aristotle's concept of prime matter). The ultimate component is both nothing and something.

In the end, there is no difference between "being in general" and "ultimate matter." Both concepts are empty, uninformative, and unintelligible. And if the real essence of everything, the real truth about the world, is to be found in either of these concepts, then the world is completely devoid of intelligible meaning. If abstract being is the ultimate reality, then there is no particularity. If abstract particularity is the ultimate truth, then there is no unity in the world. If both are somehow true, then all is chaos, and nothing is true.[26]

Another way to look at the problem is this: if, in the end, objects are defined by their relations, and relations are defined by their objects, a vicious circularity enters, so that everything remains undefined. If objects are understood by their relations and relations by their objects, how can the process get started?

How is it that this seemingly well-intentioned search for truth leads up such a blind alley? Van Til's analysis is that essentially both concepts are idols, and thus self-destructive. They are idols because they are the result of man's desire for an exhaustive understanding of the world, an understanding that only God can have. As is always the case in idolatry, we seek for an ultimate within the creation, and when we think we have found it, we discover in due course that it is utterly powerless.

In Van Til's view, unbelieving thought always sees the world as a combination of abstract unity ("being in general," or other variants of the idea) and abstract particularity (what we have called "ultimate matter"). Both abstract unity and abstract particularity are meaningless in themselves and impossible to relate to one another. As such, unbelieving worldviews always reduce to unintelligible nonsense. This is, essentially, Van Til's critique of secular philosophy (and its influence on Christian theology). We shall examine some of his examples later in this book.

They pursue abstract unity and particularity because they presumptuously seek a knowledge of the world that is available only to

---

[26]Compare this discussion with the discussion of the ways of eminence and negation in chap. 4. The issues are the same in both cases.

God, and because they fail to see that the intelligibility of the world is not due to abstract aspects of the world; rather, it is due to God's creation and direction of the world. The secularist tries to account for the world by reference to impersonal principles, but Scripture shows us that only the personal God can account for his creation. Only in God, then, is there an exhaustive and utterly intelligible rationale for the creation.

Another way to look at it is this: the unbeliever's search for unity is essentially the search for a criterion of truth, a norm or standard. But in any non-Christian worldview, the criterion of truth must be impersonal, rather than personal. Ultimately, that criterion will be a concept of "being as such" or "ultimate matter," as we have seen. But neither of these concepts can serve as a criterion of truth. Neither has any content. And neither creates an obligation to believe anything, as any ultimate criterion must do.[27]

God stands in contrast to these idolatrous concepts. His plan is perfectly unified; nothing is out of order; nothing is unknown to him. At the same time, his omniscience does not compromise the reality and intelligibility of the particulars, the individual details of his plan. Nor do the details compromise the overall unity. The ultimate unity is a person, not a principle or an abstract concept. Therefore, that unity is not without content. And the ultimate particularities, the ultimate details, are also divine, as God's plan is his own self-expression.

God's plan is a personal one and many, because his nature is one and many. The "manifoldness" of God is seen in the diversity of his attributes, his thoughts, and his plans. But it is seen preeminently in the three persons of the Trinity. There is nothing in the persons that is not in the divine unity, and there is nothing in the divine unity that is not fully expressed in the persons. In God, all particularities are fully united, and all unity is fully expressed in detail. Indeed, God's oneness *is* a unity of the richness of his nature, and God's richness is his "self-contained fullness," the richness of his uniform character.

Because God is an absolute person, he can also serve as the ultimate standard, the final criterion for the truth of creaturely thought.

In those senses, Van Til says, the Trinity is the "solution to the problem of the one and the many." It is not that somehow the Trinity

[27]Compare my argument to this effect in AGG, 89–118.

furnishes a model by which abstract unity and abstract particularity can, after all, be meaningfully joined. They cannot be meaningfully joined. Nor is it that the Trinity shows us how human knowledge of the creation can be exhaustive, after all, but on theistic presuppositions. No, human beings cannot know the world exhaustively, period.[28] When we try to do that, we run into the brick walls of abstract being and abstract particularity.

Rather, the doctrine of the Trinity calls us to look to God in faith. We are to understand that although we do not know the world exhaustively, he does. Insofar as we can know the world, it is because he gives us revelation and the ability to repeat his thoughts on an analogical, finite level. And insofar as we cannot know the world, we can trust that the world is nevertheless an intelligible whole. Things that are mysterious to us do not spring from an ultimate chaos or meaninglessness; they spring, rather, from the wonderful riches of God's thought, which transcends our understanding. And in our ignorance we may also be sure that God has at least given us sufficient knowledge to do his will. And, in the final analysis, the only reason why we should seek any knowledge at all is to do God's will.

So we are called to faith. But is this a blind faith? If so, then the Trinity really does not solve the problem in any meaningful sense. In Van Til's view and mine, our faith is not blind. In the first place, it is the most rational thing in the world to believe the Word of the world's Creator as to the structure of his work. Second, the Trinity shows us, at least in very general terms, how ultimate unity and diversity can be reconciled. They can be reconciled if they are seen not as abstract qualities, but as qualities of a person. "Being in general" does nothing to unite the particulars of our experience and therefore to illumine that experience. But it is immensely illuminating to see the world as the craftsmanship of a person who has thought everything through and given everything its proper place. Here is a unity that includes the details, a unity that is a unity of the details.[29]

I will summarize with a statement from Van Til: "My unity is the unity of a child who walks with its father through the woods."[30]

---

[28]See IST, 24.

[29]This is the way I understand Van Til's use of the term "concrete universal" in application to God, as in DF2, 26. This phrase comes from idealist philosophy, but Van Til seeks to sharply differentiate his view from theirs.

[30]WIB, 20.

Facts and Laws

The problem of the one and the many exists not only at the ultimate level, but also at the level of everyday knowledge. Some readers may protest that it is not important whether "pure being" and "pure matter" are intelligible concepts, for most people are not worried about the highest and lowest levels of abstraction. They only seek to know the middle levels. But the Van Tillian analysis affects all of human knowledge.[31]

Scientific knowledge involves grouping facts under laws, or formulating laws to describe the facts, which is the same thing. In everyday life we also seek to organize facts, to bring various kinds of data and experience together under regular categories. This pattern describes many different areas of human knowledge. Rousas J. Rushdoony, for example, indicates how politics seeks to reconcile the interest of the many to the order (unity) of society through the formulation of laws.[32]

On an unbelieving basis, however, there is no particular reason to believe that there are laws that accurately describe facts. Who is to know that reality is regular at all? If the world is ultimately the result of chance (or "ultimate matter," which is the same thing), surely it is equally likely that the world will be random or chaotic; and if our senses and reason seem to be telling us differently, why should we believe that in a world of chaos they would be telling us the truth?

And if chance is king, where do laws come from? They do not exist in the objective world, because that world is the result of chance, not the product of a designer who gives it a structure of regularity. Since Kant, most philosophers have believed that structures of order originate in the human mind. But why should we believe that such structures would have any application to the actual world? Indeed, if the world is not orderly in itself, they cannot apply to it. Are these laws not, in the end, abstractions that (like "pure being") have no application to the world?

Put these factors together: subjective laws applied to lawless facts. The situation is not only hopeless, but contradictory. It will not lead to greater knowledge, but only to skepticism about the very possibility of truth.

---

[31]Here, see Van Til's discussion in IST, 22–23.

[32]JA, 339–49.

It is also the case that scientific and everyday knowledge, like the more abstract speculation discussed in the last section, require criteria. But laws, conceived impersonally, do not impose upon us criteria, obligations to believe one thing rather than another. Much less (to recall Rushdoony's concerns) can impersonal laws claim the allegiance of persons in political society.

Therefore, it is not only metaphysical speculation about ultimates, but concrete, everyday knowledge as well, that requires a Trinitarian presupposition.

CHAPTER SIX

The Sovereignty of God

We should expect to find in Van Til a strong doctrine of the sovereignty of God from what we discussed before. We expect this, not only because of his personal and ecclesiastical background, but also from his discussions of the divine attributes and the Trinity, which we have already considered. Van Til's treatment of the divine attributes focuses on the "self-contained" nature of God. If the world were not wholly under God's control, he would to some extent be relative to things outside himself. He would not, then, be fully self-contained.

Van Til's doctrine of the Trinity focuses on the issue of correlativism. God is not a bare oneness that is relative to the pluralities of the world. He is a oneness relative only to his own Trinitarian plurality. This reinforces Van Til's emphasis on the self-containment of God. And his treatment of the one-and-many problem emphasizes that God, and nobody else, has an exhaustive interpretation of reality. But if God has eternally interpreted everything that comes to pass, then surely nothing can happen without his foreordination: "The facts and laws of the world are what they are because of God's plan with respect to them. Therefore, his knowledge of the world is involved in his plan for the world. Thus, his knowledge of the facts and laws of the world precede the existence of the world."[1]

---

[1]DF2, 11.

God's decree, then, "is the final and exclusively determining power of whatsoever comes to pass."[2] It is "the source of all substance and power in the created universe."[3]

Determinism and Freedom

Van Til denies that his position is a form of philosophical determinism. We may, I think, call Van Til a determinist if by that we mean simply that for Van Til every event in the finite world has a cause. Certainly, for Van Til, it is the case that all events in the finite world have their necessary and sufficient cause in God's decree.

But Van Til's position is different in significant ways from typical deterministic systems in the history of philosophy. For one thing, as we have seen, God's foreordination on Van Til's view is personal, while determinism in philosophy typically ascribes events to causes that are ultimately impersonal. "Philosophical necessitarianism stands for an ultimate impersonalism: consistent Christianity stands for an ultimate personalism."[4]

Another difference between Van Til's position and secular determinism lies in the distinction between primary and secondary causes. Van Til maintains that although we are never free from divine control, we are sometimes free from the "causal nexus" of the universe. This point is less explicit in Van Til, but it is implicit, for example, in a passage where he quotes Arminius as denying "that a thing which, in regard to second causes, is done *contingently* is said to be done *necessarily* in regard to the divine decree."[5] Evidently, Van Til here intends to affirm what Arminius denies, namely, that events that are foreordained necessarily according to the divine decree may nevertheless be contingent (i.e., free, not determined) in relation to finite causes.

By rejecting determinism, Van Til is able, positively, to maintain a robust view of human freedom. We should note, for example, that he sees no difficulty in maintaining both that the kingdom of God is man's highest good, and that "the ethical ideal for man should be self-

---

[2]CA, 11.

[3]IST, 247.

[4]CTETH, 35; cf. DF2, 62.

[5]CTK, 211 (emphasis his).

realization."[6] Self-realization means that *"man must work out his own will."*[7] That means that man's will must "become increasingly *spontaneous* in its reactivity . . . become increasingly *fixed in its self-determination* . . . increase in *momentum*."[8]

Remarkably, here, Van Til calls for the strengthening of the human will, not its abolition. Of course, he is not advocating an increase of willfulness or selfishness, or an attempt to sever the will's created dependence on God. Rather, he calls for an increase in the soul's resolve to do God's will. But that resolve is to become more and more spontaneous, fixed, and growing in momentum. What he means is that spiritual maturity brings more internal and less external constraint. Growing in Christ means that we become more and more willing to do his will; our obedience becomes more delightful, more the passion of our own heart. It becomes habitual, in a good sense. A mature servant of God does not need to be browbeaten (by parents, preachers, and others) into seeking God's righteousness. He loves holiness and steadily increases in it. For Van Til, then, human freedom is not a concept grudgingly conceded in the debate with Arminians. It is a fact of positive and practical importance in the Christian life.

We should keep in mind here the importance that Van Til places on the Creator-creature distinction. Often, theologians assume that any sovereignty we ascribe to God must remove spontaneity and freedom from man. This is an error both of hyper-Calvinists, who compromise human responsibility in order to maintain divine sovereignty, and of Arminians, who do the reverse. Unwittingly, both hyper-Calvinists and Arminians at this point see God and man on a common scale of being, so that anything ascribed to God must be taken from man, and vice versa.

Certainly there are some prerogatives that belong exclusively to God, for example, the right to receive religious worship and the ultimate right to take human life. Ascribing these rights to God means denying them to man. But we must beware of applying such reason-

---

[6]CTETH, 44. The term *self-realization* comes from the idealist vocabulary, though of course in its broader context Van Til's view is significantly different from idealism.

[7]Ibid., 45 (emphasis his).

[8]Ibid., 45–46 (emphasis his). See also Van Til's reference to the "spontaneity" of the biblical writers inspired by God in PDS, 25–26, and his account of the development of obedience in the Christian education of the young in ECE, 152–55.

ing to all aspects of the divine-human relationship. For example, we should not assume that because salvation is foreordained by God, human decisions are of no consequence. The Bible says that human faith is necessary for salvation. Sometimes, evidently, God's primary causality negates creaturely causality, but sometimes the former reinforces the latter. How can we tell when there is negation and when there is reinforcement? The answer is simply that the Bible tells us.

Primary causes can either negate or reinforce secondary causes because God and the world are not on a common scale of being. It is not the case that divine agency always eliminates human agency. There are two distinct levels of reality: that of the Creator and that of the creature. There are also two distinct levels of causality: divine causation and causation from within the world. Most events have both primary and secondary causes, but God may, of course, work "without, above, and against"[9] the secondary causes at his pleasure.

Perhaps the best illustration (though Van Til does not use it)[10] is this: In a well-crafted novel, the author creates a world in which events take place in meaningful causal relationships to one another. Each event has an intelligible cause within the world of the novel. But of course each event also has a higher cause, in the author's mind. Normally, such an author will try to maintain the orderly causal structure of his created universe. He may, of course, also work "without, above, and against" that causal order when he is pleased to do so. Usually, however, when an author disrupts the causal order of his novel, the narrative becomes less satisfying. Critics accuse such an author of bringing things about by a *deus ex machina*.

Because the true God is infinitely wise, his relaxations of causal regularity in the world do not corrupt, but enhance, the power of his drama. And, of course, in the case of God there is also the difference that his creation is real, not fictional. But the two cases are parallel in that in each there are two levels of causality. We may put it this way: normally, events in the world have two sets of necessary and sufficient conditions.

Thus, it is Van Til's "two-circle metaphysics," his distinction between Creator and creature, that enables him to have a strong doctrine of divine sovereignty together with a strong doctrine of human freedom.

---

[9]Westminster Confession of Faith, V, 3.

[10]It was suggested to me by Vern Poythress.

Van Til also addresses the moral responsibility of man. He argues that it is not only consistent with, but actually based upon, divine sovereignty. Unless God's will is utterly self-determinative, the world is controlled to some extent by chance. Therefore:

> As Christians we hold that determinate human experience could work to no end, could work in accordance with no plan, and could not even get under way, if it were not for the existence of the absolute will of God.
>
> It is on this ground then that we hold to the absolute will of God as the presupposition of the will of man. Looked at in this way, that which to many seems at first glance to be the greatest hindrance to moral responsibility, namely the conception of an absolutely sovereign God, becomes the very foundation of its possibility.[11]

Evil

On Van Til's view, divine sovereignty extends to all things, and therefore also to evil and sin. God is not responsible for sin, but we should deny "that anything happens in spite of him and in circumvention of his purpose."[12] In this connection he often refers to Calvin's polemic against Pighius in his treatise *The Eternal Predestination of God.* God's decree "is inclusive and permissive of the fact of sin."[13] According to Van Til, we may "speak of the permissive will of God in order to stress man's undoubted responsibility for sin, but this distinction may never lead to subversion of the clear teaching of Scripture on the all-controlling if ultimate and mysterious power of God."[14]

"Mysterious" is the operative word to describe Van Til's response to the "problem of evil," the question of how a good, all-powerful God could permit or even foreordain the presence of evil in his creation. Because of his biblical view of divine sovereignty, he is unable to "defend" God by appealing to human free will, the

---

[11]DF2, 62; cf. CGG, 140.
[12]IST, 248.
[13]Ibid.
[14]Ibid., 175.

unreality of evil, the weakness of God, etc. Positively, he says relatively little about the problem, but I think he says everything that is essential:

> The Christian claims this [with respect to the problem of evil his position is in accord with conscience] because he interprets his moral consciousness, as an aspect of his total experience, in terms of his presuppositions. He knows that the judge of all the earth must do right. All the facts and problems of evil and sin take their meaning from and find their solution in terms of the story of Scripture. The approvals and disapprovals of his conscience take their meaning from this story and from this story alone.[15]

He adds a *reductio* of non-Christian claims about evil: either the non-Christian cannot distinguish good from evil, or, if he can, he cannot hope that good will triumph: "If those who think they are good succeed in making what they think is 'good' to prevail upon earth, it can only be the suppression of the 'good' of others who also think they are 'good.' Thus power politics would forever replace all ethical distinctions."[16] This passage is almost prophetic of postmodernism, deconstruction, and the "political correctness" movements today, which relativize all moral discourse while seeking to require everybody to conform to their values. They claim that everybody else's values are relative, while theirs are absolute,[17] and theirs are to be enforced by raw power.

Here is another response by Van Til to the problem of evil:

> A Christian theodicy[18] . . . will need to start frankly from the presupposition of the self-sufficient God. It goes without saying that this self-sufficient God, who controls all things and knows all things because he controls them, can use the best means to attain his end. But what are the best means? They

[15]DF2, 218; cf. the argument with Montague on pp. 213–16.

[16]Ibid., 218.

[17]Van Til's "irrationalism" and "rationalism," respectively. See chap. 17.

[18]*Theodicy* means "justification of God." It refers to any attempted solution to the problem of evil. Van Til does not distinguish between "theodicy" and "defense," as do such writers as Alvin Plantinga.

> are those that God sees fit to use. And since they are those that God sees fit to use they may be wholly beyond the reach of human understanding. It was wholly beyond Job's understanding to know why he should suffer. . . . He found the solution only when finally he surrendered himself fully into the hands of the sovereign God. To be sure, the wisdom of God appears in the world, and man can see something of it. Yet it remains true that God is a God that hideth himself, and no man should essay to approve or condemn the deeds of the Holy One by standards of his own devising. The Reformed "theodicy" is therefore quite different from the Romanist and Arminian.[19]

Essentially, Van Til's theodicy is an appeal to God's inscrutable wisdom. God has the answer, but he has not chosen to reveal it to us, at least not comprehensively. Our thinking must be subject to his revelation, and where that revelation is silent, we must be silent as well.

At one point, Van Til appears to go beyond this appeal to mystery. Replying to Buswell's criticism, he cites Calvin's treatise *On the Eternal Predestination of God,* in which Calvin claims to absolve God from the charge of being the author of sin.[20] Calvin's argument is that God is the "ultimate" cause of sinful acts, while the wicked themselves are the "proximate" causes. Van Til quotes Calvin and Hodge at length in this connection, and with approval.[21] Although this approach to the problem of evil has some roots in Reformed tradition, I believe it is ultimately unsuccessful. I do not see how God is absolved from complicity in evil merely because his causality is once removed from the event. If I hire A to kill B, I am as responsible as A, am I not? The indirectness of my murder does not remove the guilt from me. Is it different with God? Normally, on a Reformed view of the matter, the standards that God reveals to us are standards that reflect his own nature, though there are some cases where he

[19]IST, 237–38. For an expansion of this "Jobian" response to the problem of evil, see my AGG, 149-90.

[20]Theologians rarely define "author of sin," although they always insist that the phrase does not apply to God. That creates confusion, especially between Calvinists and Arminians. I take it to mean "doer of sin," with some note of "commending sin."

[21]DF2, 183–87.

has prerogatives and rights that we do not have. Evidently he has such rights in this case. But he has revealed little or nothing to us in this connection.

In the end, the matter resolves again into mystery. The proximate-ultimate distinction does not help. Van Til would have been better off to stick with his Jobian theodicy.

Election and Reprobation

On Van Til's metaphysic, a Calvinist soteriology is inescapable:

> Even if we say that in the case of any one individual sinner the question of salvation is in the last analysis dependent upon man rather than upon God, that is if we say that man can of himself accept or reject the gospel as he pleases, we have made the eternal God dependent upon man. We have then, in effect, denied the incommunicable attributes of God. If we refuse to mix the eternal and the temporal at the point of creation and at the point of the incarnation we must also refuse to mix them at the point of salvation.[22]

Thus, "the Arminian is letting the enemy into the fort."[23] The Arminian's error does not begin with soteriology, but with the doctrine of God. He has failed to understand the fundamental relationship of God and man.

In Reformed theology, election is God's choice before the foundation of the world to save some human beings from sin. Reprobation is his determination, also eternal, to "pass by" the others, allowing them to be condemned. In Reformed circles, there is little dispute concerning election: it is by God's sovereign will, apart from anything in us. But reprobation has not been so easy to formulate. Some have resisted the notion of "double" predestination, the idea that God foreordains some to eternal life and others to eternal death. Nevertheless, Calvin and the Reformed confessions do teach this duality, and it is hard to conceive of how God could elect some eternally without at the same time reprobating all of those who are not among the elect. Scrip-

---

[22]Ibid., 19; cf. CTK, 194–95.
[23]DF2, 19.

ture also refers to reprobation in Matthew 7:23, Romans 9:13–22, and elsewhere.

Others, while accepting both election and reprobation (and thus "double predestination"), have questioned the "parallel" between the two. The Canons of Dordt, one of the major Reformed confessions, point out an asymmetry between the two: those who are elect are saved by grace, apart from anything in them; however, those who are reprobate are punished for their own works. Van Til accepts that asymmetry. He teaches that in reprobation, man's sin is the "proximate" cause of his condemnation, but God's decree is the "ultimate" cause.[24]

At the same time, as we have seen, Van Til does want to insist upon God's foreordination (but not "authorship") of the sin that leads to condemnation. Recall his exposition of Calvin on this point,[25] against Buswell, who suggests that man's sin is the only cause of his eternal state.

In this sense, Van Til affirms the "equal ultimacy of election and reprobation." G. C. Berkouwer criticizes him for this phrase, thinking that Van Til denies the asymmetry affirmed in the Canons of Dordt.[26] In my view, that criticism is not justified. When Van Til speaks of "equal ultimacy," he is not saying that election and reprobation are in every respect symmetrical. Indeed, he denies that and embraces the language of Dordt: "God's decree is not *in the same manner* back of reprobation as of election."[27] Van Til is simply saying that God's decree embraces everything that happens, and that it equally foreordains the eternal destinies of the elect and the reprobate. The decree of reprobation ensures its accomplishment just as certainly as the decree of election.

Berkouwer assumes that the phrase "equal ultimacy" has an obvious meaning, a meaning contrary to the Canons of Dordt, and does not even consider the possibility that Van Til might mean something else by the phrase. On the contrary, it seems obvious to me that the phrase is much more naturally taken in Van Til's sense than in the one Berkouwer ascribes to it. "Equal ultimacy," obviously, has to

---

[24]DF2, 182–87; cf. TJD, 45–95; CGG, 64–67.

[25]DF2, 182–87; cf. CGG, 138.

[26]*The Triumph of Grace in the Theology of Karl Barth* (Grand Rapids: Eerdmans, 1956), 390.

[27]TJD, 90.

do with *ultimate* causation, not with the presence or absence of secondary causes such as human works.

One suspects, however, that critics of Van Til's doctrine of predestination are really less concerned with the nuances of the election-reprobation parallel than they are with double predestination as such. In affirming both election and reprobation, Van Til is unhesitant and unapologetic. It is important to his epistemology and his apologetic, as well as his theology, to affirm that God has definitively interpreted every fact, including the condemnation of the lost, before the foundation of the world.

He did not, of course, see this matter as logically perspicuous. Ultimately, hell, like the lesser horrors of history, is subject to the Jobian theodicy, the theodicy of mystery. We can accept mystery in theism because the alternative is to renounce all meaning, including the very distinction between good and evil.

CHAPTER SEVEN

Analogical Knowledge

In our analysis of Van Til's "metaphysics of knowledge," we have discussed his doctrine of God and his view of the general relationship between God and the world. Now we must proceed to discuss how this metaphysical perspective bears upon human knowledge.

As we have seen, Van Til's metaphysics emphasizes (1) the distinction between Creator and creature and (2) the sovereignty of the Creator over the creature. We may well anticipate, therefore, that his epistemology will emphasize precisely those relationships in the area of knowledge: the distinction between God's knowledge and ours, and the sovereignty of God in matters of knowledge.

Van Til sums up these emphases in the term *analogy*. Human knowledge is "analogous" to God's, which means that it is (1) created and therefore different from God's own knowledge, and (2) subject to God's control and authority:

> The system [of knowledge] that Christians seek to obtain may . . . be said to be *analogical. By this is meant that God is the original and that man is the derivative. God has absolute self-contained system within himself.* What comes to pass in history happens in accord with that system or plan by which he orders the universe. *But man, as God's creature, cannot have a replica of that system of God. He cannot have a reproduction of that system.* He must, to be sure, think God's thoughts after him; but this means

that he must, in seeking to form his own system, constantly be subject to the authority of God's system *to the extent* that this is revealed to him.[1]

Van Til's choice of the word "analogical," together with the terms historically contrasted with it, namely, "univocal" and "equivocal," poses some problems.[2] Thomas Aquinas, followed by centuries of Roman Catholic thinkers, used these terms in a way quite different from Van Til. Aquinas speaks of "analogy" in terms of being, and then in terms of predication.

The "analogy of being," which Aquinas borrowed from Aristotle and Neoplatonism, is a continuum that runs from God at the top to undifferentiated matter at the bottom.[3] God has the most being, bare matter the least. Beings higher on the scale have a greater "unity between essence and existence," which means, roughly, that their nature governs their actions and experience. God's actions and experience are completely governed by himself, by what he is. Man's actions and experience are at least partly governed by factors outside himself. Undifferentiated matter, at the bottom of the scale, has no essence to express; it is strictly nonbeing or nothing.[4]

Beings at the same level on the scale are related "univocally," in Aquinas's construction. Beings at far different levels are related "equivocally." Beings at closer levels are related "analogously." There are analogies, or similarities, between being at every point on the continuum, except, perhaps, between pure matter and the beings above it. Everything is alike, at least in that it *is*.

Aquinas's doctrine of predication, or the meanings of terms, follows this analysis. A word like *wise* applies in different senses to objects at various points along the continuum. It applies "univocally" to be-

---

[1]CTK, 16 (emphasis his); cf. DF2, 39; DF1, 64.

[2]In what follows, I am borrowing heavily from Gilbert Weaver's excellent article, "Man: Analogue of God," in JA, 321–27.

[3]Certainly Aquinas did not intend to deny the Christian doctrine of creation, or the distinction between Creator and creature. But alongside his orthodox statements of these doctrines, he employed ideas from Greek philosophy that were inconsistent with these doctrines. See other discussions of Aquinas in chaps. 19 and 25 of this book.

[4]Compare my discussion in chap. 5 of the attempt to gain knowledge by ascending and descending the abstraction ladder. Van Til believes that Aquinas's continuum of being and nonbeing is essentially the same as the continuum of empty abstractions and ultimate matter.

ings who are at the same level, e.g., to Bill and to Charles. It applies "equivocally" to beings far removed from one another, e.g., to Bill and to a chess strategy. To beings closely related, but at different levels on the scale, terms are used "analogously." God's wisdom is different from Bill's, but it is also similar, although we cannot be sure precisely wherein the similarity lies. Because of God's simplicity, his unity of essence and existence, *wisdom* refers to everything God is. But Bill's wisdom may coexist with foolishness.

In Aquinas's view of language, "univocal" is more or less equivalent to "literal," and "equivocal" to "merely metaphorical." "Analogical" language is figurative language, but somehow closer to the literal than equivocal language is.[5]

Aquinas's doctrine implies a certain agnosticism about God. We can never speak univocally of God, only analogously. In our usual Bible study, when we read about Christ being a "lamb" or the "Lion of Judah," we recognize in these expressions metaphors that can (apart from literary nuance) be expressed more literally. But, for Aquinas, there is always a point beyond which such literalization cannot go. Whatever we say about God is, ultimately, figurative language that cannot be expressed literally.

Some, such as Gordon Clark,[6] have argued that this view of Aquinas amounts to skepticism. Clark's and similar arguments raise questions about what sort of meaning, if any, is carried by figurative language, apart from literal explanations of it. They also pose the question of whether there is an element of metaphor in all language. If there is, then no language is "purely literal," and the difference between literal and figurative is a difference in degree, rather than a difference between two sharply contrasted categories. And if the difference between literal and figurative is a difference of degree, then the demand for literal explanations of figurative terms raises the question, "How literal?" And the advantage of relatively literal language over relatively figurative language becomes rather hard to define.

At any rate, Clark wrote that Van Til's view of analogy was the same as that of Aquinas and therefore subject to Clark's assessment of Aquinas's position.[7]

---

[5]I am making vague distinctions. I do not believe that his own account can be made more precise than this.

[6]Clark, *A Christian View of Men and Things* (Grand Rapids: Eerdmans, 1951).

[7]Clark, "The Bible as Truth," *Bibliotheca Sacra* 94 (April 1957): 166.

On the contrary, Weaver is surely correct in arguing that Van Til's view of analogy is very different from that of Aquinas. Van Til strongly opposes Aquinas's view of the analogy of being and the view of knowledge connected with it.[8] He believes that Aquinas's view of analogy presupposes a continuum between God and man.

His own view of analogy, summarized in our earlier quotation, is that human knowledge is a "finite replica" of God's.[9] It is not God's own knowledge, nor is it on a continuum with God's knowledge. Like everything human, it is created, creaturely, finite. Nevertheless, our knowledge is a finite *replica* of God's knowledge.[10] That is to say, in human knowledge our thoughts image God's in such a way that they can be judged to be true. When we obtain knowledge, we "think God's thoughts after him."

Van Til also uses "analogous" and "analogical" to describe a method of reasoning, a method of obtaining knowledge. Note that in the quotation from *A Christian Theory of Knowledge* at the outset of this chapter and the other passages cited with it, Van Til mentions the importance of being subject to God's revelation. This is "analogous thinking" or "analogous reasoning."[11] Van Til speaks of such reasoning as "self-consciously analogical."[12] "Univocal" thinking, in contrast, presupposes human autonomy and renounces proper submission to divine authority. I shall have more to say about this later in connection with Van Til's discussions of revelation and of the ethics of knowledge.

Like Aquinas, therefore, Van Til's view of analogy expresses a metaphysical position; however, the metaphysical views of the two men were very different. Both Van Til and Aquinas also drew epistemological consequences from their respective views of analogy; the consequences they drew, however, were very different.

From his doctrine of analogy, Aquinas also drew consequences concerning the use of terms, concluding that no human language

---

[8]IST, 206–10; CTK, 16–17; SCE, 60; RP, 83–105; WSA, 32–61; GH, 267–86.

[9]IST, 206.

[10]Van Til was not absolutely consistent in his terminology. In the earlier passage quoted from CTK, he denies that we can have a "replica" of God's knowledge, while in IST, 206, he asserts that we can have a "finite replica." There is an apparent contradiction here, but I think it is plain what he is saying. The "replica" denied in CTK is clearly not the "finite replica" of IST. See the following chapter for a more complete view of Van Til's position on the relation of God's knowledge to ours.

[11]Cf. also PDS, 12–15.

[12]CTK, 16.

about God could be literal, or "univocal." That is the conclusion that Clark criticizes as skeptical. Does Van Til's doctrine of analogy entail anything similar? I think not. Weaver is right to say, "For [Van Til] analogy applies not to terms, but to the overall process of human thought: man is God's created analogue in both his being and his knowledge," and he rightly accuses Clark of the fallacy of equivocation.[13] Clark is wrong to suppose that Van Til means the same thing as Aquinas by the term "analogy." I think Weaver is also right to suggest that Van Til should have chosen a different term by which to describe his concept of finite replication. He suggests, "It might be said that man's knowledge bears an *image-relationship* to God's knowledge, or that man's knowledge is *reflective* of that of God."[14]

We might well ask at this point (though Weaver does not) whether Van Til ever discusses the possibility of literal human language about God. So far as I know, he does not. He does insist that human language about God is necessarily "anthropomorphic."[15] In these contexts his concern is to emphasize the traditional Reformed doctrine of accommodation, namely, that God speaks to us in ways that we, as finite creatures, can understand. He uses fully human language, not some mysterious intratrinitarian communication. But that leaves open the question of whether a fully human language can speak literal truth about God.

When Van Til tells us to be "fearlessly anthropomorphic," he is not telling us to be agnostic, fearing that apparently literal biblical teachings may, after all, be nonliteral. On the contrary, he is telling us to affirm the nonliteral teachings with confidence, since they contain genuine (I am tempted to say "literal") truth. In *Common Grace and the Gospel,*[16] he tells us to say fearlessly that "God's attitude has changed with respect to mankind," since Scripture represents God's attitude that way. We know, on the other hand, also from Scripture, that God "in himself is changeless." I think that Van Til would admit that the former formulation is less literal than the latter. But he wants us to take the first seriously. I gather that he believes the first formulation teaches us something important that we could not learn from the second alone. So Van Til is not calling us to greater agnosticism, as did

[13]JA, 327.
[14]Ibid. (emphasis his).
[15]IST, 205; CGG, 73; CTK, 37.
[16]P. 73.

Aquinas's doctrine of analogy, but rather to greater confidence. He is not trying to say that apparently literal expressions are really figurative, but that apparently figurative expressions contain some element of literal truth. He is telling us that even the most apparently nonliteral expressions should be set forth with confidence, as indeed Scripture sets them forth. If explanations are necessary, and those explanations are themselves scriptural, then let them be given too. This whole process leads us to true understandings of God's revelation.

Van Til's principle, "All Scripture is anthropomorphic," has the effect of narrowing the apparent gap between literal and figurative. It is not that the statement "God changed his attitude" is purely and simply figurative, while the statement "God does not change" is purely and simply literal. Both expressions partake of the limitations involved in conversations between Creator and creature—similar in some measure to the limitations in conversations between parents and small children. But the figurative expressions are not merely aesthetic decorations, easily replaced by literal truth. Rather, they convey some things that we would not otherwise know, some things that we need to add to our storehouse of literal truth. If we knew only that God did not change, we might be tempted to ignore the significance of history, the movements in time between pre-Fall and post-Fall, Old and New Testament, pre-Incarnation and Incarnation, pre-Resurrection and post-Resurrection, apostolic age and postapostolic age. "God changed his attitude" tells us that God takes these movements in time seriously, as we shall see in our discussion of common grace in chapter 16.

So Van Til's doctrine of anthropomorphism does not settle the question of whether human language can speak literally of God. I asked him once about that, and his reply was that he had never thought much about it and had not formulated a position on the question. Evidently it was not an issue he considered important to his epistemology; in that respect he is very unlike Gordon Clark. I suspect that Van Til held the view I suggested earlier, that there are degrees (and perhaps kinds) of literality and no such thing as purely literal language. Since nonliterality does not inhibit our language about the world, it cannot be said to hinder our language about God, either. Nor does literal language about God necessarily compromise his transcendence, although Aquinas thought it did. At least this sort of view would be compatible with Van Til's overall approach.

There seems to be nothing in Van Til's system that would prevent us from ascribing to language about God the same kind of (relative) literality that we regularly ascribe to language of other kinds. For example, statements about God's acts in history, like "God brought Israel across the Red Sea on dry land," are best described as literal rather than figurative. Negative statements about God, e.g., "God is not a liar," are not figurative in any useful sense; this statement distinguishes God from literal liars, not (or not only) figurative ones. And many of our positive statements, such as "God knows all things," are literal. To say that, of course, is not to deny that God's knowledge far transcends ours.

Of course, the fact that God speaks to us in "fully human" language may mean that some truths about God cannot be literally stated in revelation. Indeed, there may be some truths that cannot be stated at all in human language (Rom. 8:26; 2 Cor. 12:4). But that does not prevent some of the things that are revealed from being revealed literally.

CHAPTER EIGHT

The Clark Controversy

The discussion of analogical knowledge prepares us to look at the one ecclesiastical controversy of Van Til's ministry. It involved Gordon H. Clark, a philosopher who was also widely read in the theological disciplines. In retrospect, one would have to grant that he and Van Til together were the most important orthodox Reformed apologists of the twentieth century. Both subscribed to the Westminster Confession and Catechisms; both were, at one time, members of the Orthodox Presbyterian Church. I have the impression that at one time they were friends. For some time during the 1930s, Clark taught philosophy at the University of Pennsylvania. I have heard from one source that he and Van Til sometimes took long walks together in Philadelphia discussing various issues. Edmund Clowney, for many years a professor and the first president of Westminster Seminary, told me he first came to Westminster as a student on Clark's recommendation. Clark, then a professor of philosophy at Wheaton College, specifically wanted Clowney to get the benefit of studying with Cornelius Van Til. Other students of Clark at Wheaton also studied with Van Til at Westminster, notably Edward J. Carnell.

But during the 1940s, Clark and Van Til became antagonists in a divisive ecclesiastical battle. Following his departure from Wheaton College, Clark sought ordination in the Orthodox Presbyterian

Church, in the Presbytery of Philadelphia, of which Van Til was a member. Presbytery, at a special meeting on July 7, 1944, sustained Clark's theological examination, but a group of twelve presbyters, including Van Til, complained against presbytery's action.[1]

THE *COMPLAINT*

Their *Complaint* dealt with a number of matters, some of which will be discussed in later chapters of this volume. For now, we shall discuss the major item of controversy, what was called "the incomprehensibility of God." In my view, this phrase is somewhat misleading. Although the controversy was related to the doctrine of the incomprehensibility of God, it focused on a more specific issue, namely, the relationship between God's knowledge and man's. In other words, the controversy dealt with what we have been calling analogical knowledge.

According to the *Complaint,* Clark "denies that there is any qualitative distinction between the contents of the knowledge of God and the contents of the knowledge possible to man, but rather in so far as there is any distinction between these two the distinction is merely quantitative."[2]

The *Complaint* then attempts to show how Clark's view of the distinction is "merely quantitative." Clark, it says, believes that truth, whether in God's mind or man's, is "always propositional."[3] A proposition is a thought that can be used to make a factual assertion. It is "proposed" for consideration as to its factuality. The sentence "The window is open" asserts a proposition; the sentence "Is the window

[1]Although Van Til signed the *Complaint,* I do not believe that he wrote it. It is too far removed from his style.

[2]The complaint was denied by presbytery and sent on appeal to the Twelfth General Assembly. It was published in the *Minutes of the Twelfth General Assembly of the Orthodox Presbyterian Church* (1945), 5–30. The above quotation is from p. 13. In what follows, I shall refer to this document simply as the *Complaint.* I will be summarizing the basic argumentation of this and other documents in the controversy, but I will not be able to examine in detail the biblical exegesis and historical arguments on both sides. The argumentation of these documents is rather prolix and enters into many more or less related questions. In general, I will focus on those statements which are most relevant to our understanding and possible resolution of the issues.

[3]Ibid.

open?" does not. The proposition is not the sentence itself, but the thought behind it: "The window is open" and "La fenêtre est ouverte" express the same proposition. According to the *Complaint,* Clark holds that knowledge consists of such factual thoughts.[4] A man knows a certain number of propositions, but God knows many more. Therefore, the main difference between God's knowledge and ours is "quantitative."[5]

Further, says the *Complaint,* for Clark, "man's knowledge of any proposition, if it is really knowledge, is identical with God's knowledge of the same proposition."[6] Indeed, such a proposition would "have the same meaning for man as for God."[7]

Now Clark does, according to the *Complaint,* recognize "a difference between the *mode* of God's knowledge and that of man's knowledge. God's knowledge is intuitive while man's is discursive. . . . Man is dependent upon God for his knowledge."[8] While the complainants agree with Clark here, they deny that this affects their conclusion. The question of the qualitative distinction between God's knowledge and man's knowledge concerns only the "contents" of knowledge, they claim, not the "mode."

In the view of the *Complaint,* Clark's "quantitative" view is a serious error. Their own view of divine incomprehensibility is:

> Man may possess true knowledge as he thinks God's thoughts after him. But because God is God, the Creator, and man is man, the creature, the difference between the divine knowledge and the knowledge possible to man may never be conceived of merely in quantitative terms, as a difference in degree rather than a difference in kind. Otherwise the Creator-creature relationship is broken down at a most crucial point, and there is an assault upon the majesty of God.[9]

---

[4]To be more precise, as I assume Clark would want to be, knowledge is, in general, the justified belief that such propositions are true.

[5]The *Complaint* (p. 14) later admits that, for Clark, God's knowledge consists of an "infinite" number of propositions. The complainants insist, however, that an infinite quantity is still a quantity, and therefore that their conclusion is unaffected.

[6]*Complaint,* 13.

[7]Ibid.

[8]Ibid., 15.

[9]Ibid., 9.

THE *ANSWER*

The *Complaint* was denied by the Presbytery of Philadelphia, which approved an *Answer*, explaining its reasons for denying the *Complaint*. The *Answer* was signed by five presbyters, including Gordon H. Clark.[10]

The *Answer* does not merely seek to refute the accusations against Clark. It goes on the offensive, charging the complainants with a view that implicitly denies the possibility of divine revelation.

The *Answer* summarizes the *Complaint*'s position on incomprehensibility as follows:

> First, there is some truth that God cannot put into propositional form; this portion of truth cannot be expressed conceptually. Second, the portion of truth that God can express in propositional form never has the same meaning for man as it has for God. . . . Man can grasp only an analogy of the truth, which, because it is an analogy, is not the truth itself.[11]

Then the *Answer* summarizes Clark's position:

> 1. The essence of God's being is incomprehensible to man except as God reveals truths concerning his own nature; 2. The manner of God's knowing, an eternal intuition, is impossible for man; 3. Man can never know exhaustively and completely God's knowledge of any truth in all its relationships and implications; because every truth has an infinite number of relationships and implications and since each of these implications in turn has other infinite implications, these must ever, even in heaven, remain inexhaustible for man; 4. But, Dr. Clark maintains, the doctrine of the incomprehensibility of God does not mean that a proposition, *e.g.*, two times two are four, has one meaning for man and a qualitatively different meaning for God, or that some truth is conceptual and other truth is non-conceptual in nature.[12]

---

[10]This document was spread on the minutes of presbytery. I am working from a version published as a booklet without publication data. I shall refer to it simply as the *Answer*.

[11]*Answer*, 9.

[12]Ibid., 9–10.

To say that propositions have "qualitatively different meanings" for God and man, or to say that divine and human knowledge do not "coincide at a single point" is, according to the *Answer,* to advance a "theory of two-fold truth."[13] That is to say, there is truth for God and truth for man, but truth for God can never be truth for man, and vice versa. "According to the Complaint man can never know even one item of truth God knows."[14] Thus, revelation of truth from God to man is impossible. This view "nullifies the Bible from cover to cover."[15]

Then the *Answer* defends Clark against the *Complaint*'s charges. Clark does not, as the *Complaint* alleges, believe that God's thought is propositional.[16] Therefore, he does not believe that the distinction between God's thought and man's is "merely quantitative." Two minds can differ, not only in the number of propositions they affirm, but also in the "importance" and the logical, systematic "integration" of the propositions they believe.[17] In these latter respects, and of course also in the "mode" of their knowledge, there is indeed a qualitative distinction between God's thoughts and man's.

The *Answer* also denies that in Clark's view man's knowledge of a proposition must be "identical with" God's knowledge of the same proposition.[18] Clark's view is that in this case God's knowledge has the same object as man's (i.e., they know the same things), but that object is known in a different manner. The *Complaint,* however, has rejected the difference of "manner" or "mode" as irrelevant to the doctrine of incomprehensibility.[19] Therefore, says the *Answer,* the view of the *Complaint* must be that God and man never share knowledge of the same objects.

Putting this with the *Complaint's* denial of a common "meaning" and its denial of coincidence "at any single point," the *Answer* finds a

---

[13]Ibid., 10.

[14]Ibid.

[15]Ibid., 16.

[16]This denial is credible in the context of Clark's writings at this point in his career. Nevertheless, Clark's later writings do assert the views alleged in the *Complaint.* In *The Incarnation* (Jefferson, Md.: Trinity Foundation, 1988), 54, he defines a person as "a composite of propositions" and adds that "the definition will fail if it does not apply to God." Cf. Clark, *The Trinity* (Jefferson, Md.: Trinity Foundation, 1985), 106.

[17]*Answer,* 15.

[18]Ibid., 20.

[19]The *Answer* (pp. 23–24) later attacks this rejection as unhistorical.

clear case of "skepticism and irrationalism."[20] If this is true, then, "for all we know, perhaps Christ did *not* die for our sins."[21]

THE *REPORT*

The controversy was carried to the General Assembly of the denomination, which appointed a study committee to deal with it. The committee's *Report* has positive and negative things to say about both the *Complaint* and the *Answer*, but it generally comes down on the side of the *Complaint*.[22] It should be noted, however, that the General Assembly did not revoke Clark's ordination or declare his view to be out of accord with the Westminster Standards. Indeed, the most significant ecclesiastical result of the whole controversy was that Clark remained a minister in good standing.[23]

The *Report* emphasizes with Clark that the difference between God's knowledge and man's does not mean that God and man cannot know the same objects.[24] But with Van Til and the other complainants, it emphasizes that the difference "goes beyond the fact that human apprehension is based on revelation." Nor is it "viewed in terms of the extent of knowledge."[25] The difference is based on the fact that God is infinite and man is finite. God's knowledge always "possesses the divine qualities that can never attach to ours."[26]

The *Report* defends the *Complaint* against the charge of skepticism. While regarding some statements in the *Complaint* as "regrettably infelicitous and misleading,"[27] it argues that the "intent" of the *Complaint* was not skeptical. It points out that, except for those few infelicitous statements, the *Complaint* is not ascribing to God's knowl-

---

[20]Ibid., 21.

[21]Ibid., 23.

[22]Published in the *Minutes of the Fifteenth General Assembly of the Orthodox Presbyterian Church* (May 13–18, 1948), Appendix, 1–96.

[23]This fact is contrary to some widespread misconceptions. For example, William White, in VTDF, 128, says that the *Complaint* "carried." It did not. It was *denied* by presbytery, and that denial was upheld by the General Assembly.

[24]*Report*, 13.

[25]Ibid., 13–14.

[26]Ibid., 17.

[27]Ibid., 21, referring particularly to the statement implying different "meaning" between God's thoughts and ours, and the denial that God's knowledge and man's "coincide at any single point."

edge different "objects" or different "meanings." Rather, the difference between God's and man's knowledge is a difference in "contents," or, as the *Report* prefers, a difference in knowledge "not in the objective but in the subjective sense."[28]

The difference in "content" or "subjectivity" between divine and human knowledge cannot be reduced merely to a difference in the number of propositions, or the number of "relationships and implications" of propositions known by God and man. Rather, the difference pertains to each individual proposition held in common. Nor can it be reduced to a difference in "mode." Nor is it simply a difference between what God knows and what he has chosen to reveal to man. The difference in content pertains not only to what man doesn't know, but also to what he knows by revelation. It is a difference between God's knowledge, subjectively understood, and man's.

The *Report* points out a terminological difficulty: Clark regards "the elements of knowledge as consisting simply of *mode* and *object.*"[29] Thus, Clark does not really discuss the area of most concern to the *Complaint* and the *Report,* namely, the "content" of knowledge, or "knowledge in the subjective sense." The *Report* does consider briefly whether Clark's concept of "mode," in which he recognizes a qualitative difference between God's knowledge and man's, might be broad enough to include what the *Complaint* and the *Report* call "content." But it concludes that Clark fails clearly to affirm the difference in content that the *Complaint* is concerned about.[30]

Analysis and Evaluation

In my estimation, both the Van Til party and the Clark party had valid scriptural concerns. Van Til was concerned to maintain the Creator-creature distinction in the area of human knowledge. Clark was concerned to protect the integrity of divine revelation: to insure that it could provide a true communication from God to man. The *Report,* which generally favored Van Til,[31] did, in my opinion, do justice to

---

[28]Ibid.; cf. the discussion on pp. 24–25.

[29]Ibid., 28.

[30]Ibid., 28–29.

[31]There were several minority reports favoring Clark, which I will not discuss here.

Clark's concern about revealed truth. It repudiated the *Complaint*'s language about different "meanings" and its denial of "coincidence at a single point." In this respect, the *Report* made real progress toward a resolution of the questions.[32]

Did Clark do justice to Van Til's concerns about the Creator-creature distinction? Probably not, in my view, but that was due in large measure to the confusing way in which the Van Til party stated the question. They asked Clark to affirm a qualitative distinction between the "contents" of God's knowledge and the "contents" of man's. But "contents of knowledge" is not a clear idea. Elsewhere I have argued that the phrase can refer to differences in mental images, objects of thought, beliefs, meanings of words, fullness of understanding, or attributes of thought (e.g., divine or human attributes).[33] The *Report* helpfully indicates that the phrase does not, in its authors' view, refer to differences in objects, beliefs, or meanings. Clark certainly grants that God's thought has a greater "fullness of understanding." Neither party seems to have "mental images" in mind. I suspect that the real question was about the difference in the "attributes of thought" between God and man, which I shall expound soon. However, I wish to explore another issue first.

First Suggestion for Resolution: "Contents" as Experience

The *Report* tries to clarify the idea of "contents" by equating it with "knowledge in the subjective sense." But what does that mean? The

---

[32]Nevertheless, there has been regression in subsequent discussion. Jim S. Halsey, in "A Preliminary Critique of *Van Til: The Theologian,*" *WTJ* 39 (fall 1976), 123, reiterates the language of "no single point of identity," and on p. 129n. he insists, contrary to my formulation, that even the objects known by God differ qualitatively from the objects known by man. Indeed, he says, "Our beliefs concerning salvation, for example, are qualitatively different from God's beliefs concerning salvation." I shall indicate that this language can be taken in a sense that would make it true; but in the most obvious sense, such a statement is seriously false and is wide open to Clark's charge of skepticism (twofold truth). The Van Tillian group insisted that they did not hold such a view, and the *Report* agreed. Halsey, however, would plead guilty to Clark's charge, both for himself and for Van Til.

[33]DKG, 37–38. On pp. 38–39, I also explore some ambiguities in the phrase "qualitative difference," a phrase that I continue to regard as unhelpful in the discussion. "Qualitative difference" does not, in itself, denote a distinction between Creator and

most natural way to take it is as a reference to the experience we have in the act of knowing, to what "goes through our minds."[34] Certainly, Clark would have had no difficulty saying that God and man experience knowledge in different ways. Admittedly, this is not a characteristically "Clarkian" way to talk. Clark did (not only in this controversy, but also in his later writings) tend to see knowledge only as "object" (the proposition known) and "mode" (the manner in which it is known). In his "intellectualism," as he called it,[35] Clark had little use for talk of "experience" in a "subjective" sense, either here or in other areas of his philosophy. Such language would suggest to him an emphasis on emotion, or even an empiricist epistemology. To both of these, Clark was always staunchly opposed. His prejudice against formulations dealing with subjective experience perhaps increased the difficulty of communication among the parties. But, had he been willing to bend this prejudice a bit, I see no reason why he could not have affirmed an "experiential" difference between God's knowledge and man's. Certainly there was nothing in his theory of knowledge to rule out such a distinction. Indeed, I believe that distinction is implicit in Clark's point about the "difference in mode."

Second Suggestion for Resolution: "Contents" as Attributes

But the Van Til group insisted that the difference in mode was irrelevant to their concern. Perhaps they were wrong in saying that; perhaps they needed to rethink the concept of mode. However, let us assume that they were right, that a difference in mode was insufficient to guard their particular concern. What else could they have been thinking of when they referred to "content" and "knowledge in the subjective sense"? I have a suggestion, although it is one that apparently never occurred to anybody on either side of the controversy. In my view, the only referent of "content" and "subjective knowledge in God's mind" that fully fits the complainants' descriptions is: the divine attributes.

---

creature; rather, there are many differences within the creation that can be called "qualitative."

[34]Clearly, something more is meant here than mental imagery, though that might be included in the category of experience. I would repeat, however, that mental imagery as such is not the issue.

[35]*Answer,* 19.

According to the doctrine of divine simplicity, to which both Van Til and Clark subscribed, God's thoughts are not something separate from his nature, separate from God himself. Indeed, God's thoughts bear all the divine attributes. His thoughts are infinite, eternal, and unchangeable in their being, wisdom, power, holiness, justice, goodness, and truth, to use the language of the Westminster Shorter Catechism.[36] God's thoughts, in other words, are divine. This assertion is obviously congenial to Van Til, but it is equally congenial to Clark, who argued in *The Johannine Logos* that *logos* ("word") in John 1:1 could be translated "wisdom" or even "logic."[37] For Clark, as for Van Til, God's wisdom, his logic, his thoughts, are God.

Therefore, in one sense, the "content" of God's thoughts—all his thoughts, all his "items of knowledge," individually and collectively—is God himself. No human thought can have such divine content, and hence divine qualities. God's thoughts are omnipotent, omniscient, the ultimate creators of everything in heaven and earth. Man's thoughts are finite, created, of limited power and intelligence.

To grant this distinction is to grant all that the Van Til party was asking for: a difference in "content," based on the very distinction between Creator and creature, pertaining to all thoughts of God and man, revealed or unrevealed. The "mode" would perhaps be part of the content in this sense, but the discussion need not, on this analysis, focus on it at all. This approach would even have justified some of the more dubious statements of the Van Til group: in one sense, God's thoughts have a different "meaning" and "object" from man's, for the meaning and object of God's thoughts are God himself. His knowledge always has himself as object, for he knows the world by knowing himself.[38] And his knowledge is always an exhaustive comprehension of himself as object, including, of course, his eternal plan for the world

---

[36]Answer to Question 4.

[37]Philadelphia: Presbyterian and Reformed, 1972, p. 19. Cf. Clark's "Wheaton Lectures" in *The Philosophy of Gordon H. Clark,* ed. R. Nash (Philadelphia: Presbyterian and Reformed, 1968), 67. Van Til often disparaged Clark's translation of John 1:1, "In the beginning was logic, and logic was with God, and logic was God." Doubtless, to say the least, this rendering is not adequate to reproduce the Johannine intention. But it seems to me that unless one denies the divine simplicity, one cannot avoid identifying God's logic, i.e. his rationality, with God himself.

[38]This is not to deny that God has a direct knowledge of what happens in the created world. But even that knowledge involves his self-knowledge, since nothing happens in the created world without his permission.

and his work of Creation and redemption. We never have such exhaustive comprehension of God as an object of our knowledge. In one sense, we can even say that there is "not one single point of coincidence" between our thought and God's, because no human thought has any of the divine attributes, and no divine thought in itself is at any point creaturely. Even on my analysis, these statements about object, meaning, and coincidence are still misleading, as the *Report* rightly indicated, without a great deal of explanation, which the Van Til group wrongly failed to supply. But, on this analysis, we can understand why the complainants chose to express themselves in such odd ways, and how those odd statements can in some senses even be accounted true.

On the other hand, such a distinction, stated as I have formulated it, would not have been offensive to Clark. It would not have suggested skepticism, or "twofold truth," or the inability of God to reveal himself. God's divine attributes cannot be contained in human thoughts, but there is no reason why human language, as a vehicle of divine revelation, cannot speak truly of that divinity.

Recall from chapter 7 that Van Til's concept of analogy does not deny that human language can speak literal truth about God. Rather, it affirms that human knowledge is creaturely and thus subject to God's authority. Had the Van Tillian party made this point clearly to the Clark party, the latter group would have had no right to charge the former group with skepticism or a denial of revelation. Even in the 1940s, concepts were available in Van Til's writings that could have resolved the issue without ecclesiastical war.

I have made two suggestions for resolving the issue. Either or both would, I think, have been acceptable to both sides—at least to those on either side who would have taken the trouble to listen and understand. These suggestions are not vague compromises that leave disputed issues aside in order to achieve agreement. Rather, they are formulations rooted in Scripture and Reformed theology that clearly maintain everything that either party legitimately wished to assert and avoid the errors that each party legitimately sought to combat.

I am a bit amazed that with all the intellectual firepower expended on this issue during the 1940s, nobody made use of these or some similar formulations to bring the parties together. My educated guess, based on conversations with some of the presbyters on both sides, is that the atmosphere quickly became highly contentious and partisan. Each group was more interested in gaining "victory" than in achieving either unity or a fuller understanding. That mentality has been all too common in ecclesiastical controversies throughout history. It should be a warning to us to give closer heed to scriptural admonitions concerning contentiousness and partisanship.

Van Til's Later Response

Van Til sets forth his personal response to the controversy in *An Introduction to Systematic Theology,* chapter 13, "The Incomprehensibility of God." As my analysis would suggest, Van Til's main concern is to maintain the Creator-creature distinction. His discussion, however, does not inject any new clarity into the debate. He belabors the notions of "identity of content" and "coincidence," as if these were perfectly clear, and as if nobody could possibly object to his use of these terms except by denying the Creator-creature distinction:

> But even [the enrichment of revelation] does not imply that there is any coincidence, that is, identity of content[39] between what God has in his mind and what man has in his mind. If there is no identity of content in the first proposition that God gives to man there can be no identity of content attained by means of any number of additional propositions of revelation that God gives to man. And there could be no identity of content on the first proposition only if there were no first proposition. That is to say, if there *could* be an identity of content there *would* be and always has been an identity of content. There could and would be an identity of content only if the mind of man were identical with the mind of God.[40]

As for Clark, Van Til remains convinced that he "understood the incomprehensibility of God in a way which . . . would be in accord with the Romanist or Arminian view of it, and out of accord with the Reformed view of it."[41] He says that for the complainants, including himself, "the foundations of the Reformed faith were involved."[42]

---

[39]As if "identity of content" clarified the notion of "coincidence!"—JF
[40]IST, 165.
[41]Ibid., 168.
[42]Ibid.

Van Til quotes the four-point summary of Clark's view from the *Answer* that we noted earlier. In response to the first point, that "the essence of God's being is incomprehensible to man except as God reveals truths concerning his own nature," Van Til replies that without revelation, God is not only incomprehensible, but inapprehensible.[43] True enough, and the *Report* made the same observation, drawing the reasonable inference that the *Answer* used the word "incomprehensible" in a confusing way. But Van Til is not content to charge Clark with confusing language, as the *Report* did. Rather, he concludes that Clark "seems to hold that man may obtain a certain amount of information about God apart from revelation."[44] Presumably his argument (though he offers none) would be that since Clark used the term "incomprehensible" instead of the more appropriate term "inapprehensible," he must believe that God is "apprehensible" (though not "comprehensible") apart from revelation.

I must say that I find this criticism of Clark quite preposterous. There is no evidence that in this statement Clark was self-consciously distinguishing "incomprehensible" from "inapprehensible," as Van Til's interpretation requires. Indeed, the *Report* concluded, far more sensibly, that Clark illegitimately ignored that distinction. Furthermore, it is plain from all of Clark's writings that he believed that all human knowledge comes from revelation. Indeed, Clark's "Wheaton Lectures," cited earlier, maintain the rather extreme view that human knowledge is limited to the content of special revelation in Scripture.

Van Til does in this context mention certain problems with Clark's apologetic that suggest confusions about revelation: "Dr. Clark would appeal to certain broad a priori principles of reasoning apart from revelation in order by them to choose between 'revelations.' "[45] Those issues will concern us in later chapters. Clark's view of the relation of logic to Scripture is problematic, but I am pretty sure that he would answer Van Til by justifying the use of a priori principles from Scripture itself. In any case, there is nothing in his view of divine incomprehensibility that calls into question the view of Scripture as the fundamental "axiom" of human thought, a view that otherwise pervades his writings.

---

[43]Ibid., 168–69.
[44]Ibid., 169.
[45]Ibid.

Clark's second point was that the mode of God's knowledge is "impossible" for man. He also said occasionally that this mode was incomprehensible. Van Til, picking up on the latter formulation rather than the one he quotes, takes "incomprehensible" again to mean "inapprehensible" and says that according to Clark we do "not know anything about God's mode of knowing,"[46] from which various consequences follow. Again, I am rather shocked at Van Til's distortion of Clark's position. It is plain that Clark did not deny that anything can be known about the mode of God's knowledge. Indeed, he frequently characterized it (as an "eternal intuition"), so he clearly claimed to know something about it. Though Clark never elaborated his view of the incomprehensibility of God's mode of knowledge, it seems to me that he had in mind such obvious points as the following: (1) we do not know things the way God does; (2) we cannot imagine what it would be like to know things as God does; (3) we cannot formulate exhaustively the nature of God's eternal intuitions.

Clark's third point was that we can never know exhaustively God's knowledge of any truth with all its relationships and implications.[47] Van Til replies that since Clark has "granted the validity of a non-revelational a priori," he therefore concedes the view of non-Christian rationalism that one "must know everything or he knows nothing."[48] Thus, the "relationships and implications" of truths known to God must be exhaustively known to us or not known at all.

I deny Van Til's premise that Clark has "granted the validity of a non-revelational a priori," so I do not believe his criticism of the third point is cogent. Certainly his position as stated in the *Answer* implies no such thing. Clark's view is that we know truth about God, even though we do not know "everything."

Clark's fourth point asserted that propositions like "two times

---

[46]Ibid., 170.

[47]It is interesting that Van Til himself, in the next chapter of IST, formulates the "difference in content" between God's thoughts and man's in terms of "depth of meaning." He states: "God knows the meaning of this proposition in all the fullness of its significance because he knows it in relationship to all other propositions that he will make or not make to man" (IST, 184; cf. p. 185). Perhaps the word "known" should be understood after the two occurrences of "make." This formulation seems identical to what Clark is proposing in point three. But Van Til never acknowledges the similarity nor relates the language of this formulation to Clark's.

[48]Ibid., 171.

two are four" have a common "meaning" for God and man. Van Til replies that God and man do have a common "reference point." He does not define "reference point"; I take the phrase to mean something like "authority" or "standard," concepts that we will explore in later chapters of this book. He even seems to go part of the way with Clark in saying, "That two times two are four is a well known fact. God knows it. Man knows it."[49] It would have been more helpful if Van Til, like the *Report,* had straightforwardly conceded Clark's point that there is such common meaning. Van Til's coyness on the issue confuses matters. It is almost as if he cannot bring himself to accept Clark's wording on anything at all.

Still, he reiterates that there is no "identity of content" between God's thoughts and man's. It never seems to cross his mind that there is even a prima facie problem in saying (1) that God and man know the same mathematical proposition and (2) that there is no identity of content in their knowledge of it. He never even tries to explain the apparent contradiction. Rather, he again goes on the offensive and charges Clark with holding non-Christian assumptions about knowledge.

His coyness reaches a sort of epitome in the following:

> Suppose now that the complainants should try to "state clearly" in Dr. Clark's sense the qualitative difference between the divine and human knowledge of the proposition that two times two are four. They would have to first deny their basic contention with respect to the Christian concept of revelation. For to "state clearly" can mean nothing but to "explain exhaustively" unless one presupposes the doctrine of revelation.[50]

But there is no evidence in the materials cited that Clark equated "state clearly" with "explain exhaustively." Indeed, Clark clearly denied that we could exhaustively explain the thoughts of God. On Van Til's part, his view of divine incomprehensibility never, in any other context, prevented him from attempting to make clear doctrinal statements. Indeed, he rebuked others for their theological vagueness. So why could he not at this point simply have presented a formula such as the two suggested resolutions I proposed earlier in this chapter?

---

[49]Ibid., 172.

[50]Ibid.

He could have hedged that formula with various caveats against any claim to exhaustiveness. But such a response would have been helpful in the situation. The response I have quoted is clever, perhaps, but not helpful. It "sticks it to Clark," but it does not promote the cause of truth and understanding.

I must reluctantly conclude that Van Til's response to Clark in *An Introduction to Systematic Theology* sheds more heat than light on the controversy. With the benefit of hindsight, Van Til could have come up with formulae such as I suggested earlier that would have drawn the parties together without compromising anyone's theological concern. Instead, he went on the offensive, employing the "great gulf" language of antithesis, but with an argument so weak (in both interpretation and criticism) as to be quite unworthy of him.

Here we see Van Til as a movement leader. He was leading his troops against those of Clark with the sharpest antithetical rhetoric, taking no prisoners, admitting not the slightest shade of truth in Clark's formulations, suggesting that Clark's entire effort was marred by a false principle. In chapter 3 we found him saying that there were no fundamentals in common between himself and Stuart Hackett; here he turns the same guns on Clark. We shall see this extremely antithetical side of Van Til again. I do believe that when he gets into this sort of mood, his normally powerful intellect often fails him. Van Til is a thinker who is normally capable of making careful, even subtle, distinctions. But in his extreme antithetical mode, he tends to miss the obvious.

This is not Van Til at his best; nor, in my estimation, did Clark's performance represent Clark at his best. Further, their warfare badly divided a denomination that was already very small and could ill afford such disunity. In time, Clark and many of his followers left the Orthodox Presbyterian Church. I confess that I am appalled that at the Fiftieth Anniversary celebration of the Orthodox Presbyterian Church in 1986, one speaker lauded the Van Tillian contenders for achieving a great victory for truth. In my opinion, truth was the great loser in this battle. Evidently the only winner was pride, an unjustified pride at that.

The controversy dealt for the most part with rather technical philosophical issues that few of the OPC elders understood very well. Even Clark and Van Til were rather confused about them. Some of their disciples, even down to the present, have continued to prattle away about "qualitative differences," "propositional meaning," "identity of thought-content," "single point of identity," "twofold truth," and the like, without much idea of what they are talking about, but with the sublime assurance that they are right and that those who disagree with them are dangerous heretics. It is time for us to admit that these issues should never have been raised in such confusing terminology, that none of the confusing formulae should be made a test of orthodoxy, and that the Clark controversy was a *low* point in the life of the Orthodox Presbyterian Church and in the ministries of the two major protagonists.

Clark and Van Til are together in heaven now. I am pleased to announce that they are reconciled.

CHAPTER NINE

Revelation

As we have seen, Van Til's doctrine of analogical knowledge can be summarized by saying (1) that God's thoughts are distinct from man's, as Creator from creature, and (2) that man is to think God's thoughts after him. The controversy concerning Gordon Clark's views of the "incomprehensibility of God" dealt essentially with the first point. We must now explore the second.

For Van Til, "thinking God's thoughts after him" is first of all thinking according to divine revelation. In this chapter, we shall discuss general and special revelation. In the next chapters, we shall explore the implications of revelation for epistemology: the roles of presuppositions, reason and logic, and theological systems.

Van Til's view of revelation is essentially that of Calvin and the Reformed tradition, especially including Kuyper, Bavinck, and Warfield. There is "natural" or "general" revelation[1] in all of creation, including man, who is God's image. This revelation indicates God's nature and his moral demands (Rom. 1:18–20, 32). After man sinned, the message of God's grace was given in additional "special" revelation, communicated through theophany (including the incarnation

[1]With Van Til, I will use "natural revelation" and "general revelation" as synonymous terms. We should of course remember that "nature" in this context includes man's own nature.

of the Son of God), prophecy, and miracle, and eventually committed to writing in Scripture. Scripture is God's Word, infallible and inerrant in its original manuscripts.[2]

As Van Til relates these doctrines to his own epistemological and apologetic concerns, however, new emphases and insights emerge. In what follows, I will focus on what I take to be Van Til's distinctive contributions to the church's thinking about revelation.

General Revelation

Van Til is known for the view that all apologetic witness must be based on presuppositions drawn from Scripture, rather than on religiously neutral argument from the facts of nature alone.[3] Consequently, critics sometimes fault him for failing to do justice to general revelation.

It is important, then, to realize that Van Til has a very strong doctrine of general revelation. This is a major emphasis in his writings. He stresses that general revelation, like Scripture, is "necessary, authoritative, sufficient and perspicuous" for its distinctive purposes.[4] As we shall see, this revelation plays a central role in his apologetic. It is because of that clear, authoritative general revelation that the unbeliever "knows" God (Rom. 1:21); and it is that revealed knowledge which he seeks to suppress. It is to that clear self-revelation of God to the unbeliever, known but suppressed, that the apologist appeals.[5]

Such a strong doctrine of general revelation follows from Van Til's Reformed view of divine sovereignty. If all things come to pass by God's sovereign decree, then all things to some extent reveal that decree. Therefore, "All created reality is inherently revelational of the nature and will of God."[6] He explains:

> This God naturally has an all-comprehensive plan for the created universe. He has planned all the relationships be-

---

[2]Van Til's view of revelation is expounded in greatest detail in IST, 62–158. See also CA, 23–37; CTK, 25–71; PDS; NS; IW.

[3]We shall consider the concept of "presupposition" in the next chapter.

[4]CA, 30–37; NS, 269–83.

[5]Of course, the apologist also appeals to special revelation. More on this will follow in our discussion of Van Til's "Ethics of Knowledge."

[6]CA, 33.

> tween all the aspects of created being. He has planned the end from the beginning. All created reality therefore actually displays this plan. It is, in consequence, inherently rational.[7]

Note also, "If the whole universe was created to show forth the glory of God, as the Scriptures constantly say that it was, then it could not do this unless it was a revelation of God."[8]

A strong doctrine of general revelation is also important because the doctrine of redemptive revelation (special revelation, Scripture) presupposes it:

> Being from the outset covenantal in character, the natural revelation of God to man was meant to serve as the playground for the process of differentiation that was to take place in the course of time. The covenant made with Adam was conditional. There would be *additional* revelation of God in nature after the action of man with respect to the tree of the knowledge of good and evil.[9]

That additional revelation was a revelation of wrath (Rom. 1:18), but "together with God's wrath, his grace is also manifest." God's common grace is manifested to Noah through the sign of the rainbow. But beyond this, God proclaims saving grace in Christ. That revelation comes through prophecy and miracle. Van Til explains: "The forces of nature are always at the beck and call of the power of differentiation that works toward redemption and reprobation. It is the idea of a supernatural-natural revelation that comes to such eloquent expression in the Old Testament, and particularly in the Psalms."[10]

---

[7]Ibid., 34–35.

[8]IST, 64. On p. 110 and elsewhere, he reproaches Arminian theology because it does not see human nature itself as revelational. Since human free will, on the Arminian understanding, is independent of God's plan, it cannot be a divine revelation, the image of God. As such, general revelation is insufficient to leave man totally without excuse for sin.

[9]NS, 267–68. "Differentiation," a concept explained at length in CGG, refers to the gradual manifestation in history of the people of God in distinction from the reprobate world. See my discussion in chap. 16.

[10]Ibid., 268–69.

Van Til, therefore, insists that general and special revelation are integrated, rather than sharply distinguished. "Even in paradise," to use a common Van Tillian phrase, man "could read nature aright only in connection with and in the light of supernatural positive revelation."[11] After the Fall, that supernatural thought-communication, now a "special revelation," became all the more necessary, since fallen man naturally distorted the truth of general revelation (Rom. 1:18–32).

At the same time, supernatural thought-communication also presupposes general revelation and therefore cannot be understood without it. Natural revelation, therefore, bears the four attributes traditionally ascribed to Scripture. Like Scripture, natural revelation is necessary, authoritative, sufficient, and perspicuous.

General revelation is necessary, because "for the supernatural to appear as supernatural the natural had to appear as really natural. . . . There had to be regularity if there was to be a genuine exception."[12] And God's commandments concerning particulars of human life (Van Til speaks here of the commandment concerning the tree of knowledge in Gen. 2:17) must, if they are to serve as "examples" for our obedience in other areas, be exceptional.

The relation between the natural and the supernatural applies both before and after the Fall. But after the Fall, another distinction enters: "The natural must appear as in need of redemption. . . . The Biblical miracles of healing point to the regeneration of all things."[13] So, it is necessary to have a world cursed by sin in order to show by contrast the special plan of God's redemption. That plan is shown both by God's saving deeds and by his saving words.

General revelation is also authoritative. Evangelicals sometimes think naively that Scripture has more authority than natural revelation. But that is not the teaching of Scripture. Although Scripture has a unique role to play in the organism of revelation, as the only divinely authored written revelation, it is no more or less authoritative than God's word through nature, for both revelations, exceptional and ordinary, come from God. So, Van Til says,

---

[11]DF2, 106; cf. CTK, 29–30; IST, 68, 162, 189. But when Gordon Clark makes essentially the same point, Van Til charges him with denying the clarity of general revelation (PDS, 62–63). To read Van Til's critiques, one might imagine that Clark never said anything right!

[12]NS, 269–70.

[13]Ibid., 270–71.

> The voice of authority as it came to man in this exceptional manner was to be but illustrative of the fact that, in and through the things of nature, there spoke the self-same voice of God's command. . . . Man's scientific procedure was accordingly to be marked by the attitude of obedience to God.[14]

Even our sins are "revelational, that is, in their very abnormality."[15]

General revelation is sufficient for its historic purpose, which is, of course, to provide a proper background for supernatural redemption and revelation. It is not sufficient to communicate God's saving promises of grace, but that was not its purpose.[16]

Finally, general revelation is perspicuous, or clear. Although God is incomprehensible, and the world is cursed, nevertheless the world reveals God clearly (Rom. 1:18–21). Although clear in itself, general revelation is not properly understood by sinful man: "For any fact to be a fact at all, it must be a revelational fact. It is accordingly no easier for sinners to accept God's revelation in nature than to accept God's revelation in Scripture."[17]

To summarize, general and special revelation are equally necessary, authoritative, sufficient, and perspicuous. The uniqueness of special revelation is not that it is more authoritative (or more of the other attributes) than natural revelation. Rather, special revelation is unique because it is given for distinct purposes: (1) to guide our interpretation of general revelation, (2) after the Fall, to correct our sinful distortions of general revelation, and (3) to bring us God's promise of salvation through Christ, a message not available through general revelation.

PERSPECTIVALISM

Van Til develops in *An Introduction to Systematic Theology*[18] his ideas on the integration of general and special revelation. Interestingly, at this point he resorts to a threefold, rather than a twofold, distinc-

---

[14]Ibid., 272–73.
[15]Ibid., 275.
[16]Ibid., 275–76.
[17]Ibid., 280.
[18]Pp., 62–109.

tion: instead of the traditional general-special distinction, he refers to revelation from God, from nature, and from self.[19] Relating these to another triad, that of revelation about God, about nature, and about self, he ends up with nine categories: revelation about nature from nature, self, and God; revelation about self from the same three sources; and revelation about God from the same three sources.[20]

He argues that all three sources are involved in the knowledge of any object; but, more important, he argues that each relationship must be understood from a Christian-theistic perspective.[21] As we understand revelation about nature from nature, for example, it is important that we recognize that nature is created and governed by God; therefore, all facts are governed by laws, and all laws are related to facts.[22] And both facts and laws are what they are because of God. Apart from his plan, they could not exist in "fruitful relation" to one another. Van Til eschews both traditional empiricism and traditional apriorism: facts apart from laws and vice versa are equally meaningless. Without God to relate the facts and laws intelligibly to one another, knowledge is impossible. Thus we see that for Van Til, the knowledge of God enters even into our consideration of "revelation about nature from nature."[23]

"Revelation about nature from self" is also important, since we learn much about nature by comparing it with ourselves. But to do this properly, we must have a biblical concept of the self.[24] "Revelation about nature from God," therefore, is crucial. It is God who tells us, both in natural and special revelation, that the world is created and cursed. We may not, therefore, compartmentalize religion and

---

[19]This is reminiscent of the first page of Calvin's *Institutes,* in which he declares the inseparability of our knowledge of self from our knowledge of God. Calvin says that each is involved in the other, and he does not know which "comes first."

[20]Perhaps somewhat tongue in cheek (but perhaps not), Van Til gives to each relationship a technical title, in the manner of Kuyper's *Encyclopedia.* For example, revelation about nature from nature is physics, and revelation about nature from self is psycho-physics. The whole chart is in IST, 64–65.

[21]These insights of Van Til's are one major source (together with others) of the "perspectivalism" expounded in my DKG.

[22]Cf. chap. 5 of this volume, in which I describe the rationale for this proposition in Van Til's doctrine of the Trinity.

[23]IST, 65–66.

[24]Ibid., 66–67.

science. "Even in paradise," God expected man to study nature in the light of his spoken word.[25]

In the next three chapters of *An Introduction to Systematic Theology* (7–9), Van Til discusses the effects of the Fall upon God's revelation about nature, man, and God. We shall consider this material in Part Three, "The Ethics of Knowledge." In general, the revelation remains clear, although it reflects the curse on the earth, and although man sinfully distorts the truth, he learns from it.

Certainly, Van Til believed in *sola Scriptura* in the traditional Protestant sense: that only Scripture serves as the supreme authority for human thought and life. We shall see in the next chapter how Scripture was Van Til's "presupposition." Nevertheless, Van Til did not hold a mechanical view of *sola Scriptura,* as if we could develop our knowledge from Scripture alone, without any use of our own reason or senses. He understood that in any instance of knowledge, there is simultaneous knowledge of God, the world, and the self. We cannot know one thing without relating it to other things and to ourselves. We cannot know God rightly unless we know him as Creator of the world and as our own Creator-Redeemer. We cannot know Scripture without relating it to ourselves and to the world of our experience. General and special revelation always work together, though certainly the latter must provide the ultimate criteria for understanding the former.

We should note especially that in this scheme, revelation from nature and revelation from man are not isolated from revelation from God. Even revelation about nature from nature must be understood in a scriptural way. Indeed, nature, man, and God must all be understood in the light of one another. Even in "theology proper," the "revelation about God from God," said Van Til, "we cannot artificially separate the knowledge of God that man received or could receive by his reflection on man and the created universe in general, and the knowledge of God that man received from God by direct communication."[26] Note also:

> What God did actually reveal directly, and what God revealed naturally to man, together form one system of truth. God had one comprehensive plan with respect to the universe inclu-

---

[25]Ibid., 67–68.
[26]IST, 107.

> sive of his natural and his supernatural revelation. It is of great importance that the various aspects of revelation be regarded as implying one another. They are limiting concepts of one another.[27]

When Van Til says in the above quotation that natural and supernatural revelation are "limiting concepts of one another,"[28] I believe that he means that there is no purely natural revelation or purely supernatural revelation without admixture of the other. The natural must be understood in the light of the supernatural, and the supernatural must be understood against the "backdrop" of the natural. Apart from these contexts, they do not actually function as revelation.

I have elsewhere described this sort of view as "perspectival."[29] That is, all human knowledge is simultaneous knowledge of self, world, and God. Knowledge of one area cannot be adequate without knowledge of the other two. One cannot know the self rightly without knowing God, and similarly with the other relationships. Therefore, "self-knowledge" is really a knowledge of all three areas—self, world, and God, with a focus or emphasis on the self. Self-knowledge in this case becomes a perspective on the entire triad.

Van Til does say in the context of the last quotation that natural and supernatural theology must nevertheless be "kept distinct." The distinctness is a distinctness of content: "If we keep them distinct at this place, it will help us when we come to the question of what can, now that sin has entered the world, still be known of God by the process of natural and rational theology, and what must be reserved for theology proper."[30]

Here I believe Van Til is simply making the traditional distinction between natural theology as communicating God's nature and wrath, and revealed theology, as communicating the gospel. Natural

---

[27]Ibid., 74.

[28]"Limiting concept" is a term used by Immanuel Kant and later philosophers. Mathematical infinity is a limiting concept, because although we can use the concept meaningfully in calculations, there are no actually infinite quantities of objects in the world. Limiting concepts are useful for analytic purposes, but they do not literally represent something that exists. See chap. 13 for more on Van Til's use of this concept.

[29]In DKG, throughout.

[30]IST, 74.

and special revelation, therefore, differ in content. But to understand and to apply each one properly, we need the other. Van Til's perspectivalism must not be taken in a leveling way so that all God's messages become identical. Rather, it calls us to recognize both the integrity of each revelation and the interdependence of all God's revelations. For revelation is, after all, like creation, a manifestation of the divine Trinity.

SPECIAL REVELATION

Van Til's threefold perspectival scheme appears in a series of chapters devoted to the topic of general revelation. As we have seen, however, this scheme includes special revelation within its purview. "Revelation by God about nature, man, and God" is a category that certainly includes special, as well as general, revelation; indeed, all the categories require interpretation in the light of Scripture. So we have already seen some of what is most important in Van Til's view of special revelation: that it must rule all other aspects of human knowledge.

Nevertheless, Van Til does go on to give more focused attention to special revelation, and particularly to Scripture. We must now give attention to that discussion.

The necessity of special revelation "does not lie in any defect in the general revelation that God gave to man when he created him."[31] General revelation was, and still is, fully adequate for its purpose. Rather, the need for special revelation is found in man's sin (not, Van Til emphasizes, in his finitude). The message of grace is not found in nature. In addition, special revelation is necessary to correct our sinful distortion of general revelation.[32]

Special revelation consists not only of inspired words, but also of revelatory deeds. Van Til sees an organic relation in Scripture between theophany, prophecy, and miracle: God's saving presence, saving words, and saving deeds.[33] Each mode of revelation presupposes the other two. God's words interpret his deeds, and both "give significance to God's dwelling with man (theophany)."[34] The emphasis on

[31]Ibid., 110.
[32]Ibid., 111–12.
[33]Cf. the categories "normative," "situational," and "existential" in my DKG.
[34]IST, 119.

saving deeds keeps us from "false intellectualism";[35] our need is not a mere lack of information, but a need for personal change.

"The words corroborate the deeds and the deeds corroborate the words."[36] And in the two, God himself comes to us to save us from our sin. We cannot know one form of revelation without knowing all of them—another "perspectival" relationship.

SCRIPTURE

Speaking of Kuyper's and Bavinck's views of Scripture, Van Til remarks, "How basic and how broad was their view! The *idea* of Scripture, they said, must never be separated from its *message*."[37] "Separation" is a tricky word in theology, and some have used this idea-message relationship to criticize orthodox views of Scripture. For example, the claim is sometimes made that because the message of Scripture deals with salvation, the idea of Scripture must limit inerrancy to matters of salvation narrowly defined, thus allowing for errors when Scripture speaks of other things. Van Til, however, comes to these questions with a different concept of both the idea and the message of Scripture. The message of Scripture, for Van Til, is a message of grace from a God who is absolutely sovereign and speaks with absolute authority. If Scripture is his Word, then it must convey his ultimate authority and therefore be inerrant in all matters. Van Til describes Warfield with approval as holding that

> the classical doctrine of the infallible inspiration of Scripture was involved in the doctrine of divine sovereignty. God could not be sovereign in his disposition of rational human beings if he were not also sovereign in his revelation of himself to them. If God is sovereign in the realm of being, he is surely also sovereign in the realm of knowledge.[38]

We learn of this sovereign God from Scripture; this is part of its message. But when we learn of such a God, we realize that "such a

[35]Ibid., 130.

[36]Ibid., 131.

[37]JA, 8; cf. CTK, 31, 33, where Van Til speaks of the "interdependence of the idea of *the fact* and *the content* of Scripture."

[38]IW, 3.

God *must* identify himself. Such a God . . . identifies all the facts of the universe. In identifying all the facts of the universe he sets these facts in relation to one another."[39]

Thus, a word of God, giving his own authoritative promise of redemption, must be self-attesting. Scripture, as that Word, needs no corroboration from any source outside itself; and no such corroboration is possible, unless the other source is already subject to the interpretation and evaluation of Scripture.[40]

If Scripture is self-attesting, then it bears the traditional attributes—necessity, authority, perspicuity, and sufficiency—which Van Til expounds as follows:

God inspired Scripture as his written Word, because sinful man, if left on his own, "would be sure to misinterpret"[41] the saving deeds of God. Thus, there was the necessity for Scripture, so that God's saving message "(1) might remain through the ages, (2) might reach all mankind, (3) might be offered to men objectively, and (4) might have the testimony of its truthfulness within itself."[42]

Scripture also has authority, because, of its very nature, it must challenge man's claim to autonomy. It must convey God's claim to absolute authority—his lordship over man.

The perspicuity of Scripture means that there is no "necessity for human interpreters to intervene between Scripture and those to whom Scripture comes."[43] Teachers of the church may give us useful assistance in understanding Scripture, but Roman Catholic theology is wrong to claim that "no ordinary member of the Church may interpret Scripture for himself directly."[44] To deny the clarity of Scripture is to deny its authority, for if a human teaching authority is necessary for the proper use of Scripture, then that human authority becomes the ultimate authority in the church.

Thus, no human opinion may be added to Scripture as an authority coordinate with Scripture. In other words, Scripture has sufficiency. The Reformers, says Van Til, thought of sufficiency "particularly in opposition to all manner of *sectarianism,* as they thought of

[39]CTK, 28. Cf. IW, 1.
[40]Cf. Van Til's argument in RP, 37.
[41]IST, 133.
[42]Ibid., 134.
[43]Ibid., 135.
[44]Ibid.

perspicuity chiefly in opposition to *clericalism,* as they thought of necessity in opposition to *rationalism,* and as they thought of authority in opposition to *autonomy.*"[45] Characteristically, he adds:

> All these matters overlap and are involved in one another, and it is well to see that they do. The four attributes of Scripture are equally important because, if we did not have them all, we would have none. The whole matter centers about an absolutely true interpretation that came into a world full of false interpretation.[46]

The four attributes, too, are "perspectives."

The overall argument here is that if Scripture is the self-attesting Word of God, there must be "no admixture of human interpretation" standing between the believer and the revelation.[47] It might be objected at this point that an "admixture of human interpretation" always does intervene in our study of Scripture, since, as Van Til recognizes, we must use our own senses and reason in that process. Here, Van Til would doubtless refer to his perspectival analysis of general and special revelation: in the work of Bible interpretation, our reason, senses, and methods must themselves be brought into conformity to Scripture.[48] The "admixture" to which Van Til objects, in my judgment, is not an admixture in which human reason is governed by Scripture, but one in which that reason asserts its own ultimacy and rebelliously distorts the truth.

Is there not some sinful distortion even in the believer's study of Scripture? Yes. But the goal of the believer's study is to understand the teaching of the Word itself. Although we use our own faculties to interpret Scripture, it always stands over against us, challenging our sinful distortions. And to do that, Scripture itself must be God's pure, self-attesting Word, itself free from sinful distortion.

Van Til discusses this issue in dealing with A. E. Taylor, whose objections to the orthodox view of Scripture amount to this: "There can be no authority which is absolute, if the one who receives the message of authority is, in any way, constructive in the *reception of it.*"[49]

---

[45]Ibid., 136.

[46]Ibid.

[47]Ibid.

[48]For the issue of circularity which arises here, see chaps. 10 and 22.

[49]IST, 139. I am not clear as to why the last three words are emphasized.

This objection assumes, however, that the interpretive activity of the human mind is

> something independent of the interpretive activity of the divine mind. And if one starts with such a false assumption it is but to be expected that one cannot think of the absolute authority of God over man unless man's mental activity is brought to a complete standstill.[50]

On a Christian basis, however, the human mind was not made to be independent of the divine. I would paraphrase: the human mind does its best job of interpreting when it denies its own autonomy and "thinks analogically." If sin enters into the believer's thought, it is sin that he and the Holy Spirit are overcoming.

THE *AUTOGRAPHA*

I will not deal with Van Til's rather traditional responses to the views of Scripture of Roman Catholicism and "false mysticism,"[51] or with his scriptural argument, also traditional, for plenary inspiration.[52]

His discussion of the "*autographa*" is, however, of some interest to us. Traditional Reformed theology has argued that the infallibility of Scripture pertains strictly, not to every copy of Scripture, but to the autographs, the original manuscripts, which God directly inspired. Many have objected that if that is true, our present copies of Scripture are not infallible. And since the original manuscripts are lost, we have in fact no infallible text, and our position is no different from that of liberalism. Are we not, then, left with a Bible that is not infallible but only "reasonably reliable?"

To answer this objection, Van Til employs the illustration of a bridge covered somewhat by a flooding river:

> We can drive with comparative ease in water that is a few inches deep as long as we have a solid bottom under the water. What the idea of general trustworthiness without infallible inspiration does in effect is to say that it really makes no difference whether there is a solid bottom under us, inasmuch

[50]Ibid.
[51]Ibid., 140–45.
[52]Ibid., 148–58.

> as we have to drive through water in any case. But we have seen that man needs absolutely authoritative interpretation. Hence, if the autographa were not infallibly inspired, it would mean that at some point human interpretation would stand above divine interpretation. It would mean that man were, after all, not certain that the facts and the interpretations given to the facts in Scripture are true.[53]

In *A Christian Theory of Knowledge,* Van Til responds to the same issue by appealing to divine sovereignty:

> There would be no *reasonably reliable* method of identifying the Word of God in human history unless human history itself is controlled by God. . . . It is impossible to attain the idea of such a God by speculation independently of Scripture. . . . Such a God *must* identify himself. . . . Such a view of God and human history is both presupposed by, and in turn presupposes, the idea of the infallible Bible.[54]

The passage in *A Christian Theory of Knowledge* is suggestive, but somewhat obscure. The upshot of these two passages, however, is that unless the infallible revelation has been given somewhere in space and time, and thus is accessible in principle to human knowledge (e.g., by textual criticism), then we have no access to the pure Word of God. And without that, there can be no certainty about salvation, or, for that matter, about anything else. Indeed, without such a Word, we would know that the biblical God does not exist. For the biblical God is one who does address us authoritatively. That is the only way in which the Lord can address his servants.

Therefore, if there is no such Word, there is no God. And if there is no God, there is no such thing as "reasonable reliability." Without God, all is chance, chaos.

The Scope of Scripture

If that God does exist, revealing himself by his infallible Word, then all meaning and intelligibility in the universe is due to him. And his

[53]Ibid., 153.
[54]CTK, 28; cf. IW, 44.

Word, Scripture, is relevant to all meaning in the universe. This means, contrary to "limited inerrantists" and others, that the scope of Scripture is universal. It "speaks of everything." Van Til explains:

> We do not mean that it speaks of football games, of atoms, etc., directly, but we do mean that it speaks of everything either directly or indirectly. It tells us not only of the Christ and his work but it also tells us who God is and whence the universe has come. It gives us a philosophy of history as well as history. Moreover, the information on these subjects is woven into an inextricable whole. It is only if you reject the Bible as the Word of God that you can separate its so-called religious and moral instruction from what it says, e.g., about the physical universe.[55]

The Bible "stands before us as the light in terms of which all the facts of the created universe must be interpreted."[56]

As I indicated at the beginning of this section, many theologians have tried to show, based on the nature of Scripture's message, that the scope of Scripture is limited to certain areas of narrowly religious concern. Van Til has done the church a great service here: he has rethought the nature of Scripture's message and has concluded, rightly, that when that message is properly understood, it will require us to find in God's Word a message of unlimited scope, together with ultimate authority.

Thus Van Til unleashes the great vision of Kuyper, to bring all areas of human life under the sway of Christ (see 1 Cor. 10:31; 2 Cor. 10:5). Scripture does, after all, talk about psychology, logic, mathematics, history, science, art, philosophy, politics, economics, etc., as well as the narrowly theological disciplines. Many of Kuyper's followers have unfortunately argued that Scripture has a narrow scope and that our desire to reform society must therefore largely ignore the teachings of the Bible, although Scripture may motivate us in a useful direction. Van Til, on the contrary, opens up the great power of Scripture, not only to regenerate people, but also to instruct them for social and cultural change.

This does not mean that Van Til is a narrow biblicist. We have

---

[55]DF2, 8.

[56]Ibid., 107; cf. CA, 23–29.

seen that for Van Til, revelation is an organism, that special and general revelation must be taken together. Van Til, as we have seen, does not believe that the presence of human interpretation relativizes the authority of the Word of God. Rather, God calls us to apply our best gifts toward applying his Word to all matters, and he promises that such efforts, humbly subject to that very Word we seek to apply, will be fruitful.

CHAPTER TEN

Presuppositions

Some readers will be amazed that nine chapters of this book have passed without any concentrated attention being given to the concept of presupposition. After all, the most common name given to Van Til's apologetic is "presuppositionalist."

IS VAN TIL A PRESUPPOSITIONALIST?

Van Til himself used the concept rather sparingly. For one thing, he did not voluntarily characterize his apologetic as "presuppositionalist," although he did sometimes accommodate the use of that term by others. In discussing Floyd Hamilton's critique of his apologetics, he uses the term, sometimes in quotes, sometimes without, to allude to Hamilton's phraseology.[1] He uses it similarly in connection with James Oliver Buswell,[2] who claimed to have invented it to describe Van Til's position.[3]

For another thing, it is somewhat misleading to call Van Til a presuppositionalist, in view of the history of the concept. To summa-

[1]CTK, 255–72.

[2]Ibid., 273–309.

[3]Ibid., 276.

rize that history briefly: Western philosophers since the ancient Greeks have been concerned with the relationship between *a priori* and *a posteriori* knowledge.[4] A posteriori knowledge is knowledge gained *from* experience. A priori knowledge is knowledge possessed independently of experience—that knowledge which we bring *to* our experience in order to analyze and evaluate it.[5]

Some philosophers have tried to make the case that all our knowledge is a posteriori—that the mind begins as a "blank slate" (Locke) to be written on by experience. But we know some things that do not seem to be derived from experience. For example, the proposition that two times two is four—necessarily and everywhere in the universe—does not seem to be derivable from any experience.

Others, like Plato, and perhaps Gordon Clark, have claimed that all knowledge is a priori, and that experience gives us no real knowledge, but at best reminds us of what we know innately. But such a claim seems to give the mind free rein, removing its responsibility to conform itself to the world of our common experience.

Many philosophers in between these extremes, such as Aristotle, have argued that knowledge has both a priori and a posteriori elements. Experience is a necessary ingredient in knowledge, but that experience must be conceptualized, analyzed, and formulated by a priori concepts already in the mind. However, it has proved very difficult to distinguish purely a priori elements from purely a posteriori elements in our consciousness, for reasons such as those discussed in chapter 5.

In any case, the notion of a priori knowledge, gained to some extent independently of experience and governing experience, has been a staple of philosophical discussion for centuries. The term *presupposition,* although its common philosophical use dates back two

---

[4]Compare this discussion with the discussion of laws and facts in chap. 5. The same fundamental issues are found here, but with different terminology.

[5]*A priori* means literally "from before," suggesting temporal priority. Some philosophers may have claimed that infants are born with a priori knowledge, perhaps in "seed form." But a priori knowledge does not necessarily precede experience in time. The important thing is that a priori knowledge is independent of experience, and that it serves as a criterion for analyzing and/or evaluating it. The same point must be made regarding presuppositions. A presupposition is not a belief that one must have before (temporally speaking) one comes to believe in other things; rather, it is a belief that is independent of some other knowledge and governs that knowledge to some extent. Many critics of Van Til have erred at this point.

centuries, captures much of the meaning that philosophers have sought to include under the label *a priori*.

Immanuel Kant (1724–1804) was troubled that empiricism (emphasizing a posteriori knowledge) was leading to skepticism in the writings of David Hume, while rationalism (emphasizing a priori knowledge) was, in the writings of G. W. Leibniz and others, producing implausible speculations without any grounding in experience. As an alternative to both empiricism and rationalism, Kant developed a "transcendental method."[6] Like the empiricists, Kant denied that we have a priori knowledge of the world "in itself" apart from our experience. But he also agreed with the rationalists that some kind of a priori knowledge was necessary if we are to make any sense out of experience. That a priori knowledge was discovered "transcendentally," that is, by asking, What are the preconditions of meaning and rationality? Granting that knowledge is possible, in other words, what must we presuppose to be true? Kant concluded that we must make certain assumptions about space and time and about the "categories" (unity, plurality, cause, effect, etc.) that the mind applies to experience.

Idealism in Germany (Fichte, Schelling, Hegel) and Britain (Green, Bradley, Bosanquet) continued Kant's transcendental approach, although it reached different conclusions about the preconditions of knowledge. It was in the idealist literature that *presupposition* became a common philosophical term. Van Til wrote his doctoral dissertation on the idealist concept of God, and, doubtless, picked up the term from that school of thought, even though he was very critical of idealism in general.

Through the twentieth century, idealist influence on philosophy has waned, but others have emphasized the importance of presuppositions in human knowledge, with or without using the term. Phenomenologists and existentialists have emphasized the importance of the "life-world," the world of ordinary experience, which supplies the presuppositions for theoretical activity. Ludwig Wittgenstein taught that acceptance of a "form of life" or "language game" was prior to knowledge of anything within that form of life or language game. Philosophers of science have often emphasized the presuppositions of scientific theorizing: e.g., Michael Polanyi's "tacit knowledge" and

---

[6]Van Til also called his method "transcendental" (SCE, 10–13). I shall discuss that concept in connection with his "Argument for Christianity," especially in chap. 23.

Thomas Kuhn's "paradigms." Marxists have insisted that commitment to a certain life-project or praxis is prior to all theorizing. Some hermeneutical theorists have emphasized the need of prior commitment to a "story." And deconstructionists have found so much bias in human communication that, in the view of their critics, they have entirely denied the possibility of objective content in language, reducing language entirely to the assertion of presuppositions.

Clearly, then, any twentieth-century apologist worth his salt would have to deal in a serious way with the concept of presupposition, distinguishing it from other aspects of human knowledge, and distinguishing his own view from the many other possibilities available. Van Til undertook this task, but in this respect he was no different from many other apologists, even from many who would prefer to be called "evidentialists" or "classicists."[7] Certainly, one's concern for the preconditions of knowledge does not in itself justify one's being labeled a presuppositionalist.

That label may connote a kind of apriorism, which either denies a posteriori knowledge or minimizes its importance relative to the a priori. Gordon H. Clark was certainly a presuppositionalist in this sense, and he welcomed that label. He denied that anything could be learned from sense experience. But Van Til was not an apriorist in this sense. He approved of empirical, factual study and believed that the study of factual evidence was important to apologetics.[8] In general, he took this position:

> I do not artificially separate induction from deduction, or reasoning about the facts of nature from reasoning in *a priori* analytical fashion about the nature of human consciousness. I

[7]Thomas Reid, the nineteenth-century founder of the school of philosophy called Scottish commonsense realism, argued that philosophy must make certain commonsense assumptions that are not strictly provable, such as the reliability of sense experience and the reality of the world external to ourselves. Reid's thinking became the basis of the "Old Princeton" apologetic, and it is reflected in many forms of evangelical apologetics today. See appendix A, in which I indicate that the book *Classical Apologetics,* by R. C. Sproul, John Gerstner, and Arthur Lindsley (Grand Rapids: Zondervan, 1984) claims this kind of presuppositional basis. In my estimation, however, they are far less sophisticated than Van Til in their account of how presuppositions function in apologetic argument.

[8]See our later discussion of Van Til's "Argument for Christianity" (pt. 4, chaps. 18–24). Some references on this point are IST, 146–47; SCE, 7–13.

> do not artificially abstract or separate them from one another. On the contrary I see induction and analytical reasoning as part of one process of interpretation.[9]

He even said, with somewhat less balance, that human beings "must reject every form of a priori reasoning and base themselves upon the revelation of God from the start."[10]

As we have seen, Van Til's epistemology is multiperspectival: it seeks a balance between facts and laws, a balance between revelation in word, act, and divine presence. He coordinates revelation from and about God, the world, and the self, and he finds them interdependent. Similarly, we see in this context that Van Til seeks a balance between a priori and a posteriori elements in knowledge. The Trinity is not a mere oneness or a mere threeness, but always three in one. So the creation is unity in plurality, fact in law, law in fact. There is no pure a priori or pure a posteriori. The search for either is fruitless and idolatrous, being the search for an absolute criterion apart from God. Therefore, if presuppositionalism denotes apriorism, Van Til is not a presuppositionalist.

However, Van Til may be called a presuppositionalist in another sense. Certainly he believed that God's revelation has absolute authority (and thus a certain priority) over all human thought. We have seen that his concept of analogical knowledge requires us to "think God's thoughts after him." We have seen that, in Van Til's view, revelation must serve as our ultimate criterion of truth in all areas of life.

This revelation is given to us a priori, in a sense. It governs our interpretation of experience, and that is one traditional function of a priori knowledge. But we discover it partly through our experience, unlike a priori knowledge in the traditional sense. We learn about God by reading the Bible (under the illumination of the Holy Spirit) and by observing his handiwork in creation and in ourselves. That is, we receive revelation through experience. This is why Van Til is able,

---

[9]DF1, 258. This is followed by an endorsement of "historical apologetics," with the caveat that discussions of fact should include challenges to the unbeliever's philosophy of fact.

[10]IST, 170, in response to Clark. As we have seen, Van Til tended to "lose his balance" when he dealt with Clark. Surely he should have objected here, not to a priori reasoning as such, but to apriorism as a theory of knowledge, to the denial of a posteriori knowledge, or to a priori reasoning apart from revelation.

in the previously quoted passage, to draw a sharp contrast between a priori reasoning and basing ourselves upon the revelation of God.

So, we may or may not choose to call Van Til a presuppositionalist. But it is more important in either case to understand in what ways Van Til affirms, and in what ways he rejects, traditional apriorism.

THE MEANING OF *PRESUPPOSITION*

Van Til uses the term *presupposition* to indicate the role that divine revelation ought to play in human thought. I do not believe that he ever defines the term. I have tried to define it for him as a "basic heart-commitment." For the Christian, that commitment is to God as he reveals himself in his Word. Non-Christians substitute something else—another god, themselves, pleasure, money, rationality, or whatever—as that to which they are ultimately committed and that which governs all of life, including thought.[11] Our ultimate commitment plays an important role in our knowledge. It determines our ultimate criteria of truth and falsity, right and wrong. As long as we consistently maintain our ultimate commitment, we cannot accept anything as true or right that conflicts with that commitment.

There are a few instances in Van Til's writings in which he uses the term *presupposition* differently. For example, he urges the apologist to show "the non-Christian that even in his virtual negation of God, he is still really presupposing God."[12] Clearly, when the unbeliever "presupposes" God in this sense, he is not acknowledging God as his ultimate commitment. Van Til's point here is that, in assuming the intelligibility of the world, the unbeliever implicitly concedes the existence of the God he explicitly denies. This lesser sense of *presuppose* is related to Van Til's more common use of the term, but it is somewhat different. For the unbeliever to presuppose God in this context is for him to think, say, or do something, contrary to his own inclination, that indicates at some level of his consciousness a recognition of God's reality and significance.

There are also passages in Van Til in which the word *presuppose* is used, not of persons, but of things: arguments, methods, knowledge, academic disciplines, states of affairs (like the intelligibility of

[11]DF2, 83, 216.
[12]CTK, 13.

the universe).[13] In such contexts, that which is presupposed is a necessary condition or that which legitimizes. Perhaps we can relate these uses to our basic definition by saying that if *x* presupposes *y*, then *y* is that to which a person must be committed if he is to give an intelligible account of *x*.[14]

Van Til sometimes uses other phrases as equivalents to *presupposition,* especially "starting point" and "reference point." These latter phrases are, in my estimation, less clear.[15] "Starting point," in particular, suggests a temporal sequence which, as we have seen, is not necessary to the concept of presupposition.

Finally, there is the phrase "reasoning by presupposition," which for Van Til designates the "transcendental argument" for Christian theism. Because he advocates this sort of argument, Van Til may certainly in one sense be called a presuppositionalist. We shall discuss this form of argumentation in chapter 23.

MISUNDERSTANDINGS

Some writers understand a presupposition to be a mere supposition, assumption, or postulate—a belief chosen arbitrarily, with no rational basis.[16] This is not Van Til's understanding, and it should not be assumed in discussions about him. For Van Til, Christian presuppositions have the strongest possible rational ground, namely, the revelation of God. Indeed, Christian presuppositions are even *provable* in a sense, as we shall see in our examination of Van Til's argument for Christianity. Nor does Van Til use *presupposition* to refer to a hypothesis adopted for consideration, as does, for example, Edward J. Carnell.[17] For Van Til, presuppositions are categorical, not hypothetical. Nor should we emphasize the *pre-* in *presupposition* to suggest that a presupposition must be held at some point in time prior to all our other knowledge. The *pre-* in *presupposition* refers to the "pre-eminence" of the presupposition with respect to our other

---

[13]Examples: science (CA, 24), consciousness of self and objects (DF2, 77), and methods (DF2, 100).

[14]For Van Til's concept of "reasoning by presupposition," see chap. 23.

[15]See DKG, 125–26.

[16]E.g., Mark Hanna, *Crucial Questions in Apologetics* (Grand Rapids: Baker, 1981), and Sproul, Gerstner, and Lindsley, *Classical Apologetics.*

[17]See the discussion in chap. 21.

beliefs. Van Til says, "Man's consciousness of self and of objects presuppose for their intelligibility the self-consciousness of God. In asserting this we are not thinking of psychological and temporal priority. We are thinking only of the question as to what is the final reference point in interpretation."[18]

The question is sometimes asked, How can people be expected to presuppose God's revelation before they have come to believe in God? The answers are: (1) Everyone knows God already by virtue of natural revelation (Rom. 1:21). Those who choose not to believe in him do so contrary to their own better knowledge. (2) Even if presupposing God did require knowledge in addition to what we have, the lack of such knowledge would not invalidate the obligation to presuppose God. Rather, that obligation would entail the further obligation to gain that additional knowledge. (3) Even if the requirement to presuppose God's revelation were in some sense impossible for man to obey, that fact would not invalidate it. Calvinism typically teaches that God commands what depraved man cannot do apart from grace.

Proximate and Ultimate

In the preceding sections, I have reserved the word *presupposition,* as Van Til usually does, for a person's ultimate commitment. The example of the non-Christian's presupposing God was an exception.

There are other exceptions: "If then the human consciousness must, in the nature of the case, always be the proximate starting point, it remains true that God is always the most basic and therefore the final reference point in human interpretation."[19]

Some have objected that we cannot ask people to presuppose or "start with" God in their thinking, for they must always "start with" whatever is most immediate to them, namely, their own consciousness. This objection becomes less plausible when we reply that Van Til's "start with" in such a context does not have a temporal meaning, but simply refers to that which has supreme authority over a person. If we do treat the question as a temporal one, the answer is that we can "start with" anything. It does not matter in what order we consider the various items we think about.

[18]DF2, 77.

[19]Ibid; cf. IST, 72.

But, more importantly, even if we do begin with our own consciousness, we will not be able to interpret that consciousness rightly apart from God. Indeed, a true insight into our own consciousness brings us face-to-face with God, for we are his image. Hence Calvin emphasized the interdependence of our knowledge of God and of the self. Therefore, even in the temporal sense, a true encounter with consciousness will simultaneously be an encounter with God.

And even if we must "start with" the consciousness in a temporal sense, that does not mean that we must accept as normative the present standards or criteria that that consciousness affords us. The temporal question and the normative question must be kept distinct. The term *start with* confuses that distinction, and therefore is not a good synonym for *presuppose.*

Van Til's formulation is that the self or consciousness is the "proximate" starting point or presupposition, while God is the "ultimate" one. We know our own consciousness, and we must presuppose that self-knowledge when we come to know anything else.[20] But our ultimate presupposition must be God alone. The apostle assumes that relationship when he writes, "Whenever our hearts condemn us, God is greater than our hearts, and he knows everything" (1 John 3:20).

[20]Of course, it is also the case that we cannot know ourselves without at the same time knowing something of our finite environment. So knowledge of self is not prior to knowledge of the things outside ourselves. Self, world, and God are known simultaneously, as perspectives on each act of knowledge. That does not mean that the three are identical to one another, only that they are known together. This is my formulation, but I think it is in accord with Van Til's overall perspectivalism.

CHAPTER ELEVEN

The Primacy of the Intellect

We will now look at Van Til's view of human reason. I do not believe that Van Til defines *reason* anywhere, but it is clear that he views it primarily as a human capacity or faculty. Specifically, reason is the capacity of a person to think and act according to logical norms, including the capacity to form beliefs, draw inferences, and formulate arguments. The adjective *rational* can pertain to such thinking (and the resulting beliefs, inferences, and arguments) and acting, as well as to the person and his intellectual faculty.

Although Van Til does not point this out, it is important for us to understand that *reason* and *rational* are used in both descriptive and normative senses. All thinking is "rational" in the descriptive sense. But in the normative sense, thinking is "rational" only when it formulates true beliefs, draws valid inferences, operates according to proper criteria, and so on.

Ultimately, for Van Til, the norms of reason are found in the revelation of God. Like all human activities, reasoning is subject to the norms of divine revelation. Thus, "the intellectual itself is ethical."[1] The human mind is created, and therefore not ultimate or self-sufficient.[2] We must submit our reasoning, like every other activity, to

[1]DF2, 46; cf. pp. 17–18.
[2]DF2, 90.

God.[3] In Van Til's thought, as we have seen, human thinking is to be "analogical," accepting God's revelation as the ultimate presupposition or "reference point" for all human knowledge. Ultimately, truth is correspondence with God's "self-complete nature and knowledge."[4] So, "if man is not autonomous, if he is rather what Scripture says he is, namely, a creature of God and a sinner before his face, then man should subordinate his reason to the Scriptures and seek in the light of it to interpret his experience."[5]

Van Til looks more closely at the functions of reason[6] by interacting with the views of the nineteenth-century Princeton theologian Charles Hodge. Hodge lists three functions of reason in theology: to receive revelation, to judge contradictions (possibilities and impossibilities), and to judge the evidences of revelation.[7]

We might expect Van Til to agree with Hodge on the first point and simply reject his second and third points. But his response to Hodge is more subtle than that, and his discussion introduces three of his main concerns: the primacy of the intellect, the place of logic, and the role of evidence. We shall consider these in turn. This chapter will deal with the primacy of the intellect.

Hodge argues that revelation is directed specifically to the mind, and therefore may be received only by intellectual beings, not "brutes" or "idiots." Van Til takes this to mean that it is the intellect, rather than the will or the emotions, which receives the revelation of God. He describes Hodge as holding to "the primacy of the intellect."

The doctrine of the primacy of the intellect is not found in the Reformed creeds, but it is advocated in the writings of various Reformed theologians, including J. Gresham Machen and Gordon H. Clark, as well as Hodge. The Clark controversy, besides dealing with the incomprehensibility of God, also dealt with the relation of intellect to will and emotions, both in God and in man. The *Complaint* charges Clark with (1) denying that God has emotions and (2) believing that the human intellect has a far greater religious importance than the human will or emotions.[8] According to the *Complaint,* Clark makes

---

[3]IST, 192.

[4]CA, 10.

[5]DF2, 108; cf. pp. 31–35.

[6]I.e., reasoning in theology. But Van Til does not draw a sharp distinction between theology and other fields: see IST, 14–16.

[7]Ibid., 31–42.

[8]P. 16.

intellectual contemplation of God the highest form of glorifying and enjoying him, and he subordinates will and emotions to intellect as means to an end. The *Complaint* concedes that Clark does commendably resist separating these faculties in either God or man; Clark wishes to maintain a unity among these faculties so that the mind (whether divine and human) always thinks and acts as a whole. Nevertheless, says the *Complaint,* when we seek to describe, relate, and evaluate these different "aspects" of the unity of personality, Clark would have us attribute "primacy" to the intellect. The *Complaint* considers this view out of accord with the Scriptures and the Reformed faith.[9]

The *Answer* replies that Clark denies emotions to God because he defines them as among the "passions" that are denied to God in the Westminster Confession of Faith, II, 1.[10] Clark, however, does not deny that God feels. He only insists that God's feelings are not, in Dabney's words, "ebbing and flowing accesses of feeling."[11] The *Answer* argues that unless we assert the primacy of the intellect, "it would be a matter of indifference whether one followed one's anger or his sober judgment of truth."[12]

Van Til does not, to my knowledge, address the question of emotions in God, even in the part of *An Introduction to Systematic Theology* where he discusses the divine attributes.[13] But in discussing the primacy of the intellect in man, he makes two distinctions: one between Christian and non-Christian views of the primacy of the intellect, and one between ontological and economic primacy.

The Christian view of the primacy of the intellect, according to Van Til, is "based on the Creator-creature distinction."[14] Sproul, Gerstner, and Lindsley, in *Classical Apologetics,* object that "if any primacy is based on something else, it does not have primacy."[15] This

---

[9]The *Complaint* also alleges that Clark makes an inadequate distinction between the believer's and the unbeliever's use of reason. I shall not specifically discuss Clark's view of that distinction, but Van Til's view will be discussed in the chapter on "Antithesis."

[10]*Answer,* 26.

[11]Ibid., 27. Should "accesses" be "excesses?"

[12]Ibid., 29. The General Assembly's *Report* did not discuss this issue.

[13]I suspect that if he had, he would have urged us to be "fearlessly anthropomorphic" in accepting the existence of divine emotions.

[14]IST, 31; cf. p. 161.

[15]R. C. Sproul, John Gerstner, and Arthur Lindsley, *Classical Apologetics* (Grand Rapids: Zondervan, 1984), 227.

objection fails to see that the primacy alleged in the phrase "primacy of the intellect" is a primacy with respect to other faculties of the mind, not a primacy of the mind with respect to authorities outside itself. Intellect may be prior to will or emotion, without being prior to God's revelation and without being its own ultimate standard of truth. Van Til's point, however, is one that I think even the authors of *Classical Apologetics* would concede after a little reflection, namely, that any Christian view of the primacy of the intellect must be consistent with the relationship between God and man as revealed in Scripture.

Van Til then argues that the relations between the various faculties of the human mind are analogous to the relations between the persons of the Trinity.[16] As Father, Son, and Holy Spirit are ontologically equal, so are the human intellect, will, and emotions.[17] Not one is better or worse than the others; not one is inherently more or less prone to error or sin. Nevertheless, as the Son and Spirit relate "economically" to the creation in voluntary subordination to the Father, so the human intellect has an "economic" primacy over the will and emotions.[18] Van Til explains: "The will of man cannot function unless it knows in relation to what to function. Man must know the truth if he is to react with his will and feelings to it."[19]

Van Til does not attempt to develop his Trinitarian analogy from Scripture itself; that would be difficult to do. But there is a legitimate scriptural point here. In Scripture, all human faculties have the purpose of glorifying God, for that is the purpose of human life itself. When Adam fell, his whole personality fell. All his faculties were involved in his sin. Scripture is quite explicit on this point: in Genesis 3:6, Satan perversely stimulates Eve's emotions, intellect, and will. Through Christ, we ourselves, as whole persons, including all our faculties equally, are redeemed, regenerated, and sanctified.

---

[16]See chap. 5 for his overall perspective on this analogy.

[17]As we saw earlier, Van Til takes the Creator-creature distinction to imply that there are only two levels of being. This implies that there are only two kinds of ontological status: God's and the world's. Everything in the world has the same ontological status: see DF2, 26–27. Van Til's metaphysic does not rule out the presence of hierarchy within the creation, but it does not encourage hierarchical thinking, as does the Greek philosophical scheme of traditional Roman Catholicism.

[18]IST, 32.

[19]Ibid.

Van Til contrasts this view with a non-Christian approach "which hails from the ancient philosophers."[20] That approach denies both the Creation and the Fall. It holds that man's intellect is divine and unfallen, but that emotions are "inherently unruly."[21] Wicked human behavior comes, on this view, not from comprehensive depravity, but from following emotions rather than intellect. Improvement comes, not through comprehensive redemption, but through a determined attempt to follow reason rather than emotion.[22]

EVALUATION

Van Til is right, I think, in denying this philosophical view and in saying that all human faculties are equally subject to sin and redemption. Neither sin nor redemption involves the elevation of one faculty above another; rather, both sin and redemption equally affect all of our faculties. Some Christians have erred at this point, particularly trichotomists, who typically argue that sin involves a primacy of body and soul over spirit, and that redemption restores the primacy of spirit.

Did Clark err at this point?[23] Not so far as I can see, judging from the evidence available at the time. There was certainly no evidence that Clark regarded the human intellect as divine or unfallen. Clark did insist that one should follow one's sober judgment of truth rather than his anger or other momentary emotions, but Van Til says virtually the same thing in describing the "economic" primacy of the intellect.

On Van Til's side, he surely recognized that the role of the intellect is relevant to redemption. Redemption does not consist of a rearrangement of our faculties. But to "follow one's anger" instead of "sober judgment" is certainly one form of sin, and the reversal of that pattern is one of the goals of redemption. And, as Clark maintains, if we do not reverse these patterns, we fall into skepticism. This sort of change is not the whole of redemption, nor the key to sanctification,

---

[20]Ibid.

[21]Ibid., 34.

[22]Van Til also formulates this argument in SCE, 58; CTEV, 112; PR, 67.

[23]Van Til indicates in IST, 35, n. 1, that Clark is one of his targets.

but it is surely one aspect of our growth in grace. It would certainly be wrong to charge Clark with deifying the intellect simply because he believes that in such cases the will and the emotions ought to follow the intellect.[24]

Van Til's analysis, therefore, is insightful, but it is not successful as a critique of Clark. We have seen several times in this book how Van Til seems to be at his worst when he interacts with Clark. That suggests to me that the difference between them was not merely theological or academic. But I would not care to speculate as to the precise nature of the problem between them.

I do think that Van Til's basic distinctions, between Christian and non-Christian approaches and between ontological and economic relations, are sound as far as they go. Certainly nothing in these constructions justifies the charge that Van Til is an irrationalist. Nor does Van Til's position justify the opposite criticism of Dooyeweerd and Knudsen that he is a rationalist.[25] Dooyeweerd bases this criticism on the fact that Van Til seeks to derive philosophical concepts from Scripture. Knudsen's argument is that Van Til speaks of God's self-knowledge as "analytical" and thus uses the human "analytical judgment" as a model of divine thought, rather than recognizing God's mind as transcendent to all human rationality.

Dooyeweerd's point reveals defects in his own view of Scripture rather than any problems with Van Til. Van Til, as we have seen, insists that Scripture speaks to all areas of life, including philosophy; Dooyeweerd evidently denies that. Knudsen's argument fails to take adequate account of Van Til's own explicit definition of "analytical" (namely, that God's knowledge does not depend on anything outside himself). In the light of Van Til's interaction with Clark, it is a bit strange for somebody to accuse him of identifying God's thought with human reason.

As to the relationship of the various human mental faculties with each other, I think it best to go beyond both Clark and Van

---

[24]On the other hand, there are pantheistic implications (doubtless contrary to his intention) in some of Clark's later writings. First, he asserted that there must be an identity rather than a mere correspondence between idea and object in human knowledge, *Language and Theology* (Phillipsburg: Presbyterian and Reformed, 1980), 29. What does this say about human knowledge of God? Second, he argued that a person is a composite of propositions (see chap. 8) and that some human propositions are identical with God's.

[25]JA, 74–127, 275–305; HDRA; see chap. 27.

Til.[26] It is interesting that both of them insist on the unity of human personality and suggest that there are dangers in dividing the human mind sharply into faculties such as intellect, will, and emotion. Nevertheless, this agreed premise of the unity of personality plays no role in the *Complaint,* the *Answer,* or in Van Til's *Introduction to Systematic Theology.* Van Til and Clark, rather, carry on their argument as if the three faculties were each self-contained and separate from the others, each competing for flat-out dominance within the mind.

On the contrary, it seems evident to me that our feelings supply legitimate data for our intellectual judgments, that our intellectual judgments influence our feelings, that to some extent we choose what to believe and feel (so that the will influences beliefs and feelings), that our beliefs and feelings influence the will, and so on. Thus, our "faculties," if we choose to call them that, are highly interdependent, not self-contained.

Furthermore, "following one's anger over one's sober judgment" (assuming we are talking about what the Bible calls sinful anger) may be called a choice of emotion over intellect, but it may also be described as the choice of one emotion (anger) over another (our affection for God's will), or as the choice of one belief (that sinful anger will have good results) over another (that sinful anger will be counterproductive to any good purpose). Each rational decision has emotional characteristics, and each emotional decision has rational characteristics.

These considerations make emotions, intellect, and will very hard to distinguish. Indeed, it is to some extent a matter of arbitrary choice as to what we call "emotion" and what we call "intellectual conviction." Our acts, in other words, are acts of the whole person. They may be characterized intellectually, volitionally, emotionally, and perhaps in other ways as well.[27] But the intellect itself has emotional and volitional aspects, etc. Perhaps it is best to see intellect, emotions, and will as perspectives on the whole personality.[28]

---

[26]I will not discuss Dooyeweerd's view in this connection, beyond this brief comment: Dooyeweerd, too, emphasizes the unity of personality. Dooyeweerd rejects even the soul-body distinction of traditional Reformed orthodoxy as the product of Greek dualism. It is a good thing to emphasize unity of personality, but Dooyeweerd is wrong thereby to oppose any theological analysis of the aspects of personality.

[27]Van Til, interestingly, correlates reason and intuition in IST, 91.

[28]See my DKG, 328–46, where I have worked out this approach in some detail.

On this sort of analysis, we can make the obvious points about how people should follow their sober judgments rather than their momentary inclinations. It is unimportant for present purposes whether we describe these judgments and inclinations as intellectual, emotional, or volitional. They do not, after all, come with labels on them, and they always have all three aspects. At the same time, we can avoid seeing the intellect as a kind of master sergeant, subduing and bossing around the other "faculties" up in our heads. More important, on this basis we can avoid the temptation to confuse the ethical with the metaphysical—to see salvation as the elevation of one human faculty rather than the transformation of the whole person.

I think it is advisable for Reformed theologians to avoid advocating the primacy of the intellect. The phrase can, to be sure, be used to make some legitimate points about "following anger" and so on. And its use in Reformed theology is understandable in light of the challenges of liberalism and neo-orthodoxy, which denied any propositional or intellectual element in revelation, leaving us with empty "feeling" or "encounter." And, of course, Reformed theology has also had to contend with various kinds of emotionalism within evangelicalism, and not only within the charismatic movement. However, the primacy of the intellect is rather misleading as a general concept of human psychology.

I believe this concept has also encouraged an unfortunate intellectualism in some Reformed circles. In those circles, sanctification, guidance, worship, preaching, discipleship, counseling, and ministerial preparation have often been too easily and closely assimilated to the model of academic learning. Cultivating godly emotions and ministering to the emotional needs of people, even the development of pastoral skills, have often been neglected—and even treated with a kind of smug contempt.[29] This sort of attitude has much more in common with rationalistic philosophy than with the Bible.

---

[29]For an example, consider Richard Muller's *The Study of Theology* (Grand Rapids: Zondervan, 1991) in the light of my critique, "Muller on Theology," *WTJ* 56 (spring 1994): 133–51. Muller's reply to me, "*The Study of Theology* Revisited: A Response to John Frame," *WTJ* 56 (fall 1994): 409–17, is even more smug than his book. I will not be permitted to publish an additional response in *WTJ*, so I will say briefly here that (1) in the reply Muller seems more interested in discrediting a critic than in making progress on the issues, and (2) he writes, well, like a man who knows that his opponent will not be permitted to reply.

The Bible is a very emotional book, as well as a book with profound intellectual content. It does not reveal the truths of God merely as academic propositions. It tells stories, issues commands, repeats itself, sings songs, offers prayers, gives us visual aids (symbols, especially the sacraments), and calls upon us to greet one another with a holy kiss. Paul breaks off from logical arguments in Romans to shout praise. I do believe that Reformed people need to regain their perspective in these areas.

CHAPTER TWELVE

Logic

We continue our discussion of Van Til's view of reason by considering the subject of logic. In the last chapter, we focused on his interaction with Hodge's view of the place of reason in theology. The first of Hodge's three points was that reason has the function of "receiving" revelation. Van Til took that as asserting the primacy of the intellect, and we dealt with that in the last chapter. Hodge's second point is that reason is the *judicium contradictionis*, the judge of contradiction. Hodge says that reason has "the prerogative of deciding whether a thing is possible or impossible. If it is seen to be impossible, no authority and no amount or kind of evidence can impose the obligation to receive it as true."[1]

Persons with a little familiarity with Van Til's thought might expect that he would simply disagree with Hodge here. Certainly, our first impression of the discussion is that Van Til is setting Hodge up for a fall. Eventually, surely, Van Til will insist that reason has no right to judge what is possible; only God does.

Van Til does accord to God the ultimate right to make such judgments, but here he does not simply disagree with Hodge; rather,

[1]IST, 36, quoting Charles Hodge, *Systematic Theology* (Grand Rapids: Eerdmans, n.d.), 1:51.

the tone of his response is surprisingly positive. Basically, he agrees with what Hodge says, but he tries to clarify the question by pressing the distinction between (Christian) theistic and nontheistic views of logic.[2] Ultimately, Van Til's conclusion is that reason does indeed have the right to judge the logical consistency of revelation, but reason itself must be subordinate to God.

The main difference between theistic and nontheistic views of logic is that the theist finds the foundation of logic to be the nature of God, while the nontheist believes that logic "operates independently of God."[3] If some god exists for the nontheist, that god "has his source in possibility" rather than the reverse.[4] The same can be said for probability.[5]

For Van Til, God's nature is rational. In him is an absolute system of truth.[6] Our own rationality is created, but it expresses God's: the law of contradiction is *"the expression on a created level of the internal coherence of God's nature."*[7]

Unbelievers, though they repress the truth,[8] nevertheless retain

> some remnant of the knowledge of God and consequently of the true source and meaning of possibility and probability. It is to this remnant of a truly theistic interpretation of experience that Hodge really appeals when he speaks of the laws of belief that God has implanted in human nature. It is, of course, not only quite legitimate, but absolutely imperative to appeal to the "common consciousness" of men in this sense.[9]

---

[2]In CGG, 183, Van Til seems to reject Hodge's position flatly: "The Princeton method, so far as it worked by this method of appeal to the reason of man as such as the judge of the possible and the impossible, was flatly opposed to the Princeton theology." However, the phrases "so far as" and "as such" imply that Hodge's point could be taken in a good sense. On p. 184, it is plain that here, as in IST, Van Til criticizes Hodge mainly for failing to distinguish Christian from non-Christian views of reason.

[3]IST, 37.

[4]Ibid., 38.

[5]Ibid.

[6]DF2, 43; CGG, 142.

[7]IST, 11 (emphasis his).

[8]We will explore in detail the differences between believer and unbeliever in chap. 15.

[9]IST, 11.

Taking logic in the theistic sense, it is quite correct to say, "It is impossible that God should do, approve, or command what is morally wrong."[10] Nor is it possible that "God should command anything that 'contradicts the laws of belief which He has impressed upon our nature.'"[11] God is not illogical, for he is consistent with the laws of his own nature.

Van Til critiques Hodge, however, for failing to draw a distinction between logic as used by a Christian and logic as used by a non-Christian. In this respect, Hodge makes the same error that Van Til attributes to Gordon H. Clark, Edward J. Carnell, Wilbur M. Smith, J. Oliver Buswell, Jr., and C. S. Lewis.[12]

Non-Christians, says Van Til, have very different ideas from Christians about what is possible and impossible, and about what contradicts and what does not contradict our moral and rational natures. Therefore, we must not ask unbelievers to "apply the law of contradiction *as they see it* to the gospel *as they see it,*"[13] for then they would reject the gospel.

Compare Van Til's comment about Warfield, the great Old Princeton theologian of the next generation: "To be sure, if Warfield's appeal to the natural man were of an *ad hominem* nature, then it would be well. Christ does ask the natural man to judge with respect to the truth of his claims. But then he asks them to admit that their own wisdom has been made foolish by God."[14]

Van Til's discussion of logic in this particular context is somewhat abbreviated. It leaves certain important questions unanswered, and so we must look at what he says elsewhere on these issues. Does Van Til want to say, for example, that unbelievers have no ability to think logically? No, says Van Til. The antithesis between believer and unbeliever is ethical, not metaphysical. Even the lost in hell "have not lost the power of rational and moral determination."[15] Van Til is saying that the unbeliever may be very competent in logic, just as he may have other natural gifts in abundance. Believers do not necessarily excel unbelievers in intelligence; indeed, the opposite is often true:

---

[10]Ibid., 39.
[11]Ibid., 40.
[12]Ibid., 39.
[13]Ibid., 41.
[14]PDS, 61.
[15]Ibid., 254.

not many wise are called (1 Cor. 1:26). But the unbeliever uses his natural gifts to repress and attack the truth. Here Van Til's famous illustration of the buzz saw is helpful: the unbeliever is like a buzz saw that is very sharp and efficient, but has been set in the wrong direction.[16]

Does regeneration give to believers new laws of logic, or new rules for constructing syllogisms? Certainly not. "I do not maintain," he says, "that Christians operate according to new laws of thought any more than that they have new eyes or noses."[17] The differences between believer and unbeliever in the area of logic are rather, as we saw in the discussion of Hodge, in the philosophy of logic[18] and the use of logic.

How should we respond to unbelieving challenges on these matters? Philosophically, the unbeliever seeks a nontheistic foundation for logic. But in a nontheistic world, logic can be nothing more than purely abstract laws, which man seeks to connect with meaningless facts. As Van Til illustrates, "His logic is merely the exercise of a revolving door in a void, moving nothing from nowhere into the void."[19] Elsewhere, he presents the unbeliever as facing "the dilemma of absolute ignorance or absolute omniscience":[20] either the unbeliever knows the truth already and thus cannot learn anything new, or else he is ignorant and cannot even ask the questions that would lead to the truth. These are forms of the one-and-many problem that we explored in chapter 5. In a universe of chance, there is no logical order, except one that man creates out of his own mind. If man creates it, then in principle he must know it omnisciently. But there is no reason to suppose that that humanly imposed order has any relation to actual facts. Nor can the facts themselves be intelligible in such a worldview. Hence, man is left with absolute ignorance. Van Til's overall philosophical conclusion is that logic presupposes a Christian worldview.

The unbeliever also uses logic differently than the believer. The unbeliever employs his logic to attack Christian theism, bringing to

---

[16]DF2, 74.

[17]DF1, 296; cf. CGG, 27–29; IST, 254.

[18]DF1, 296.

[19]CTK, 299.

[20]DF2, 90; cf. pp. 86–90; IST, 167. See chap. 17 on the unbeliever's combination of rationalism and irrationalism, which is equivalent to the dilemma discussed in this passage.

bear nontheistic standards of possibility and impossibility. He tries to show that Christianity is logically inconsistent by bringing up paradoxes like the Trinity and the relationship of divine sovereignty to human responsibility. The Christian should not answer such objections, says Van Til, by trying to show that Christianity is consistent by the unbeliever's standards. Rather, he should appeal to "analogical" consistency.

To understand this principle better, we should explore further Van Til's frequent references to the "apparent contradictions" in the Christian faith.[21] We saw in chapter 5 that Van Til refuses to accept any easy resolution of the Trinitarian paradox: one God in three persons. He does believe that the Trinity is not really contradictory. Yet he also maintains that it is not possible to fully remove from our formulations the *appearance* of contradiction. The doctrine of the Trinity obviously appears contradictory on an unbelieving view of logic, but this apparent contradiction also exists on a Christian view of logic. The same thing is true with another form of unity and diversity in God, the relation between God's nature and his attributes.[22]

Van Til similarly sees a limit to human logic in dealing with the problem of necessity and freedom in God. If God's will is directed by his intelligence, then it seems that his free acts, such as Creation and redemption, become necessary: God had to create and redeem us. If, however, God's free acts are truly free, then it would seem that they must be unconnected with his intelligence and therefore random: God just happened to create. Neither alternative is biblical. Scripture requires us to affirm both the intelligence and the freedom of God's acts of Creation and redemption. Van Til does suggest that we should distinguish two kinds of necessity: the necessity of God's nature and that necessity by which his free acts come about. But he does not explain these two kinds of necessity, which might remove the appearance of contradiction. Rather, he breaks off the discussion: "This is as far as our finite minds can reach."[23]

Van Til's paradigm case of apparent contradiction in the relationship between God and the world is what he calls "the full bucket difficulty":

---

[21]Here I return to some of the territory I explored in 1976 in VTT.

[22]IST, 229; DF1, 26.

[23]IST, 249; cf. pp. 176–78.

> To the non-Christian our position may be compared to the idea of adding water to a bucket that is already full of water. "Your idea of the self-sufficient ontological trinity," he will say, "is like a bucket full of water. To God nothing may be added. He cannot derive glory from His creatures. Yet your idea of history is like pouring water into the full bucket. Everything in it is said to add to the glory of God."[24]

Van Til also notes other areas of "apparent contradictions." There is the problem of evil: God brings evil to pass, but he is not to be blamed for it.[25] Van Til sees apparent contradictions in God's secret and revealed wills;[26] prayer and the counsel of God;[27] the image of God in the "wider" and "narrower" senses;[28] mankind existing and not existing in Adam;[29] sin being able, yet unable, to destroy the work of God apart from common grace;[30] unregenerate man being able, yet unable, to know the truth;[31] the deity and humanity of Christ;[32] and the free offer of the gospel.[33]

During the Clark controversy, the issue of paradox was raised in connection with divine sovereignty and human responsibility. The *Complaint* agreed with Clark in saying that divine sovereignty and human freedom were not actually contradictory. But it also asserted that "there are difficulties here which [Reformed theologians] are unable to solve."[34] Among these is the problem of reconciling comprehensive foreordination and concurring providence with the denial that God is the author of sin.[35] The complainants find it "amazing" that Clark thinks he can solve such problems, when the greatest theologians of the past have confessed their inability to do so.[36] In the

[24]CGG, 10; cf. pp. 27, 73; DF1, 61–62; IST, 63–64.
[25]IST, 248; NS, 271; CTETH, 36, 139.
[26]CGG, 27.
[27]Ibid.; DF1, 61.
[28]CTETH, 46; DF1, 29.
[29]DF1, 249–51.
[30]CGG, 199–200.
[31]IST, 26–27, 112–13. See my discussion of "Antithesis" in chap. 15.
[32]DF1, 205.
[33]CGG, 10.
[34]*Complaint,* 22.
[35]Ibid., 23.
[36]Ibid., 24.

end, they believe that Clark's solution to the problem does violence to human responsibility.[37]

The *Answer* replies that the Westminster Confession itself encourages logical inference from Scripture, and therefore, presumably, also intends to encourage resolution of apparent logical contradictions.[38] Further, it says: "He who claims that a given paradox cannot be solved, logically implies that he has examined every verse in Scripture, that he has exhausted every implication of every verse, and that there is no hint of a solution. . . . This is a claim to an exhaustive knowledge of all Scripture."[39] Clark's claim, on the contrary, is that Scripture itself provides hints for a solution of the problem, which amounts to denying free will in the traditional Arminian sense.[40]

Van Til, however, was not persuaded by the *Answer*. Certainly he had no interest in defending the Arminian concept of free will. But he did not believe that Clark had fully solved the paradox, either. What, specifically, is unresolved? That is hard to say. Van Til says, "That all things in history are determined by God must always seem, at first sight, to contradict the genuineness of my choice."[41] That phrase, "at first sight," might seem to suggest that the problem can, in fact, be resolved—"at second sight." But that is not Van Til's view. He holds, in fact, that human beings never reach the point where these matters no longer appear contradictory. What about heaven? Will we there discover solutions to the paradoxes? Probably not, according to Van Til, since our inability to solve them is related to our finitude. And, of course, in heaven we remain finite.

Perhaps what Van Til means to say is that Christians grow in their ability to appreciate the goodness and wisdom of God's ways. If our first impulse ("at first sight"), in contemplating divine sovereignty, is to claim that it contradicts human responsibility, we may nevertheless have better impulses ("at second sight") as we grow in grace. The problem is never actually resolved, but we gain the spiritual maturity to appreciate that God has an answer, and we do not go around complaining about an unresolved contradiction. This is, I believe, a spiri-

---

[37]Ibid., 26.

[38]*Answer*, 35.

[39]Ibid., 36.

[40]Ibid., 36–37. The *Report* of the General Assembly committee did not discuss this particular issue.

[41]CGG, 10.

tual, rather than a logical, point that Van Til wants to make about apparent contradictions.[42]

Van Til, then, would insist that even with spiritual maturity, the logical problem remains. What is the problem? In this example, it is a problem with the "genuineness" of my choice in a God-ordained universe. But is Van Til right in describing this problem as an "apparent logical contradiction"? Once we reject the Arminian concept of free will, we do not then affirm anything that actually contradicts the comprehensiveness of divine sovereignty. Also, once we reject the Arminian construction, we must also deny that a "genuine" choice must be an uncaused or autonomous choice. On a Calvinistic basis, all human choices are genuine choices. So why is there a problem with genuineness? And why does Van Til insist that the problem is a problem in logic?

We need to look a bit deeper. Van Til sees this problem as a form of the full bucket problem. As we have seen, that problem is that nothing can be added to God's glory, yet he makes creatures to glorify himself. Applied to "choice," this means that God's choices have fully determined the course of history, yet human choices are, somehow, also important or significant—what Van Til calls, somewhat awkwardly, "genuine."

So the question of "genuine choice" boils down to the question of how God's glory precludes, yet demands, addition. This is indeed a logical problem of sorts, but it is important for us to see what kind of logical problem it is.

It is, I think, similar to the logical problem connected with the Trinity. Scripture tells us that God is three and that God is one. From that teaching, one might allege that because God is three and not-three (or one and not-one), the doctrine of the Trinity is a logical contradiction. But, as I indicated in my earlier discussion of the Trinity, such a judgment would be premature, to say the least. It is common in discussions of logic to note that an apparent contradiction may be resolved through consideration of ambiguities in the terms: if God is three in one respect and one in a different respect, then there is no contradiction. The church has always made the claim that God is one and three in different senses, and, as we saw in the earlier discussion, Van Til does not dispute this claim. But he does claim that

[42]As we shall see in other connections, Van Til often makes penetrating observations on issues of spiritual life and interpersonal communication, but he tends to reduce them all to issues of logic and theological principle.

we do not know precisely how God is one and precisely how he is three; so we cannot *demonstrate* the logical consistency of the doctrine. For that reason, some appearance of contradiction remains.

The same is true of the full bucket problem. God's glory doubtless precludes addition in one sense and permits it in another. But we do not know enough about God's relation to history to define precisely what those senses are. Therefore, apparent contradiction remains in God's relation to history and specifically with respect to divine foreordination and the genuineness of human choice.

Since there is apparent contradiction in the basic nature of God (the Trinity) and in the fundamental relation of God to the world (the full bucket), Van Til sees apparent contradiction in all revelation and in all human knowledge: "Now since God is not fully comprehensible to us we are bound to come into what seems to be contradiction in all our knowledge. Our knowledge is analogical and therefore must be paradoxical."[43] "While we shun as poison the idea of the really contradictory we embrace with passion the idea of the *apparently* contradictory."[44] *"All teaching of Scripture is apparently contradictory."*[45]

Understandably, some Christians respond to these statements very harshly. For Reformed Christians, logical contradiction is a very serious matter. Clark is right in citing the Westminster Confession as authorizing us to affirm the logical entailments of biblical teachings. But if the Bible is full of contradictions, even apparent ones, how can we derive such entailments?

Logic textbooks tell us that from contradictory premises, any and all conclusions validly follow. Consider the following argument:

1. God is one. (Premise)
2. Either God is one or the moon is made of green cheese. (Follows from point 1 by the logical operation called addition. If a statement is true, then the statement or any other statement is true.)
3. God is not one. (Premise)
4. Therefore, the moon is made of green cheese. (Follows from points 2 and 3. Since point 3 denies the first half of the "or" statement, the second half must be true.)

---

[43]DF1, 61.

[44]CGG, 9.

[45]Ibid., 142 (emphasis his); cf. DF2, 44–46.

This example shows how from contradictory premises (points 1 and 3 in this case) any manner of nonsense will follow validly. (Any statement whatever could have been substituted for "the moon is made of green cheese.") Therefore, once we allow that Scripture contains contradictory teachings, we must also admit that anything at all may be validly deduced from Scripture. Indeed, if Scripture contains even one contradiction, it implicitly teaches everything, and therefore nothing. The presence of contradictions in Scripture would entirely invalidate the statement of the Westminster Confession that the counsel of God is to be found in the "good and necessary consequences" of Scripture as well as in Scripture's explicit statements. If there are contradictions in Scripture, then everything, and therefore nothing, is a "good and necessary consequence."

Of course, Van Til does not teach that Scripture is contradictory—quite the reverse. What he says, however, is that all Scripture is apparently contradictory. However, apparent contradiction poses the same problems as real contradiction for the logical analysis of Scripture. Let us say that in the illustrative argument presented above, points 1 and 3 are only apparently contradictory, which is in fact Van Til's claim about the Trinity. Nevertheless, Scripture does teach that God is one and that God is three. If we are to draw logical inferences from Scripture, as the Westminster Confession prescribes, will we not find ourselves in the same bind, deducing nonsense from apparently contradictory premises?

One reply might be this: since we know that there is some unclarity about the senses of "one" and "not one" in points 1 and 3, we should simply avoid constructing arguments of this kind. The ambiguity in the terms should make us reluctant to draw any inferences at all from these particular premises.

But if "*all* teaching of Scripture is apparently contradictory," then *any* logical deduction from scriptural premises would seem to be ruled out. Since there are apparent contradictions not only in the doctrine of the Trinity, but also in the doctrine of the divine attributes and the doctrine of God's overall relation to the world, how can we draw any logical inferences at all from biblical teaching?

To answer these questions, we will have to look into Van Til's ideas of "limiting concept" and "analogical system." These will be the topics covered in the following chapter.

CHAPTER THIRTEEN

The Analogical System

For all of the problems Van Til raises about the use of logic, his overall attitude toward logic and the building of intellectual systems of thought is remarkably positive. God is "exhaustively comprehensible to himself"[1] and can therefore be described as an "absolute system."[2] Since he has planned and controls all things, "All created reality displays this plan. It is, in consequence, inherently rational."[3]

God's rationality vindicates human rationality. His knowledge is exhaustive, and his intention is for us to know him and the world. Since we are creatures, our knowledge cannot be exhaustive, but it can be a genuine possession of the truth.[4] Our knowledge of God, in particular, is not only true, but also certain, which is simply to say that God is clearly revealed in creation and especially in ourselves.[5]

As we have seen, Van Til regards Scripture as internally consistent, a system of truth. And he also believes that our own formulations should reflect that consistency. We should not affirm contradictory doctrinal formulations. Note the following:

---

[1]NS, 277.
[2]DF1, 61; cf. IST, 10.
[3]NS, 277.
[4]DF1, 60–61; IST, 24, 164; NS, 277.
[5]IST, 114–15; CA, 13; NS, 278–79.

> But I do, of course, confess that what Scripture teaches may properly be spoken of as a system of truth. God identifies the Scriptures as his Word. And he himself, as he tells us, exists as an internally self-coherent being. His revelation of himself to man cannot be anything but internally coherent. When therefore the Bible teaches that God controls by his plan whatever comes to pass, it does not also teach that God does not control whatever comes to pass. If such were the case, God's promises and threats would be meaningless.[6]

In these passages, Van Til grants the logical point made in the last chapter, that contradictory formulations produce intellectual chaos. And, indeed, he seems also to be granting the point that apparent contradictions also lead to meaninglessness. Surely Van Til intends by these statements to encourage us in the practical work of theological formulation and communication. So he is speaking not only about the Bible "in itself," but also about how it appears to us. And as we come to read and understand the Scriptures, we learn that God controls whatever comes to pass and therefore does not fail to control his creation. Our understanding of divine sovereignty logically justifies our denial of creaturely autonomy.

We have also seen that in Van Til's own theological formulations, he is one of the most systematic of thinkers. He stresses logical relationships among doctrines more than almost any other recent theologian.[7] He speaks of some doctrines as being "central" or "fundamental" to others.[8]

And what is often most striking about Van Til's theology is that he constantly insists that one doctrine necessarily follows from another. For example, if God is self-contained, then revelation must be self-attesting.[9] If God is a Trinity, then man's knowledge must be analogical.[10] Man's knowledge is true "because," not "in spite of" the fact that, it is analogical.[11] Man's being and action are genuinely his own "because of" (again, not "in spite of") "the more ultimate being and

---

[6]DF1, 205; cf. CTK, 38–39, 200–202; CGG, 76; IST, 251.

[7]Gordon Clark is, of course, an exception.

[8]CA, 4; CTK, 12; DF1, 28, 59, 229; IST, 1, 29, 206; TJD, 76.

[9]DF1, 203; IST, 62; IW, 3, 36–37; CTK, 70.

[10]SCE, 48, 97. I have traced the development of this argument in chaps. 5–10.

[11]SCE, 48, 97. The "because, not in spite of" motif is frequent in Van Til's writings.

activity on the part of the will of God."[12] The absolute God, the absolute Christ, and the absolute Scriptures "go hand in hand. We cannot accept one without accepting the others."[13] The "absolute personality of God," as we have seen, becomes the key to avoiding both determinist and indeterminist errors.[14] Denial of the self-sufficient holiness of God entails denial also of the temporal Creation and the historical Fall.[15] "God is free not in spite of but because of the necessity of his nature."[16] "Deny the doctrine of creation and you have denied the Christian concept of God."[17] The creation of man in God's image is at the same time a "presupposition of revelation" and a "corollary from the notion of an absolutely self-conscious God."[18]

No other American theological writer gives his readers such a profound sense of the unity of Christian truth. Again and again, we learn that to affirm one doctrine is to affirm another and to affirm the whole; to deny one doctrine is to deny another and to deny the whole. All doctrines are interdependent: the whole depends on the parts, and the parts depend on the whole. Other theologians should give extended attention to these suggestions; each could be made the subject of a treatise. Why is it that the self-contained nature of God implies that his revelation be self-attesting? Van Til only sketches the reason; I tried to expand that sketch a bit in a previous chapter. But it would be edifying for some theologian to develop an extended analysis of this relationship.

In our eclectic age, it becomes all the more important to stress these interconnections. It is important to show that we cannot concoct new theologies by taking a bit of Lutheranism here, a touch of Calvinism there, an idea from Arminius over here, and blending them together uncritically. It is no accident that each of these schools of thought has maintained a fairly constant "package" of doctrines down through the years. For the most part, such packages are held together by logical bands, bands that eclecticism tends to ignore.

---

[12]CA, 11.

[13]CTETH, 28.

[14]SCE, 67–68; CTETH, 35, 48; DF1, 29, 59.

[15]IST, 244.

[16]Ibid., 177.

[17]DF1, 231.

[18]IST, 63. Other examples of Van Til's strong insistence on relations of logical dependence among doctrines: PDS, 35, 37; DF1, 202, 207, 267–69; SG, 63; IST, 139, 239; TJD, 118–19, 122; CTK, 47, 200; CGG, 65–68, 73; CA, 62, 73.

Of course, this concept of logical unity can be taken too far. We must also be critical of the theological packages bequeathed to us by tradition, testing everything by the Word of God. Theologians in the past have not been perfect exegetes or perfect logicians. If we Calvinists, for example, are to be true to the *sola Scriptura* of the Reformation, we must be prepared to criticize our received doctrines by Scripture, even as Luther and Calvin did not hesitate to analyze critically the theological traditions of their day.[19] But such analysis may not ignore the logical relationships of Scripture itself, many of which have been noted in our theological traditions.

There is real growth in theological maturity when someone moves from saying "God is absolute and Scripture is self-attesting" to saying "God is absolute and therefore Scripture is self-attesting." In that development there is growth in insight, certainty, and power to communicate. We can grow much in this way by reading Van Til.

At any rate, it is plain that Van Til is not indifferent to logical relationships in Scripture and in theology. Indeed, those logical relationships are among his main emphases. That fact raises even more pointedly the problems we raised in the preceding chapter: How can Van Til stress these logical relationships while also asserting that "all teaching of Scripture is apparently contradictory"?

To bring this problem into sharper focus, consider Van Til's critique of Francis Pieper, a Lutheran dogmatician. Van Til calls Pieper's approach "irrationalist" because Pieper teaches that God decrees all things, yet that the divine decree can be resisted.[20] "God can reveal only that which is consistent with his nature as a self-identified being," says Van Til.[21] Could not Pieper reply that his position, the position of Scripture as he sees it, is only "apparently

[19]Van Til suggests in IST, 4, that a creed should never be revised in such a way as to "tone down" specific doctrines into "vague generalities." That may be a valid criticism in the case he cites, the 1925 credal revision in the United Presbyterian Church of North America. But it would be wrong, I think, to adopt as a general principle the idea that a creed should never be revised in the direction of generality. Such a principle would mean that once a church (say, the Roman Catholic Church) adopts a specific doctrinal position, it may never change its mind. On the contrary, we must listen to Scripture, whether it tells us to be more specific or calls us to abandon specific positions previously held.

[20]CTK, 200. In context, Van Til also argues that Pieper is a rationalist, because Pieper appeals to a logical principle higher than the counsel of God.

[21]Ibid., 202.

contradictory" and therefore theologically permissible even on Van Til's terms? What, then, would make Pieper's appeal to "apparent contradiction" less legitimate than Van Til's? In other words, how can Van Til insist on maintaining apparent logical consistency when he makes such liberal allowance for apparent logical contradiction?[22]

CHRISTIAN LIMITING CONCEPTS

Van Til frequently speaks of "limiting concepts." The phrase comes from the philosophy of Immanuel Kant. Kant argued that the "noumenal world," the world as it really is apart from our experience, cannot be known by man, but that the idea or concept of a noumenal world does have a legitimate purpose in human thought: "The concept of a noumenon is thus a merely *limiting concept,* the function of which is to curb the pretensions of sensibility; and it is therefore only of negative employment."[23] In Kant's thought, a limiting concept has no positive content. For Kant, "God" is a limiting concept, and this means, not that God actually exists, but only that the term *God* may properly be used in describing the limitedness of our experience. For him, our experience is limited as if by God, whether God actually exists or not.

Mathematicians speak of limits in similar ways. Mathematical infinity is a quantity we cannot actually reach by counting finite numbers. It is a "limit" that we may approach indefinitely without ever actually reaching it. There are also limits within the system of finite numbers. The number one, for example, is the limit of the series 1/2 + 1/4 + 1/8. . . . The series approaches one without ever actually reaching it. Unlike infinity and the God of Kant, the number one can be known actually to exist in the finite world. But, like infinity and the Kantian God, it never becomes a member of the series of which it is a limit. In some ways, however, we treat mathematical limits *as if* they were the highest members of the series which they limit.

[22]I will leave it to the reader to evaluate in the light of the above data this statement of John Robbins: "Nearly every reference to logic in [Van Til's] books is a disparaging reference. He continually criticizes, belittles, and deprecates logic, not the misuse of logic, but logic itself." *Cornelius Van Til: The Man and the Myth* (Jefferson, Md.: Trinity Foundation, 1986), 23. He follows this statement with all of two examples.

[23]Kant, *Critique of Pure Reason,* tr. Norman Kemp Smith (New York: St. Martin's, 1929), 272.

Van Til's concept is somewhat similar to the others I have mentioned, but also significantly different from them. Van Til's limiting concepts have an "as if" character about them, but they may also convey knowledge of the real world, unlike Kant's limiting concepts. They are not merely abstract, as are the limits of mathematics: they can convey truth about concrete things, persons, and events. Here is an example:

> We have to speak *as if* sin would have destroyed the work of God. That was certainly its ethical intent. But we know that this is not an ultimate metaphysical possibility, for it was already, from all eternity, a part of the plan of God that sin should be defeated through the work of the Christ.[24]

Now Van Til's concern is this: somebody might start with the premise that sin cannot destroy the work of God, and then deduce from that premise the conclusion that sin needed no common-grace restraint in history. Or, one might start from the premise that sin is a serious threat to the fulfillment of God's plan and conclude that God did not foreordain sin's defeat. Both of these logical deductions are plausible, but both are badly mistaken, in Van Til's view.

Or, to make it simpler: one might use the concept of divine sovereignty to deny human responsibility, or vice versa. That sort of deduction is plausible to many; both hyper-Calvinists and Arminians see these two concepts as opposed to one another. The hyper-Calvinist opts for divine sovereignty and denies or compromises human responsibility; the Arminian does the reverse.

Van Til disparages this sort of argument as "deductivism."[25] The system of Christian thought is not a "deductive" system, he says. To my knowledge, Van Til never defines "deductive" in this sense, but evidently he means to say here (1) that we should not try to develop a theological system by deducing everything from one "master-concept" such as the sovereignty of God[26] and (2) that theology ought not to make deductions from one or more doctrines, the conclusions of which contradict other scriptural teachings.[27]

---

[24]CGG, 199–200.

[25]CTK, 38; DF1, 204–5, 227; PDS, 123; IST, 257; CGG, 202.

[26]SCE, 20; DF2, 7–8.

[27]See references in the previous notes; also IST, 256; JA, 126.

Rather, we should treat each biblical doctrine as a "limiting" or "supplementative" concept.[28] The theologian's thinking should be

> always and only an attempt to integrate the various aspects of biblical teaching. In doing so he is deeply conscious of the fact that every "concept" he employs must be limited by every other "concept" he employs, and that therefore his "system" is an effort to restate in his confession the truth as it is in Jesus.[29]

Therefore: "When man makes a 'system' for himself of the content of revelation given him in Scripture, this system is subject to, not independent of, Scripture. Thus the idea of system employed by the Christian is quite different from the idea of system as employed in modern philosophy."[30]

It follows that our doctrines are "'approximations' to the fullness of truth as it is in God."[31] Van Til emphasizes that he is not speaking of approximations to abstract truth, as in non-Christian thought. That concept of approximation is based upon an ultimate skepticism. The Christian view, rather, is based upon the incomprehensibility of God. God is knowable, but, because he is incomprehensible, our concepts do not exhaust the fullness of his being.

What, then, are Christian limiting or supplementative concepts? From the above descriptions—characteristically, Van Til gives no definition—I would say that these are concepts which, to be properly understood and employed, must be balanced by other concepts. In the theological case, the teachings of Scripture are limiting concepts, because each must be read in the light of other scriptural teachings. If

[28]He uses these two terms interchangeably. By the way, in this discussion I am following Van Til and ignoring the philosophical distinction between concepts and propositions (doctrines and teachings being groups of propositions). Most of Van Til's statements about concepts can be translated into language about propositions and vice versa.

[29]SCE, 20.

[30]CGG, 200. Interestingly, he cites G. C. Berkouwer as one who has contributed to our understanding of Christian limiting concepts. I would also note at this point that Van Til sometimes refers to this method of returning over and over to Scripture as the "method of implication." This phrase comes from idealist philosophy, but Van Til criticizes the idealist use of it. See SCE, 6–10, 200–201; JA, 302; CTETH, 203.

[31]CGG, 11.

we do not do that, we fall into the danger of "deductivism," drawing conclusions from one doctrine that might well contradict another biblical truth.

To read each biblical doctrine in the light of the others will sometimes restrain our drawing of logical deductions. Van Til argues that if we understand divine sovereignty in the light of human responsibility and vice versa, we will not draw the inferences from these doctrines that are drawn by the hyper-Calvinists and the Arminians. For the fully biblical doctrine of divine sovereignty does not contradict the fully biblical view of human responsibility, nor the reverse.

But do these considerations rule out all use of logical deduction from biblical premises? Van Til evidently did not think so, for he engaged in quite a bit of logical deduction, as we have seen. However, to my knowledge, he never answered this question explicitly, nor did he attempt to show that his own use of logical deduction was not deductivist. I think, though, that the following explanation fits in with his overall epistemology:

Sometimes, when we interpret one doctrine in the light of the others, we are restrained from making deductions that we might be tempted to make if we were looking at each doctrine in isolation from the others. That is the case in Van Til's examples concerning divine sovereignty and human responsibility. But there are other times, when that process of comparing doctrines motivates us toward performing logical deductions. For example, when we understand the doctrine of Scripture's self-attestation in the light of God's self-contained fullness, we learn that indeed it is possible (with some additional premises) to deduce the former from the latter. In these cases, indeed, we have an obligation to perform the requisite deductions. Pieper's refusal to draw the proper deductions from divine sovereignty is, given Van Til's exegesis, properly described as "irrational." Van Til would say to Pieper that if he had a fuller biblical understanding of divine sovereignty and of the will of man, he would not hesitate to draw the same logical inferences that Calvinists do.

The analogical system, then, is not a system devoid of logical inference. It is rather a system in which logical inference is governed by careful, contextual interpretation of the Scriptures. Logicians all know that logical inferences will not work if the meanings of crucial terms vary through the argument. Sound principles of interpretation, therefore, are a necessary prerequisite for logical inference. It is easy to come up with logical arguments that look plausible, even persuasive, but which miss the nuances, or even the central points, of biblical teaching.

Apparent Contradiction Again

We must return to the questions of the previous chapter. If we are to think analogically, using Christian limiting concepts, we should not deduce from God's unity that he cannot be three, or vice versa. Nor should we reason that because God has foreordained all things, finite beings cannot bring glory to him. Insofar as these paradoxes influence everything we say about God and man, they inject "apparent contradiction" into all of our theology.

But we can make many deductions from God's unity that do not compromise his triune nature. For example, since the true God is one, and we must worship only a true God, it follows that we must not worship many gods. And to reason that since God foreordains all things, he foreordains the fluctuations of the stock market, does not compromise the full bucket paradox. Therefore, to acknowledge apparent contradictions is not to renounce all use of logic. To be sure, we must always ask ourselves whether our attempts at logical deduction run afoul of the general paradoxes pertaining to the divine nature and the Creator-creature relationship. Some such attempts do; some do not. If we have asked this question in a responsible way, then nothing prevents our free use of logical deduction.

It should surprise nobody that interpretation is in one sense prior to logical deduction.[32] Even the classical syllogism, "All men are mortal; Socrates is a man; therefore, Socrates is mortal," works only if the words of the premises are taken in certain senses. It will not work, for example, if "man" in the second sentence refers to a chess piece. In this respect, Van Til is not saying anything new or profound.

Theologically and spiritually, however, the point is important. We must, as theologians, continually go back to the Word of God, over and over again. We never reach a point where we can construct a system through our logical skills alone, without asking again and again, "What did God say in Scripture?"

---

[32]Of course, logic is also part of interpretation. The two disciplines are mutually dependent.

MULTIPERSPECTIVALISM

Another way to consider the logical structure of the analogical system is to think of it as multiperspectival. This is not Van Til's term, but I consider it a good description of Van Til's typical way of relating various aspects of his system to one another and to the whole. One element of the system is perspectivally related to another or to the whole, when, upon reflection, it is seen to include the other, or even to include the whole. Since many elements of the system have this characteristic, the whole can be seen from various perspectives.

We have already seen a number of these relationships. In chapter 9, I presented Van Til's view of the four attributes of revelation, namely, necessity, authority, clarity, and sufficiency. In Van Til's analysis, each of these implies the others. Thus, the four aspects constitute a whole which can be seen from any one of the four. In chapter 10, we saw that Van Til makes similar points about a priori and a posteriori reasoning, induction and deduction. Rather than seeing these as rigidly distinct, as philosophers sometimes have, Van Til regards them as united in a single act of interpretation. In chapter 11, we saw Van Til make a similar suggestion about the relations between intellect, emotions, and will in human psychology. He sees these as aspects of a unified human self, not as autonomous, competing "faculties." I sought, in response, to represent these even more perspectivally, as "involved in one another" and quite inseparable, thus making untenable the traditional concept of the primacy of the intellect. Later in this book, we will see that in Van Til's apologetic, the starting point, method, and conclusion are involved in one another, creating an inevitable circularity. And in chapter 16, we will see that in Van Til's doctrine of common grace, "earlier" and "later" are perspectivally related.

The root of these perspectivalisms is Van Til's doctrine of the Trinity, which we considered in chapter 5. Father, Son, and Spirit are "mutually involved," without losing their distinctness. Each embodies the complete divine essence, so each is God from a particular perspective. Lest we embrace modalism, of course, it is also important for us to say that the perspectives represent genuine eternal distinctions within the one Godhead, not just the subjective viewpoints of those who come to know God.

Since the Trinity is perspectival, the world is also. This is another way of stating Van Til's view of the relation between the eternal one-and-many and the temporal one-and-many. The world, too, has many aspects that reflect one another, connect with one another, and mirror the whole.

Negatively, perspectivalism discourages us from finding absolute priorities among the divine persons, or among the elements of creation. Of course, there is an absolute priority of God to the world, embodied in the concepts of foreordination, Creation, providence, and redemption by grace. But Scripture warns us against putting one person of the Trinity above another.

One does have to employ this principle with some care, rather than unthinkingly rejecting every sort of priority. The name Father does suggest some kind of primacy of the first person to the others, which has been expressed theologically by the concept of "eternal begetting." This idea is very difficult to define, although it is plain in Scripture that the Father is related to the Son as Father through all eternity. What is clear is that the economic subordination of the Son is not inappropriate to his ontological status. Somehow, it is eternally right that the Son "comes to do the Father's will." Nevertheless, Christian theologians have always insisted that there is no eternal, ontological subordination within the Trinity as to power or glory. All three persons are fully God and share the divine lordship. Nor, as Calvin emphasized with his doctrine of *autotheiotes,* is the deity of the Son derived from that of the Father. Each of the persons is "in" the other two.

And, in God, no attribute is prior to any other. Each belongs to all the others in the unity of the divine essence.

It is similar with creation. While Scripture does not entirely exclude priorities—hierarchical relationships within the world—the general structure of creation is not hierarchical (as in Neoplatonism and Scholasticism) but perspectival. All creatures are fundamentally equal before God. God may give them different roles and different levels of authority, but as the servants obey their masters, so the masters serve their servants. It is remarkable how the biblical doctrine of authority repeatedly emphasizes this reciprocal responsibility, while affirming genuine distinctions of role: see Matthew 20:26–28; Romans 12:3–21; 1 Corinthians 7:1–4; 11:7–12; 12:1–14:39; Ephesians 4:1–13; 5:22–6:9; Colossians 3:18–4:1; 1 Peter 2:13–3:9.

It is also similar with philosophical questions of metaphysics and epistemology. As we saw in our discussion of facts and laws, it is wrong to seek an absolute starting point for human thought within the creation, apart from God's revelation. Some have sought this starting point in abstract law, others in abstract particularity. But there is no pure law without particularity, or vice versa. Indeed, the concepts of "pure law" and "pure particularity" are unintelligible. The laws are unintelligible apart from the particulars; they are an aspect of the particulars—and vice versa. The same is true for the relationships of logic to fact, or reason to experience. In human knowledge, the subject, the object, and the norm are inseparable. Our knowledge of one affects our knowledge of the others.[33]

Thus, in Van Til's concept of a Christian analogical system, there are no absolute beginnings and endings, except for the subordination of the entire system to God's revelation. It is interesting that Van Til tends to be very casual about matters of "encyclopedia," the relationships between various intellectual disciplines. Van Til's Dutch predecessors and contemporaries, particularly Kuyper, and even more Dooyeweerd's school, were very meticulous in defining the exact boundaries of every science. Dutch Christian philosophers have seemed to believe that encyclopedia was the major philosophical problem—that once one determines the precise subject matter for every science, one will have solved most philosophical problems.

In the light of this background, Van Til's attitude toward such questions seems shockingly loose. He begins *Christian Apologetics* by defining the difference between apologetics and evidences: apologetics deals primarily with theism, and evidences with Christianity, but "the whole matter is a question of emphasis. That the whole question can be no more than one of emphasis and never one of separation is due to the fact that Christian theism is a unit. Christianity and theism are implied in one another."[34]

It is a difference in "emphasis," and only that, because the two disciplines are perspectivally related in the unity of Christian theism as a whole. Similarly, you cannot "separate the so-called religious and moral instruction of the Bible from what it says, e.g., about the physical universe."[35] And "defense and positive statement go hand in hand."[36] Apologetics and theology, too, are interrelated. Theology consists mainly of positive statements and apologetics of defense, but you really cannot do one without the other. Hence, "the place of

[33]CTETH, 131, passim; CFC, 96; CC, 3:28; DF2, 67; IW, 23, 25.
[34]CA, 1.
[35]Ibid., 2.
[36]Ibid., 3.

apologetics cannot be very closely defined."[37] The best we can do is to use figures: the apologist is a "messenger boy" who facilitates communication between different theological disciplines. Or, he is a "scout," "to detect in advance and by night the location and, if possible, some of the movements of the enemy."[38] But that is about as much as we can say. "This really completes the story of Christian encyclopedia."[39] What took Abraham Kuyper three volumes to describe, Van Til completes in three pages!

And we can, of course, forget Warfield's idea that apologetics must somehow lay the theistic foundation before the edifice of Christian theology can be built. On Van Til's view, apologetics itself must presuppose the completed edifice of theology if it is to know what it is to defend.[40] Nor can theology deal with God without simultaneously dealing with the world and with man; the traditional divisions of systematic theology are also only "differences in emphasis."[41] And Van Til informs Frederick Howe in *Jerusalem and Athens* that he does not care for Howe's sharp distinction between *kerygma* and *apologia* (preaching and defense), for the two are quite inseparable.[42]

Contra Dooyeweerd, the distinction between naive experience and theoretical thought, around which Dooyeweerd builds his entire system, should be regarded as a difference in degree.[43] The same is true for theology and philosophy.[44] It does not matter, he says, whether one begins with metaphysics or epistemology.[45]

There are, of course, various doctrines that Van Til considers central or crucial to the Christian system. However, these are indeed various; there are many "centers"! The historical Fall is crucial to a sound theology.[46] So is the temporal Creation.[47] Predestination is the

---

[37]Ibid.

[38]Ibid.

[39]Ibid.

[40]IST, 2–3.

[41]Ibid., 1–2.

[42]JA, 445–52.

[43]CC, 2:3, p. 6.

[44]SCE, 193; CTETH, 5.

[45]SCE, 29, contra Jim Halsey, who suggests in a critique of my VTT that Van Til always insisted on beginning with metaphysics rather than epistemology. See his "A Preliminary Critique of *Van Til: the Theologian*," *WTJ* 39 (1976): 120–36.

[46]IST, 29.

[47]DF1, 229.

"central doctrine of the Reformation."[48] The Trinity is the "heart of Christianity."[49] But if there are many centers, they would seem to be perspectivally related. Each major doctrine provides a perspective in terms of which the whole of Christianity can be viewed.

Thus, one doctrine frequently necessitates another, as we saw early in this chapter. In general, "a truly Protestant method of reasoning involves a stress upon the fact that the meaning of every aspect or part of Christian theism depends upon Christian theism as a unit. . . . [T]he whole claim of Christian theism is in question in any debate about any fact."[50] Again, "The starting point, the method, and the conclusion are always involved in one another."[51]

In the previous section, I emphasized that interpretation is in one sense prior to inference (and, of course, vice versa!). In this section, we are showing concretely how interpretation warrants logical inference. Perspectivalism is the logical structure of biblical doctrines, and perspectival relationships are frequently the biblical warrant for logical inferences. The "system" of Christian truth, therefore, is not a deductive system like Euclid's axioms, but a perspectival unity of various revealed truths, which on reflection can be seen to presuppose and imply one another. As we see that this is indeed the structure of God's revelation, we lose that hesitancy about using logical inference described in the previous section. Although there are apparent contradictions in revelation, there are also many cases in which Scripture legitimates logical inference, and the overall structure of biblical truth strongly encourages it.

Van Til's emphasis on the unity of the Christian-theistic system is remarkably edifying. We grow in our appreciation of God's wisdom when we see how each doctrine follows from and implies the others. Each of these interdoctrinal relationships teaches us something more about the doctrines so related. Thus, Van Til's importance as a dogmatician, even apart from his more specifically apologetic ideas, should not be underestimated. A book could be written, for example, about how the denial of Creation entails the denial of God. Van Til does not belabor the point; he simply sets it before us. But if it is true, it is enormously significant, for it would profoundly

[48]TJD, 76.
[49]DF1, 28.
[50]CA, 73.
[51]Ibid., 62.

affect the way many people today think of Creation and about God. Van Til does this sort of thing over and over again, leaving an enormous legacy of theological ideas of enormous potential value to the church.

Van Til's approach also has another interesting ramification. In the last two centuries, there has been much concern in theology over the "central focus" of the Christian revelation. I suspect that the main reason for this is that since scriptural authority in the orthodox sense has been abandoned by "mainstream" theologians, they have sought to find something authoritative *in* Scripture that they could separate from the content they deem unbelievable. They tend to call that authoritative element of scriptural teaching the "central focus" of Scripture. Of course, there has also been among orthodox thinkers a concern to identify the central emphases of the Word of God. At any rate, many theologies have arisen attempting to persuade us of the "centrality" of something or other in the Christian faith. There have been theologies of the Word, of crisis, of personal encounter, of divine acts, of history, of hope, of self-understanding, of celebration, of covenant law, of doxology, and so on.

Van Til, however, reminds us that, as we saw above, there are many "central" doctrines, perspectivally related. God does not give us a single axiom from which everything else must be deduced; rather, he gives us a complex revelation of many truths in unity. We cannot pick one doctrine out from the complex, set others aside, and expect to have sufficient conceptual resources to construct a complete Christian theology. In Christianity, the "central" doctrines do not become central by canceling out other scriptural teachings, as in the liberal theologies. Rather, they undergird, support, and necessitate these other doctrines.

We can see, now, concretely, how a genuine system of Christian truth is possible. It does not come about through autonomous reasoning, which picks and chooses among biblical doctrines and seeks some autonomous starting point outside biblical revelation altogether. Rather, it comes from immersion in the organism of revelation, an organism that presents apparent contradictions to our minds, while also overwhelming us with its own logical unity.

CHAPTER FOURTEEN

Evidence

In chapter 11, I began to analyze Van Til's view of reason by discussing his critique of Charles Hodge's three points about the function of reason in theology. So far I have discussed two of them, the primacy of the intellect (chap. 12) and logic (chap. 13). We must now move on to the third, "Reason as Judge of the Evidences of a Revelation."[1]

In chapter 5, we discussed the relationship between facts and laws. In epistemology, that relationship is reflected in the distinction between logic and evidence. Logic sets forth the laws of human thought at the most abstract level. Evidence is the data with which logic deals. Evidence supplies the premises for logical arguments, while logic supplies the rules of inference.

In Van Til's thought, logic is coordinated with law, and evidence with fact. Logic formulates the broadest laws of thought, which are also the most abstract laws of the universe, so as to direct us in the thinking process. Evidence states the facts of experience in such a way that they can serve as premises for arguments. So Van Til regularly

[1]IST, 41. I recommend Thom Notaro's *Van Til and the Use of Evidence* (Phillipsburg, N.J.: Presbyterian and Reformed, 1980) as an excellent and fuller discussion of this issue.

correlates evidence and fact, and in this chapter we will be discussing both concepts.[2]

Hodge says that it is a "legitimate use of reason" for it to "judge the evidences of any revelation that comes to it." Faith, he argues, is "an intelligent reception of the truth on adequate grounds," and Scripture never demands faith "except on grounds of adequate evidence."[3]

As I said in connection with Hodge's view of logic, one who knows a little about Van Til might expect him simply to disagree with Hodge at this point. It does not sound Van Tillian to speak of reason "judging" revelation, either by logic or by evidence. Van Til's position, however, is not so easily predicted. He does not deny Hodge's assertion. Rather, as in the case of logic, he criticizes Hodge for a sin of omission—for failing to distinguish between Christian and non-Christian uses of evidence.

In general, Van Til's attitude toward evidence, like his attitude toward logic, is quite positive. On the same page, Van Til speaks of "the truth for which Hodge is contending," suggesting that Hodge's statement (considered apart from its omissions) is in itself true. He also agrees with Hodge's successor, B. B. Warfield, that "Christian faith is not a blind faith but is faith based on evidence."[4] He is even able to say that "Christianity meets every legitimate demand of reason."[5]

Van Til believes that all people know God from the created world and from themselves as God's image (Rom. 1:18–21). With regard to the existence of God and the truth of Christian theism, there is "absolutely certain proof."[6] That proof is so clear that we can be certain of God's existence.[7] The evidence itself is certain, not merely "possible" or "probable."[8] There is a cogent "theistic proof."[9] Indeed, every fact proves God, since no fact can be understood intelligibly without presupposing God.[10]

This point must be stressed, because critics of Van Til persist in overlooking it. It is widely alleged that he simply denies the legiti-

---

[2]Compare the discussion of facts and laws in chap. 5.

[3]IST, 41, quoting Hodge, *Systematic Theology,* 1:53.

[4]CTK, 250.

[5]CGG, 184.

[6]DF2, 103; CA, 64.

[7]IST, 114–15; CA, 13; NS, 278–79.

[8]IST, 114–15; CA, 13; NS, 278–79.

[9]IST, 102–4, 196; DF1, 196; CTK, 292; CGG, 179–80, 191–95; SCE, 109–10.

[10]IST, 14, 17.

macy of proof or evidence, resorting to a pure fideism.[11] Clark Pinnock, for example, says, "Although the majority Christian view over the centuries has been that Christian theism could be securely grounded by means of rational arguments and empirical considerations, Van Til refuses to have anything to do with it."[12] According to him, Van Til "cannot escape the charge of fideism, the view that truth in religion is ultimately based on faith rather than on reasoning or evidence."[13]

In fact, Van Til has often spoken against fideism, in very strong terms. In his evangelistic pamphlet *Why I Believe in God,* he apologizes to his unbelieving friend for the fideistic approaches of some Christians:

> In our great concern to win men we have allowed that the evidence for God's existence is only *probably* compelling. And from that fatal confession we have gone one step further down to the point where we have admitted or virtually admitted that it is not really compelling at all. And so we fall back on testimony instead of argument. After all, we say, God is not found at the end of an argument; He is found in our hearts. So we simply testify to men that once we were dead, and now we are alive, and that once we were blind and that now we see, and give up all intellectual argument.
>
> Do you suppose that our God approves of this attitude of His followers? I do not think so. . . . A testimony that is not an argument is not a testimony either, just as an argument that is not a testimony is not even an argument.[14]

It is not Christian faith, but non-Christian "faith" that is blind.[15] Christian faith claims to be both rational and in accord with the facts.[16]

---

[11]Fideism is the view that our knowledge of God is based on faith apart from any evidence or rational considerations. Van Til, on the contrary, agrees with Hodge and Warfield that Christian faith is based on evidence, ultimately the evidence of divine revelation.

[12]JA, 421.

[13]Ibid., 423; cf. p. 425.

[14]P. 16; cf. RP, 65–66; CTEV, 34–35. Notice the perspectival relationship between argument and testimony.

[15]PDS, 52; cf. CGG, 184.

[16]JA, 20.

Van Til often endorses detailed study of scientific and historical evidences for Christianity.[17]

People accuse Van Til of fideism because he criticizes certain traditional concepts of evidence. As with logic, Van Til's concerns pertain to both the "philosophy" and the "use" of evidences. In his discussion of Hodge, he says: "On the surface at least [Hodge's] manner of statement again seems to assume that all men, regenerate and non-regenerate, agree on the nature of reason and evidence. But this is contrary to fact."[18] In passing, let me note the qualifications "on the surface" and "seems." It appears that Van Til here is somewhat unsure that Hodge is actually subject to his criticism, but that he chooses to discuss it anyway because of its importance. However, as we have seen before, Van Til evidently does not want to take issue with Hodge's major and explicit point, that reason has the right to judge the evidences of revelation. He is rather concerned with the omissions in Hodge's discussion.

The first omission is in the area of the philosophy of evidence. Like logic, evidence is grounded in God's nature, his eternal plan, and his creative and providential activity. As we have seen, Van Til holds that because God is sovereign, he is clearly revealed in all his works—in all of creation, including ourselves.

We have also seen that since the creation reflects the Trinity, facts and laws are correlative. There are no "brute" facts. In Van Til's vocabulary, "brute" facts are facts uninterpreted by God and therefore meaningless, the constituents of a universe of pure chance.[19] Philosophers and scientists have sometimes sought to base their thinking on "brute fact," because they have wanted to find a starting point for human thought outside of God's revelation. Since, on their view, human thought is ultimate, it must be based, not on God's prior thought, but on something prior to all thought, namely fact. These brute facts must be utterly independent of the laws imputed to reality by human thought, if they are to be the justification for human thought.

---

[17]DF1, 258; CTK, 293; CTEV, 64–65; IST, 146.

[18]IST, 41.

[19]CTEV, 51. It is important that we keep Van Til's definition in mind. The phrase "brute fact" is sometimes used merely to mean "objective fact." If we confuse the two definitions we will misunderstand Van Til, taking him in a subjectivist sense. We may also be tempted to use his critique against those who are merely using the phrase to assert objectivity, which, of course, Van Til also wants to assert.

But such a fact is a meaningless fact, as we saw in our discussion of facts and laws in chapter 5.[20]

On the contrary, Christians *"appeal to facts, but never to brute facts.* We appeal to *God-interpreted* facts."[21]

It is thus that Van Til raises the question of the "philosophy" of fact and evidence. We must, he says, not only claim that Christianity is factual, but also clarify what we mean by fact. We must address the philosophical question.[22]

The philosophical issue has implications for our use of evidences. Van Til says:

> I see induction and analytical reasoning as part of one process of interpretation. I would therefore engage in historical apologetics. (I do not personally do a great deal of this because my colleagues in the other departments of the Seminary in which I teach are doing it better than I could do it.) Every bit of historical investigation, whether it be in the directly biblical field, archaeology, or in general history, is bound to confirm the truth of the claims of the Christian position. But I would not talk endlessly about facts and more facts without ever challenging the unbeliever's philosophy of fact. A really fruitful historical apologetic argues that every fact *is* and *must be* such as proves the truth of the Christian position.[23]

It is important that we distinguish here between Van Til's philosophical and his strategic recommendations. His philosophy of evidence, I believe, is entirely biblical and therefore normative for Christians. To call it "fideistic" is either to misunderstand it or to accept the unbelieving ("brute fact") alternative. There is, of course, more to be said about this issue. I shall discuss in a later chapter the charge that this view of fact leads to circular argument. But no Christian, certainly, can deny that the facts are what God says they are. No Christian can properly think of facts as some sort of ultimate foundation for would-be autonomous human knowledge.

---

[20]Cf. Van Til's discussion in CTEV, 50–65; CGG, 1–9.

[21]CTEV, 57 (emphasis his). On the same page, Van Til identifies this procedure with his method of "implication into God's interpretation."

[22]Cf. DF2, 7–8; CTEV, vii–ix.

[23]CTK, 293.

Van Til's strategic recommendation is that we should not talk "endlessly" about facts "without ever challenging the unbeliever's philosophy." Well, nobody wants to talk endlessly about anything! And it is certainly true that the crying need today (as in Van Til's time), in intellectual discussions, is for a serious challenge to the basic methodology of unbelieving thought.

However, not all Christian witnessing is on such an exalted intellectual level. Many people with whom we share Christ are not capable of understanding philosophical issues. Must we give philosophical instruction to every unsophisticated inquirer? Perhaps to some, but I do not think that is always necessary. Some people, after all, are converted through relatively simple presentations of, say, the evidences of Jesus' resurrection, or even through a simple "testimony."

If someone asks me what evidences there are for the Resurrection, I will simply tell him. If, then, he raises epistemological objections (such as Hume's objection that there can never be sufficient testimony to establish a supernatural event), then I will try, either in technical language or by simple illustration, to deal with the philosophy of fact. But that is surely not necessary for every presentation of the gospel. Scripture itself does not do it in any explicit way.

Nor did Van Til's colleagues, whom he commends in the above-quoted passage for their work in historical apologetics. Members of Westminster's biblical departments, such as Robert Dick Wilson, Oswald Allis, Edward J. Young, Meredith Kline, Ned Stonehouse, John Skilton—and, indeed, J. Gresham Machen—did considerable work in historical apologetics, but rarely spoke about the philosophy of fact.

I am not sure what Van Til would have thought about the previous three paragraphs. Typically, he did not think in such "practical" terms. He was interested in the large-scale intellectual conflicts of his age, not in witnessing strategies for one-to-one encounters,[24] nor even in the detailed defense of the Bible. From his macrocosmic viewpoint, he saw that both Christians and non-Christians needed to become aware of the great philosophical differences over the use of evidences.

We should not assume in Van Til's thought a direct correlation between macrocosmic and microcosmic, general and particular, broad strategy and argumentative detail. Van Til is quite right, at least, about

[24]He did quite a bit of one-to-one witnessing, however.

the big picture. It is still vitally important for us to communicate, to believer and unbeliever alike, that there are two philosophies of fact, and that the unbelieving philosophy must not be taken for granted.

Another of Van Til's recommendations for the proper use of evidences is negative: do not separate fact from meaning. Some have argued that we can prove that God exists without first establishing what kind of God exists.[25] Others have tried to prove the fact of Christ's resurrection without discussing its meaning.[26] Van Til evidently believed this rule followed from his correlation of fact and meaning, fact and interpretation.

But if all facts are laden with meaning, then it is simply impossible to separate fact from meaning, no matter how much we may try. We cannot even talk about the "fact of the Resurrection" without having some meaning in mind. A resurrection, after all, is a resurrection, not a storm at sea. And nobody tries to prove the existence of God, even the existence of "a god," without having in mind something of what he is seeking to prove. When somebody says he is proving that God exists without defining what kind of God he is talking about, he is nonetheless trying to prove the existence of a god, not the existence of unicorns; so the concept will always have some defining content.

On the other hand, it is also plain that no argument for God's existence, or for Jesus' resurrection, will exhaustively define what is meant in the proof by "God" or "resurrection." To say that we cannot know God without knowing everything about him is an idealist notion which Van Til rejects. He insists that our knowledge, both of God and the world, can be true, although it can never be exhaustive.[27]

So it seems that the emphasis on "that" and "what" is a matter of degree. The argument seems to be about *how much* theological definition of *x* needs to be included in a proof of *x*. In my opinion, Van Til does not present enough argument to require a particular degree of definition in an apologetic proof.

Nevertheless, there is certainly some point in Van Til's concern here. Historically, it has been difficult for apologists to reason from the general conclusions of the theistic proofs to the specific, distinctive character of the Christian God. That difficulty may not be evaded

---

[25]SCE, 116–31; RP, 94–98.

[26]RP, 48.

[27]DF2, 43–44.

in a system of apologetics. It is unnecessary, I think, for a theistic proof to establish the whole of the biblical doctrine of God, but among all the proofs and arguments of an apologetic there must be sufficient basis to establish the distinctives of the Christian position. Otherwise, the apologetic is not worth its salt. Of course, that "sufficient basis" might be an appeal to Scripture.

And the apologist must also take account of the fact that the resurrection of Jesus is more than a mere "strange event." Its theological interpretation is crucial. The whole biblical interpretation of the Resurrection is unlikely to be established by a single argument. But the apologist must understand in his own mind at least how the inquirer is to ascertain the full content of theological interpretation.

I would conclude this chapter by urging my fellow Van Tillian apologists, including myself, to give students better training in Christian evidences than has usually been the case in our circles. We have seen that Van Til's method encourages, rather than discourages, the use of evidence, although some of his language may suggest otherwise. Typically, however, he did not give his students much instruction in the actual, detailed evidences for Christianity. That, I am convinced, was a mistake, even though that omission was partly remedied by the work of Van Til's colleagues. Pastors frequently get opportunities, in the form of direct questions, to present evidences for the historical truth of Scripture. We should not miss such opportunities for witness.

PART THREE

The Ethics of Knowledge

CHAPTER FIFTEEN

Antithesis

In the preceding chapters, we considered Van Til's concept of the metaphysics of knowledge. That is, we asked how the fundamental Christian worldview, the Creator-creature distinction, affects human knowledge. Since this fundamental metaphysical relationship was not changed by the Fall, I did not have to say much about sin, except occasionally to contrast believing and unbelieving worldviews.

On this basis one can maintain a distinctively Van Tillian view of knowledge while disagreeing substantially with his view of the noetic effects of sin. Chapters 4 to 14 include quite a lot of content: the doctrine of God, the Trinity, divine sovereignty, human responsibility, analogical reasoning, revelation, presuppositions, intellect, logic, evidence. Certainly anyone who largely accepts Van Tillian views in these areas must be considered a Van Tillian, even if he differs from Van Til in other areas.

That is somewhat my own situation. I do find excellent insights in Van Til's ethics of knowledge, his view of the effects of sin and regeneration on human knowledge. But I confess that I am rather more critical of him in this area than I was in the area of the metaphysics of knowledge.

At any rate, we should now proceed to analyze his views regarding the relation of sin and regeneration to human knowledge. The most conspicuous feature of Van Til's position is the "antithesis" between believing and unbelieving thought. We saw in chapter 3 that Van Til is, following Kuyper and Machen, a kind of apostle of antithesis. This antithesis is the diametrical opposition between belief and unbelief and therefore between belief and any compromise of revealed truth.

The concept of antithesis is one of Van Til's major concerns, and it is the element in his thought that has brought him the most severe criticism. In the present pluralistic theological climate, it seems particularly difficult to draw lines sharply enough to support Van Tillian talk of antithesis: lines between denominational traditions, between liberal and conservative, between Christianity and other religions, between belief and unbelief. Universalism is taken for granted in contemporary liberal theology, and conservative Christian thinkers, if not going that far, often tend nevertheless to play down the differences between themselves and others. Is it necessary, or even possible, to maintain Van Til's emphasis in our time and to repudiate all these tendencies toward accommodation? Or did Van Til overstate his case, unnecessarily inhibiting biblical ecumenism? Or is the truth to be found somewhere between these two evaluations?

As we consider the matter of antithesis, we must simultaneously consider the doctrine of common grace, which teaches that God restrains sin in the unregenerate. On the basis of common grace, Van Til maintains that unbelievers know some truth despite their sin and its effects. It might seem at first glance that antithesis and common grace are opposed to one another, at least in the sense that one limits the other. Whether or not that is the best way to look at it, it is certainly true that there are temptations to imbalance on either side. In this chapter, I shall discuss common grace as a limit on antithesis, or (perhaps better) as a factor that helps us to define antithesis better. In the following chapter, I shall discuss other aspects of common grace.

In his ethics of knowledge, Van Til seeks to describe concretely how the Fall affects human thought. Sinful man, according to Van Til, "sought his ideals of truth, goodness and beauty somewhere beyond God, either directly within himself or in the universe about him."[1] He "tried to interpret everything with which he came into contact without reference to God."[2] In this connection, Van Til often refers

[1]DF2, 15.
[2]Ibid., 47.

to the process described in Romans 1: fallen man suppresses what he knows to be true about God, exchanging it for a lie.

Instead of presupposing God's revelation as the ultimate criterion of truth, the sinner presupposes (as Kant advocated so clearly and explicitly) that his own autonomy is the ultimate principle of being and knowledge. Thus, fallen man stands in antithesis to God and to God's people as well.

In regeneration, the human consciousness "has *in principle* been restored to the position of the Adamic consciousness."[3] The qualification "in principle" implies that "the relatively evil" remains "in those who are absolutely good in principle."[4]

Van Til also asserts that there is "relative good in those who are evil in principle."[5] Thus, he defends the doctrine of common grace. The noetic implications of common grace are as follows:

> But in the course of history the natural man is not fully self-conscious of his own position. The prodigal cannot altogether stifle his father's voice. There is a conflict of notions within him. But he himself is not fully and self-consciously aware of this conflict within him. He has within him the knowledge of God by virtue of his creation in the image of God. But this idea of God is suppressed by his false principle, the principle of autonomy. This principle of autonomy is, in turn, suppressed by the restraining power of God's common grace. Thus the ideas with which he daily works do not proceed consistently either from the one principle or from the other.[6]

An important problem, however, emerges at this point. Although Van Til affirms the ambiguity of the unbeliever's position under common grace, he nevertheless often writes as though the unbeliever knows and affirms no truth at all and thus is not at all affected by common grace. Note these statements:

> The natural man cannot will to do God's will. He cannot even know what the good is.[7]

---

[3]Ibid., 49.
[4]Ibid.
[5]Ibid., 50.
[6]Ibid., 170.
[7]Ibid., 54.

> It will be quite impossible then to find a common area of knowledge between believers and unbelievers unless there is agreement between them as to the nature of man himself. But there is no such agreement.[8]
>
> But without the light of Christianity it is as little possible for man to have the correct view about himself and the world as it is to have the true view about God. On account of the fact of sin man is blind with respect to the truth wherever the truth appears. And truth is one. Man cannot truly know himself unless he truly knows God.[9]
>
> [The unbeliever] interprets all the facts and all the laws that are presented to him in terms of [his unbelieving] assumptions.[10]

The unbeliever does not even find Christian truth to be meaningful: "It is precisely Christianity as a whole, and therefore each of these doctrines as part of Christianity, that are meaningless to him as long as he is not willing to drop his own assumptions of autonomy and chance."[11]

And since the unbeliever's depravity excludes all common notions, we can be sure, and can safely predict, what the unbeliever will do with an apologetic argument. When a Christian presents the historical argument for the Resurrection, a pragmatist philosopher, says Van Til, "will refuse to follow this line of reasoning. Granted he allows that Christ actually arose from the grave, he will say that this proves nothing more than that something very unusual took place in the case of that man Jesus."[12] Contrary to Hodge, who speaks of "reason" as "something that seems to operate rightly wherever it is found," Van Til insists that "the 'reason' of sinful men will invariably act wrongly. . . . The natural man will invariably employ the tool of his reason to reduce these contents to a naturalistic level."[13] Note here the twofold "invariably."[14]

---

[8]Ibid., 67.

[9]Ibid., 73.

[10]Ibid., 201.

[11]Ibid., 150.

[12]Ibid., 8.

[13]Ibid., 83.

[14]Cf. CTK, 297–98. For similarly extreme statements of the antithesis, see DF1, 203, 228; IST, 14, 22, 56, 75, 146, 189; CTK, 262, 293.

On this extreme antithetical view, it would almost seem as if no unbeliever can utter a true sentence. It would also seem as if no communication is possible between believer and unbeliever. Unregenerate man cannot know what the good is, so how can he understand sin and the need for redemption in Christ? Since he cannot know his own nature, and cannot know God, and since truth is one, he literally cannot know anything. But how does a Christian present a witness to somebody who literally knows nothing? And why should we witness? For we can be safely assured that the unbeliever will be quite indifferent to any facts we set before him. Is there any role at all here for common grace to play?

I believe that Van Til was at least sometimes sensitive to the difficulty of the problem, though at many points in his writings he seems quite unaware of it. The peak of his awareness of this issue can be found in *An Introduction to Systematic Theology,* pages 26–27, where he uncharacteristically admits to having some difficulty in formulation. Here he concedes that the fact that unbelievers have knowledge that is "true as far as it goes" "has always been a difficult point," and he even adds: "We cannot give any wholly satisfactory account of the situation as it actually obtains. . . . All that we can do with this question as with many other questions in theology, is to hem it in in order to keep out errors, and to say that truth lies within a certain territory."[15] His conclusion:

> The actual situation is therefore always a mixture of truth with error. Being "without God in the world" the natural man yet knows God, and, in spite of himself, to some extent recognizes God. By virtue of their creation in God's image, by virtue of the ineradicable sense of deity within them and by virtue of God's restraining general grace, those who hate God, yet in a restricted sense know God, and do good.[16]

A "mixture"! But that view of the unbeliever's mentality provides a rather weak basis for all the strong antithetical language. If there is such a mixture, how can we be so sure that the unbeliever

[15]IST, 26. Compare his statement on p. 25 that this is a matter of "great complexity."

[16]IST, 27. The last sentence of this quotation would be clearer if it read: ". . . those who hate God nevertheless know him, in a restricted sense, and do good." On the

might not agree with us, at times, about flowers and trees, or even about the good, or the nature of man, or the existence of God, or that the Resurrection was more than a "strange event?" How can we declare in advance what the unbeliever will or will not agree with?

As we have seen, Van Til is aware of this problem. His statements in *An Introduction to Systematic Theology*, page 26, and *The Defense of the Faith* (rev. ed.), page 170, indicate a certain agnosticism as to its precise solution. Yet he does not leave this matter as a paradox, as he urges us to do in connection with other matters. Rather, he tries to alleviate it by describing the situation more concretely, using various concepts, illustrations, and images.[17] One problem, however, is that there are quite a number of these explanations, and they are rather different from one another. Van Til's intent is that they should be taken as supplementary, perhaps as perspectivally related to one another, though he does not use that language. My evaluation is that, nevertheless, these formulations are not altogether consistent with one another, and some of them can be rejected on other grounds. Thus, if we are to build upon Van Til's work, we will have to adopt or modify some of these formulations and reject others.

These formulations are strategies for reconciling antithesis with common grace. I classify them in five categories: (1) extreme antithetical formulations, (2) normative formulations, (3) situational formulations, (4) existential formulations, and (5) practical formulations.

EXTREME ANTITHETICAL FORMULATIONS

We have already seen that Van Til often speaks in ways that suggest that the unbeliever knows no truth at all and therefore has literally no area of agreement with the believer. This extreme position is reflected in some of his strategies for reconciling antithesis and common grace.

a. Obligation Versus Actual Knowledge. Sometimes Van Til suggests that the unbeliever has an obligation to know the truth, but in fact

"mixture" idea, cf. DF2, 170: "Thus the ideas with which [the unbeliever] daily works do not proceed consistently either from the one principle or from the other."

[17]I suspect that his inner perception of the issue varied considerably from time to time during his career. The apparent agnosticism of IST, 26, and DF2, 170, is hard to reconcile with the sense of assurance that permeates many of his discussions of this issue.

refuses to fulfill that obligation. The situation is "that *all* men *ought* to see God in nature since he is clearly revealed there, but that only he who is given the regenerated heart actually does see this to be the case."[18] This distinction should perhaps be taken to refer to saving knowledge rather than to the knowledge referred to in Romans 1:21, which the unbeliever suppresses. In any case, it is rather unclear. If it refers to common-grace knowledge, then it is inconsistent with Van Til's insistence that this knowledge is actual and not merely potential. If the unbeliever is obligated to know, but does not actually know, then he has no knowledge.

b. Revelation Versus Interpretation. Van Til sometimes asserts that divine revelation is given to all, but that the unbeliever always interprets it wrongly. We have already seen this in earlier quotations. Note also:

> By using the term "general revelation" we emphasize the fact that this revelation is accessible to all men and valid for all men even though only believers interpret it truly.[19]

> When the unbeliever *interprets* the world, he interprets it in terms of his assumption of human autonomy. . . .
> The unbeliever is the man with yellow glasses on his face. He sees himself and his world through these glasses. He cannot remove them. His *interpretation* of himself and of every fact in the universe relating to himself is, unavoidably, a *false* interpretation.[20]

On this account, common grace, if there is any role for it at all, would be seen only in God's gracious provision of revelation. There is, evidently, no divine restraint of sin in the unbeliever's process of interpretation.

To my knowledge, Van Til never defines "interpretation," but I gather he uses the term fairly broadly to describe all of a person's activity in his attempts to understand the world. The contrast, then, is between the revelation inherent in the creation and the distortion

[18]PDS, 72 (emphasis his).
[19]IST, 75.
[20]CTK, 258–59 (emphasis his); cf. pp. 265, 301–2.

that enters whenever the unbeliever tries to understand that creation. Van Til's assertion that all the unbeliever's efforts to know (as all his efforts generally) are tainted by sin is simply an application of his Reformed view of total depravity and thus may be accepted as cogent in the present context. But does that depravity entail, as Van Til suggests, that all the unbeliever's interpretive activity results in false conclusions? To say that it does is not part of the historic doctrine of total depravity, nor is it consistent with Van Til's own view of common grace. On this strategy, there is no "mixture," only unmitigated falsehood.

Of course, one can try to patch up this strategy by employing some of the others listed below. One can say that the unbeliever's interpretation is incorrect on an ultimate level, or insofar as he is self-conscious, etc. My present point, however, is that the distinction between revelation and interpretation is not in itself sufficient to describe the relation of antithesis to common grace. Common grace is not merely an objective revelation of God. Rather, it is, if anything, a divine restraint upon the sinful activity of the unbeliever. In this context, it must be a divine restraint upon the unbeliever's sinful distortion of revelation. To deny that restraint, as Van Til appears to do in the present context, is to deny common grace itself.

c. Metaphysical Versus Epistemological. In *The Defense of the Faith,* Van Til asks how unbelievers can agree with believers as to weights and measures. He answers:

> If sin is seen to be ethical alienation only, and salvation as ethical restoration only, then the question of weighing and measuring or that of logical reasoning is, of course, equal on both sides. All men, whatever their ethical relation to God, can equally use the natural gifts of God. . . . As far as natural ability is concerned the lost can and do know the truth and could contribute to the structure of science except for the fact that for them it is too late.[21]

Here he argues that weighing and measuring are created human capacities and that, as such, they are not affected by the Fall. This is similar to his illustration of the buzz saw,[22] which he uses to

[21]DF2, 171.
[22]Ibid., 74.

indicate that the unbeliever's created faculties (such as the logical faculty) may work very efficiently while working in the wrong direction. On this analysis, common grace would be seen in God's preservation of the metaphysical situation, the unbeliever's epistemic faculties, and antithesis would be seen in that the unbeliever always makes a faulty use of his created equipment.[23]

However, this view contradicts Van Til's emphasis elsewhere that common grace is not needed to preserve the metaphysical situation, and is not the source of the unbeliever's natural knowledge of God.[24] And Van Til also takes issue with Abraham Kuyper's view of weighing and measuring by saying, "Weighing and measuring are but aspects of one unified act of interpretation."[25] Therefore, weighing and measuring cannot be taken as natural, metaphysical abilities that are somehow prior to and independent of that interpretive activity which is affected by sin. To the extent that all epistemic or interpretive activity is affected by the Fall, weighing and measuring must also be affected.

d. Form Versus Content. Often, Van Til describes the unbeliever's knowledge as "formal." In criticism of C. S. Lewis's concept of "the *Tao,*" an objective knowledge common to all men, Van Til replies, "But surely this general objectivity is common to Christians and non-Christians in a formal sense only."[26] The non-Christian can "formally understand" the truth,[27] and even give "formal assent" to the "intellectual argument for the existence of God."[28] But it is wrong to say that the unbeliever has, concerning God, "correct notions as to content, not merely as to form."[29]

Van Til uses the word *formal* to describe cases in which two people use the same words, but with different meanings, and thus tend to misunderstand one another. He points out that "there can be no intelligible reasoning unless those who reason together understand what

---

[23]I take the term "epistemological" here to be roughly synonymous with the term "interpretive" discussed in the preceding section. I believe also that the "psychological-epistemological" contrast found in CGG, 52–53, is more or less synonymous with the distinction under consideration.

[24]CGG, 159.

[25]Ibid., 44.

[26]DF2, 59.

[27]Ibid., 74.

[28]IST, 198.

[29]CTK, 296; cf. IST, 194.

they mean by their words."[30] He adds that although the unbeliever may actually construct theistic proofs, the god whose existence he proves will always be something different from the God of Scripture. Indeed, the unbeliever differs with the believer over the meaning of *soul,*[31] the meanings of *is* and *is not,*[32] and the meaning of *supreme* in the phrase "supreme being."[33] As for *miracle,* there is "nothing but formal agreement between the scientist and the Christian."[34] Traditional apologists err because "they attribute to the natural man not only the ability to make formally correct statements about 'nature' or themselves, but also to mean by these statements what the Christian means by them."[35]

Put all of these statements together, and the conclusion seems to be that Christians and non-Christians speak entirely different languages. Although both groups use words like *God, soul, nature, miracle, self,* and even *is,* the meanings of these words differ radically between them. But how, then, is communication possible between believers and unbelievers? If I say "Good morning" to you and mean by that "Hooray for the San Diego Padres," what have I communicated?

Indeed, Van Til himself insists that the unbeliever's knowledge is *not* merely formal. In a context which, oddly enough, directly adjoins one of the above passages, he says this against Lockean empiricism:

> Accordingly we cannot say that the innate knowledge of God in man is the merely formal ability, the capacity or potentiality, in view of man's creation as an intellectual being, to recognize revelation if and when it comes. There can be no finite human consciousness that is not stirred to its depths by the revelational content within itself as well as about itself. Thus the innate knowledge deals with a thought content, and not with a mere formality. The finite human consciousness is itself revelational of God.[36]

---

[30]DF2, 77. He does not actually use the word *formal* in this context.

[31]CTK, 265–72.

[32]IST, 37.

[33]Ibid., 194.

[34]Ibid., 114.

[35]Ibid., 113.

[36]Ibid., 195; cf. p. 196, where he makes some fairly tortuous distinctions in this regard.

One might defend Van Til's consistency at this point by saying that for him the unbeliever has a true, revealed thought content in his *knowledge,* but never expresses it in words except "formally." However, that would be a highly artificial distinction, one that Van Til, to his credit, never makes explicitly.[37] It would certainly be hard to justify from Scripture. Jesus, for example, commends the words of the Pharisees in Matthew 23:2–3, not just their inner knowledge, and Paul speaks similarly about pagans in Acts 17:28 and Titus 1:12–13.

It is this insistence of Van Til that the unbeliever is in "actual possession" of revealed knowledge[38] that leads me to reject all of these "extreme antithetical formulations," at least in their obvious senses. For if any of these formulations is true, then it cannot be maintained that the unbeliever has an actual knowledge of God. To have knowledge, it is not enough to be exposed to revelation, to have efficient epistemic capacities, or to be able to speak with formal correctness. Subhuman creatures are exposed to revelation, animals and computers have efficient epistemic capacities, and parrots can speak with formal correctness. But none of these has a knowledge of God in the sense of Romans 1. We must say something more about the unbeliever if we are to credit him with a genuine knowledge of God (even a knowledge suppressed by sin).

I shall try later to indicate why I think Van Til was so fond of these extreme formulations. I shall also indicate a certain sense in which these formulations can be judged true, though nevertheless misleading. All in all, however, I believe that apologists should avoid this sort of formulation.

Normative Formulations

Van Til often expresses the antithesis as an opposition between "two principles" at war with one another.[39] The unbeliever is in principle sold out to Satan; the believer belongs to God. But neither is perfect in his allegiance: "As the Christian has the incubus of his 'old man' weighing him down and therefore keeping him from realizing the

---

[37]However, see later discussion of Van Til's half suggestions that the unbeliever's knowledge is somehow subconscious.

[38]CGG, 173; cf. DF2, 91–92.

[39]DF2, 209.

'life of Christ' within him, so the natural man has the incubus of the sense of deity weighing him down and keeping him from realizing the life of Satan within him."[40] Therefore, "insofar as men are aware of their basic alliances, they are wholly for or wholly against God at every point of interest to man."[41]

That "insofar" is crucial to what I am calling Van Til's "normative" formulations. In these formulations, the antithesis is essentially between two "principles," "systems," "allegiances," or "norms." Individual unbelievers are opposed to Christianity only "insofar as" they are true to their "principle." Note: "But *to the extent that* [the unbeliever] interprets nature according to his adopted principles, he does not speak the truth on any subject."[42] Van Til criticizes S. J. Ridderbos because he fails to distinguish

> clearly between the knowledge of the natural man that comes from his creation and his knowledge as it is implied in the idea of autonomy. He thinks it is a mistake to distinguish between common notions derived from the image of God in man and common notions that proceed from the idea of autonomy. Thus he cannot take the principle of autonomy in its full seriousness of opposition to the truth.[43]

Autonomy is the unbeliever's "principle." Insofar as he is true to that principle, says Van Til, he knows nothing truly.

This kind of formulation is very important in Van Til's thought. When I was his student, I wrote a paper quoting and criticizing what seemed to me to be rather extreme expressions of antithesis in his writings. Alongside my quotations, Van Til wrote several times in the margin "according to their principle," "in their systems," etc. Note: "And it is of these systems of their own interpretation that we speak when we say that men are as wrong in their interpretation of trees as in their interpretation of God."[44]

---

[40]IST, 27. In response to John Murray's criticism, Van Til came to abandon this idea as a theological formulation, but it still serves as a good illustration of how Van Til understood the nature of the unbeliever's knowledge of God. It is, to the unbeliever, as sin is to the believer, a distraction from the main direction of his life.

[41]Ibid., 29.

[42]Ibid., 113 (emphasis mine).

[43]DF2, 170.

[44]IST, 84.

It should be noted, however, that this strategy for reconciling antithesis and common grace is very different from those extreme antithetical approaches noted in the previous section. Under the normative approach, there is no suggestion that believer and unbeliever are speaking different languages, or that all the unbeliever's interpretive activity will lead to false conclusions, or that the unbeliever will never utter a true sentence except "formally." Rather, Van Til recognizes quite explicitly here that the unbeliever may well grant many truths of Christianity. All that antithesis requires in this strategy is that when the unbeliever speaks such truth, we should regard him as inconsistent with his own principle.

And the unbeliever is indeed inconsistent. To the objection that Van Til is denying that the unbeliever can discover truth, he replies, "We mean nothing so absurd as that. The implication of the method here advocated is simply that non-Christians are never able and therefore never do employ their own methods consistently."[45]

This formulation does not make the antithesis a dead letter. Certainly the concept of antithesis has the very practical function of warning apologists not to assume too much about the unbeliever. He is operating on a basic assumption or presupposition opposite to that of the Christian. And the unbeliever has a strong motivation to interpret all of reality according to his own presupposition. Thus, when the unbeliever finds in his own thinking some uncomfortable bit of Christian truth, his inclination will be somehow to twist it, suppress it, deny it, domesticate it, or simply change the subject.

I believe that this formulation is much more scriptural than those listed in the first section, although we shall see in subsequent sections that it needs to be supplemented. As Van Til establishes in his metaphysics of knowledge, God expects us to honor him as the ultimate source and standard of knowledge. The nature of sin is to deny such honor to God. The unbeliever seeks, through his words and thoughts, to deny God's rightful honor. Thus there is antithesis. But there is no need to assume that either believer or unbeliever is fully consistent with his principle. Rather, the opposite is the case.

This formulation has some significant consequences. On this formulation, as opposed to the extreme antithetical formulations, we cannot predict the response of the unbeliever to an apologetic, whether

---

[45]Ibid., 103; cf. pp. 173–75; IST, 27, 60.

that apologetic be traditional or Van Tillian. As we have seen, Van Til always thought that the unbeliever's response was in general predictable. He insisted, for example, that the unbeliever will necessarily reject the evidences for the Resurrection. But that may not be so on a normative interpretation of the antithesis. For one thing, the unbeliever may simply be inconsistent in such a situation, and because of that inconsistency he may grant the evidential arguments.[46] For another thing, of course, special grace may intervene: the Holy Spirit may choose to regenerate a person on the occasion of such an apologetic presentation.

A somewhat parenthetical observation: Van Til often uses the noetic effects of sin to show that the Christian apologist should always go beyond the presentation of evidence and present a transcendental, presuppositional argument. His contention is that the unbeliever will always repress the evidence, and so something other than evidence must also be presented. Although I do believe in the use of transcendental argumentation,[47] and I accept some of Van Til's other justifications for it, I do not defend it on this particular ground. We do not know for sure that the unbeliever will reject the evidence. And sin may lead the unbeliever to repress the force of a transcendental argument just as much as it leads him to repress evidence.

Situational Formulations

Another type of Van Tillian strategy for reconciling antithesis with common grace is represented by the following:

> It should be remembered that the universe has actually been created by God and is actually sustained by his providence. This precludes the possibility of any non-Christian philosopher, however profound, offering a system of interpretation of the universe that would seem satisfactory even to himself.[48]

---

[46]We shall see, and Van Til recognized this, that unregeneracy is compatible with a certain amount of doctrinal orthodoxy, the Pharisees and Satan being cases in point.

[47]See chap. 23.

[48]IST, 75. In this connection, he refers to Job 28:12–14, 20–22.

Here, the unbeliever's suppression of the truth is limited in the very nature of the case. Since this is God's world, no unbelieving system can adequately account for it; such a system, therefore, will of its own nature generate problems. The main problem, of course, is that it will miss what is obvious, since God is clearly revealed in creation.

Together with this, we should note Van Til's statement that "even in [the non-Christian's] virtual negation of God, he is still really presupposing God. . . . [H]e cannot deny God unless he first affirm him, and . . . his own approach throughout its history has been shown to be destructive of human experience itself."[49] Here the word "presupposing" is used with a meaning different from Van Til's usual concept of presupposition. Usually, Van Til uses *presupposition* to indicate the fundamental religious direction of a person's thought. Here it cannot mean that. However, it does mean at least that the unbeliever's natural knowledge of God cannot be entirely suppressed. Nor does it fail to influence the unbeliever's explicit thoughts and words. One cannot deny God without affirming him, because apart from God denials are meaningless. So, to use Van Til's frequent illustration, the unbeliever is like a child slapping her father while being supported by his lap.[50]

Although Van Til does not enumerate here the specific types of problems that inevitably arise from an attempt to construe the world nontheistically, we may assume that they include inconsistencies (as we saw earlier), factual inaccuracies, existential dissatisfactions, etc. Where the unbeliever's antitheism is inconsistent, there is by logical necessity some affirmation of the truth, for the contradiction of antitheism is theism. Whatever may be the type of inadequacy, Van Til tells us here that the unbeliever himself is capable of recognizing that inadequacy to some extent, for his system will not "seem satisfactory even to himself."

When Van Til recognizes such insight in the unbeliever, he is, as in the normative formulations, contradicting his own more extreme antithetical formulations. The situational formulations are, however, compatible with the normative ones. In both of them we have a picture of the unbeliever attempting to understand reality apart from God, and yet failing to do so. The situational formulations add to the normative, first, that the unbeliever's thought is deficient

[49]CTK, 13.

[50]JA, 98, and elsewhere.

in more than logical consistency. Second, they add that these deficiencies are not merely accidental or simply the result of the unbeliever's intellectual failures. Rather, they are necessitated by the very nature of the situation. An unbelieving system cannot adequately describe God and his world. Third, they add that just as the unbeliever's depravity affects everything that he thinks and says, so does common grace.

Because of the third point, the relationship between truth and falsehood in the unbeliever's consciousness is somewhat paradoxical. It is not simply the case that the false assertions of unbelievers manifest the noetic effects of sin, and that their true assertions manifest common grace. Depravity attaches to everything the unbeliever says and does, for depravity is total in its extent. And common grace also attaches to everything, for everything the unbeliever thinks and says "presupposes" truth in the atypical sense noted above.

The normative formulation alone might encourage us to distinguish sharply between the unbeliever's denials of revelation, which reflect depravity, and his inconsistent affirmations of it, which reflect common grace. On the situational formulation, however, the unbeliever is not only inconsistent in certain assertions he makes, but in his thought as a whole. For everything he thinks and says "presupposes" a truth that all his thought seeks to deny.

Existential Formulations

Still another approach to the relationship between antithesis and common grace is found in Van Til's examination of the unbeliever's heart condition. Consider the following:

> The question of knowledge is an ethical question at the root. It is indeed possible to have theoretically correct knowledge about God without loving God. The devil illustrates this point. Yet what is meant by knowing God in Scripture is *knowing and loving* God: this is *true* knowledge of God: the other is *false*.[51]

Knowing God, then, is not merely an intellectual matter. It includes love; it is also closely connected with the emotional component

[51]DF2, 17 (emphasis his).

of regeneration. Notice how Van Til uses Charles Hodge's exegesis of Ephesians 4:24 and Colossians 3:10: "Regeneration secures right knowledge as well as right feeling; and right feeling is not the effect of right knowledge, nor is right knowledge the effect of right feeling. The two are inseparable effects of a work which affects the whole soul."[52]

Therefore, the antithesis is regeneracy versus unregeneracy, a good heart versus a bad one—and that, as Van Til always insists, is an ethical issue. As he explains in *Christian Theistic Ethics,* the works of the unbeliever are not done to the glory of God, based on the scriptural standard, and motivated by faith. So it is with knowledge, for, in his view, "the intellectual itself is ethical."[53] Knowledge itself must be sought with the proper goal, standard, and motive if it is to be true in the fullest sense. Recall Van Til's statement, quoted earlier, that knowledge and love are not separable.

So, the unbeliever may say many things that in themselves the believer cannot fault; but those things, like all the words of sinful man, spring from sinful motives within. Even the Devil has knowledge after a fashion, as we have seen. The unbeliever, like his father, the Devil, speaks truth, but falsifies it by the way he lives: "Formal assent to the intellectual argument for Christianity, and pharisaical punctiliousness in living up to the form of the law, are in themselves perhaps the most diabolical falsification of the truth."[54]

Van Til often speaks of the unbeliever giving "intellectual assent" to the truths of Christianity: "We may hold that [the children of Cain] 'knew' the truth intellectually as fully as did the children of God."[55] Evidently, some unbelievers, like the Pharisees or the Devil, can be quite orthodox!

We might be inclined here toward a formulation like the following: Unbelievers may accept the truth intellectually, but are morally opposed to it. Their problem is "not intellectual but moral." This is the way Sproul, Gerstner, and Lindsley formulate the noetic

---

[52]Ibid., 75. Here Van Til is quoting Hodge's *Systematic Theology* (Grand Rapids: Eerdmans, 1952), 3:36. Cf. our discussion in chap. 11 of this book and my perspectival treatment of intellect, will, emotions, and other human faculties in DKG, 335–40.

[53]DF2, 46.

[54]IST, 198.

[55]Ibid., 78; cf. DF2, 299; CTK, 19, 226, 292.

effects of sin in their *Classical Apologetics*.[56] Certainly there is much truth in this formulation. Van Til would agree with its intention to place the unbeliever's depravity in the ethical, rather than the metaphysical, realm. The buzz saw illustration mentioned earlier teaches that the intellectual capacities of the unbeliever as such may work quite efficiently. Sin does not destroy them physically or metaphysically; rather, it keeps them from operating in the right direction.

However, Van Til also says,

> When we say that sin is ethical we do not mean, however, that sin involved only the will of man and not his intellect. Sin involved every aspect of man's personality. All of man's reactions in every relation in which God had set him were ethical and not merely intellectual; the intellectual itself is ethical.[57]

Similarly: "It will not do to separate the logical powers of man from his moral powers and say that though man is morally unwilling to serve God, he can intellectually know God aright."[58] In this context, he concedes that in one sense Satan and human sinners like Cain know God very well: "But herein exactly lies the contradiction of Satan's personality that though he knows God he yet does not really know God. His very intellect is devising schemes by which he thinks he may overthrow God, while he knows all too well that God cannot be overthrown."[59]

Thus, like the situational formulation, the existential formulation is paradoxical. We cannot neatly divide the personality of the unbeliever into one portion that is affected and another that is unaffected by the Fall. To be sure, sin does not destroy our rational capacity to formulate propositions and make inferences; review in this connection chapters 12 and 13. Unbelievers may and often do exceed believers in those capacities. But in all the unbeliever's assertions and

---

[56](Grand Rapids: Zondervan, 1984), 52; cf. my critique in "Van Til and the Ligonier Apologetic," *WTJ* 47 (fall 1985): 279–99, reprinted in my AGG, 219–43, and in appendix A of this volume.

[57]DF2, 46.

[58]IST, 92.

[59]Ibid.

reasoning, he acts as a sinner—and, in all his assertions and reasoning, he reflects God's common grace.

At the same time, the unbeliever knows God in one sense and fails to know him in another. The two senses of knowledge here are difficult to define and distinguish.[60] Perhaps the most helpful elucidation of this distinction is for us, with Van Til in the preceding quotation, simply to observe the biblical figure of Satan: brilliant and knowledgeable, but brought by his sinful hatred into a hopelessly stupid project, the project of trying to overthrow the kingdom of the living God. The interplay of his brilliance and stupidity is exceedingly difficult to describe, except by the narratives of Scripture and history. But it rings true. We have all known brilliant people who have in this way made fools of themselves. Satan is like them, to the nth degree, and non-Christians in general are like him in turn.

Of course, there are important differences between Satan and human unbelievers and between some unbelievers and others. One difference to which Van Til often refers is a difference in self-consciousness. "There is therefore a gradation between those who sin more and those who sin less self-consciously."[61] Self-consciousness in this sense is sometimes a function of learning: unbelievers tend to be more explicitly antagonistic to Christianity when they are philosophizing than when they are speaking from common sense.[62] Sometimes it is also a function of historical differentiation:

> Paul speaks of the ignorance of men to whom the gospel has not been preached. There is therefore a gradation between those who sin more and those who sin less self-consciously, as some are closer and others are further removed in history from the original direct supernatural revelation of God to men.[63]

Here the normative and existential formulations overlap. Here Van Til speaks of "self-consciousness." Earlier we saw that he often speaks of the "systems" or "principles" of the unbeliever being the

---

[60]For an attempt to do this roughly and approximately, see DKG, 49–61.

[61]CTK, 46.

[62]DF2, 82.

[63]CTK, 46. Cf. the account in CGG of the process by which unbelievers and believers become more and more clearly differentiated from one another as history

specific locus of noetic sin. I take it that these formulations are pretty much equivalent: see Van Til's own equation of them in *An Introduction to Systematic Theology,* pages 83–84. To say that the unbeliever's suppression of the truth is "in his system" or "insofar as he is true to his principle" is the same as saying "to the degree that he is epistemologically self-conscious."

Still, this is not to say that sin has no effects upon people who are relatively unself-conscious or relatively unsystematic in their thought. For in such people we still find knowledge without love, which is the heart of noetic sin.

Van Til occasionally uses formulations that press the concept of self-consciousness in a psychological direction, as if the unbeliever's knowledge of the truth were unconscious or subconscious. For example, "[The Reformed apologist] must seek his point of contact with the natural man in that which is beneath the threshold of his working consciousness, in the sense of deity which he seeks to suppress."[64] However, Van Til also writes, "We should, however, be on our guard not to make too much of the distinction between preconscious and self-conscious action . . . [as if intuition] were something quite different and something more elemental than ratiocination."[65]

In general, Van Til does not insist that all of our agreements with unbelievers must be limited to their subconscious beliefs. Rather, when he talks about an unbeliever's level of self-consciousness, he is talking about the unbeliever's intentions and sophistication, not his psychological self-awareness. Depravity and common grace are both displayed at all levels of psychological consciousness, as is clearly implied by the normative and situational formulations.

Depravity and common grace are both pervasive realities. That being so, we can understand why Van Til makes use of extreme antithetical formulations. If depravity is pervasive, it will not do to suggest without qualification that the unbeliever knows a collection of

progresses to its consummation. I confess I have reservations about the scripturality of this theological construction, which I will note in the following chapter. But I do not doubt that people repress the truth with different degrees of self-consciousness.

[64]DF2, 98. Van Til frequently appeals to what is "deep down" in the heart of the unbeliever (pp. 94, 231). Cf. also his emphasis on the "involuntary" nature of the unbeliever's recognition of truth, as in IST, 88.

[65]IST, 90.

truths that he holds in common with the believer. There is no commonality without difference.

On the other hand, we can also understand why the extreme antithetical formulations are inadequate without considerable qualification. First, they suggest that the unbeliever errs literally in every statement he makes. As we have seen, depravity does not necessarily work that way. It works in various ways. Sometimes it does lead unbelievers literally to deny the teachings of Scripture. Sometimes, however, it leads them to affirm those teachings hypocritically—without love, without a heart to serve God. Second, those formulations suggest that the specifically intellectual aspects of human depravity always appear in the discrete statements that the unbeliever makes, rather than in the direction of his entire life. Third, they fail to convey that the unbeliever's very denial of the truth is in some respects an affirmation of it. It is inconsistent and therefore conveys truth along with error (normative formulation); it presupposes the truth (situational); it recognizes the truth intellectually while responding to it foolishly (existential).

Practical Formulations

We have seen that Van Til's view of the unbeliever is actually very complex. He appears to deny this complexity in his extreme antithetical formulations, but we certainly must take them into account if we are to build well on his foundation. Bearing this complexity in mind, how shall we prepare ourselves practically for apologetic encounters? What should we expect of the unbeliever?

I questioned earlier Van Til's assertion that we can predict how the unbeliever will respond to an apologetic challenge (e.g., by twisting the evidence for the Resurrection into a naturalistic scheme). I believe it is evident now that no such prediction is possible. The unbeliever may or may not twist the evidence in this way. He may confess that Jesus is risen, but do so hypocritically or with hatred of the God who so triumphed over his lord, Satan. These are alternatives within the sphere of common grace. We should recognize also that special grace may intervene and use the presentation of such evidences to bring conversion. Thus, the actual response of the unbeliever to an apologetic argument is quite unpredictable.

Van Til's most practical formulations, then, are formulations that (contrary to the extreme antithetical formulations) leave the situation fairly open and flexible. I referred earlier, for example, to his assertion that there is a "mixture" of truth and falsehood in the unbeliever's mentality. The non-Christian's statements "do not consistently proceed from the one principle or the other."

In the same vein, Van Til often urges apologists to avoid the assumption that the unbeliever can form a "basically proper judgment on any question."[66] He states that, on a biblical epistemology, the unbeliever's "claim to interpret at least some area of experience in a way that is essentially correct, is mistaken."[67] "Basically" and "essentially" seem like rather vague terms. In a thinker as conscious of principle as Van Til, one would not expect to find that sort of vagueness. We ask, Are the unbeliever's judgments proper or improper? When the issue is principial, how can we introduce terms that suggest differences of degree?[68]

But Van Til does use such terms, and perhaps that is where we should leave the matter for practical purposes. Unbelievers do speak truth sometimes, but their overall understanding of the world is "basically" wrong. Nor can this basic wrongness always be demonstrated in a purely conceptual way. Is Einstein's relativity theory wrong because it was devised by a non-Christian? Is it "basically" wrong? To say so without further explanation would be misleading. The wrongness of an unbeliever's mentality is essentially a wrongness of the heart, and that wrongness of the heart may be expressed actively and conceptually in various ways. A non-Christian scientist may discover facts and report them accurately; the wrongness of his perspective may appear in his use of those facts, or in his inner motivation for discovering them, rather than in his statement of them. His theory as such may be "basically right," although his overall outlook on life will be "basically wrong."

When the apologist approaches an unbeliever, he should expect to find one who represses the truth of God in one way or another, so that the overall configuration of his life is wrong and wrongheaded.

---

[66]DF2, 83.

[67]Ibid., 93.

[68]Cf. also IST, 32: "Formally and incidentally, [unbelievers] have said many things that are true." We discussed "formally" earlier. "Incidentally" suggests that unbelievers speak truths, but not on the main drift of a topic of conversation.

But the specific forms that this repression takes are so many and so varied that it is not possible to predict just how an apologetic confrontation will go. To use a currently popular phrase, apologetics must therefore be "person variable." It must deal with each inquirer according to his own special needs, concerns, interests, and problems.

Van Til himself thought it was possible to predict the course of such encounters. But his own account of the complexities of the unbeliever's consciousness cannot be reconciled with such predictability.

And it may be that he was actually not so rigid on this question as some of his formulations might suggest. As a student, I used to press him on the literal force of his view of antithesis. It seemed to me then that a literal account of it (e.g., "We may never agree with an unbeliever") would require all sorts of absurdities. Van Til would not even have the right, for example, to accept Hume's critiques of some of Butler's arguments, which he certainly wanted to do. When I raised this issue, Van Til's replies to me were always of a rather commonsense variety. Of course, he said, we can agree with Hume, or Kant, or Plato, or Aristotle, about this or that, but not about their "basic" ideas. He was not hesitant to express agreement with unbelievers on various points, such as the importance of the one-and-many problem.[69] He could even speak of "the lofty ethics of idealism,"[70] and he speaks of how we should "apply the method of idealist logicians in a way that these idealist logicians, because of their own anti-Christian theistic assumptions, cannot apply it,"[71] thus implying some level of agreement with the idealists as to how concepts cohere in a system of thought. He could praise elements of the Greek *paideia* and agree with observations made about it by the secular writers Kroner and Jaeger.[72] He could agree with the secular scientists about "details."[73] Non-Christians, he says, can teach much that is good, right, and true.[74] Modern theologians have even made great contributions to biblical studies.[75] Nor was

[69]DF2, 24.

[70]Ibid., 64; CTETH, 59.

[71]DF2, 115–16; cf. IW, 18.

[72]CTETH, 219.

[73]CTEV, 64, 114; PR, 1, 69, 71. Note PR, 78–80, where he struggles for words to articulate this distinction.

[74]ECE, 83; but on p. 202 he says that no teaching is possible except in Christian schools!

[75]TJD, 23; cf. also Gordon Lewis's comments in JA, 352–54.

Van Til embarrassed to speak of "a certain admission on the part of the sinner that his own gods do not meet the needs of his intellect, his emotions or his will."[76]

But Van Til felt that the "basic" structure of these philosophies was antithetical to Christianity, and he presented cogent argumentation to show that that was so. He would challenge me to find one case in the history of non-Christian philosophy in which someone attained an authentically theistic worldview. I was, of course, unable to produce any examples.

His point seemed to be, not some rigid conviction that we must never agree with unbelievers on any proposition, but rather the empirical observation that, as a matter of fact, depravity tends to produce systems of thought that deny biblical truth in significant ways. Perhaps there are a few unbelievers, such as the Pharisees may have been, who repress the truth more subtly than that, devising intellectual systems that actually affirm biblical truth, but who hold that truth hypocritically. That is possible, and it may have happened, but we must agree that it does not happen very often.

I would suggest that although Van Til's talk of antithesis often appears very rigid (perhaps necessarily so, since we are talking about differences in "principle"), his use of the concept was fairly flexible. Following the example of his practice rather than of his more extreme formulations, we may (and, in my judgment, should) do the same.

Conclusion

Thus far, I have discussed five ways in which Van Til describes the relation of antithesis and common grace. Putting together what we have learned, I would suggest that the extreme antithetical formulations with which his thought is most commonly identified and for which it is most commonly criticized do not represent him at his best or at his most typical. Nor do they represent the full complexity of his thinking on these subjects. Indeed, it would, I believe, be very wrong for us to go into apologetic encounters taking these statements literally and acting on the basis of them.

No doubt Van Til himself was fond of his more extreme antithetical formulations. To those he devoted his greatest eloquence, his

[76]IST, 120.

greatest illustrative cleverness (the buzz saw, the man made of water, the jaundiced eye). Why? In my view, he saw himself as the heir to Kuyper and Machen, and he felt responsible to maintain the mentality of antithesis in the Machen movement and promote it throughout the larger church. His greatest concern was that that sense of opposition to unbelief might lose its sharpness. Further, his more careful analyses of antithesis (normative, situational, existential, and practical) did warrant the view that the effects of depravity upon the unbeliever were comprehensive, so that it could be said that in one sense the unbeliever "knows nothing truly." He very likely felt that these considerations justified his extreme formulations.

But, as we have seen, although the noetic effects of sin are comprehensive, we must give attention to the nature of those comprehensive effects. It is simplistic to hold that they amount to a propositional falsification of the unbeliever's every utterance. Van Til recognized that in his better moments, but his formulations do not always reflect that level of insight.

The point is not that we (that is, we Van Tillians) must deemphasize Van Til's doctrine of antithesis in favor of his doctrine of common grace. To do that would be to rob Van Tillian thought of all its distinctiveness. Rather, what we must do is to understand and make use of the full dimensions of Van Til's thinking about the antithesis, rather than practice a "Van Tillian apologetics" that simply takes his most extreme formulations at face value. Such extreme and literalistic uses of Van Tillian antithesis actually tend to weaken Van Til's teaching in this area, for they tend to describe "antithesis" largely in intellectual terms, as if it were merely about one group of propositions logically contradicting another. In fact, Van Til's "antithesis" is far more than that. It is a teaching about the whole life of man, believing and unbelieving, about the conflict of the ages between the kingdom of God and the kingdom of the Wicked One. This conflict embraces the intellect, but it also embraces every other area of human life. And we do not adequately see *how* the antithesis affects the intellect until we see how sin places the intellect, together with all the rest of life, into the service of an idol.

When we understand the antithesis in its full dimensions, we see more fully the legitimacy of the "great gulf" language in certain contexts. To be sure, there is a great gulf between Christianity and unbelief, and between authentic Christianity and deformations of it. Is there also a "great gulf" between Reformed Christians and non-Reformed

Christians, or between Van Tillian apologists and non–Van Tillian apologists? I confess I would be more conservative than Van Til was with this kind of language, maintaining that the chief antithesis is between belief and unbelief as such rather than between varieties of belief or various formulations of the truth. Arminianism and non–Van Tillian systems of apologetics are erroneous in some measure, I would say, but they have much in common with the Reformed faith at the deepest level. Thus, we should not criticize them in the same terms that we use to criticize unbelief.

Do Reformed believers really have "no fundamentals in common" with Arminian Christians like Stuart Hackett?[77] In my view, statements like this are unwise and untrue if taken in their natural meaning. The issue of antithesis is essentially an issue of the heart, and I am confident that Reformed believers are, in general, of one heart with their Arminian brothers and sisters.

The problem is this: Van Til sometimes forgot that his doctrine of antithesis was a doctrine about the human heart. He sometimes thought that he could identify it exhaustively with various conceptual oppositions. In this belief he was wrong. If we are to maintain fully Van Til's "presuppositionalism of the heart" in our own day, we must avoid such confusion.[78] Of course, I am not saying that one's doctrine has nothing to do with the condition of one's heart. Doctrine proceeds from the heart, as do all of our words (Matt. 12:34). But, as we have seen, the precise relationship between heart condition and verbal confession in individual cases is rather complex.

The notion is abroad in some circles that Van Til's thought forbids us to seek to learn anything at all from unbelievers, or even from non-Reformed Christians.[79] Van Til's extreme antithetical formulations do give some aid and comfort to that position. I take it, however, that my analysis decisively refutes such applications of Van Til's thought. Van Til himself learned much from non-Christian and non-

---

[77]Recall our discussion of this in chap. 3. We shall see other examples of this extreme language in chaps. 22, 25, and 27.

[78]See my AGG, 57–88, where I attempt to show some other ways in which Van Til confuses heart-attitudes with propositional formulations.

[79]Understandably, this sort of view is not usually found in print, but I think many readers will recall private conversations and presbytery speeches to this effect. For one published example, see the exchange between William Dennison, the late William White, and myself, in *Journey*, September–October 1987; March–April, May–June, and July–October 1988; January–February 1989.

Reformed thinkers, and he taught his students to do the same. Wooden application of Van Til's more extreme antithetical statements misses entirely the subtlety of Van Til's teaching. We ought not to take as our starting point those statements of Van Til which are least defensible scripturally and which contradict Van Til's own fuller formulations.

Still, in my view, the great need in our time is for more, not less, recognition of antithesis. Here, Van Til can continue to make an important contribution to Christian thought, as long as we focus on the richness of his teaching rather than carelessly repeating his more colorful formulations.

CHAPTER SIXTEEN

Common Grace

In the preceding chapter, I discussed common grace as a limit to antithesis. Common grace is that which gives to the unbeliever a nonsaving, but nonetheless genuine, knowledge of God. It is that knowledge against which he sins and which therefore renders him responsible for his actions.

There is, however, much more to the doctrine of common grace, which was a major focus of Van Til's interest. His doctrine of common grace was in effect his philosophy of history. We must, therefore, look at that doctrine more systematically.

The doctrine of common grace was developed by John Calvin to show how unregenerate, totally depraved sinners could do things that were good for human society.[1] Abraham Kuyper wrote a three-volume work on the subject, *De Gemeene Gratie,* still untranslated into English. Kuyper's influence provoked a lively debate over the subject in Dutch Reformed circles; there has been no comparable discussion in English-speaking Presbyterian churches.

---

[1]For Calvin's views, the standard study is Herman Kuiper, *Calvin on Common Grace* (Grand Rapids: Smitter, 1928). In my opinion, the best exegetical study of the doctrine available in English is John Murray's 1942 essay, "Common Grace," reprinted in *Collected Writings of John Murray,* 4 vols. (Edinburgh: Banner of Truth, 1976–82), 2:93–119.

The Christian Reformed Church, of which Van Til was a member until 1936, went through a period of serious controversy concerning common grace. A number of ministers, including the brilliant dogmatician Herman Hoeksema, denied the existence of common grace. Van Til explains: "Hoeksema and Danhof argue that it is inconceivable that God should be in any sense, and at any point, graciously inclined to those who are not his elect. The wicked do, to be sure, receive gifts from God. But rain and sunshine are not, as such, evidences of God's favor."[2] In 1924, the denominational Synod, meeting at Kalamazoo, Michigan, "virtually condemned"[3] the views of Hoeksema and Danhof by affirming three points of doctrine. Van Til includes the text of these in *Common Grace and the Gospel,* pages 19–22. They may be summarized as follows:

1. There is a "certain favor or grace" of God which he shows to his creatures in general.
2. God restrains sin in individuals and in society.
3. God enables the unregenerate to perform "civic good," that is, things that promote the welfare of others.

Van Til was too young to be a major participant in the discussions of the early 1920s, but the debate did stimulate him to comment frequently on the issue in later years. He had friends on both sides of the controversy and he regretted the divisiveness of it. He sought in his writings to get beyond the standard positions on either side and to make some real progress in theological understanding.[4] In this effort he acknowledged the value of contributions by S. G. De Graaf and Klaas Schilder, with some criticisms of the latter.[5]

Van Til's booklet *Common Grace,* subsequently published as the first three chapters of the collection *Common Grace and the Gospel,* is rather difficult to follow. There are all sorts of comparisons and contrasts between Calvin, Pighius, Kuyper, Bavinck, Schilder, Hepp, Hoeksema, De Graaf, Greydanus, and Zwier, and many digressions and excursuses about science, theistic proofs, apologetic methodol-

---

[2]CGG, 18.

[3]Ibid.

[4]Note his comments in CGG, 12–13. His goal was to provide sympathetic, critical analysis of both sides.

[5]CGG, 23–29.

ogy, paradox, logic, analogical thinking, and so on, some of which I refer to elsewhere in this volume.

I will bypass most of this here and attempt to summarize and evaluate the main thrust of Van Til's proposal. That proposal begins with an emphasis upon the correlativity of universals and facts in the world, reflecting the Trinity. Granted such correlativity, the facts are meaningful and the meanings are factual. This is true also of historical facts, facts about moments in time. "Because of this correlativity there is genuine progress in history; because of it the Moment has significance."[6]

Therefore, "to make progress in our discussion we must, it seems, learn to take time more seriously than we have done."[7] We should do this by "stressing the idea of the *earlier* and the *later*."[8] All parties to the debate are Calvinists and therefore agree that the final destinies of men are settled eternally in the counsel of God. But, he continues: "The difference obtains with regard to the meaning of the historical. And here the problem is, more specifically, to what extent we should allow our notion of the earlier to be controlled by our notion of the later. We think that the notion of the earlier must be stressed more than has been done."[9]

To be "controlled by our notion of the later" is to say that God's favor to someone is determined exclusively by that person's foreordained final destiny. On this view, if a person is finally saved, then everything God does for him in history is favor, for in every event God is preparing the way for that person's final salvation. But if the individual is finally lost, then everything God does for him during his life is wrath: in history God does nothing but prepare that person for his final condemnation.

There is a certain logic about this. Certainly God and his plan are unchanging; thus, it seems to make sense to picture his attitude toward each individual as unchanging as well. And certainly everything that God does in history helps to realize the consummation of his plan, including the blessedness of the elect and the eternal punishment of the lost. Thus, it makes some sense to see God's attitude throughout history toward the elect as favor and toward the nonelect as wrath.

---

[6]Ibid., 64.

[7]Ibid.

[8]Ibid., 72 (emphasis his).

[9]Ibid.

But there is something scripturally wrong with this way of thinking. For Scripture does speak of God showing mercy and kindness to all his creation.[10] Therefore, his treatment of the nonelect is at least in some respect favorable. Scripture also speaks of transitions in history between God's wrath and his grace. All are genuinely lost in Adam, under a "common curse." That wrath of God is genuine wrath, so genuine that only the death of Christ could satisfy it.[11] In Christ, that wrath is genuinely averted, and there is a transition from wrath to grace. Similarly, the wicked are under God's favor in Adam, and in the Fall they go through a transition—in this case from favor to wrath. But that wrath is not wholly unmixed until the Last Judgment, which is their historical transition to unmitigated wrath.

Van Til does not entirely deny the view of history that is "controlled by the later." It is true, he says, that both the saved and the lost are moving through history toward their final destiny.[12] But he resists drawing from this view the conclusion that there are no genuine transitions in history, and therefore that there is never any divine wrath upon the elect or favor upon the lost.

It is not surprising that Van Til relates this issue to the full bucket problem that we considered earlier.[13] For the essence of the full bucket problem is that "God's plan is exhaustive, yet history is significant." Everything is settled in advance, but nothing is settled until it actually happens. Everything is worked out in advance, but in history there are "downs and ups."[14] The road from God's plan to its consummation is not a straight line. There is temporary, yet real, divine wrath upon the elect, and similar favor to the reprobate.

Does this mean that God and his plan do change, after all? Van Til does not deal with that question specifically, but the theological tradition (doubtless supported by Van Til) would say this: God does not change, but as creatures change, his relation to them changes. In the sunlight, a man receives the warmth of the sun; away from the sunlight, he does not. The change is not a change in the sun, but in

[10]Van Til deals with four significant passages in CGG, 29–33; cf. Murray's more elaborate treatment in "Common Grace" (see note 1 above).

[11]CGG, 31.

[12]Ibid., 31–32.

[13]Ibid., 10.

[14]Ibid., 31.

the man. Similarly, God is unchanging in himself, but he can be said to change in relation to his creatures.

As for the plan of God, it does not change, but it determines change. The changes in this world are part of God's plan, foreordained by God. It is not that God's plan is changing, but rather that God has a plan for change. God's unchanging plan includes change.

Yet there is paradox, in the sense that we discussed it in chapters 12 and 13. For God has not told us why his unchanging plan includes change. Why should it include time and change? Why should God not simply wrap up everything in a moment? What importance can this long history of change have for God, for whom everything is eternally settled?

In any case, the divine plan does not render history meaningless. Rather, "history has meaning, not in spite of, but because of, the counsel of God who controls whatsoever comes to pass."[15] Change and transition are real and significant, because God has planned for them to be real and significant.

So, while the view of history "controlled by the later" has some value, it misses the important transitions from wrath to favor and from favor to wrath. Van Til, therefore, suggests "that the notion of the earlier must be stressed more than has been done heretofore."[16] The idea here seems to be, to use my terms rather than Van Til's, that God is as much concerned with beginnings and middles as with endings, somewhat like a human composer or novelist. God is interested in the whole historical process, not only with the consummation. Therefore, we must affirm that his love for the whole human race at its creation in Adam was a genuine love, that his wrath upon humanity following the Fall was a genuine wrath, that his good gifts to the reprobate in history are a genuine divine favor, and that redemption is a genuine transition in history from wrath to grace.[17]

Note that Van Til here uses the language of degree. It is not that we should simply abandon the perspective (as we might call it) of

---

[15]Ibid., 73.

[16]Ibid., 72.

[17]It is interesting that Van Til frequently criticizes Barth in terms of Berkouwer's observation that for Barth there is no "transition from wrath to grace in history." It might be said that that is Van Til's most fundamental criticism of Barth; see our discussion in chap. 26. Van Til does not charge Hoeksema with being a Barthian, but he clearly takes this issue of transition very seriously.

"the later" and replace it entirely with "the earlier." Rather, he says, the earlier "must be stressed more." It is a matter of stress, of emphasis. The two perspectives supplement one another.

Van Til agrees with Bavinck that neither supralapsarianism, which stresses the later perspective, nor infralapsarianism, which stresses the earlier, is in itself scripturally adequate. Supralapsarianism "led to a virtual denial of second or historical causes," while infralapsarianism "led, sometimes, to a virtual denial of God's plan as the first or last ultimate cause as controlling all finite causes."[18] These positions are not wrong in themselves; Van Til knew of writers on both sides whom he would not have wished to criticize in this way. What is wrong, he says, is what these positions sometimes "lead to," particularly in extreme formulations like those of Hoeksema.

Van Til recommends that we follow Bavinck and resist choosing between supra- and infralapsarianism. Instead, he believes, we should keep the earlier and the later perspectives in balance. In my own view, and I think in Van Til's as well, this balance is not impossible to achieve, for the two positions are not inherently contradictory. Supralapsarianism says that everything God does in the world advances the purposes of election. Infralapsarianism says that as God advances the purposes of election in history, there are real transitions and changes, and God's plan includes those as well.

The Free Offer of the Gospel

But how can we describe common grace in a way that emphasizes "the earlier"? First, it will emphasize human solidarity in Adam and God's love for the human race as his creatures. It will also emphasize the solidarity of the human race under God's wrath following the Fall. Van Til continues: "But *after the common, in each case, comes the conditional.* History is a process of differentiation. Accordingly, the idea of that which is common between the elect and the reprobate is always a limiting concept. It is a commonness for *the time being*. There lies back of it a divine *as if*."[19]

By "the conditional" Van Til means a "well-meant offer of salvation to a generality of men, including elect and non-elect."[20] The free

[18]CGG, 146.

[19]Ibid., 74 (emphasis his).

[20]Ibid., 75.

offer of the gospel was also a matter of debate between Hoeksema and his opponents. It was also discussed in the Clark controversy; evidently Clark was reluctant, during his theological examination, to accept the terminology of a "sincere" general gospel offer, recognizing that that terminology had been used by Arminians to oppose the Calvinistic view of election.[21] The complainants feared that he was hyper-Calvinistic, denying the legitimacy of a general gospel offer. In my estimation, the reply of the *Answer* was sufficient. But the General Assembly's *Report* included a very useful analysis entitled "The Free Offer of the Gospel," authored by John Murray with some assistance from Ned B. Stonehouse.[22]

Van Til's exegetical position is essentially in agreement with this article, but his discussion of the subject adds some conceptual nuances:

> [Valentine] Hepp speaks as though it were already known who are and who are not elect. He speaks as though a preacher may approach a certain individual whom he knows to be reprobate, and tell him God has no pleasure in his death. But this is to forget the difference between the earlier and the later. The general presentation comes to a generality. It comes to "sinners," differentiated, to be sure, as elect and reprobate in the mind of God, but yet, prior to their act of acceptance or rejection, regarded as a generality. To forget this is to move the calendar of God ahead.[23]

Van Til then goes on, in a discussion of the Calvin-Pighius controversy, to emphasize that the gospel offer to all men is *conditional.* Of course, God has unconditionally elected those whom he intends to save. But God's unconditional purpose is not inconsistent with human responsibility. God achieves his eternal purposes in part through finite, secondary causes. He ordains means as well as ends, and those means include human faith-responses to the gospel offer. Apart from such means, there is no salvation. Faith-responses are among the historical transitions that we emphasized earlier.

---

[21]See *Answer,* 38–39.

[22]This was published in the *Minutes of the Fifteenth General Assembly of the Orthodox Presbyterian Church* (1948) and later as a pamphlet. It can also be found in Murray, *Collected Writings,* 4:113–32.

[23]CGG, 75–76.

From the passage quoted immediately above, it appears that Van Til regards not only acceptance of the gospel (i.e., saving faith), but also rejection of it, as a significant historical transition. Before that acceptance or rejection, elect and nonelect are not differentiated from one another. Differentiation comes with their conscious response to the gospel. The actual preaching of the gospel assumes, then, a nondifferentiated situation, and therefore it is directed equally to all.

At this point I begin to have problems with Van Til's analysis. Doubtless he is on solid biblical ground when he tells us to take history seriously and to recognize the earlier as well as the later. Certainly any analysis of common grace must take account of genuine historical transitions and therefore recognize the importance of secondary causes as well as ultimate divine causes. Coming to saving faith is always a significant historical transition in the life of an individual.

But what do we make of the unbeliever's rejection of the gospel? Is that, as Van Til suggests, a historical transition of similar magnitude? It certainly is a significant event in the unbeliever's life history. Rejection of God's Word can lead to hardening, according to Isaiah 6:9–10 and the allusions to that passage elsewhere in Scripture.[24] Yet it is not a spiritual reversal, as is faith. Faith marks a transition from wrath to grace, but rejection of the gospel is only a transition from wrath to more wrath.

Van Til almost suggests in the quoted passage that the unbeliever is spiritually neutral until his rejection of the gospel definitively places him in Satan's camp. That, of course, is certainly not Van Til's view, but it is hard to make sense of this particular formulation on any other supposition.

The fact is that the gospel is not addressed to a "generality," but to particular people. And these people are not merely "as yet undifferentiated," but are already really under God's wrath. It is to those actual individuals that the promises, offers, commands, and invitations of the gospel come.[25] And it is to them that God says that he does not desire their death. On this point, Hepp is right and Van Til wrong. Here I believe that Van Til fails, despite his best intentions, to take history seriously.

It is certainly true that the universality of the gospel offer reflects

[24]Matt. 13:13–15; Mark 4:12; Luke 8:10; John 12:40; Acts 28:26–27; Rom. 11:8.

[25]Van Til, citing Calvin, rightly denies any significant difference between these (CGG, 77).

God's general intentions for the human race. It certainly does reflect God's love for the whole human race in Adam and his desire to reestablish that race in Christ as its new head. "God so loved the *world*, that he gave his only Son" (John 3:16). But it also expresses his desires for individuals.

Some have objected that God cannot sincerely desire the salvation of one whom he has not determined to save. But that objection fails the test of historical seriousness. The fact is that throughout the history of revelation God expresses desires for things that, according to his eternal counsel, do not take place. God did not want Cain to kill his brother, but he ordained that he would do so. He did not want Israel to worship idols, but he foreordained that they would.

To deal with such matters, theologians have distinguished between God's decretive and preceptive wills: the decretive will controls all things; the preceptive will expresses God's commands and preferences to rational creatures. Both can be described as God's "desires," but they somehow represent different sectors of the divine psychology. This distinction can be useful, but, as Van Til would say, it leaves much mystery. God is, after all, one. His mind is not neatly divisible into psychological compartments. To say the least, it is not clear how God could want, and at the same time not want, sin to enter the world. Here we must invoke Van Til's doctrines of paradox and analogical thinking. But, as Van Til often tells us, we should not deny one side of the paradox in order to embrace the other side, for Scripture clearly teaches both.

In his strange idea of preaching the gospel freely to a "generality," Van Til himself seems to have violated his own principle. He evidently resorts to this formulation on the grounds that God could not desire the salvation of an actual reprobate person, only of a generality including elect and reprobate together. But that assumption is unbiblical and quite unnecessary if we follow Van Til's earlier advice and take seriously the transitions of history. Following the transition of the Fall and preceding the transition of the Last Judgment, God wants all individuals to repent, whether or not he has foreordained for them to do so.

Daane's Critique

It is interesting to note that Van Til's doctrine of common grace has been subjected to two book-length critiques—exceeding by far the critical analysis available on any other aspect of his teaching. Later we will look at Gary North's *Dominion and Common Grace;* here we will briefly consider James Daane's *A Theology of Grace.*

Daane's book is very thorough and ingenious, but in the final analysis it is rather bizarre. Daane was originally impressed with Van Til's emphasis "upon the necessity of taking time and dates seriously in our doctrine of common grace, and because of his emphasis on the equal ultimacy of universality and particularity in the principle of the ontological trinity."[26] He published two articles supporting Van Til's ideas, but then had second thoughts. In the book, he claims to have "laid bare" the "philosophical categories" underlying Van Til's formulations.[27]

Van Til has sometimes been accused of criticizing others unfairly on the basis of his speculative reconstructions of philosophical categories supposedly underlying their thought.[28] If those accusations are true, then in *A Theology of Grace* Daane has given Van Til a dose of his own medicine! He takes Van Til's talk about generalities and so on to reflect philosophical idealism and various dialectics between being and nonbeing. He focuses much attention on this text from Van Til: "If we make the earlier our point of departure for the later, we begin with something that believers and unbelievers have in common. That is to say, they have something in common because they do not yet exist. Yet they do exist. They exist in Adam as their common representative."[29]

Daane pounces on the clause "because they do not yet exist" and belabors it over and over again throughout his book. He construes Van Til's position to be that *"the only thing that the elect and reprobate have in common—without a difference—is their non-existence."*[30] Their commonality, therefore, is supratemporal and mystical. Even Adam himself "does not exist" as a historical figure. Van Til reduces Adam, says Daane, to a mere generality.[31] Common grace is given only to nonexistent people; once they come to exist, there is no common grace. As

---

[26]Daane, *A Theology of Grace* (Grand Rapids: Eerdmans, 1954), 7.

[27]Ibid., 8.

[28]See, e.g., G. C. Berkouwer, *The Triumph of Grace in the Theology of Karl Barth* (Grand Rapids: Eerdmans, 1956), 386.

[29]CGG, 72.

[30]Daane, *Theology of Grace,* 21 (emphasis his).

[31]Ibid., 39–42.

Van Til criticizes Hoeksema and Barth for denying any real significance to historical events, so Daane makes the same charge against Van Til.

I said that Daane's critique was rather bizarre. That should be plain to anybody who has even a slight knowledge of Van Til's writings. His emphasis on the actual historical existence of Adam and the significance of redemptive events in history requires no documentation.

I do think that the sentence about nonexistent people in Adam could have been better formulated. Certainly it is true in one sense. When we were judged in Adam, we did not exist as distinct individuals. And it is true that people who do not exist have their nonexistence in common! But that is really irrelevant to Van Til's argument, and, cute as the point is to philosophical readers,[32] he should never have made it. The commonness of common grace, for Van Til, is not based upon the *nonexistence* of individuals in Adam; rather, as Van Til hastens to add, it is based on their common *existence* in Adam as their representative and their continued *existence* through the temporal transitions of history.

Van Til's talk about "generalities" is also unfortunate, as I indicated earlier in this chapter,[33] and it is contrary to the main thrust of his book. His main argument is in essence a plea for the importance of historical particularities, not generalities, and for the importance of temporal transitions.

Daane's first thoughts about Van Til's *Common Grace* were far sounder than his second thoughts. Van Til's utterances about nonexistence and generalities are unfortunate lapses, not keys to the discovery of vast ranges of heresy in his thought. Daane makes the mistake of elevating jokes, obiter dicta, and unfortunate misstatements to the status of programmatic pronouncements. Then he rather violently forces everything else Van Til says into the mold of this alleged philosophical program. Daane's remarkable performance illustrates the need for more sense of proportion—and more sense of humor (with which a sense of proportion is closely linked)—in Reformed theology.

---

[32]I believe that Van Til was often led astray by the opportunity to employ a cute but misleading phrase or a fetching illustration. We saw that tendency in the extreme formulations of antithesis discussed in the previous chapter.

[33]Of course, as I said, there are "general" facts about the human race that are relevant to the doctrine of common grace.

The Process of Differentiation

The next step in understanding Van Til's view of common grace is to observe the direction in which the process of differentiation is moving:

> All common grace is earlier grace. Its commonness lies in its earliness. . . . It pertains to all the dimensions of life, but to all these dimensions ever decreasingly as the time of history goes on. At the very first stage of history there is much common grace. There is a common good nature under the common favor of God. But this creation-grace requires response. It cannot remain what it is. It is conditional. Differentiation must set in and does set in. It comes first in the form of a common rejection of God. Yet common grace continues; it is on a "lower" level now; it is long-suffering that men may be led to repentance. . . . Common grace will diminish still more in the further course of history. With every conditional act the remaining significance of the conditional is reduced. God allows men to follow the path of their self-chosen rejection of Him more rapidly than ever toward the final consummation. God increases His attitude of wrath upon the reprobate as time goes on, until at the end of time, at the great consummation of history, their condition has caught up with their state.[34]

To paraphrase: God's favor to the nonelect diminishes over time, becoming nonexistent at the final judgment. This happens because, as history progresses, the nonelect become more and more hardened in their wickedness. They become more and more like the perfectly wretched souls in hell that they finally will be. Each time they reject God's revelation, they place themselves more decisively upon that path. Toward the end there will be an acceleration of apostasy.

It is scripturally true, as I indicated in my earlier citation from Isaiah 6 and its New Testament allusions, that some human decisions bring hardening. There are downs and ups, as Van Til says, but that does take place. But I doubt if it can be established scripturally that

[34]CGG, 83. He adds that the reverse is true for the elect: an *increase* of divine favor, perfected at the consummation.

throughout history there is an increase in wickedness and hence a gradual decline of divine favor to the reprobate. For one thing, God's favor to the wicked, his common grace, exists in spite of their sin. It exists to some extent as a witness against them. So sin, in and of itself, does not diminish or extinguish common grace. There is no reason to suppose that there is an inverse relationship between the amount of sin in the world and the amount of divine favor to the reprobate (if such things could even be quantified!).

Furthermore, it is questionable whether the world is becoming more and more wicked as the result of a divinely ordained "process of differentiation." That is, of course, the position of some traditional eschatological viewpoints, but it is by no means generally accepted in Reformed theology.

Apart from theological positions about the end times, can we really say with confidence that there is more wickedness in the world today than, say, during the period of the fall of Rome? And are we sure that God is less gracious to the wicked today than he was then? A case could be made for saying that God is more long-suffering in his dealings with the wicked today than he has ever been, and that he gives more good gifts than ever to those who hate him.

I do think Van Til is right to say that common grace is "earlier" in that it derives from a historical situation prior to the Final Judgment, ultimately from God's good creation of Adam. At all points in history, it takes account of the unfinished nature of God's plan. However, I do not see in Scripture any smooth historical continuum from the Fall to perdition. Rather, as with the redemption of the elect, there seems to be a rich drama of ups and downs.

NORTH'S CRITIQUE

The second book-length critique of Van Til's doctrine of common grace is Gary North's *Dominion and Common Grace*.[35] North is one of the leading theonomist or Christian reconstructionist writers, and, like others in that school, quite Van Tillian in his epistemology. Yet

---

[35]Tyler, Tex.: Institute for Christian Economics, 1987. As I indicated in chap. 2, North dedicated this book to me, with a slightly ironic inscription. I mention this again so that the reader may make an informed judgment as to possible bias on my part.

he regards *Common Grace* as "without question the worst book [Van Til] ever wrote. It is also one of the most confusing books he ever wrote, granted the relative simplicity of the topic."[36] This confusion, North thinks, is partly for the stylistic reasons we noted in chapter 2. Van Til's *Common Grace* is "cluttered up with extraneous material."[37] The clutter, especially the preoccupation with epistemology and other philosophical issues, steers Van Til away from the main issue, which, in North's view, is eschatology.[38]

North simply denies the first point of the Kalamazoo Synod, that God shows "favor" to the reprobate. North believes that God hates them throughout history, with perfect hatred, "without compromise or shadow of turning."[39] What of the biblical passages that suggest otherwise? "Without exception, they refer to *gifts* of God to the unregenerate. They do not imply God's favor."[40] God gives them "favors," not "favor." Why does he give favors to people he hates? These favors are the overflow from the favors God gives to his own people, the "crumbs that fall from the master's table that the dogs eat."[41] Nevertheless, God has a distinct purpose in permitting this overflow: *"God gives ethical rebels enough rope to hang themselves for all eternity."*[42]

In this sense, even Satan receives common grace, a conclusion that is impossible on the traditional understanding. God gives to Satan gifts and powers that will in time lead to his more severe condemnation. Of course, for him there is no "free gospel offer."[43]

As for the process of differentiation, North cites the parable of the wheat and the tares to emphasize that the separation of saved and lost occurs at the end of history, not within it. The course of history, he argues, is postmillennial, not amillennial, as Van Til assumes. Therefore, the church will experience eventual victory through history, rather than progressive defeat, though the progress does not follow a "straight line."[44] North accuses Van Til of an implicit contradiction:

---

[36]*Dominion and Common Grace,* 9.
[37]Ibid., 14.
[38]Ibid., 15.
[39]Ibid., 18.
[40]Ibid., 20.
[41]Ibid., 6, citing James Jordan.
[42]Ibid., 29 (emphasis his).
[43]Ibid., 34–46.
[44]Ibid., 100–103.

as an amillennialist, he believes that the wicked will be victorious over the course in history, but how can they be victorious if the gifts of common grace are gradually withdrawn?[45]

North thinks Van Til's discussion is centered too much on epistemology, when the most important issues are ethical. God gives unbelievers good gifts of knowledge, but they are ethically unable to make the best use of those gifts. That is why they will be defeated, not only in the final judgment, but in history as well.[46]

More significantly, as the gospel goes through the earth, North says, God's law comes to rule society, and that brings benefits to believers and unbelievers alike. Unbelievers cannot make the best use of those benefits, so they will in time be defeated, after a brief final period of rebellion. But they enjoy its blessings for a time. Indeed, those blessings increase as the gospel gains ground. Therefore, on North's view, common grace is not earlier, but later grace—"future grace."[47]

North's analysis of the issue is helpful in raising some additional issues. Certainly, some account must be given of the powers God gives to unbelievers, by which they accomplish their sinful purposes in history. North's account focuses on that question, while Van Til largely ignores it. And North also makes the important point that at least many of the benefits given to the reprobate are a kind of "overflow" from the blessings given to the righteous.

However, in my view, North's discussion of "favor," like many other discussions of it, is somewhat confused because of ambiguities in the term. *Favor* can refer to a kindly disposition, or it can refer to advocacy, as in "I favor the Republican candidates." God never favors the wicked in the sense of advocating their purposes or desiring them to accomplish their goals. God does, however, have a kindly disposition toward all his creatures, as is plain in Psalm 145:9 and Matthew 5:43–48. These passages do not refer only to divine gifts; they also refer to the divine disposition underlying the gifts. And, as we have seen, God does have a genuine desire that the wicked be saved.

The first point of the Kalamazoo Synod uses *favor,* I think, in the sense of "kindly disposition," rather than in the sense of "advocacy." It is the concept of kindly disposition that Van Til endorses. North has not given us any reason to reject it.

---

[45]Ibid., 85–87.

[46]Ibid., 103–11.

[47]Ibid., 98.

As for "earlier" and "later," again there seems to be some terminological confusion. Van Til and North are answering different questions here. Van Til asks why God would wish to give anything good to reprobate sinners who ultimately deserve only hell. He answers that God loves the whole human race in Adam and recognizes that their progressive depravity has not reached its conclusion. North asks a different question, namely, how do the reprobate gain the gifts they have? He answers that they receive the overflow from the blessings God gives to the church. But the two concepts are not logically incompatible. It may well be the case both that God is motivated as Van Til describes, and that blessings are given to the reprobate in the way that North describes.

As for postmillennialism and the church's victory in history, I shall not try to solve that question here. The topic warrants further study! I do agree with North that there is no straight-line progress in history from the Fall to the Last Judgment.[48]

Many others have criticized *Common Grace*. James Oliver Buswell's and Floyd Hamilton's objections are discussed in *A Christian Theory of Knowledge*. Van Til responds to many criticisms by Christian Reformed writers in the original edition of *The Defense of the Faith*. We must, however, move on to other subjects.

[48]Since you asked, my view is that, as the amillennialists teach, the period between Christ's resurrection and his return is a time for Christians to suffer in persecution and poverty. However, it is also, as the postmillennialists teach, a time in which the blood of the martyrs is the seed of the church, which grows through history both in numbers and in social influence. Scripture and history both warrant that twofold viewpoint upon this age. Is there truth in premillennialism? Well, this age is also, perhaps preeminently, a time of waiting for Jesus. And the Last Judgment might take a thousand years.

CHAPTER SEVENTEEN

Rationalism and Irrationalism

We have explored Van Til's view of the antithesis between believer and unbeliever and the ways in which he qualifies that view by means of his doctrine of common grace. My critique may be summarized in this way: (1) Van Til often exaggerates the epistemological implications of the antithesis beyond what is warranted by his own doctrine of common grace. (2) His doctrine of common grace, while insightful, (a) compromises its historical focus in its notion of a gospel offer addressed to a "generality," and (b) includes an unbiblically rigid concept of progressive differentiation (between the elect and the nonelect) down through history. I have also argued that Van Til exaggerates the predictability of the unbeliever's responses to Christian witness. God's sovereignty in both common and special grace makes it more difficult than Van Til thinks to know exactly how every unbeliever will respond to a given testimony.

Nevertheless, it will still be useful to make at least some rough generalizations as to how unbelievers think. Or, more precisely, we may ask what a thoroughly unbelieving epistemology would be like—granted, of course, that no unbeliever is ever perfectly consistent in his unbelief. Does the quest for autonomy lead naturally to certain kinds of intellectual beliefs and commitments? And do those beliefs play a dominant role in the history of unbelieving thought?

Van Til thinks it is possible to make a general characterization of unbelieving thought. That might seem to be an unrealistic expectation; after all, non-Christian thought takes so many different forms. Some non-Christians are rationalists and others are irrationalists, in addition to mystics, religious, irreligious, skeptical, dogmatic, sophisticated, unsophisticated, monists, pluralists, pantheists, deists, and so on. There have been a great number of philosophical, religious, scientific, political, economic, and other systems and nonsystems in the history of non-Christian thought.

Nevertheless, Scripture does warrant Van Til's attempt to define a general structure for unbelieving thought. For all their diversity, unbelievers are at least united in one thing: their desire to repress the truths of divine revelation (Rom. 1:18–32). That is, they are united in their unbelief, united in holding, at some level of their consciousness, beliefs that are opposite to the teachings of Scripture.

So one way to determine the general structure of unbelieving thought is simply to determine what beliefs are directly contradictory to the Christian worldview. Chief among these would be the denial that the biblical God is the sovereign ruler of all things and the supreme authority over human thought and life. As Van Til puts it: "Here is the heart of the matter: through the fall of Adam man has set aside the law of his Creator and therewith has become a law unto himself. He will be subject to none but himself. He seeks to be autonomous. . . . He makes himself the final reference point in all predication."[1]

He sets himself up as "the ultimate standard of right and wrong, of the true and false."[2] We should note, however, that Van Til qualifies these statements by adding that God (in his common grace) restrains the unbeliever's purposes, so that "he cannot carry out his principle to its full degree." Therefore, unbelievers "can yet discover much truth."[3]

Van Til holds that to deny the biblical God is to hold that the universe is ultimately meaningless—the product of chance, or "pure contingency." If God exists at all, the world is as mysterious to him as it is to us. In the Fall, Eve, then Adam, questioned whether God really knew the truth about the forbidden tree:

---

[1]CTK, 42.
[2]Ibid., 47.
[3]Ibid., 43–44.

> No one had as yet had any experience with eating of this tree; there were no inductively gathered records to indicate even as much as a tendency to evil being involved in the use of the fruit of this tree. It was the "inductive method," with its assumption of ultimate mystery involved in pure possibility, that Adam introduced. This was utter irrationalism. It was therefore by implication a flat denial of God's being able to identify himself. It was in effect a claim that no one, neither God nor man, can really know what he is or who he is. How could there be any ultimate or final distinction or preference made in an ocean of Chance?[4]

Therefore, the general structure of unbelieving thought includes an ultimate epistemological irrationalism, correlated with a metaphysic in which reality is reducible to chance.

"But there is another side to the story of the fall of man," continued Van Til:

> How could man be sure that he could safely ignore the command of God? How did he presume to know that God did not know what would come to pass should he eat of the forbidden tree? If there was to be any seeming sense to such an action, it would have to be on the assumption that man himself knew that the evil threatened would not take place. Satan told man that the issue would be quite otherwise than God said it would be. He said that God knew that it would be otherwise. Satan suggested that God too knew that man would be as God, knowing good and evil if man should eat of the tree. Reality, said Satan in effect, is wholly lit up, lit up for the "creature" as well as for the "Creator." Man therefore does not need to live by the authoritative assertions of the Creator. He can discover by his own independent inspection, by *Wesensschau,* what will take place in the course of time. Man as well as God can ascertain the laws of being by means of the laws of rationality in his mind. . . .
>
> It was thus that man, in rejecting the covenantal requirement of God became at one and the same time both irratio-

[4]Ibid., 48.

> nalist and rationalist. These two are not, except formally, contradictory of one another. They rather imply one another. Man had to be both to be either.[5]

The reader might usefully compare the above discussion with our exploration in chapter 5 of the implications of the doctrine of the Trinity. There I mentioned Van Til's view that the Trinity solved the "problem of the one and the many," the problem of the relation of universals to particulars. Van Til says that because unity and diversity are equally ultimate in God, they are also equally ultimate in the creation. There is no "ultimate matter," "pure particularity," or "brute fact" underlying and therefore uninterpreted by any conceptual thought. Nor is there any "pure concept" that exists apart from any particular applications of it. Non-Christian thought, lacking belief in the biblical God, seeks absolutes elsewhere, either in the purely abstract concept or in the purely abstract particular or both. We may relate that discussion to the present one by saying that for Van Til the search for utterly abstract concepts represents the rationalist impulse; the search for utterly uninterpreted brute facts represents the irrationalist impulse.

Van Til analyzes the history of non-Christian thought, particularly Western philosophy, in these terms: "In ancient philosophy the rationalistic motif seemed to dominate the scene; in modern times the irrationalistic motif seems to be largely in control. But the one never lives independently of the other."[6]

In Greek philosophy, we find some figures, like the Sophists, who were predominantly irrationalistic; yet the Sophists' insistence that "man is the measure of all things" shows their rationalistic side, and Plato was able to show that their skepticism was itself a dogmatic assertion, offered as a sure, universal truth. Others, like Parmenides, sought to understand everything in terms of timeless logic, but he needed to resort to mythology to explain the "illusions" that did not cohere with his rationalistic worldview. The irrationalistic Sophists were also rationalists; the rationalistic Parmenides was also an irrationalist.

Plato combined these motifs explicitly. He was rationalistic about

---

[5]Ibid., 48–49. Van Til's treatment of the same topic in DF2, 123–28, is a useful supplement to his discussion in CTK.

[6]CTK, 50.

our knowledge of the world of forms or ideas, yet irrationalistic about our knowledge of the world of sense experience. His problem was in fitting the two worlds together. Van Til offers an interesting and, I think, profound analysis of Plato's vacillations between the two motifs.[7] The same critique bears upon Aristotle. For him, form and matter are not found in different worlds, as in Plato, but rather are complementary aspects of the world in which we now live. But, like Plato, Aristotle understood form and matter antithetically: as pure universality and pure particularity. Thus, their relationship is as problematic as that of Plato's two worlds.

The medieval theologian and philosopher Thomas Aquinas, whose thinking had official status in the Roman Catholic Church for many centuries, adopted an epistemology based in part upon Neoplatonism and Aristotle. Van Til attributes to that compromise many of the doctrinal and apologetic errors of the Roman Catholic tradition.[8]

Van Til finds rationalism emphasized in the modern era by Descartes, Spinoza, and Leibniz, but from an irrationalistic basis. The opposite is true of Locke, Berkeley, and Hume. Immanuel Kant (1724–1804), like Plato, sought to develop a viewpoint that did equal justice to both motifs. In order to accomplish this, he set up a division between two realms: the "noumenal" realm, of which nothing can be known by man, and the "phenomenal" realm, in which autonomous reason reigns supreme. Kant was, in other words, irrationalistic about the noumena and rationalistic about the phenomena. In attempting to reconcile the concerns of rationalism and irrationalism, he advocated human autonomy even more explicitly and consistently than did his predecessors. The human mind became the source of the categories that supply the structure of the phenomenal world.[9] In Kant, Van Til finds a key to all the more recent philosophies.[10] Modern theology, as well—both liberal and neo-orthodox—

[7]SCE, 24–43.

[8]Van Til discusses Roman Catholicism and its traditional Scholastic philosophy often in his writings. See my discussions in chaps. 19 and 25.

[9]Ibid., 103–15.

[10]Van Til discusses the idealist philosophy of Hegel, Bradley, Bosanquet, Pringle-Pattison, and others at great length, reflecting his doctoral studies in that field: see CI and SCE, 114–82. Nevertheless, he evidently believed that Kant's thought was more significant than idealism as an intellectual turning point. Idealism and pragmatism, he wrote, "are both elaborations of Kant's creativity theory of thought which has set

is essentially Kantian: Barth's *Geschichte* is Kant's noumenal realm.[11]

In later chapters we will look more closely at Van Til's critiques of various thinkers. My purpose here has been to present his overall approach in broad strokes. In my view, Van Til's analysis of the history of non-Christian thought in terms of rationalism and irrationalism, together with its theological justification, is one of his best accomplishments. It is scripturally based in its accurate account of the Christian worldview and the unbeliever's negation of it. It is confirmed by analysis of the secular texts themselves. And it gives to the Christian a wonderful insight into the structure and dynamics of intellectual movements.[12] This insight is immensely important both to the task of interpretation and to the work of apologetics.

Van Til's analysis provides a good perspective from which to understand the twists and turns of the history of thought. Every several years, one hears the claim that contemporary thought has become radically different from anything that has gone before. The latest claim of this sort is made for "postmodernism." We are told that thirty years ago or so, our culture rejected the rationalistic assumptions of the Enlightenment and came to recognize that "linear, scientific, objective" thinking is largely an expression of bias. Therefore, contemporary postmodern thought rejects all the assurances of the past and opens itself up to various non-Western, nonlinear influences, such as Eastern religions, occultism, and so on. It "deconstructs" language to lay bare its essential use—not as a means of rational communication from one mind to another, but as a means of social power, to control and oppress.

When the molders of opinion announce such radical changes in the intellectual climate, Christians often wonder how they can deal with this new challenge to their faith. Evangelical leaders argue that some utterly new approach is needed. Christians need to prepare for dialogue by reading all the new literature, seeing all the new plays, listening to all the new music, and so on.

Van Til always endorsed the idea that Christians, or at least the apologists among them, should be well informed as to what is going

---

up the temporal categories as the ultimate standard of interpretation" (SCE, 114). Idealism is "built upon the same Kantian presuppositions" (SCE, viii).

[11]See NM, CB, and TG.

[12]These ideas can be fruitfully applied to disciplines other than philosophy. Cf. Rousas Rushdoony on politics in JA, 339–48, and the various essays on mathematics,

on in the intellectual and cultural world. But he also comforted us by saying that there is no need to panic. Were he alive today, he would say that the "new thinking" of our time is really nothing drastically different from what has been going on since the Garden of Eden. Essentially, it is rationalism and irrationalism. The latest contemporary ideas are essentially no different from those of the ancient Greeks, the modern rationalists and empiricists, Kant, Hegel, and the others. Postmodernism, insofar as it is really a change from what has gone before, is a shift from a rationalistic to an irrationalistic impulse. Its rejection of "linear objectivity" is something we have seen before, among the Greek Sophists, in Hume's critique of objectivity, in Kant's critique of metaphysics, and in Hegel's attempt to achieve truth through negation and synthesis.

In this respect, Van Til's analysis of the history of philosophy is more accurate, and, I think, more profound, than that of his student Francis Schaeffer, though there is much profitable teaching in Schaeffer's thought (see chap. 28). Schaeffer argues that the Greek philosophers believed in objective truth, and that that conviction pervaded Western philosophy until the coming of Hegel, who taught that truth and falsity could somehow be combined dialectically to achieve a supralogical level of insight. After that, says Schaeffer, Western culture "escaped from reason," despairing of ever discovering "true truth."[13]

Van Til, on the contrary, finds the Greeks just as irrationalistic as the moderns. The Sophists' "man is the measure," Heraclitus's "everything flows," Plato's "realm of opinion," Aristotle's "prime matter," the Gnostic realm of error—all are, to Van Til, classic statements of the irrationalist impulse—which, to be sure, was combined in their thought with the rationalist impulse. But, says Van Til, even Greek rationalism did not possess the sort of objectivity that Christians should applaud. Greek rationalism was based on human autonomy, and therefore on empty concepts rather than the riches of divine revelation.

Unlike Schaeffer, therefore, Van Til did not commend the objectivity of the Greeks; nor did he see some drastic shift to irrationalism in the philosophy of Hegel. Plato was both a rationalist and an

---

education, psychology, history, economics, etc., in G. North, ed., *Foundations of Christian Scholarship* (Vallecito, Calif.: Ross House Books, 1976).

[13]Schaeffer, *The God Who Is There* (Downers Grove, Ill.: Inter-Varsity Press, 1968), 1–29.

irrationalist, and so was Hegel. The differences between the two were differences in detail and historical perspective, not differences in underlying commitment.

Van Til, therefore, gives us the courage to take "cultural seachange" in stride, not to be terrified by every new ideology that comes down the pike. In a fundamental sense, there is nothing new under the sun. And students who learn their apologetics from Van Til, if they learn it well, will be prepared for the next development when it comes; they will not have to learn their apologetics all over again.

My only caveat is that we should avoid using this analysis in a wooden way, insensitive to the diversity among non-Christian thinkers. Nor should we assume that everything in non-Christian thought can be exhaustively explained by the rationalist-irrationalist dialectic. Once we are aware of this apologetic tool, we may be tempted to mechanically categorize everything in a philosopher's thought as either rationalism or irrationalism. But some assertions by unbelievers may have a different character entirely. As Van Til notes in his more moderate formulations, unbelievers do sometimes discover and acknowledge truth "in spite of themselves." We must not routinely reject everything they say. Rather, we must be sensitive to distinguish between the ideas they have learned from God's revelation and the ideas they are using to suppress that revelation.

Indeed, there is a certain complication here: a thinker's words often reflect both revelational insight and suppression of the truth at the same time. When Plato says that the real world is rationally apprehensible, he is expressing revealed truth. The world is rationally knowable, first to God, then to us by revelation. But he is at the same time expressing his own rational autonomy, for the process of rational apprehension to Plato is far different from that of biblical analogical thinking. It would be wrong to disagree with Plato merely because he is an unbeliever; to do so would be an instance of the genetic fallacy, i.e., judging something on the basis of its origin. On the other hand, it would be equally wrong to think that this statement in no way expresses Plato's suppression of the truth.

As we saw in chapter 15, Van Til does acknowledge that unbelievers have insight, even though at times his extreme formulations of the antithesis and his exaggeration of the predictability of non-Christian thought come dangerously close to the genetic fallacy. On the whole, however, his rationalist-irrationalist analysis of non-Christian thought is a powerful apologetic tool.

PART FOUR

The Argument for Christianity

CHAPTER EIGHTEEN

The Traditional Method: The Church Fathers

Up to this point, we have discussed Van Til's theology, rather than his specifically apologetic teaching. That we could spend so much time in this area—profitably, I hope—vindicates the provisional judgment I made twenty years ago in *Van Til: The Theologian* concerning the significance of Van Til as a *theologian*. Thus, I have subtitled this volume "An Analysis of His *Thought*" rather than "An Analysis of His *Apologetic*."

And, of course, Van Til's thought is of such a nature that the first priority for any interpreter is to get the theology straight. Van Til's apologetic is thoroughly determined by his theological commitments. Indeed, he believed that the most important and distinctive aspect of his apologetics was its consistency with Reformed theology.

We must now move on to his ideas about "apologetics proper." Knowing what we do about the metaphysics and ethics of knowledge, how should a Christian approach a non-Christian to bear witness for Christ? In chapters 22 and 23, I shall discuss that question directly. In this chapter and the following three, we shall consider Van Til's view of how *not* to do it—what he calls "the traditional method."

Van Til explains the traditional method by describing the history of apologetics. That history itself, in his estimation, contains both good and bad elements. But the apologetic method that came to prevail in the church was, he believes, a compromise between Christian and non-Christian principles of reasoning.

That compromise began, according to Van Til, in the thinking of the earliest church fathers:

> Here then we have these two facts, together constituting two aspects of one fact (a) the charge of rationalism and determinism lodged against the church Fathers was answered by means of the non-Christian idea of indeterminism, and (b) the charge of indeterminism lodged against them was answered by means of the non-Christian idea of determinism. They confused the Greek notion of determinism, or system, with the Christian idea of God's control of all things, which is the Christian system. Again they identified the non-Christian idea of indeterminism, namely, that of free will or human autonomy with the Christian idea of man's being a responsible creature of God.[1]

Let me state at the outset my thesis about Van Til's analysis of the history of apologetics. (1) He rightly finds unscriptural elements in the theologies of the various apologists. (2) He shows that their apologetics could have been stronger if it had been fortified with a self-consciously presuppositional epistemology. (3) However, he does not succeed in showing how these deficiencies invalidate the arguments that the apologists have actually used. Of course, those arguments may be unsound for other reasons. But Van Til is not successful at connecting problems (1) and (2) with the actual apologetic arguments.

Clement, Justin, Athenagoras

First, we shall look at Van Til's critique of the apologetics of the early church fathers. Regarding Clement of Rome, he says this:

> But when he wants to present Christ and the resurrection to unbelievers he seeks to win them by showing that they need

[1]CTK, 75. Compare also on these matters the more elaborate discussion of the history of apologetics in CC.

> not accept a new principle of continuity at all when they come to Christ. Is not the resurrection of Christ easy to believe? Every spring all of us witness the resurrection of a new season. Is it not easy to believe in our own future resurrection! Surely, you have heard of that bird Phoenix. It rises repeatedly from the dead.[2]

Justin Martyr, in the second century, confuses the biblical God with Plato's "nameless one" and adopts the Greek view of freedom as human autonomy. He confuses Christ with the Greek Logos, that impersonal principle of rationality present in the world and in the human mind.[3]

Athenagoras, roughly contemporary with Justin, confuses a Christian with a non-Christian concept of possibility:

> In his brief treatise *On the Resurrection* Athenagoras argues that since God has created all things it should not be impossible for him to raise men from the dead. This is in itself true. But Athenagoras did not realize that, according to the views of Plato and others, God did not create all things. He apparently did not appreciate the fact that when he argued for the possibility of the resurrection in terms of the philosophy of his opponents he himself was no longer true to his own position.[4]

Van Til is right to say that there was compromise in the apologetics of the second century. Justin in particular adopted forced interpretations both of Scripture and of Plato in order to make them agree with one another. And these men certainly did endorse nonbiblical Greek ideas, particularly the "nameless God" and human autonomy.

However, Van Til is less cogent when he is dealing with more practical, less philosophical, forms of apologetics. The phoenix aside, is Clement really wrong to say that various phenomena in creation are similar to the Resurrection in some way? To be sure, the resurrection of Christ is a unique event compared to the coming of spring, but

---

[2]Ibid., 76.
[3]Ibid., 78–79.
[4]Ibid., 79–80.

do not those events have something in common?[5] The coming of spring is a provision of the Noahic covenant (Gen. 8:22), which symbolizes the postponement of divine judgment, the replacement of death with newness of life. Does not the coming of spring in that way anticipate the Resurrection?

Furthermore, Clement, on Van Til's account, is in effect charging unbelievers with inconsistency. They acknowledge, however superstitiously, the resurrection of the phoenix. But they dogmatically refuse to accord such credibility to the report of Jesus' resurrection. Is it not right to challenge this failure of logic? As we shall see, Van Til himself tells us to adopt the presuppositions of unbelievers "for the sake of argument" in order to show that those presuppositions reduce to absurdity. Surely Clement, implicitly, is doing that very thing. Is it necessary to do this explicitly rather than implicitly? Perhaps that is what Van Til wants to say, but I don't know how he would argue for it.

Of course, it is not "easy" for a non-Christian to believe in the Resurrection. If Clement really thought it was, he was wrong.[6] The unbeliever cannot come to the truth on his own; only supernatural regeneration will suffice. But it *ought* to be easy—because, as Van Til tells us, the non-Christian way of assessing the evidence self-destructs upon examination. Insofar as Clement shows that self-destructiveness of unbelief, he does indeed indicate that inherently easy way to the truth.

I do not doubt that Stoic moralism has influenced Clement's letter. It shows a higher regard for pagan virtue than the New Testament warrants.[7] (Recall, however, Van Til's own statements

---

[5]Nothing is absolutely unique. Absolute uniqueness would be "ultimate matter," totally beyond any conceptualization or description, and therefore equivalent to nothingness. Even God's nature is not unique in such a way that it cannot be truly presented in nature and special revelation. On the other hand, everything is relatively unique, in the sense that nothing is identical to anything else. On a Van Tillian, Trinitarian metaphysic, identity and uniqueness are limiting concepts of one another, neither found without the other.

[6]The accuracy of Van Til's interpretation of these thinkers is another area deserving critical analysis. I have a few questions in this area, but not very many. In general, Van Til seems to understand the historical texts well. In any case, I shall for the most part set aside that range of problems and leave them to people more expert than I in the history of Christian thought. My problems are more along these lines: granted the general accuracy of Van Til's paraphrases and interpretations, are his criticisms fair?

[7]CTK, 77; cf. CC, 1:1, p. 21.

about the "lofty ethics of idealism."[8]) It is not obvious, however, that the logic of Clement's actual argument is invalidated by Stoic influence. Van Til, I think, often confuses the issue of influence with the issue of validity. That confusion is sometimes called the genetic fallacy, namely, evaluating the truth of a statement on the basis of the factors influencing a person to make it. Certainly the presence of bad influences upon an apologist can legitimately arouse our suspicions about his work. But bad influences do not in themselves invalidate an apologetic argument. For example, idealist philosophy is undoubtedly an influence upon Van Til. But that influence in itself does not invalidate any of Van Til's positions. The same could be said even if Van Til had adopted some idealist positions inconsistent with Scripture,[9] for the presence of some error would not invalidate everything else in his thought.

Van Til's critique of Athenagoras is even more debatable. Note his admission that Athenagoras's argument about the Resurrection is "in itself true." If God created all things, he can also raise the dead. So why was it wrong for Athenagoras to use that argument? Van Til's reply is that non-Christians deny the premise. They do not believe in Creation. But that is an odd point for Van Til to make. Does not Van Til himself urge us not to be intimidated by the unbeliever's denials? Does he not urge us to argue on Christian presuppositions, whether or not the unbeliever accepts them?

Perhaps Van Til's point is that Athenagoras's argument was not well contextualized—that it did not effectively address the intellectuals of the time. It would have been more effective, for example, if he had, like Van Til, developed an internal critique of the Greek form-matter scheme. Well, perhaps, but we do not know that Athenagoras had such a sophisticated audience in mind. Certainly, at a practical level there can be no legitimate Van Tillian objection to pointing out that if one grants the Christian doctrine of creation, one should have no trouble with the possibility of resurrection. And Athenagoras's argument can also be used to make a more sophisticated point: as Van Til would put it, we can ask the unbeliever to consider the Christian presupposition (creation) "for the sake of argument" and show him that, granted that presupposition, the doctrine of resurrection is consistent.

---

[8]CTETH, 59; DF2, 63.

[9]In my opinion, that did not happen.

In any case, Van Til does not seem here to be accusing Athenagoras of bad strategy or poor contextualization. (In general, Van Til had very little interest in such questions.) Rather, he is accusing Athenagoras of compromise. He says that Athenagoras was arguing for the Resurrection "in terms of the philosophy of his opponents." But how was he doing that? Van Til gives no quotation or reference that would suggest such a critique. From his paraphrase of Athenagoras's argument, precisely the opposite conclusion follows: Athenagoras is arguing for the Resurrection in terms of the *Christian* philosophy of creation.

What Van Til seems to be saying is that since Athenagoras fails to distinguish explicitly between the Christian and the non-Christian views of possibility (a sin of omission), he has in effect conceded the non-Christian view (a sin of commission), even though he explicitly tells us otherwise.

I confess that I am not persuaded by this kind of critique. It seems to assume that the apologist must always make an explicit distinction between Christian and non-Christian epistemology as part of his apologetic witness. Without such a distinction, Van Til implies, any otherwise true statements and valid arguments are worthless and constitute compromise. My own view is that such distinctions are often helpful and important, but not for every audience or in every situation. If somebody asks me whether the Resurrection is possible, I think it best to respond exactly as Athenagoras does. That may be sufficient, since many people today are willing to concede the doctrine of Creation, either because they are Christians or because they acknowledge Creation "in spite of themselves," using "borrowed capital," etc. If, then, the inquirer informs me that he does not believe in Creation, then the discussion will shift to that topic. But I see no need of answering, say, the question of a twelve-year-old child with a philosophical distinction between Christian and non-Christian epistemology.

Van Til would certainly agree that the presentations of God's truth in Scripture itself are adequately "presuppositional." It always challenges unbelief at the most fundamental level. But Scripture never distinguishes between believing and unbelieving systems of thought in any technical way, and it often presents its message without any explicit distinction between them. For example, Jesus did nothing of the kind with the woman of Samaria, yet he powerfully convicted her of sin and of his messiahship.

Irenaeus and Tertullian

In his survey of the church fathers, Van Til goes on to discuss Irenaeus and Tertullian, fathers from the later second century whose chief opponent was Gnosticism. He deals primarily with the theological views of these men, views that were in some degree influenced by Greek philosophy. Irenaeus and Tertullian did, in Van Til's analysis, make progress toward more scriptural views in some matters, even in epistemology (i.e., Irenaeus's emphasis on the canon of Scripture and Tertullian's opposition between Athens and Jerusalem). But they also compromised with some non-Christian philosophical conceptions: autonomous freedom, wholly other deity, and Logos speculation.

Van Til says nothing in *Christianity in Conflict* and very little in *A Christian Theory of Knowledge* about Irenaeus's actual arguments against Gnosticism. A few of them, as he describes them, sound very Van Tillian. Irenaeus, for example, asks the Gnostics whether the philosophers from whom they get their speculations know or do not know the truth. If they know the truth without Christ, then there is no need of Christ; if they do not know it, then why do the Gnostics claim that their speculations are true?[10] That certainly sounds like Van Til's argument that autonomous philosophy is a hopelessly inadequate basis for knowledge of God. Irenaeus, in effect, confronts the Gnostics with the "paradox of the wholly omniscient and the wholly ignorant," otherwise known as the rationalist-irrationalist dialectic.

In a similar way, Irenaeus attacks the Platonic doctrine of reminiscence. Since Plato is in the body, and therefore, according to his own philosophy, "in a state of oblivion," how can he know about a state of knowledge preceding that oblivion?[11] Here Van Til might have credited Irenaeus with recognizing the rationalist-irrationalist dialectic in Plato. Platonic philosophies destroy human knowledge, but they make pretentious claims to know absolute truth. But Van Til's conclusion is that Irenaeus thought of "a general theism maintained by many men who are not Christians and of Christianity as something that is added to this general theism."[12]

For one thing, the charge of "general theism" does not seem to arise out of the arguments of Irenaeus that Van Til cites. Rather, in

---

[10]CTK, 80–81.
[11]Ibid., 81.
[12]Ibid.

those cases Irenaeus emphasizes the sharp distinction between the Christian and the non-Christian positions. Nor is it clear how advocacy of general theism would discredit the arguments mentioned above.

But is it necesarily wrong to maintain a general theism to which Christianity is "added"? As for general theism, in chapter 14 I discussed Van Til's rule that we may not prove "that" God exists apart from establishing "what" he is. I argued that there is some truth in that distinction, but that it should be seen as a matter of degree rather than a black-and-white issue, for we can have different degrees of knowledge as to what God is, and we can never know that exhaustively. The question of whether we are permitted to argue for a general theism is essentially the same issue in different words. In both cases, the question is, *How much* of the biblical doctrine of God must be proved by our argument?

As for supplementation, Van Til teaches, as we have seen, that all men know the true God through natural revelation, to which special revelation adds supplementary content. In that sense, the model of supplementing general theism accords perfectly with Van Til's own view. His point, of course, is that the unbeliever suppresses the truth and exchanges it for his own lies; accordingly, Greek theism is anti-Christian, not a foundation for a Christian supplement. But we have seen that Van Til also qualifies his view of suppression. He does not claim that every statement of the unbeliever is simply wrong. Is it not possible that Plato or some other philosopher might have uttered statements in accord with Scripture, which an enterprising apologist might employ as a basis for establishing further Christian truth? If so, in such a case the Christian would indeed be supplementing the non-Christian's ideas.

Now, as a matter of fact, I agree with Van Til that Irenaeus and other church fathers overestimated the theism of the Greeks. Their equation of Greek ideas with biblical truth was indeed extremely misleading. But I am concerned for the moment with the formal question, Is it always wrong for an apologist to think in terms of supplementing a non-Christian's ideas? Certainly in everyday, practical situations we do that all the time. An unbeliever objects to a God who foreordains all things, thinking that such an idea destroys human dignity. We reply by supplementing his understanding of predestination. He is right that God foreordains all things; but he needs to know more about second causes, the nature of human responsibility, and the meaninglessness of free will in a universe of pure chance. Of course, in such a conversation the apologist is not merely supplementing the unbeliever's knowledge; he is also rebuking unbelief and demanding comprehensive rethinking. But, among other things, he is offering a supplement. And such supplementation can often be effective.

Irenaeus does, of course, teach the Logos theology, which was common among the church fathers, in which the Logos, the Son of God, is the divine reason found in all men.[13] I would agree with Van Til that this construction is unscriptural. Van Til's critique is correct, but he has not demonstrated that Irenaeus's theological errors invalidate his arguments against the Gnostics.

Van Til's critique of Tertullian is similar. Tertullian, despite seeing a radical opposition between Athens and Jerusalem, nevertheless believed that the heathen had knowledge of God and his law similar to Christian knowledge. Van Til says:

> The basic difficulty with the apologetic of Tertullian at this point is that he does not realize that the "truths" recognized by the heathen are "truths" by which they seek to suppress the truth about themselves and the world. Tertullian seeks largely to connect Christian thought with heathen thought; there is, to him, a great difference between paganism and Christianity, but the difference remains one of gradation rather than of contrast.[14]

Well, there is a difference of gradation between the kitchen sink and the Pacific Ocean, but there is certainly contrast between them as well. Gradation and contrast are not always opposed. But, more seriously, Van Til's argument here seems to assume his extreme formulations of antithesis, that is, that everything the unbeliever says must be opposed. Otherwise, one could well imagine, as in our discussion of Irenaeus, an apologist taking statements of unbelievers and supplementing them to present the gospel.

Indeed, Van Til's own arguments against unbelief can often be construed as supplementation. For example, at one point he applauds the growing interest in child psychology in secular circles, and he

[13] Ibid., 82.
[14] Ibid., 89.

commends the growing understanding in these circles that the child is not merely a miniature adult, but has his own distinctive psychology. Van Til then remarks that these insights could have been presented "in the interest of Christian theism."[15] Modern psychology is also interested in the unconscious. Even this emphasis "has good elements in it."[16] Of course, he goes on to show that the psychologists use these insights to suppress the truth, to argue that impersonal developmental patterns, not the God of Scripture, govern human psychology. But his argument certainly employs, in a broad sense, supplementation: secular psychologists have certain insights, but they lack the knowledge of God to enable them to use these insights correctly.

Perhaps the real point Van Til wishes to make is that something more than supplementation is necessary—that supplementation must be supplemented! We must not only supplement the unbeliever's knowledge, but also distinguish his presuppositions from ours and attack his at the most fundamental level. That is to say, the church fathers are guilty of sins of omission (alongside their theological errors).

I agree with Van Til that the early apologists would have given a stronger witness if they had engaged in such presuppositional reasoning in a more systematic way. But it is not that they never did this. Irenaeus's arguments against the Gnostics and Tertullian's contrast of Athens and Jerusalem, I believe, strike at the presuppositions of unbelief at a fundamental level. But, of course, Irenaeus and Tertullian were not Van Til. They did not work out a thorough, distinctively Christian epistemology.

That epistemology, as Van Til developed it, is immensely important. But, as I have said before, not every apologetic situation requires explicit discussion of epistemological antithesis. That depends on the nature of the encounter, the sophistication of the inquirer, the particular questions asked, etc.

Granted the sophistication of their opponents, and the nature of the questions at issue, Irenaeus and Tertullian would have been better off to argue in a more Van Tillian way. Certainly, their actual theology should have been more in accord with Scripture. But even beyond that, their apologetic should also have been more presuppositional. However, it is not wrong for someone to present Christianity as a

---

[15]CTEV, 114.

[16]Ibid., 116.

supplement to the ideas of an inquirer, nor must every apologetic encounter deal with epistemological presuppositions and antithesis. The problem with the apologetic of these church fathers was rather that their arguments were inadequately contextualized; that is, they were inadequate for their Gnostic audience.

Van Til, in my opinion, often confuses issues of practice with issues of apologetic theory. He rarely deals specifically with the former. If he did, he might admit more flexibility in the nature of apologetic witness than he appears to allow in this sort of context.

In conclusion, Van Til is correct to point out unscriptural elements in the theology of these men and to criticize them for inadequately confronting the unbelief of their time.[17] However, in making these valid criticisms, he invokes questionable principles that presuppose an extreme, rather than a nuanced, view of antithesis. At points he appears to insist that attacks on unbelieving presuppositions must be explicit rather than implicit. That approach seems to me to be unfair and unwarranted by Van Til's overall presuppositional methodology.

Augustine

I will pass over Van Til's discussion of the Alexandrian fathers, Clement and Origen. They had almost no sense of antithesis between Christian and non-Christian principles of knowledge, and I agree with Van Til's negative evaluation of their contribution to apologetics.

Augustine, however, the great fourth- and fifth-century Christian thinker (354–430), is another matter. In Van Til's view (and mine), Augustine made great progress in understanding the biblical doctrines of the Trinity, of salvation by grace, and of God's sovereign election. Van Til also rightly credits Augustine with a more fully personalist view of our relation to God and with an "antithetical" view of history in his *City of God*.[18]

However, some elements of Augustine's thought were not biblical: his derivation of evil from the "slenderness of being" in the human will, and his understanding of the authority of the church hierarchy.[19]

---

[17]I have no doubt that the second problem arises out of the first, as Van Til says.

[18]CTK, 135–42.

[19]Ibid., 132–35.

But our concern is with epistemology and apologetics. In these areas, his most influential writings come from his earlier years, when he was still somewhat under the influence of Neoplatonism. Van Til finds in these writings elements of rationalism and irrationalism:

> In his early writings, Augustine was largely rationalistic in his defense of theism and largely irrationalistic in his defense of Christianity. . . . That is to say, he tended in this direction. Throughout his argument both for theism and for Christianity there appears a tendency to reason in a better way, a way that is more in accord with his own final theology. But then he had not yet worked out his final theology and it could hardly be expected that he should, therefore, at once be able to work out a true method of apologetics.[20]

Van Til finds rationalism in Augustine's defense of theism: "Augustine seems to think that a true theism is found among the Greeks and that he can use the arguments given for the defense of theism as these have been worked out by the philosophers."[21] Like Irenaeus, Augustine defends a "bare theism,"[22] which he believes Christians hold in common with Greek philosophers. The theistic argument of Augustine that Van Til discusses is the argument from the imperishability of truth: "If truth perishes, it is still true that truth perishes and so truth still exists."[23] Ultimate truth, that which provides the criterion[24] for all knowledge, must be eternal and imperishable. But eternal truth must lodge in an eternal mind, and so God exists.

This argument is essentially Platonic, and I would not recommend its use by Christian apologists without considerable elaboration. Plato held that truth was eternal, but as an abstract form. Augustine uses the same argumentation as Plato to prove the existence of a personal God. But is it therefore wrong for Augustine to do so, as Van Til argues?

Again, it is insufficient to rebut Augustine's argument merely by pointing out that he got it from Plato. As we have seen, Van Til him-

---

[20]Ibid., 118–19.
[21]Ibid., 119.
[22]Ibid., 120.
[23]Ibid., 123.
[24]Ibid., 120.

self did not claim that everything in Plato was incorrect. To argue that Platonic origin in itself invalidates Augustine's reasoning is an obvious example of the genetic fallacy.

So the question is, Does Augustine's argument work, given biblical presuppositions? Or does that argument necessarily presuppose a Platonic view of truth as an abstract form? Well, the premise that truth is necessarily eternal is certainly biblical. On a Christian worldview, it is surely impossible that truth should perish. If truth were to perish, the result would be chaos, irrationality, or nonbeing, not the world that God created. And indeed, as Plato said, it is contradictory to assert as truth that there is no truth.

Does the imperishability of truth imply the existence of God, granted Christian presuppositions? Yes it does, for, as Van Til emphasizes, without God there could be no intelligible predication.

No doubt Augustine can be faulted for being inadequately critical of Plato's overall epistemology and for failing to place the scriptural view more sharply over against Plato's. But do those failings invalidate the argument that he actually presented? The worst we can say about Augustine, I think, is that he formulated his argument in a way that may have misled readers to overestimate the common ground between Christianity and Platonism. But we cannot, I think, fault him for using the argument he used.

Van Til finds irrationalism in Augustine's view that signs and words cannot communicate truth unless that truth is already innate.[25] Of course, as Van Til points out, the Platonic doctrine that all knowledge is innate might also be cited as evidence of rationalism. In any case, in Van Til's view, Augustine is skeptical about sense experience and human communication, in order to be rationalistic about innate knowledge.[26] Thus, says Van Til, "It is this intellectualism, involved in a Platonic type of *a priori*, that requires for its correlative the idea of brute factuality."[27] But, says Van Til, if that view were carried out consistently, it would require the denial of historical truth. The events of history would have no significance except to remind us of what we know already. That view would be manifestly unbiblical.

---

[25]Ibid., 125–27.

[26]The reader may notice a convergence between these views of Augustine and those of Gordon H. Clark. I suspect that the similarity of Augustine's views to Clark's may have prejudiced Van Til somewhat against Augustine (see chap. 8).

[27]Ibid., 127.

This skepticism about sense experience and language also makes it necessary for human beings to gain their religious knowledge from authority. Our finitude makes us ignorant, and so we must seek the truth from those who know it. We must seek our expert authority within the Christian church, because "there are more Christians, than if the Jews and idolators be added together."[28] Among the Christians, we must turn to the teachers of the Catholic Church, since they are generally agreed to be most expert. Rightly, Van Til indicates that Augustine's view here is closer to a Roman Catholic than to a Protestant view of authority.

On these matters I am inclined to agree with Van Til. In Scripture, knowledge of the gospel of salvation is good news. It is learned through Word and Spirit, not through innate knowledge. And Augustine's argument about seeking out the views of the most prestigious teachers within the most numerous religion is rather ludicrous. On that basis, we would today have to direct inquirers to secularist authorities. But Scripture does not warrant the view that the majority is always right—quite the contrary.

Certainly, Augustine's epistemology is defective in these areas. But it is not clear to me what all of this has to do with apologetic method. I doubt that Augustine ever replied to inquirers merely by telling them to consult their innate knowledge or to look up their local priest. He presented arguments, as we have seen. And he would have advised the local priests to present arguments, not merely to pontificate. And those arguments, as his writings indicate, were of various kinds—philosophical, historical, biblical, logical. To evaluate Augustine's actual apologetic, we must evaluate those arguments, not merely his epistemology. It will not do to say that epistemological errors must produce bad arguments. To say that is to assume that in every apologist there is a perfect consistency between his epistemological theory and the arguments he employs. It is also to assume that every epistemological error logically requires the use of a bad argument. Those assumptions are false. We must, therefore, evaluate epistemologies and apologetic argumentation somewhat independently.

In any case, Van Til's discussion does not show that Augustine's epistemological errors contaminate his actual apologetic. In discussing Augustine's "rationalism," Van Til cites an argument that he thinks

[28]Ibid., 133.

is invalidated by that rationalism. I have given reasons for rejecting that evaluation. In discussing Augustine's "irrationalism," Van Til cites no serious arguments at all that are invalidated by the epistemological error. (I do not consider the appeal to numbers and to the Catholic authorities a serious argument.) Therefore, I am not persuaded by Van Til's contention that Augustine employed, in his early years, a defective apologetic method.

My conclusion is that although the church fathers made some serious theological errors, Van Til has not proved that they employed a particular apologetic method that Christians must reject in toto. Many of their actual arguments, however influenced by pagan thought, are quite consistent with Christian presuppositions. Van Til is right, however, to point out that the church fathers could have made a more powerful case for Christianity had they been more self-conscious and more articulate about the radical differences between Christian and non-Christian thought.

CHAPTER NINETEEN

The Traditional Method: Thomas Aquinas

In the previous chapter, we began to look at Van Til's account of the traditional method in apologetics, over against which he has developed his alternative method. Van Til's critique of the church fathers, in summary, is that their theological errors invalidated their apologetic methods and arguments. Although I agree with Van Til's theological evaluations, he has not persuaded me that their theological errors generally discredit their apologetic reasoning. At most, he has shown a significant error of omission in their apologetic work: a failure to attack explicitly and systematically the fundamental epistemological presuppositions of non-Christian thought.

That omission is significant. But it does not entirely discredit their apologetic effort. Although they did not attack unbelieving presuppositions explicitly and systematically, they did so implicitly and unsystematically. Many of their specific arguments are insightful and worthy of our emulation.

But we must follow further Van Til's critical analysis of the history of apologetics, for we have not yet discussed the most influential figures in that history. Van Til often refers to the traditional method of apologetics as the Aquinas-Butler approach, so we should give special attention to Van Til's discussions of Thomas Aquinas (1225–74) and Joseph Butler (1692–1752). In this chapter we shall look at the former figure.

Thomas Aquinas was a brilliant Dominican theologian, who, in his short lifetime, wrote several bookshelves full of highly technical, densely written, often profound treatises. He was canonized by the Roman Catholic Church, and his philosophy has been recognized as the official philosophy of Roman Catholicism. His views continue to carry great weight today, in both Catholic and Protestant circles.

Like other medieval theologians, Aquinas was under the influence of Neoplatonism, especially through the writings of Pseudo-Dionysius. What is new in Aquinas, compared to his predecessors, however, is a pervasive use of Aristotelian philosophy. New editions and translations of Aristotle in Aquinas's time had caused a substantial problem for the church, for Aristotle denied temporal Creation, God's knowledge of and love for the world, and other elements of biblical theism. Aquinas argued that Aristotle's thought should not simply be dismissed, nor its study forbidden; rather, his philosophy could provide major assistance in the development of a Christian philosophy and theology.

Van Til criticizes both the Neoplatonic and the Aristotelian elements of Aquinas's theology. According to Neoplatonism, there is a chain of being from God at the top to the material world at the bottom, and a continuum of beings between them. In these respects, there are many formal parallels between Neoplatonism and Gnosticism, although the two movements differ greatly in mood and style. Neoplatonism is pantheistic in its teaching that all reality is an "emanation" of God, but deistic in its view that God is somehow "wholly other" than any of his emanations. Van Til equates the tension between pantheism and deism with the rationalist-irrationalist dialectic. The union between God and his emanations amounts to rationalism: the identity of the human mind with the divine. The separation between God and the world implies irrationalism: the ignorance of finite minds, their utter incapacity to know God.[1]

Aristotle's God was the prime mover of the universe, but not its Creator in the biblical sense. For Aristotle, the world has existed eternally, without any beginning in time. Yet every sequence of causes, through every period of time, has its beginning in God. God is pure form, the only being in the universe in whom form exists apart from

[1]Van Til's most elaborate discussion of these matters is in CC, 2:1, 2:2, pp. 1–15.

matter. Because he is pure form, he cannot interact with the material objects of our world. He does not know them or love them. How does he cause them to move? They move as they long after him, but he does not know they are longing after him. He can think of nothing but himself, and then only of his own thought: thought thinking itself. In Van Til's view, Aristotle's philosophical deduction (apart from revelation) of pure thought, the ultimate cause of all events, is rationalistic. But in the end Aristotle's God is ignorant of the world of matter, a world that is essentially unstructured, unformed, and therefore chaotic; thus Aristotle is also irrationalistic.[2] The "pure thought" of Aristotle's God is, in Van Til's analysis, an "empty universal," having no content except itself. Aristotle's "prime matter" is Van Til's chief example of brute fact.

Now Van Til recognizes that Aquinas is neither a pure Neoplatonist nor a pure Aristotelian. Indeed, much of Aquinas's thought is governed by Scripture. But Van Til believes that Aquinas's theology and his apologetics are fatally flawed by his compromises with these non-Christian philosophies. In this chapter, we shall discuss Van Til's view of Aquinas's argument for the existence of God. In chapter 25, we shall discuss more broadly the Scholastic synthesis between Christianity and Greek philosophy.

Aquinas "begins his identification of God . . . by means of the natural reason."[3] "Natural reason" is reason operating without the assistance of divine revelation. In practice, for Aquinas, it is equivalent to the reasoning of the Greek philosophers, particularly Aristotle. According to Van Til, this approach is flawed:

> So then Thomas thinks he has the right to argue from effect to cause without first inquiring into the differences in meaning between the idea of cause when used by Christians and the idea of cause when used by those who do not take the Christian position.
>
> And it is this uncritical assumption that vitiates the entire argument for the existence of God that he offers, and in fact vitiates his approach to every other problem in philosophy and in theology.[4]

---

[2]Ibid.
[3]CTK, 169.
[4]Ibid., 173.

How does Aristotle's concept of cause differ from the Christian concept? Van Til says, "For Aristotle the idea of cause is not that of production. It is rather that of a principle of explanation."[5] Therefore, for Aristotle, the fact that God is "first mover" does not mean that he created the world. Nor is Aristotle's God personal or self-conscious. "He" is really an abstract principle, correlative with pure chance. Such a being is not the self-contained, self-attesting God of Scripture. Therefore, when Aquinas seeks to prove the existence of God as first cause and first mover, he proves, if anything, the existence of a God other than the God of Scripture. Van Til continues:

> All this is not to say that as a Christian theologian Thomas does not hold in some sense to Christian teaching. It is to say that the natural theology as worked out by him fits in with the natural theology of the official documents of the Roman Catholic church and is, therefore, inherently inimical to the Protestant idea of Scripture.[6]

Etienne Gilson, the great Roman Catholic scholar and defender of Aquinas, argues a sharply different view of the relation between Greek philosophy and Christianity:

> For my part I see no contradiction between the principles laid down by the Greek thinkers of the classical period and the conclusions which the Christian thinkers drew out of them. . . . If medieval thought succeeded in bringing Greek thought to its point of perfection it was at once because Greek thought was already true, and because Christian thought, in virtue of its very Christianity, had the power of making it still more so.[7]

To Gilson, the basic relation of Christianity to Greek philosophy is that Christianity supplements and corrects Greek thought by adding deeper insight to it. Certainly there are occasions on which the Christian must simply deny a Greek idea, such as Aristotle's view of

---

[5]Ibid.

[6]Ibid., 175.

[7]Etienne Gilson, *The Spirit of Medieval Philosophy* (New York: Scribner's, 1936), 81–82. Van Til interacts with Gilson in some detail in CC, 2:2.

the eternity of the world. But there are also important truths in Greek thought that the Christian should recognize and build upon.

Once we grant that there is both truth and falsity in Aristotle, the language of supplementation and correction has legitimate application. We supplement Aristotle's truth with Christian truth, and we correct his falsity with Christian truth. We saw in the previous chapter that Van Til does not like the language of supplementation in these contexts. Yet I do not believe he can reject that language altogether unless he is willing to claim that Aristotle's philosophy is literally false at every point. But that would be a view of extreme antithesis,[8] which, though cohering with some of Van Til's rhetoric, is contrary to his more careful and biblically accurate formulations.

So, the differences between Van Til and Gilson are a matter of degree. Still, I am inclined to side more with Van Til's pessimism than with Gilson's optimism about the value of Greek philosophy for Christian theology and apologetics. There can be no doubt but that Aristotle's God is far from the God of Scripture. Any supplementation of Aristotle to turn his God into the Christian God would have to be a drastic supplementation indeed.

But our main concern in this chapter is apologetic. And, therefore, the relevant question is whether the great difference between the worldviews of Aristotle and Scripture "vitiates the entire argument for the existence of God that [Aquinas] offers, and in fact vitiates his approach to every other problem in philosophy and in theology."[9]

For all his relative optimism, Gilson admits that the Greek thinkers did not believe in the Christian God.[10] And he admits that the philosophers were very far from holding distinctively Christian insights: "What Aristotle lacked in order to conceive creation was precisely the essential principle and starting-point."[11] Even the theistic proofs in Aristotle undergo profound changes in meaning when they enter Aquinas's system, according to Gilson.[12]

---

[8]See chap. 15.

[9]CTK, 173.

[10]*Spirit of Medieval Philosophy,* 44–48, 65, 111.

[11]Ibid., 68–69. For other "antithetical" language in Gilson, see pp. 74, 158, 332, 357.

[12]Ibid., 72; cf. pp. 76–77: "The Thomist proof . . . has a meaning altogether its own."

Van Til, then, believes that Aquinas's commitment to Greek philosophy vitiates his apologetic arguments. Gilson, rather, believes that Aquinas radically transforms the Aristotelian proofs under the influence of the Scriptures.

Aquinas's apologetic is chiefly known for its "five ways" of proving the existence of God. They are summarized briefly in his *Summa Theologica*. There are many other such arguments in his other writings. Of the five ways, the one that is most obviously influenced by Aristotle is the first, the proof from motion. Like Aristotle, Aquinas seeks to prove the existence of God as the "first mover." He uses the Aristotelian categories of "potentiality" and "actuality." Motion, he says, is change from potentiality to actuality. To use Aquinas's example, when something gets hot, it changes from being potentially hot to being actually hot. If something is only potentially hot, it can become actually hot only by some other cause that is itself actually hot. Since it cannot itself be both potentially and actually hot, it cannot warm itself. It must be warmed by something else, and that something must be warmed by something else, and so on. The sequence must begin somewhere; else, "then there would be no first mover, and, consequently, no other mover."[13] I think what this means is that without a first mover, the sequence would never have gotten underway—or, to put it differently, it would have no adequate explanation.

Now my purpose here is not to ask whether this proof is valid or sound. Many responses have been offered, pro and con. My only interest, for the moment, is to ask if there is anything in this argument that is incompatible with the Scriptures. In other words, I am asking whether Aquinas's commitment to Aristotle's philosophy, evident in this very proof, "vitiates" his apologetic at this particular point.

As we saw in earlier chapters, Van Til does believe that God's existence can be proved: "I do not reject 'the theistic proofs' but merely insist on formulating them in such a way as not to compromise the doctrines of Scripture."[14] On the other hand, "The fact that [Calvin] places all possible emphasis on the fact that man can know nothing unless he knows what he knows on the presupposition of the existence and revelation of the triune God of the Bible, is calculated to

[13]*Summa Theologica*, Question 2, Article 3. My source is *Basic Writings of St. Thomas Aquinas*, ed. Anton C. Pegis (New York: Random House, 1944), 1:22.

[14]DF2, 197.

destroy the proofs as historically formulated."[15] Doubtless, the phrase "as historically formulated" refers to the proofs of Aquinas and his successors.

Van Til's problem with the proofs is that "if followed out logically, they would have to lead to the notion of a finite God. Nothing else could be obtained from them for the reason that they were usually built upon the presupposition of the ultimacy of the human mind and the ultimacy of the facts which the mind meets in the world."[16] Therefore, "Instead of crying that God exists, as Hepp says they do, they cry that God, namely, the God of Christian theism, does not exist."[17]

To be more specific, "If you start with the ideas of cause and purpose as intelligible to man without God . . . then you cannot consistently say that you need God for the idea of cause and purpose."[18] Doubtless Van Til would say that in the argument we summarized above, Aquinas assumes that motion, potentiality, and actuality are "intelligible to man without God." He would probably claim as well that Aquinas in this proof is "presupposing the ultimacy of the human mind and the ultimacy of the facts which the mind meets in the world."

But is that criticism fair to Aquinas? Does he, first of all, assume that motion, potentiality, and actuality are "intelligible to man without God"? "Intelligible" is an ambiguous term. No doubt Aquinas does assume that the language of his proof is intelligible enough for fruitful communication. But surely any apologist, including Van Til, must make this assumption; otherwise, how could any apologetic be put into words? Van Til himself, as we have seen, grants that the unbeliever can understand intellectually the argument for Christianity. Therefore, both Van Til and Aquinas agree that a sound proof will be intelligible to the unregenerate in that sense. When the apologist speaks of motion, potentiality, actuality, and such things, the inquirer will not simply dismiss it as gibberish.

Evidently, Van Til is talking about another kind of intelligibility. In the following passage, he talks about a legitimate form of the cosmological argument: "Men ought to realize that nature could not

[15] SCE, 99.
[16] IST, 56.
[17] Ibid., 57.
[18] DF1, 252.

exist as something independent. They ought to sense that if anything intelligible is to be said about nature, it must be in relation to the absolute system of truth, which is God."[19] But does this principle actually vitiate Aquinas's argument? Aquinas would certainly agree that "men ought to realize that nature could not exist as something independent." That is the whole point of Thomas's proofs—to show that nature cannot be independent.

Would Aquinas also agree that intelligibility in nature "must be in relation to the absolute system of truth, which is God?" "In relation to" is a bit vague; evidently Van Til's point is that nature is intelligible *because* it is the result of God's plan and purpose. But Thomas Aquinas certainly believed that the intelligibility of the world finds its cause in God's plan, Creation, and providence. Van Til sometimes gives the impression that Aquinas held a libertarian view of human freedom, because, like Aristotle, he supposedly believed that ultimate matter was irrational. Of course, some Roman Catholic thinkers have held that sort of view. Aquinas's doctrine of predestination, however, is no less comprehensive than that of Calvin.[20] Van Til might wish to argue that Aquinas should have held a Pelagian view of the human will, because of his dependence on Aristotle, but he did not actually hold such a view.

Does Aquinas's argument prove "the existence of a finite God"?[21] If it is successful, it proves that there is a first mover. The question of finitude or infinity does not arise in this particular argument as such, although Aquinas certainly believed that the first mover was infinite, and he sought to prove that through other arguments. Scripture certainly warrants the conclusion of the argument, namely, that God is the ultimate cause of motion in the world.

In chapter 14, we considered Van Til's view that every apologetic argument ought to prove the whole of Christian theism, the "what" as well as the "that." I shall have more to say on this point in chapter 23. I believe, however, that proving the whole of Christian theism is a pretty tall order for a single apologetic argument. We shall

---

[19]IST, 102.

[20]See *Summa Theologica,* Question 19, Article 6, pp. 203–5; Questions 23, 24, pp. 238–58. See also Question 83, pp. 786–92, which acknowledges that God is the first cause of our free choices. His doctrine of grace and salvation, however, is to some extent synergistic.

[21]IST, 57.

ask later whether Van Til himself does that successfully. We should not, of course, be content to bring an inquirer only to embrace part of the truth. It is best to develop a system of arguments that establishes as best we can the truth of the full biblical message. But I do not believe that every apologetic syllogism must conclude with the full richness of biblical revelation. Therefore, I am not scandalized by the fact that Aquinas's argument for the first mover does not also prove God's infinity.

Recall my argument in chapter 14 that "that" and "what" are matters of degree. No argument proves everything that God is; no argument proves bare existence without any additional definition. If Van Til objects to Aquinas on these grounds, he should show how much "whatness" is required in an argument for God's existence, and precisely why that degree of definition is required.

Do the premises of Aquinas's argument require that the cause of motion be finite? There is a problem here, which arises in connection with Aquinas's doctrine of analogy (see chap. 7). Aquinas reasons from finite movers to the first mover. If the argument is to succeed, the first mover must move things in the same sense that the finite movers move things. But Aquinas elsewhere denies that predicates can be applied to God and to creatures in the same sense. Granted Aquinas's doctrine of analogy, therefore, it might be objected indeed that within his system his premises can lead only to a finite (but "first") mover. However, there are other aspects of his system that dictate that the first in a causal series be radically distinguished from the other members of it. The first mover or first cause is unconditioned and self-sufficient in a way that the other members are not. Aquinas uses such considerations, following his theistic proofs, to establish some of the attributes of God. Indeed, without some such additional considerations, the argument from motion fails. For if the first mover is not radically different from the later movers, then another mover is required to explain its own motion.

Perhaps the most that can be argued is that Aquinas is inconsistent here. But of course that inconsistency can be overcome, if we reproduce Aquinas's argument in terms of Van Til's epistemology. For Van Til, as we have seen, does not deny that terms can be predicated of God and of creatures in the same "literal" sense. Therefore, there can be no objection, granted a Van Tillian epistemology, to saying that God "moves" objects in the same sense in which finite persons and forces "move" objects. Of course, God moves things in ways that are mysterious to us, but nevertheless he does move them, in the usual sense of "move"; he is the sufficient cause of their movements.

Our evaluation of Aquinas's argument, therefore, depends on the extent to which we look at it as part of a system of thought. We have seen that the argument creates some problems for Aquinas, taken in conjunction with other ideas of his. But, taken by itself and used with other epistemological assumptions, the argument seems unobjectionable.

Van Til, of course, tended to look at every item as part of a "system"—perhaps because of his heritage from philosophical idealism. It can be persuasive to say that everything in a thinker's writings must be related to everything else if we are to evaluate it properly. In this case, that outlook would lead us simply to reject Aquinas's argument because it leads to inconsistencies elsewhere in his system. And then we would have to reject *every* element of the system, because every element is part of a system that as a whole is inconsistent.

That kind of criticism has its value. It is useful to see how different elements of a system interact with one another and cause problems for one another. But that kind of analysis needs supplementation. We must look at the parts as well as the whole. The parts are not merely functions of the whole, nor vice versa. Indeed, we cannot even conceive of a whole without some specific attention to the parts. Specific ideas are to some extent independent of the system containing them, and they deserve independent evaluation, as well as evaluation in terms of the whole system. Therefore, the problems arising from the relations of Aquinas's argument to other elements of his system are not necessarily fatal to the argument itself.

It must be remembered that all of us, including Van Til, have made mistakes. If every mistake invalidated one's whole system of thought, and therefore every argument in that system, then none of us could claim to have formulated a sound argument about anything.

Interpreting Aquinas in terms of his system, one might say that the argument from motion is worthless, because it is inconsistent with other elements of his thought. To adopt the argument on this view would be to adopt the whole system, and we cannot do that. However, if we look at Aquinas's ideas one by one, in piecemeal fashion, we might find the argument of some value.

If we simply take the argument literally, I see nothing about it that would be inconsistent with a Van Tillian theory of knowledge.

Therefore, there is a greater degree of agreement between Van Til and Aquinas than Van Til recognizes. Of course, that agreement is not perfect by any means. There are very substantial differences. Chief among them is the relation of faith and reason. When Aquinas says that man can know God by "natural reason," he gives virtually a blank check to Aristotelian epistemology. Although Aquinas gives Scripture a kind of veto power in the realm of natural reason, and therefore, e.g., denies Aristotle's view of the eternity of the world, he does not allow Scripture to function significantly in the development of his own theory of knowledge. Thus, as Van Til says, he does attempt to impose the Christian worldview on top of Aristotle's scheme of abstract form and chaotic matter and the Neoplatonic scheme of wholly other deity and chain of being.

As I mentioned in connection with logic, any manner of nonsense can be derived from inconsistent premises. Since Aquinas's system is inconsistent on the above understanding, it is possible to derive all sorts of absurdities from it. Yet we must be careful not to attribute to Aquinas all the absurdities that might be logically derivable from his system. That sort of analysis is neither fair, nor illuminating, nor useful to the progress of Christian apologetics. As I argued above, piecemeal analysis must supplement systematic analysis. As the one and the many are equally ultimate in God and in creation, so in analyzing a system we must not allow the structure of the whole to wipe out the individuality of the parts, or vice versa.

Coordinating systematic with piecemeal analysis may lead to critiques that are somewhat messy. We may find ourselves rejecting a system as a whole and recognizing the systematic relationships between the whole and the parts, yet finding some parts that are nonetheless of positive value. Or, conversely, we may accept a system as a whole, while critiquing parts of it. That kind of criticism tends to lack symmetry and elegance. It leads us to say things like "portions of this book are good, other portions are questionable, but the topic warrants further study," to repeat Gary North's bit of satire.[22] But at times this is the best we can do.

Van Til does speak of "incidental" truths within otherwise false systems, as we saw in chapter 15. But, on the whole, his style of criticism is rather unbalanced. It is very systematic, hardly ever piecemeal. When Van Til criticizes a thinker, he sees that thinker's system

[22]See chap. 1.

as a unit, everything related to everything else. Therefore, the system must be accepted or rejected as a whole. Even for biblical theism, in which there is no discrepancy between the whole and the parts, that approach is inadequate, for, as Van Til himself points out, there are apparent contradictions in Scripture. Even in Christian theism we must, to some extent, believe and practice the various parts of divine revelation without knowing how they fit together systematically. The analysis of human systems of thought needs even more of a piecemeal approach. No human writer is absolutely consistent. There is always good amid the bad and bad amid the good.

As for Aquinas, Van Til sees his thought as a seamless robe—as a system that is false and that therefore vitiates all of Aquinas's individual theistic arguments. Granting much of Van Til's critique of Aquinas, I cannot press it that far. Aquinas is wrong to claim so much common ground with the Greek philosophers and to incorporate so much of their thought into his own system. He is not wrong to perceive, as Aristotle did, that motion implies a first mover, nor to perceive, as Aristotle did not, that the first mover is nothing less than the God of the Bible.

Aquinas is often considered the father of the traditional apologetic, although we have seen anticipations of his methods in the church fathers discussed earlier. Van Til typically treats this traditional apologetic as a unit: a system that includes a claim of common ground with non-Christian thought, theistic proofs, probability arguments, etc. That traditional method, in Van Til's view, should be rejected in toto. But this is another example of Van Til's overly systematic thinking. In my view, the tradition contains both good and bad: claims of religious neutrality (bad), insightful arguments (good), etc.

CHAPTER TWENTY

The Traditional Method: Joseph Butler

The cofounder of the Aquinas-Butler method was Joseph Butler (1692–1752), an Anglican bishop. His most famous apologetic work was *The Analogy of Religion Natural and Revealed to the Constitution and Course of Nature,* published in 1736. The book defends traditional (theologically Arminian) Christianity against the deists. The deists taught that God had turned the reins of the universe over to an impersonal system of natural laws. Thus, on their view, God did not perform miracles or otherwise involve himself directly with human history. The deists believed that natural revelation was sufficient to tell us what we need to know about God. On their view, the content of natural revelation is simple: God exists, he desires worship, and he requires and rewards good moral behavior. Deism has no place, therefore, for special revelation, for authoritative Scripture, or for Scripture's message of sin and redemption. Despite the heterodoxy of the deists, Butler did consider his belief in God to be common ground with them. Thus he was able, in his book, to assume "that God has made and controls the 'constitution and course of nature.'"[1] "Assume" here is

[1]CTEV, 2. My references to Butler will usually cite Van Til's references in CTEV, although I do have access to Butler's own volume, which I will cite in a few instances. I do this because (1) my intention is primarily to evaluate Van Til's own argument,

not to be taken in the sense of a Van Tillian presupposition. Butler "assumes" the existence of God merely because he and his particular opponents both acknowledge it. Actually, he appeals to rational argument as the ground of his belief in God.[2]

Butler seeks to develop an "analogy" between natural and special revelation. He wants to show the deists that if one believes in God on the basis of natural revelation, one should also have adequate grounds for believing in special revelation. Nature, Butler argued, gives intimations, not only of Creation, but also of redemption. And if there are difficulties in Scripture, there are parallel and equivalent difficulties in natural revelation as well. Of course, no analogy is perfect. In every analogy, the items compared are both similar to and different from one another. Therefore:

> When Butler applies these principles of reasoning to the question of Christianity he makes a twofold use of them. He makes, first, a positive use of them. It is based upon the idea that we can legitimately make conclusions about the unknown, assuming that it will be *like* the known. In the second place, he makes negative use of them. The unknown, though we may expect it will be like the known, may also be *unlike* the known.[3]

Butler makes much of the distinction between "probable" and "demonstrative" evidence. "The former admits of degrees from mere presumption to moral certainty, while the latter brings immediate and absolute conviction."[4] Probable evidence may be sufficient to determine action. Even in the absence of demonstration, prudence dictates that we do what, according to our best judgment, seems most conducive to happiness. "Probability is the very guide to life."[5] Notice that Butler is concerned less with theoretical certitude than with practical certainty, the certainty by which we make our daily decisions.

"Probability in daily life rests upon analogy."[6] Analogical reason-

---

and (2) my readers should be able to find CTEV more easily than they can find my particular edition of Butler's *Analogy*.

[2]CTEV, 7–8.

[3]Ibid., 4.

[4]Ibid., 1.

[5]Butler, *Analogy of Religion* (New York: Harper and Bro., 1898), 84.

[6]CTEV, 2.

ing, for Butler, is reasoning about unknown possibilities from the known "constitution and course of nature." This "constitution and course of nature" is our starting point as far as the facts from which we reason are concerned.[7]

Following John Locke, Butler takes a generally empiricist view of knowledge. He expresses disapproval of the rationalism and apriorism of René Descartes and Samuel Clarke, who, in his view, allowed their reasoning to stray far beyond known fact. Butler's method is "to join abstract reasonings with the observation of facts, and argue from such facts as are known to others that are like them."[8] "With the empiricists in general," Van Til says, "Butler wishes to make a certain reasonable use of reason."[9]

But this apparently modest use of reason has considerable force: "Let reason be kept to: and if any part of the Scripture account of the redemption of the world by Christ can be shown to be really contrary to it, let the Scripture, in the name of God, be given up."[10]

Butler argues for human immortality by pointing out that "although we have in our lifetime undergone much change, we have still survived. Therefore, it is likely that we will survive death."[11] Van Til observes:

> This passage affords an excellent illustration of the principle of likeness or *continuity* on which Butler rests his reasoning from the known to the unknown. His positive argument for a future life depends upon the observed principle of continuity. In the immediately following section he deals with the main objections against the idea of a future life. In meeting these objections he uses his celebrated argument from unlikeness or *discontinuity*.[12]

The argument from discontinuity is an argument from ignorance: we do not know enough about death to say that it involves a loss of our present powers.

---

[7]Ibid.
[8]Ibid., 3.
[9]Ibid.
[10]Ibid., 5.
[11]Ibid., 6.
[12]Ibid.

Van Til comments about these arguments from ignorance: "It becomes apparent from such an argument as this that it is the *bruteness or dumbness of the facts that is of basic importance for Butler*. . . . His principle of unlikeness or discontinuity is based on the idea of pure contingency as pervasive of all reality."[13]

Van Til then goes on to consider Butler's argument for the specific doctrines of Christianity. He points out Butler's Arminian theology.[14] In his argument, Butler "finds an analogy in nature for the vicarious suffering of Christ,"[15] for in human life it does happen that the innocent suffer for the guilty. On the other hand, the argument from ignorance is that we should not "expect to have the like information concerning the divine conduct, as concerning our own duty."[16]

Butler then investigates the historical evidence for miracle and fulfilled prophecy. He summarizes by saying that natural religion is corroborated by Scripture and vice versa, the two blending together. All of the "probable proofs" in the book "not only increase the evidence, but multiply it," since so many different lines of evidence wonderfully come together.[17]

Van Til replies to Butler by describing the criticisms of Hume and Kant against this type of argumentation and, of course, by adding his own comments. Theologically, he criticizes Butler's view of freedom, the Fall, and human ability. I shall refer to Van Til's theological critique of Butler briefly in the next section, in connection with the notion of brute fact. Van Til's specifically apologetic critique of Butler centers on the concepts of brute fact, probability, analogy, and rationalism, which we shall examine in order.

Brute Fact

It is important to recognize that Butler was not a theoretical epistemologist, as were Aristotle, Aquinas, Hume, Kant, and Van Til. Although he was a fairly sophisticated thinker, he did not enter profoundly into the technical debates between apriorists and empiricists,

[13]Ibid., 7 (emphasis his).
[14]Ibid., 8–13.
[15]Ibid., 14.
[16]Ibid.
[17]Ibid., 15.

nominalists and realists. He was interested in describing how we do, and should, make our decisions in practical life.

Ironically, however, this practical emphasis was prophetic of various movements to come among philosophers, even among those far more concerned than Butler with the technicalities of epistemology. David Hume himself, after he reduced to skepticism the empiricism of Locke, argued that most of our causal and other judgments were, and should be, governed by custom. Thus, he recommended a practical epistemology, rather than any one of the traditional technical theories. Kant, after demolishing the rationalistic pretensions of "pure" or "theoretical" reason, argued that we need to make assumptions of a metaphysical type,[18] governed by something called "practical" reason. He was followed by Thomas Reid's philosophy of "common sense" (which was so influential upon nineteenth-century Princeton theology) and twentieth-century movements such as pragmatism, phenomenology, existentialism (with its emphasis on "lived experience"), Wittgensteinian ordinary language philosophy (limiting the function of language to its ordinary social context), and present-day deconstruction (seeing language and knowledge as tools for achieving power in society).[19]

In any case, it is important that we understand Butler's formulations in the practical context in which he has chosen to write. I fear that Van Til sometimes failed to observe this principle. A case in point is the references to "brute fact" and "pure contingency" cited above in connection with Butler's argument from ignorance. In Van Til's technical vocabulary, "brute fact" is uninterpreted fact or "ultimate matter"—fact uncreated, uncontrolled, and unknown by God, and therefore unintelligible. But Van Til has supplied no evidence at all that Butler thinks of fact in this way. In the context cited by Van Til, Butler appeals only to human ignorance of the nature of death, not to any ultimate brutishness of facts.

Indeed, the ignorance in view, although Butler treats it sympathetically, is the ignorance of the unbeliever, rather than that of all men generally. Certainly Butler is not saying that Scripture leaves believers ignorant concerning life after death. So he is really calling

---

[18]These assumptions are "regulative," not "constitutive"; that is, they function, not to tell us about ultimate reality, but to help us make decisions in our practical life.

[19]Going back before Butler, this practical emphasis is perhaps foreshadowed in the famous "wager" of Blaise Pascal.

on the unbeliever to recognize his own state of ignorance. The unbeliever does not know, so he cannot object to, the Christian position. Within the non-Christian system of thought, there is no basis for any such objection. But that is a perfectly Van Tillian point. Van Til would say that the unbeliever, on his presuppositions, has no basis from which to challenge the claims of the believer.[20]

I believe that Van Til would reply to my analysis with the observation that Butler is an Arminian, and that it is characteristic of Arminian theology to advocate "brute fact" in some measure.[21] Arminians believe that man's will is not always subject to the sovereign plan of God. Therefore, they believe that the free choices of men are "brute facts," unplanned and uninterpreted by God.[22] I suppose that Van Til would also add that a theology that finds one brute fact is likely to find others; therefore, the facts of death and the future life must also be brutish for Butler.

That, however, does not follow. In any case, Arminian theology certainly does not maintain that all facts are brutish in this sense. Therefore, we should not charge Arminians, on the sole ground of their theology of free will, with an epistemology based on brute fact.

Furthermore, classical Arminian theology is inconsistent in its view of the human will, rather than consistently autonomist. Although Arminianism insists that the human will is at some point independent of God, it nevertheless teaches also that God determined before the foundation of the world which human persons would be created, and that, in creating them, he had exhaustive foreknowledge of what their decisions would be.[23] Thus, the Calvin-

---

[20]A Van Tillian might also reply to Butler that the unbeliever knows of his immortality as part of his natural knowledge of God (Rom. 1:18–21). It is an interesting question whether the reality of a future life is given in natural revelation, but I shall pass that one by. The important point here is that Van Tillian epistemology accounts both for the knowledge of the unbeliever and for his ignorance. Van Til cannot simply argue that any reference to the ignorance of the unbeliever compromises the clarity of natural revelation. In important senses, unbelievers are ignorant, as the apostle Paul emphasizes in Acts 17:22–31.

[21]Van Til explores Butler's Arminian commitments in CTEV, 3, 8–13. In DF2, 202, he relates his criticisms of Butler directly to his Arminian theology.

[22]They are, however, planned and interpreted by the independent human will. That point introduces some complications for Van Til's analysis, but I will pass over them.

[23]I understand that some recent Arminians, seeking to avoid the problem I am describing, have denied God's exhaustive foreknowledge. That seems to me to be a

ist believes in divine "foreordination of all things" and the Arminian in "creation with exhaustive foreknowledge." The distinction between those two ideas is not easy to draw. What it all boils down to is that Arminianism inconsistently believes in both human autonomy and divine foreordination. The former position entails the existence of some brute facts in Van Til's sense. The latter denies that there are any. Thus, the worst that can be said about Butler on the basis of his Arminianism is that he does not consistently oppose the notion of brute fact. Arminianism, like the philosophy of Aquinas, is, from a Reformed point of view, an inconsistent mixture of Christian and non-Christian thought.

However that may be, Butler's references to human ignorance of the future life may not be read as affirmations of the existence of brute facts or as advocacy of a brute fact epistemology. Lacking evidence to know precisely where Butler would go with his inconsistent principles, it would be best for us to give him more benefit of the doubt than Van Til does.

PROBABILITY

Butler's thought has been a major source of the probabilistic argumentation that has been emphasized in evangelical apologetics. Van Til takes sharp issue with this kind of argument in these passages:

> The traditional method therefore compromises the *clarity* of God's revelation to man, whether this revelation comes through general or through special revelation. Created facts are not taken to be clearly revelational of God; all the facts of nature and of man are said to indicate no more than that *a* god *probably* exists.[24]

> It is an insult to the living God to say that his revelation of himself so lacks in clarity that man, himself through and through revelation of God, does justice by it when he says that God *probably* exists.[25]

---

fairly drastic step, putting them into obvious conflict with Scripture. But, of course, their position is not that of traditional Arminianism or, specifically, of Butler.

[24]DF2, 258; cf. pp. 241–59.

[25]Ibid., 197.

> Christians are interested in showing to those who hold that "God" *possibly* or *probably* exists but possibly or probably does not exist, that the words possibility and probability have no meaning unless the God of Christianity actually exists. It is their conviction that the actuality of the existence of *this* God is the presupposition of all possible predication.[26]

Thus, for Van Til, God's existence is not merely possible or probable, but absolutely certain. Not only that, but our apologetic argument for God's existence must also claim certainty. There is "absolutely certain proof for the existence of God and the truth of Christian theism."[27] The Reformed apologist "maintains that there is an absolutely valid argument for the existence of God and for the truth of Christian theism. He cannot do less without virtually admitting that God's revelation to man is not clear."[28] Note also: "We should not tone down the validity of this argument to the probability level. The argument may be poorly stated, and may never be adequately stated. But in itself the argument is absolutely sound. Christianity is the only reasonable position to hold."[29]

In this discussion, it seems to me, a more careful distinction needs to be made between evidence and argument. Van Til is certainly right to argue that the *evidence* for Christian theism is clear (Rom. 1:18–21; Ps. 19:1) and therefore certain. Scripture holds the unbeliever responsible for his rejection of that revelation, and he could not be responsible for rejecting the truth if it were never revealed to him in a clear fashion. Van Til is also right, I believe, to emphasize that Christian theism is the only basis for intelligible predication. To reject Christian theism is foolishness (Ps. 14:1; Prov. 1:7; 1 Cor. 1–2). As we have seen, the alternative to Christian theism is ultimate impersonalism, which offers no intelligible explanation for the order and value of the world. Ultimate impersonalism, in turn, requires ultimate explanation in terms of abstract laws and/or ultimate matter, neither of which is in itself an intelligible concept, and neither of which is suited to serve as an explanatory basis for other phenomena.

---

[26]CA, 13.

[27]DF2, 103.

[28]Ibid., 104.

[29]CGG, 62. Van Til thinks highly enough of this formulation to quote it in DF2, 197.

On the other hand, Van Til himself admits that our apologetic *argument* may not be adequate to establish that certain conclusion. Remarkably, he even says, in the last passage quoted above, that the argument may never be adequately stated. But if the argument is never stated adequately enough to justify the certainty of its conclusion, then on what basis may the apologist claim certainty for his argument?

Evidently, Van Til has in mind a kind of ideal argument that may never be adequately stated by an actual apologist. What he seems to be saying is that if there could be an argument that would perfectly reproduce the inherent clarity of God's revelation, that argument would be absolutely sound, valid, and certain.[30] But it is possible (!) that no actual argument, including Van Til's, has ever measured up to that standard.

But then it is illegitimate for him to demand that all actual (as opposed to ideal) apologetic arguments claim certainty for their conclusions. Rather, an apologist, recognizing that he is not presenting the full evidential force of divine revelation, ought to be honest and admit that his argument conveys something less than absolute certainty. Another way of making that admission is to state that the argument is "probable."

Of course, the goal of all apologetic argument is to approach the cogency of the ideal argument. Approaching that level of cogency, however, may sometimes require many arguments, or (which is the same thing) a single argument that is very complex. Van Til claims that his "transcendental" or "presuppositional" argument, showing the impossibility of any intelligibility except on the presupposition of Christian theism, generates an absolutely certain conclusion.[31] We shall look at that argument in more detail in chapter 23. But that argument, if it is to be clearly and cogently articulated, necessarily requires a great many subsidiary arguments. Certainly it is not obvious, at first reading, that the intelligibility of the universe presupposes Christianity. Clarifications must be made, objections must be answered, and

[30]Van Til uses *sound, valid,* and *certain* more or less interchangeably, passing over the distinctions among these terms commonly made by philosophers.

[31]Or does he? As we have seen, he also states that the argument generating such certainty may never have been adequately stated (presumably even by him). If that is the case, then his own argument is not, after all, entitled to a claim of absolute certainty. I sense some inconsistency here.

logical connections must be displayed. If it is difficult to insure the certainty of a single argument, it is even more difficult to insure the certainty of a complex system of arguments of this sort. At each point in that system, the argument may fall short of cogency. And, at that point, the proper claim, if the argument is still thought to have any value at all, is one of probability.

Recall our discussion in chapter 13 of "limiting concepts," in which Van Til says that our doctrinal formulations are, in one sense, approximations to the truth as God knows it. In this discussion, Van Til recognizes the difference between the data of the Word of God and our doctrinal formulation of that data. Granting that difference, we may not demand that our apologetic formulations convey the full force of the revealed evidential data.

Certainly Butler is right that many of our decisions in life, even some of the most important ones, are made on the basis of arguments that yield only probable conclusions. When a person becomes a Christian, he is, to be sure, confronted with the certain evidence of divine revelation, driven home to him by the illumination of the Holy Spirit. But insofar as apologetic argument plays a role in such conversion—as a tool of the Spirit—it may, and indeed will, convey something less than the fullness of the revelation itself.

If an unbeliever objects that an apologetic offered to him has, after all, only probable force, it is not wrong to reply that he himself relies on probability in making many of the decisions (including the larger ones) of his life. As I defended earlier Butler's argument from ignorance, so here I defend his argument from probability; the two are virtually the same. Neither ignorance nor probability keeps people in everyday life from making decisions. Indeed, it is foolish, and often even immoral, to demand absolute certainty before taking any action. As with the argument from ignorance, we may describe this argument as a *reductio* of the unbeliever's inconsistency: he has no basis to oppose the Christian argument.

It would be quite absurd to reject all apologetic argument that falls short of certainty. For example, Christians have often admitted that there are problems in Scripture to which the answer is uncertain. Various hypotheses have been suggested to show the consistency and factual accuracy of the Bible in response to these problems. But often, even the most devout scholars are uncertain as to what hypothesis is correct. For example, E. J. Young, for many years professor of Old Testament at Westminster Seminary and a long-time colleague of Van

Til's, speaks of "possible and plausible" solutions to problems, although he also affirms very clearly a Van Tillian epistemology.[32] Van Til, as we have seen (chap. 14), endorses the use of historical and scientific evidence in apologetics, but much of that evidence consists of probable conclusions from historical and scientific data.

Van Til's critique of probabilism is legitimate up to a point. Some apologists, perhaps including Butler (though Van Til does not give textual evidence of this), have claimed that the evidence for Christianity is only probable, and that the unbeliever is therefore right, up to a point, to have doubts about it. Van Til is correct to insist that we should not give the non-Christian such a justification for his unbelief. But Van Til overstates his case when he insists, or appears to insist, that every apologetic argument should claim certainty. It is not wrong to offer to the non-Christian an *argument* claiming only probability. But we should not at the same time give him the impression that the *evidence* is less than fully cogent.

And, of course, Van Til is also right to suggest that when the subject of probability comes up, the Christian has the opportunity to show that the very idea of probability makes sense only on the basis of Christian theism. But to argue thus is certainly not to renounce probability altogether; it is rather to affirm it.[33]

Analogy

As we recall, Butler employs both analogy and disanalogy in his apologetic, what Van Til calls continuity and discontinuity, respectively. Analogy tries to show that special revelation is analogous to natural revelation. Disanalogy, or the argument from ignorance, tries to show that the unlikeness of the supernatural invalidates unbelieving objections: the unbeliever does not know enough to object to scriptural teaching. This too is, in Butler's estimation, a practical kind of argument, like those by which we make decisions in everyday life. He presses the non-Christian to be consistent: admit in the religious debate the same continuities and discontinuities that you freely recognize elsewhere. When you do that, he tells the inquirer, you will see that special revelation has the same cogency that you accept in natu-

---

[32]E. J. Young, *Thy Word Is Truth* (Grand Rapids: Eerdmans, 1957), 172–85, 192–93.

[33]For more considerations on probability, see DKG, 134–36, and AGG, 77–82.

ral revelation. And if there are problems in special revelation, they are no greater than the problems of natural revelation. Since you are able to bear with the latter, you should be able equally to bear with the former. It is because of these problems in both realms that we must in all of life be satisfied with probability.

W. J. Norton suggests a problem with this kind of reasoning:

> There are some readers of Butler who affirm that this use of analogy is a two-sided sword that cuts both ways. They maintain that you do not gain plausibility for your disputed facts by showing that they are like undisputed facts; instead, you show that the arguments of your opponents are effective in more fields than one, and that the undisputed facts now become as doubtful as the disputed ones.[34]

One might paraphrase this objection as follows: Someone might use the principle of continuity where he uses the principle of discontinuity and vice versa. Recall Butler's argument for a future life, cited earlier in this chapter. The objector might use a principle of continuity based on the analogy between body and soul: since the body is clearly extinguished in death, we should presume that the soul is extinguished also. When the Christian objects that life after death is nonetheless possible, the unbeliever might assert the principle of ignorance: we do not know what follows death.

This is essentially the argument of David Hume, which Van Til discusses in chapter 2 of *Christian-Theistic Evidences.* Van Til finds Hume's point cogent against Butler. To Butler's analogies, Hume opposes disanalogies. In addition, Hume suggests alternative analogies that, in his view, weaken the types of arguments offered by Butler. For example, could not the world be more like a vegetable organism than a product of design?

Butler, however, is not without a response to this sort of attack. That response is as follows:

> But it has always been allowed to argue, from what is acknowledged to what is disputed. And it is in no other sense a poor thing, to argue from natural religion to revealed, in the man-

[34]W. J. Norton, *Bishop Butler, Moralist and Divine* (New Brunswick, N.J.: Rutgers University Press, 1940), 308–9.

> ner found fault with, than it is to argue in numberless other ways of probable deduction and inference, in matters of conduct, which we are continually reduced to the necessity of doing.[35]

In other words, he says, there are problems in any argument from analogy, but we must nevertheless use such arguments, as they are the only principles by which we can make practical decisions. Butler would have found Hume's arguments subversive of these practical principles, in fact subversive of all human knowledge. Hume himself was tormented by the skeptical implications of his arguments; in the end, he too took refuge in practical life, or "custom."[36]

I am not interested in defending Butler's specific argumentation. I do not find his argument about the future life persuasive, for example, nor do I think that his analogy between the mother hen protecting her chicks and the redemptive work of Christ carries much apologetic weight. But his general method does not seem to me to be wrong. In any kind of practical apologetic encounter, we must reason from the known to the unknown. It is important to show the non-Christian that there are analogies between what he claims to know and what we seek to teach him. That is simply a matter of sound pedagogy. It is also important to convince the unbeliever that he does not know as much, in certain areas, as he thinks he does.

Van Til himself endorses these strategies, in different language. To "argue from ignorance" is, in Van Til's terms, to attack unbelieving rationalism. To "point out analogies" is, in Van Til's terms, to attack unbelieving irrationalism. Butler, does not, of course, set forth Van Til's analysis of the rationalist-irrationalist dialectic in unbelieving thought. He would have been more convincing if he had done so, in my estimation. But that is to say that he did not develop the proper theory to support his practice; it is not to invalidate his practice.

RATIONALISM

However, there is one remaining concern about Butler, namely, his subjection of revelation to reason. He is, of course, an empiricist, and

---

[35]Butler, *Analogy of Religion,* 304.

[36]See Hume, *Treatise of Human Nature* (New York: E. P. Dutton and Co., 1911), 1:252–54.

therefore critical of the pretensions of reason. Yet, as we have seen, he does advocate a "reasonable use of reason." And recall our earlier quotation from him that if any Scripture be found really contradictory to reason, Scripture must—in the name of God!—be given up. That is a very misleading comment to make in the hearing of an unbeliever. It certainly suggests that the human mind is the final authority and that God's Word must submit to human judgment.

Although the comment is misleading, it is not literally wrong. In our earlier discussion of reason (chaps. 11–14), we saw that Van Til does not actually dispute Hodge's statement that reason is the proper judge of the consistency and the evidences of a revelation. He merely criticizes Hodge for not adding that Christians and non-Christians use reason very differently. Reason, in Van Til's view, is a human capacity, created by God in us, for making judgments and inferences. We must use it in making judgments even about Scripture. Van Til's point, however, is that we must not make those judgments autonomously.

Indeed, Van Til does not hesitate to argue both that Christianity is in accordance with the facts and that it is rational.[37] Believing as he does that God's revelation is clear, he commends B. B. Warfield, Hodge's successor, for his emphasis on the rationality of divine revelation. On that point, he commends Warfield over against Abraham Kuyper.[38] Note also:

> Positively, Hodge and Warfield were quite right in stressing the fact that Christianity meets every legitimate demand of reason. Surely Christianity is not irrational. To be sure, it must be accepted on faith, but surely it must not be taken on blind faith. Christianity is capable of rational defense.[39]

Of course, in the contexts of these quotations are various warnings to distinguish between Christian and non-Christian uses of reason. But these statements, taken by themselves, say nothing more or less than Butler's quoted statement.

Butler does add the rhetorical twist about giving up Scripture in the name of God, but that is only a rhetorical twist. Neither Butler

[37] JA, 20.
[38] CTK, 243–44.
[39] CGG, 184.

nor Van Til believed that Scripture was irrational. The condition "if any part of Scripture is contrary to reason" is clearly intended to be contrary to fact. Such rhetorical formulations are always dangerous in controversial writing. In most cases it is better to avoid them, and I think Butler should have avoided this one here. But the fact that he did use this language does not make his statement literally false.

Van Til, from the standpoint of his legitimate theological assumptions, has the right to criticize Butler's rhetoric and its misleading character in an apologetic situation. He also has the right to ask Butler, as he asked Hodge and Warfield, to add to this emphasis a distinction between Christian and non-Christian forms of reasoning. I agree with those criticisms. But Van Til should not give the impression that Butler's statement is in itself false or that it amounts, in itself, to a theological compromise.

I would draw four conclusions about Butler. First, he does not clearly teach a doctrine of brute fact. Second, his use of probability arguments is not in itself wrong. Third, although his specific analogies and disanalogies are not always persuasive, the use of such reasoning is unavoidable in apologetics. Fourth, although his rationalistic rhetoric, without suitable qualifications, is highly misleading, it does not, when literally interpreted, violate any principle of Scripture.

CHAPTER TWENTY-ONE

The Traditional Method: Edward J. Carnell

To complete our analysis of Van Til's critique of the apologetic tradition, we should look at his response to the evangelical apologetics of his own time. Van Til dealt with many apologists who came after Butler. We have discussed his response to Hodge and Warfield, who developed the Old Princeton apologetic. We have also discussed in some detail his critique of Gordon H. Clark. Van Til also discussed many other nineteenth- and twentieth-century apologists in his books, syllabi, and book reviews—including James Orr, William Brenton Greene, James Oliver Buswell, Floyd Hamilton, Wilbur Smith, C. S. Lewis, Carl F. H. Henry, Bernard Ramm, Stuart Hackett, and Francis Schaeffer. We cannot look at all of these discussions, so I have chosen one that is especially interesting and that shows the general pattern of Van Til's interaction with other apologists. The most interesting of these interactions, in my opinion, was that between Van Til and Edward J. Carnell.

Carnell (1919–67) was one of Van Til's most promising students at Westminster, after studying with Gordon Clark at Wheaton College. Van Til says the following about him: "May I tell you that Carnell was a student of mine for four years and that he was a friend as well? His Master's examination was a brilliant one and there was in it every indication that we were in agreement regarding apologetic methodology."[1] Within my hearing, Van Til often reflected on his friendship with him. Carnell, for all his intellectual brilliance, was prone to emotional and psychological difficulties. He also had theological difficulties: for a time he was taking instruction in Roman Catholicism. Van Til invested many hours counseling Carnell, and he had great expectations that Carnell would continue in his footsteps.

However, Carnell went on to further graduate study and thence diverged somewhat from Van Til's apologetic method. Gordon Lewis describes his development as follows:

> From Cornelius Van Til at Westminster Theological Seminary he took his starting point, the existence of the triune God of the Bible. However, this tenet is not an unquestioned presupposition for Carnell, but a hypothesis to be tested. His test of truth is threefold. At Wheaton College, in the classes of Gordon H. Clark, Carnell found the test of noncontradiction. The test of fitness to empirical fact was championed by Edgar S. Brightman at Boston University where Carnell earned his Ph.D. The requirement of relevance to personal experience became prominent during Carnell's Th.D. research at Harvard University in Søren Kierkegaard and Reinhold Niebuhr.
>
> These pieces began to fall into place to form a single picture in 1948 when Carnell published his prize-winning volume, *An Introduction to Christian Apologetics*.[2]

An Introduction to Christian Apologetics is, from a Van Tillian perspective, a curious volume. It is highly eclectic, hard to pin down as to its specific apologetic approach. Carnell uses a lot of language that is recognizably, even distinctively, Van Tillian. He reflects on the self-authenticating authority of Scripture: "If the Word required something more certain than itself to give it validity, it would no longer be

[1]Van Til's response to Gordon R. Lewis in JA, 361.

[2]Gordon R. Lewis, *Testing Christianity's Truth Claims* (Chicago: Moody Press, 1976), 176. Some readers may find it interesting to compare this "threefold test" to the "three perspectives" of my DKG. In my view, the two triads are related, but should not be equated.

God's Word."[3] Carnell speaks of the "problem of the one" and the "problem of the many."[4] He speaks of the Creator-creature distinction as fundamental.[5] He speaks of the Trinity as the "logical starting point" for Christian thought.[6]

At the same time, much of this language becomes problematic when Carnell describes his Christian starting point as, in Lewis's words, "not an unquestioned presupposition . . . but a hypothesis to be tested." For example, how can Scripture be self-authenticating and still be subject to Carnell's threefold test? This is not to say that a Van Tillian epistemology rejects all testing of Scripture. As we have seen, Van Til grants the right of reason to judge the consistency and evidence of revelation. But what does Carnell mean to deny that Scripture is the believer's "unquestioned presupposition"? And how does his threefold test relate to the self-authentication of Scripture?

There is also language, both in this book and in Carnell's other writings, that almost seems intended to offend Van Til. Van Til often quotes this passage: "Bring on your revelations! Let them make peace with the law of contradiction and the facts of history, and they will deserve a rational man's assent. A careful examination of the Bible reveals that it passes these stringent examinations *summa cum laude*."[7] Van Til used this passage for years as the clearest possible example of what the apologist should *not* do: to make the Bible subject to the opinions of fallen man, abstract principles of logic, and brute facts.

There are other things, too, like this statement of Carnell in critique of fundamentalism: "Nothing can be learned from general wisdom, says the fundamentalist, for the natural man is wrong in starting point, method, and conclusion. When the natural man says, 'This is a rose,' he means 'This is a not-made-by-the-triune-God rose.' Everything he says is blasphemy."[8]

---

[3]Edward John Carnell, *An Introduction to Christian Apologetics* (Grand Rapids: Eerdmans, 1948), 66 (emphasis his). Van Til quotes this passage appreciatively in JA, 361–62; he also notes favorably passages from pp. 40, 72, 194, and 212 of Carnell's book.

[4]Ibid., 34–41.

[5]Ibid., 40.

[6]Ibid., 124.

[7]Ibid., 178. See Van Til's references to this in CFC, 7, 70; IST, 41; DF2, 246–47; RP, 58.

[8]Edward John Carnell, *The Case for Orthodox Theology* (Philadelphia: Westminster, 1959), 119.

This is an odd statement. The triad of starting point, method, and conclusion is a triad found often in Van Til's writings and is typical only of Van Til. The reference to a rose comes out of the Clark controversy, in which both parties were constantly speaking about roses, and propositions involving roses, as items of knowledge. Therefore, it seems that this statement really applies, even as satire, only to Van Til. "Fundamentalism" in 1959 generally referred to dispensational Baptists and Independents, not to confessional Calvinists, though the usage of that term was fairly loose. No typical fundamentalist, certainly, would have said anything like what Carnell here attributes to the fundamentalist. But why should Carnell choose this kind of context, a critique of fundamentalism, to vent a bit of nastiness about Van Til? For it is certainly nasty. As we saw in chapter 15, Van Til's view of the unbeliever's knowledge is far too complicated to be summarized, or even mocked, by this sort of gibe.[9]

It seems sometimes that Carnell just had a chip on his shoulder regarding Van Til. Van Til was, I believe, greatly saddened by this. It seems that the problem between the two men was more than an intellectual or even a theological difference. I have no idea what was going on; perhaps the Clark controversy, raging during the 1940s, had something to do with it.

Van Til gave as good as he got. He said that Carnell's method of defending the Christian faith "requires the destruction of Christianity"[10] and leads to "the rejection of the whole body of his Christian beliefs."[11] We may not be able to determine the reason for the rhetorical extremes of these statements. But after a few more introductory considerations, I will try to pin down the actual differences between the two men concerning apologetic method.

Carnell's brilliance and his eclecticism made him an interesting thinker. He wrote several books on apologetics, each approaching the inquirer from a somewhat different angle: logic, ethical value, the

---

[9]Van Til comments on this in CFC, 137. Note also, in Carnell's *Christian Commitment* (New York: Macmillan, 1957), 137, the reference to "zealots" who deny "that God and man have anything in common."

[10]CFC, 82.

[11]Ibid., 85. Recall Van Til's statement about Stuart Hackett, quoted early in this book, that "the issues between us are total. There are no 'fundamentals' in common between us. . . . Hackett's Christian faith and my Christian faith, which we both desire non-Christians to accept, are radically different. They are different not only in their *content* but also in the very *method* of their construction" (JA, 15–16).

"judicial sentiment," the law of love. Probably no evangelical apologist in the twentieth century has used such a broad range of data and arguments in his presentations. He was not as theologically and epistemologically penetrating as Van Til, nor as logically cogent as Clark. But Carnell had a fascinating writing style and many ideas for apologetic strategies that deserve reflection and further development. For these reasons, too, it will be more interesting for us to look at Carnell than at any of Van Til's other rival apologists.

Van Til's main critique of Carnell is found in *The Case for Calvinism*. In the mid-1950s, Westminster Press published three volumes representing different theological positions: *The Case for Theology in Liberal Perspective*, by L. Harold DeWolf; *The Case for a New Reformation Theology*, by William Hordern; and *The Case for Orthodox Theology*, by Carnell. In *The Case for Calvinism*, published not by Westminster Press, but by Presbyterian and Reformed Publishing Company, Van Til reviews all three books and presents his own alternative, "Calvinism."[12]

Van Til points out that both Carnell and DeWolf are under the influence of Edgar S. Brightman and other "Boston Personalists." DeWolf's "comprehensive coherence" and Carnell's "systematic consistency" reflect at least formally Brightman's program to coordinate logical consistency with factual adequacy. These efforts may be compared with Butler's attempt to combine abstract reasoning with empirical fact. Van Til argues that DeWolf's epistemology, like Hordern's, is based on the post-Kantian freedom-nature scheme, in which autonomous man seeks to investigate a natural world ruled by abstract laws and irrational facticity. As such, they reject the historical character of divine revelation and self-attesting Scripture.[13]

Carnell's intention, Van Til grants, is to tell the biblical "story," not to advance the post-Kantian alternative.[14] Nevertheless, he defines his method of systematic consistency very much like the way Brightman and DeWolf define their own tests of truth, without pointing out any substantial difference between his and theirs.[15]

Van Til surveys the content of Carnell's apologetic works. In *An*

---

[12]There is a bit of irony in the title of CFC. To his family and close Dutch-American friends, Van Til was known as "Kees," pronounced "Case."

[13]CFC, 49–60.

[14]Ibid., 65, 84.

[15]Ibid., 62–69.

Introduction to Christian Apologetics, Carnell appeals to the "rational man" by means of the law of noncontradiction. In *A Philosophy of the Christian Religion,* he appeals to the "free man" on the basis of the values of the heart. In *Christian Commitment,* he appeals again to the "free man" by virtue of the "judicious sentiment." In *The Kingdom of Love and the Pride of Life,* he appeals to the law of love, as it is known by a "happy child." Happy children know that love, not money or success, is the source of happiness.[16] His basic contention is that "if good men are only consistent in the use of the method involved in their own position, then they will end up reverencing Christ."[17]

Carnell seeks to resolve even theological differences among Christians, such as those between Roman Catholicism and Protestantism, by means of "systematic consistency" rather than by biblical exegesis as such.[18]

These appeals to human rationality and morality do not explicitly distinguish between regenerate and unregenerate people. Carnell appeals to men as men—as rational, moral, judicious, and loving. His justification for such an appeal is the doctrine of common grace.[19]

Van Til finds in this pattern of argument the Kantian "primacy of the teleological over the mechanical." That is, Carnell is arguing that our worldview must be governed by our practical, heartfelt sense of reality rather than by some abstract logical system. Even the appeal to the law of noncontradiction is an appeal to the needs of the "rational" man who is also the "free" man. According to Van Til, this is the same pattern of argument found in DeWolf's book, and it is not essentially different from the approach of Hordern.

For Kant and DeWolf, however, this type of argument substitutes the authority of the free, autonomous man for divine authority, and it places the locus of salvation within autonomous man rather than in history. This autonomous "rational man," or "good man," or "moral man," is not fallen in Adam as Scripture teaches. Salvation, then, is essentially salvation through one's own resources. God rewards the good man for his goodness.[20] Van Til thinks that Carnell's appeals to the native rationality and goodness of the unregenerate

[16]Ibid., 69–77.
[17]Ibid., 70.
[18]Ibid., 85–88.
[19]Ibid., 85.
[20]Ibid., 78–85.

capitulate to this model: "Carnell Tends to Reduce the Ethical Status of Sin to that of Metaphysical Tension," reads one subtitle.[21]

Van Til describes Carnell's method as follows:

> [Carnell's] method is to start with man as autonomous. Starting from man as autonomous, Carnell worked up a modern form of natural theology under the guise of common grace. Starting from man as autonomous and therefore as inherently good Carnell was compelled to cater to the Kantian idea that God is, in some utterly unintelligible fashion, an omnipotent being who will reward those who are recommended to him as good by the "good man." Similarly, we now note, starting with the idea of human autonomy Carnell again caters to the idea that God is identical with the projected ideals of the "good man." And these three points are, naturally, involved in one another.[22]

Because he appeals to autonomous man, "Carnell's Method would Require him to Create God in Man's Image."[23] And, "It is obvious that in all this it is Carnell's method that seeks to frustrate the electing and sovereign love of God for man in terms of the abstract and indiscriminate principle of love."[24]

We may summarize Van Til's critique of Carnell as follows: (1) Carnell "starts with God" as a hypothesis to be tested, rather than as an unshakable presupposition, as Van Til does. (2) Carnell's tests for truth are identical to those of DeWolf, Brightman, and Kant, which presuppose human autonomy. (3) These appeals to autonomy implicitly (though contrary to Carnell's intention) deny the entire Christian worldview and gospel message.

God as Hypothesis

Gordon Lewis, the student of Carnell and critic of Van Til to whom we referred earlier, takes Van Til to task for failing to recognize that

---

[21]Ibid., 91.

[22]Ibid., 95.

[23]Ibid. (another subtitle). Note the word "would." Van Til is still trying to maintain the goodness of Carnell's intentions while asserting the bad logical consequences of his method.

[24]Ibid., 103.

Carnell affirms the same "starting point" that he does.[25] But then he admits the significant difference between Van Til and Carnell: Carnell starts with the Bible as a "hypothesis," while Van Til starts with it as a "presupposition."[26] Certainly! But that is a rather large difference, is it not? It is indeed, but there is more to be said.

At least on the face of it, Van Til appeals to Scripture as his ultimate criterion and test of truth, while Carnell appeals to logic, experience, and subjective adequacy of various kinds. "Starting point" is, as I have argued elsewhere in this volume, a rather ambiguous expression, even when we distinguish "logical" from "synoptic" starting points, as do Lewis and Carnell.[27] In my view, the phrase should be left out of the discussion. The relevant question is, What is the ultimate test of truth? Van Til's answer is clear. What of Carnell's?

Although Carnell's answer often appears to be opposite to Van Til's, that answer is not unambiguous. We have seen that he affirms the self-attestation of Scripture and denies that there is any authority superior to it. In those passages, he certainly seems to be affirming Scripture as something more than a "hypothesis." Yet he also says things like the "Bring on your revelations" quotation, which seem to subject Scripture to man's logical and rational tests. Is there some way to find consistency among Carnell's formulations?

I have pointed out in connection with Hodge, Butler, and others that it is not wrong in every sense, even on Van Til's view, to test Scripture by reason. Thus, in the last chapter, I discussed Butler's statement that, if anything in Scripture is really contrary to reason, we should at that point give up Scripture in the name of God. I pointed out that that statement was highly misleading, but not strictly false, granted the contrary-to-fact character of the condition. Even for Van Til, Scripture is rational and "meets every legitimate demand of reason." Van Til's only concern is to emphasize, as Butler does not, that Christians and non-Christians use reason in different and contrary ways. Thus, Butler's statement, taken without proper qualification, tends to mislead people into thinking that there is a greater area of common ground between believers and unbelievers than there really is.

Carnell's "Bring on your revelations" is equivalent to Butler's statement, although it is more rhetorically excessive. Like Butler's

---

[25]JA, 350–52.

[26]Ibid., 351. Van Til puts the issue the same way in his reply on p. 363.

[27]Ibid., 352.

statement, it is not strictly false. Van Til agrees that Christianity passes the legitimate tests of logic and facticity; indeed, he thinks that no other system does. The only question is, What constitutes a legitimate test?

It is not that Van Til wants to eliminate the tests of logic and evidence. In previous chapters, we have seen his positive statements about both. He only wishes to call our attention to the fact that unbelievers, in their repression of the truth, use false standards in judging logical and factual adequacy.

It is hard to imagine that Carnell would disagree with Van Til on this point. All Christians surely recognize that unbelievers resort to illegitimate logical and empirical appeals in order to oppose the gospel, although we also recognize (as Van Til does, in chap. 15) that non-Christians know much truth. Yet Carnell never explores the noetic effects of sin in any systematic way, and that plays no role in his apologetic presentation.

Lewis is correct, therefore, when he points out some parallels between Van Til and Carnell. Both men presuppose Scripture as God's Word, and both men allow the testing of that Word by reason and factual evidence.[28] The difference is that Van Til presents far more clearly the epistemological role of Scripture, and that he takes account, while Carnell does not, of the noetic effects of sin. In this regard, Van Til's overall approach is far superior to that of Carnell. But the difference between the two is a difference in clarity and completeness—not in substance, as Van Til thinks. Carnell is not denying Scripture when he attempts to test it by reason and experience.

Nor is he wrong to present these tests to the unbeliever, even without discussion of the noetic effects of sin. Scripture does not require us to bring up this issue in every evangelistic conversation. Lewis says that "the precise point of Van Til's criticism is that Carnell *utilizes* these points of contact in his apologetic."[29] Van Til does sometimes sound as though he is saying that, but, as Lewis points out, Van Til also presents rational and empirical arguments to the unbeliever. I agree that Van Til's language on this point is sometimes loose (chap. 15, again). But his most carefully considered view of this is that yes, we may present such evidences, but we should not do so in such a way as to support the unbeliever's would-be autonomy.

---

[28]Ibid., 351, 353–56.

[29]Ibid., 354.

Again, it is not wrong to test Scripture in these ways. But we should perform these tests, and present them to inquirers, in ways that do not mislead them as to the teaching of Scripture itself. The legitimate force of Van Til's critique is that Carnell is not adequately clear in this respect. But Van Til is wrong to think that his formulations as such implicitly deny the truth of Scripture.

Van Til is here really addressing questions of strategy, formulation, communication, and contextualization: How can we best communicate the gospel so that people today will understand what we are saying? His difference with Carnell is not so much over what we say, as over how we say it. I grant that the "what" and the "how" cannot be entirely separated. A true message so poorly stated that it gives a false impression is not much different from a false message. But we do, in a rough-and-ready way, distinguish between people who speak falsehood and those who speak truth unclearly. Van Til tends to avoid questions of communication and to restrict his attention to matters of scriptural principle. But in doing so, he tends to *reduce* questions of communication to questions of principle.

Carnell's errors, in my view, are serious errors of presentation. Because of their tendency to mislead audiences, they approach being matters of truth and principle. Therefore, I am sympathetic with Van Til's criticisms, although I believe that he has rather drastically overstated them. Both he and Carnell are guilty of a rhetorical excess that is not good for the cause of Christian unity or the cause of apologetic clarity.

Carnell and Kantian Thought

Van Til's second criticism of Carnell is that his tests of truth are identical to those used by unbelieving philosophy, especially Kantian philosophy. Lewis calls this criticism "fallacious guilt by association."[30] I am inclined to agree with Lewis.

We saw in the last section that these tests of truth are not illegitimate, although in the present climate of thought the apologist should seek to remove common misunderstandings about them. They do not presuppose human autonomy, although the rhetoric in which they are stated often, misleadingly, suggests such autonomy.

---

[30] Ibid., 356.

The tests of logical, empirical, and subjective adequacy have been used by both Christian and non-Christian thinkers for centuries, including the argument about the "primacy of the teleological over the mechanical."[31] They are not, in themselves, unique to the Kantian and post-Kantian periods. We have seen such tests functioning in the church fathers and Aquinas, and especially in Butler. Van Til uses them too, and recommends them, although warning us to use them in a clearly Christian way.

Carnell, once again, is not clear at this point. But although his language is very similar to that of Brightman and DeWolf, it certainly cannot be said that he endorses their view of human autonomy. None of Van Til's citations from Carnell justifies that conclusion. The fact that Carnell appeals to man's logic, or rationality, or moral sense, does not imply that he appeals to *autonomous* logic, rationality, or moral sense.

Again, Van Til would have been more persuasive if he had criticized Carnell's clarity, rather than the substance of his arguments. Certainly, when Carnell uses language that is similar to liberal or dialectical theology, some are likely to misunderstand him. Of course, the question does arise as to what audience Carnell is addressing here and whether that particular audience would be misled. But, as a general rule, in addressing twentieth-century people with college educations, as Carnell usually does, greater clarity is needed.

Implicit Denial of Christianity?

The third point in our summary of Van Til's critique of Carnell may therefore be dismissed without much discussion. To say that Carnell's arguments implicitly deny the gospel is an enormous logical stretch. It is possible, of course, for a writer to be so unclear that his readers uniformly derive a meaning directly contrary to his intentions. Carnell may lack clarity, but it is not as extreme as that.

As we saw earlier in the case of Clark, Van Til tended to be at his

[31]Since this world is created and controlled by a personal God, the teleological is prior to the mechanical, even if Kant did say it! Kant's view of these concepts is very different from that of Scripture. But if anything, it is Kant who is appropriating traditional Christian language, rather than Christians who are appropriating Kantian language.

worst in dealing with rival apologists. That is the case here, as it was with Stuart Hackett in the passage quoted earlier. I do not entirely understand this failing in Van Til. Perhaps personal factors made effective communication impossible among these men. Perhaps, like many creative thinkers, Van Til overestimated his originality and therefore the differences between himself and all other apologists of the past and present. Perhaps Van Til's vision of Kuyperian and Machenite antithesis illegitimately spilled over into his relations with fellow Christians, even those fellow Christians closest to him in theological commitments and apologetic purpose. To our shame, the fiercest battles, often based on misunderstandings, frequently occur within families. In this respect, I urge readers not to follow Van Til's example.

But Van Til is a reliable guide to the overall *emphasis* that is most needed in apologetics today. When dealing with educated people, we will often, perhaps usually, find it inadequate merely to present standard logical and evidential arguments. Those arguments may be sufficient for some, and we should not despise those who present them simply and naively. But among those who are culturally aware, we must challenge unbelieving presuppositions; otherwise, we will be misunderstood as reinforcing them.

Conclusions on the Traditional Method

What have we learned in these past four chapters? Let me make some summary statements.

1. Throughout the history of apologetics, Christians have, with some inconsistency, honored Scripture as God's infallible Word, and therefore as the ultimate standard of truth.

2. At the same time, Christians have appealed to logic, fact, and subjective adequacy in various ways to confirm the truth of Scripture.

3. In Van Til's view, these appeals are not wrong, but they must be carried out in a scriptural way, in subordination to Scripture itself.

4. Nevertheless, Van Til does sometimes refer to these appeals as if they were, in themselves, evidence of compromise. He should not have done this without also presenting evidence that they were made on an unscriptural basis.

5. To show the illegitimacy of such an appeal, it is not sufficient to show that the apologist's language resembles, or is influenced by, a non-Christian thinker. For (a) non-Christians do sometimes speak

truth, contrary to Van Til's "extreme antithetical formulations," and (b) Christians often legitimately use the language of non-Christian thinkers to make biblical points, as Van Til does with the language of idealism.

6. It is important to communicate effectively with our age. The strongest criticism of the apologetic tradition is that in its zeal to persuade non-Christians, it has often failed to communicate to them the full antithesis between Christian and non-Christian presuppositions.

7. Van Til's observations often address most cogently the questions of communication. Unfortunately, he misleadingly insists on presenting these concerns as matters of theological substance, ignoring entirely the dimension of communication. Thus, his own communication is hindered.

8. In our apologetic work today, we should not mislead inquirers by formulations, however literally true, that in the present cultural context suggest an autonomous use of reason. Aquinas's distinction between faith and reason, Butler's "Let reason be held to . . . ," and Carnell's "Bring on your revelations" are examples of such misleading formulations.

9. Nevertheless, the history of apologetics furnishes us with many useful rational tools, including theistic proofs, evidential arguments, and appeals to logic, probabilities, and human subjectivity. Such appeals do not, in themselves, violate any biblical principle.

10. The history of apologetics does not reveal the existence of a "traditional method" that uniformly presupposes human rational autonomy and that we must today reject in toto. Rather, that history contains both good and bad, including bad in the best and good in the worst.

11. In judging our predecessors and contemporaries in the field of apologetics, we should not overestimate the importance of our own insights at the expense of others. Nor should we interpret other writers in the worst sense possible, as Van Til has sometimes done. Rather, we should give them the benefit of the doubt, as we would wish others to give that benefit to us. "Innocent until proven guilty" is a valid principle of theological debate, as it is of criminal law.

CHAPTER TWENTY-TWO

Spiral Argument

At long last, we come to Van Til's positive argument for Christian theism. We have spent many chapters discussing the theological, metaphysical, epistemological, and ethical background to this argument, as well as the historical background against which Van Til presents his nontraditional approach. These background chapters have been necessary, I believe, in order to understand Van Til's positive apologetic. However, the fact that so much of Van Til's writing is concerned with such background issues shows that he is as much a theologian as an apologist. Perhaps he is more the former than the latter, insofar as the two can be distinguished.

This point can be made in qualitative, as well as quantitative, terms. I have made no secret of my view that Van Til is at his best in discussing the metaphysics of knowledge and at his worst in discussing traditional apologetics and some aspects of the noetic effects of sin. Therefore, his most significant contributions are more fittingly described as theological than as apologetic.

Nevertheless, Van Til's writings provide substantial insights even in those areas where he is weakest. And no apologist can afford to ignore the argument for Christian theism that Van Til proposes.

Reviewing Some Basics

First, let us review a bit, for I have already laid in place some of the basic building blocks of Van Til's positive apologetic:

1. There is an "absolutely certain proof" of Christian theism (chap. 14). Van Til renounces fideism, the view that faith is blind or irrational. Fideism denies or ignores the clarity of revelation—revelation that provides a rational basis for faith. Indeed, Christian theism is the *only* rational position to hold.

2. All reasoning, including apologetic reasoning, must presuppose divine revelation. Reasoning is never religiously neutral (chaps. 7, 9, and 10).

3. Therefore, our reasoning must presuppose the self-contained, tripersonal God, who exercises absolute and total rule over the world through exhaustive foreordination, Creation, and providence (chaps. 4–6).

4. Our reasoning must take into account both the noetic effects of sin and common grace. We should reckon on the fact that the unbeliever's intent is to suppress the truth (chaps. 15–17). He is not a neutral or unbiased inquirer.

5. The unbeliever suppresses the truth by substituting for Christian theism a dialectic of rationalism and irrationalism: the world is uncreated and therefore without meaning and structure, a chaos, yet somehow made intelligible by purely abstract, logical principles based on the autonomous thought of man (chaps. 5, 12, 14, and 17).

6. We may freely use logical arguments and present evidences for the truth of Scripture. But we should not "endlessly"[1] discuss facts and logic without challenging the unbeliever's philosophy of fact and logic (chaps. 5, 12, and 14). Certainly, we should never ourselves appeal, as the unbeliever does, to "abstract logic" or "brute fact" (chaps. 20 and 21).

7. We should always seek to prove Christian theism "as a unit." This means, for example, that we should not separate the "that" from the "what"—trying to prove *that* God exists without establishing *what* God we are talking about. Our argument should never conclude merely that *a* God exists (chap. 19).

8. Our argument should claim absolute certainty for its conclusion, never mere probability (chap. 20).

[1] CTK, 293.

9. We should not produce arguments that purport merely to supplement the unbeliever's knowledge. Rather, we should seek to overturn the very foundations of his thinking (chaps. 18–21).

Next, let us review my responses to Van Til's principles:

1. I have suggested that we distinguish between the certainty of the *evidence* for Christian theism, which is absolute, and our human *arguments* for Christian theism, which are fallible and often uncertain. Van Til makes this distinction but ignores some of its important implications.

2. With this point I agree with enthusiasm.

3. Again, I agree with enthusiasm.

4. I agree, but I resist the literal use of Van Til's more extreme formulations of the antithesis between Christians and unbelievers. His own account of the matter correctly requires us also to take account of true statements made by unbelievers.

5. Agreed.

6. Agreed, with the proviso that we be permitted to vary our approach depending on the nature of our audience and the specific questions being discussed. Not every apologetic confrontation requires an explicit discussion of epistemology.

7. There is some truth in this principle, but it needs to be qualified. We should not reason as if the nature of God were indeterminate, or as if the nature of God were not clearly revealed. Nevertheless, we are not required by Scripture to prove the entire biblical doctrine of God in a single syllogism. To some extent it is legitimate to prove one fact about God at a time, being careful not to distort the whole in expounding the parts.

8. See the first point, above. It is legitimate in some cases, and even unavoidable, to use arguments that claim only probability.

9. If we reject the idea of extreme antithesis (see point 4), then we must recognize that there will be elements of truth in unbelieving thought. On that assumption, it follows that one function of apologetics is to supplement that truth. This is not to deny the importance of overturning the foundations of unbelieving thought, for the elements of truth in unbelieving thought are at variance with its foundational commitment.

Circularity

When we seek to employ the above principles in actual apologetic discussion, we immediately face the problem of circularity. On Van

Til's principles, the Christian must presuppose the truths of divine revelation in his apologetic arguments. But the unbeliever does not grant those truths. So how can the apologist legitimately presuppose the truths of Scripture when those very truths are being contested? Does not that procedure introduce a vicious circularity into the argument?

Van Til admits that his approach is circular in some sense: "To admit one's own presuppositions and to point out the presuppositions of others is therefore to maintain that all reasoning is, in the nature of the case, *circular reasoning*. The starting-point, the method, and the conclusion are always involved in one another."[2] Of course, "involved in" is not a precise term. It will be helpful to define more sharply what kind of circularity Van Til is referring to.

In its most vicious form, circularity exists when the conclusion of an argument is explicitly included among the premises. Here is the most obvious sort of example:

Example 1

Premise: There are green people on Mars.
Conclusion: There are green people on Mars.

But circularity is usually less explicit. One slightly less obvious example:

Example 2

Premise 1: Either 1 + 1 = 4, or there are green people on Mars.
Premise 2: It is not the case that 1 + 1 = 4.
Conclusion: Therefore, there are green people on Mars.

Although premise 1 does not actually state the conclusion, it virtually does that, by placing it in disjunction with an obvious falsehood.

Arguments actually charged with circularity are more often like the following:

Example 3

Premise 1: If there are yellow buildings on Mars, there are green people on Mars.

[2]DF2, 101 (emphasis his); cf. SCE, 12, 201–2.

Premise 2: There are yellow buildings on Mars.
Conclusion: There are green people on Mars.

Proof of premise 2:

Premise 1: On Mars, green people always build yellow buildings.
Premise 2: There are green people on Mars.
Conclusion: Therefore, there are yellow buildings on Mars.

Here, the actual argument is not circular in any formal way. But when we spell out the argument for premise 2, the larger argument becomes circular.

Of course, people rarely use arguments that are as obviously circular as those in the previous three examples. More commonly, arguments charged with circularity are arguments like the following:

Example 4

Premise 1: The effects of government welfare programs are always harmful.
Premise 2: Programs with exclusively harmful effects should be abandoned.
Conclusion: Government welfare programs should be abandoned.

This argument is not circular in the ways that any of the first three examples were circular.[3] Still, an opponent of the conclusion might not find the argument very cogent, for the first premise would not be accepted by somebody who did not already accept the conclusion. At best, the argument presents a kind of outline for discussion. Most of the discussion would not be about the conclusion as such, but about the first premise. If the truth of the first premise can be established, then the argument is certainly a sound one. But if the truth of the first premise can be established, the argument itself is scarcely necessary.

An opponent of the conclusion in example 4 (call him Johnny) might ask a proponent of the argument (call him Justin) to substitute an argument that does not presuppose the conclusion in this way.

[3]In DKG and AGG I distinguish between "broad" and "narrow" circularity. In the present context, example 1 is the narrowest, example 4 the most broad.

But what often happens in such cases is that any premise Johnny selects will be questioned by Justin. There is a clash between two broad systems of thought. The search for significant common ground between them can be difficult indeed. Of course, the two parties will agree on the truths of logic and mathematics, and perhaps to some propositions about welfare. But the disagreement is so great that it is hard for them to find propositions that are both held in common and significant in leading to greater agreement.

Justin's suggestions will often seem circular to Johnny in the sense that they presuppose items from Justin's "system" that Johnny is unwilling to grant. Justin may oblige by trying to find common ground, but that search may finally be unsuccessful.

Is Justin, then, guilty of circularity? Well, one can define *circularity* any way one likes, and it is not uncommon to see the word used in this kind of situation. But we should note that this kind of circularity is not necessarily a bad thing. For one thing, where there is a clash of systems, it is usually the case that such circularity exists on both sides. If Justin's case is circular, so is Johnny's. So the circularity is unavoidable. And if it is unavoidable, the term *circularity* should not be used as a reproach. It is not necessarily Justin's fault that Johnny fails to agree with his premises. Certainly Johnny has no right to require Justin to use premises acceptable to him, nor vice versa. Neither can be expected to choose premises that violate his fundamental assumptions.

In such difficult political issues, it is hard to find common ground. But it is even more difficult when the matter under dispute is the ultimate criterion of truth. Obviously, one party will try to use only premises acceptable on his criterion, and the other party will try to use only premises acceptable on his. If those criteria are contradictory, and if the disputants are both consistent with their own presuppositions, there will be no common ground at all, no common premises. Each will claim that the other's arguments are circular.

There are examples of this phenomenon outside of what is usually considered the field of religion. In *Apologetics to the Glory of God* (pp. 11–12), I mention the case of a paranoid who lives in an unreal world. He may have his own distinctive concepts of logic and fact—concepts that are quite unacceptable to normal people. On the other hand, the concepts of normal people are unacceptable to him. Again, there are competing circularities, disagreeing about the ultimate nature of truth. And one does not help a paranoid by agreeing with his demented presuppositions. As one helps a drowning person only by giving him a firm rope to grasp, so when somebody is drowning in illusion, we can help only by firmly maintaining the truth of the real world.

The religious case is much more like example 4 than like the others. Van Til, who sometimes accepts and sometimes rejects the phrase "circular reasoning," puts it this way:

> Yet we hold that our reasoning cannot fairly be called circular reasoning, because we are not reasoning about and seeking to explain facts by assuming the existence and meaning of certain other facts on the same level of being with the facts we are investigating, and then explaining these facts in turn by the facts with which we began. We are presupposing *God,* not merely another fact of the universe.[4]

That is, unlike example 3, where the yellow buildings prove the green men and the green men prove the yellow buildings, Van Tillian argument does not reciprocally verify facts on "the same level." Rather, the circularity is between God, who is the ultimate determiner of truth and falsehood, on the one hand, and all the facts governed by him, on the other.

Van Til has taught us that the debate between Christians and non-Christians is, among other things, a debate over the ultimate criterion of truth. Therefore, in his more extreme antithetical formulations, he declares that there is no common ground at all between believers and unbelievers. Of course, as we have seen, there is common ground, because the unbeliever is never consistent in his unbelief. There is no common ground in principle, but there is common ground in actual debate. But even if the unbeliever were consistent, the Christian would have no choice but to be true to his own presuppositions and argue according to his own convictions. He must always utilize the biblical criterion of truth, not the unbiblical criterion of unbelief.

It is in this sense, and this sense only, that Van Til's apologetic is circular. But that cannot be grounds for criticism. As I have noted, this kind of circularity exists in other kinds of debate to some degree; the religious case is unique only because it deals with what by definition are the most fundamental differences in values. Such circularity is unavoidable, and it exists on both sides of the debate.

---

[4] SCE, 201.

Two questions about Van Tillian circularity now deserve our attention. First, does circular reasoning make it impossible for us to learn anything new? And second, does circularity make communication with unbelievers impossible?

The first question arises because the conclusion is assumed in the premises of a circular argument. Therefore, it seems, the premises cannot lead to any new knowledge. However, even on non–Van Tillian views of the matter, every valid syllogism is circular in the sense that the conclusion is implicit in the premises. That is what validity means. So, in one sense, no deductive syllogism adds to our knowledge. If we know the truth of the premises, we know the truth of the conclusion.[5]

This kind of circularity does not, of course, rule out the possibility of learning something new. For the premises of arguments must themselves be verified, and that verification at least sometimes involves the introduction of new data into the system.

In the religious case, the Christian presupposes what he knows about God's revelation. But his knowledge of God's revelation is not static. It grows, and occasionally declines. Our knowledge grows as we presuppose the basics and apply those presuppositions to the analysis of data new to us, both from Scripture and from creation.[6]

Therefore, Van Til sometimes prefers to speak of "spiral" rather than "circular" reasoning:

> The method of implication as outlined above is circular reasoning. Or we may call it spiral reasoning. We must go round and round a thing to see more of its dimensions and to know more about it, in general, unless we are larger than that which we are investigating. Unless we are larger than God we cannot reason about him any other way, than by a transcendental or circular argument.[7]

The illustration of "going round and round a thing"—say, a tree—is helpful. Each time we go around, we presuppose the things

[5] I grant, of course, that we may know the truth of premises without being psychologically aware of the truth of the conclusion.

[6] See DKG for an account of the epistemological process that I believe is implicit in Van Til's thought.

[7] SCE, 12.

we learned on the previous trip and apply those presuppositions to the new data. Sometimes, of course, the new data will require us to unlearn things that we thought we knew before. In the religious case, we may have to revise our interpretation of God's revelation in some areas, but our confidence in the more fundamental matters should direct us through the more questionable territory.

The second question is whether circularity makes communication impossible between believer and unbeliever. This is the question raised by John W. Montgomery's fascinating article, "Once upon an A Priori."[8] Using characters from an animated French television series, he develops an apologetic parable, featuring a confrontation between "Shadoks" and "Gibis":

> The two positions are logically incompatible, needless to say, so both of them cannot be true (though they can both be false—a possibility not seriously entertained by either protagonist, however!). Each position is formally similar to the other and thoroughly presuppositionalist (since a Shadok always starts from his world-perspective and a Gibi from his). Shadoks have their doctrine of election (Election-Sh), their inerrant Scripture (Bible-Sh), and their self-attesting inward experience of salvation produced by the immanent work of their God (Holy Spirit-Sh); Gibis affirm their opposing religious tenets on the basis of similar claims (Election-G, Bible-G, and Holy Spirit-G).[9]

The dialogue, then, proceeds, along the following lines:

> *Shadok:* You will never discover the truth, for instead of subordinating yourself to revelational truth (Bible-Sh), you sinfully insist on maintaining the autonomy of your fallen intellect.
>
> *Gibi:* Quite the contrary! [He repeats exactly the same assertion, substituting (Bible-G) for (Bible-Sh).] And *I* say what I have just said *not* on the basis of my sinful ego, but because I have been elected by God (Election-G).[10]

[8]JA, 380–92.
[9]Ibid., 384.
[10]Ibid., 385.

Thus the dialogue proceeds, each appealing to his own Bible, experience, election, and Holy Spirit, and each denying the corresponding appeals of the other on the basis of his own. Montgomery's point is that this kind of dialogue obviously gets nowhere. The only way to make progress is to appeal to facts that are available to both. But Van Tillian circular argument, Montgomery contends, eliminates any real communication between believer and unbeliever.

By way of reply, first of all, it is not wrong to appeal to facts. As we have seen, Van Til does not object to facts, but only to brute facts. And, in my view, he exaggerates the extent to which apologists in the past have appealed to brute fact. The facts of redemption are indeed publicly available and are important to the work of apologetics. But Montgomery knows as well as anybody that unbelievers often evaluate factual arguments very differently from Christians. Van Til is right: the issue is not only fact, but also philosophy of fact. Thus, the appeal to fact is not an alternative to presuppositional argument, but only a different form of it. We could well expand Montgomery's parable to include Shadok facts (Facts-Sh) and Gibi facts (Facts-G). The introduction of facts into the dialogue would not, in itself, be of much help.

Furthermore, the debate between believer and unbeliever, if Van Til is right, is not at all like the dialogue between Shadoks and Gibis. The logical structure of Christianity is not formally parallel to unbelief in the way that Shadokism is formally parallel to Gibiism. Non-Christians do not believe in a Trinitarian, sovereign, Creator God who redeemed his people from sin through the work of his Son and revealed his will in a holy book. There are *some* formal parallels—particularly in non-Christian movements influenced by the Bible, like Judaism and Islam. And, of course, there is the formal parallel that both Christians and non-Christians have presuppositions. But no non-Christian system contains all the content of the Christian message.

And if one of them did, what would we say about it? We would only say that it was Christianity, expressed in a different language.

Moreover, Van Til does not call upon apologists merely to shout their dogmas at people. He tells us to use factual and logical arguments, governed, of course, by Christian presuppositions. And, as we shall see in the next chapter, he tells us to show the unbeliever that predication is impossible on his premises.

Can the unbeliever reverse these arguments against the Christian? He may try, but he cannot ultimately be successful, because the unbeliever, at some level, *knows* the truth. He is in touch with objective reality, however much he may resist it. Christian witness communicates by reminding the unbeliever of what he knows at this deep level. Besides, Christian witness has a supernatural dimension. As God chooses to do so, his Holy Spirit empowers the word unto salvation. An unbeliever might claim to have such supernatural power on his side, but that does not matter. What matters is not what people claim, but what is the case. What matters is not the talk, but the power. As in the contest between Elijah and the priests of Baal, God settles the dispute.

Practically speaking, Christian witness, even by Van Tillian apologists, rarely looks much like the dialogue of the Shadoks and Gibis. Occasionally, there will be an impasse that somewhat resembles that parable. It sometimes happens that somebody who knows a little of Van Til's apologetics walks off in frustration, saying, "Well, we cannot talk any more. You have your presuppositions, and I have mine, and that's the end of it." But at that point, the inexperienced Van Tillian is at fault, for he is not using the full resources of Van Tillian apologetics. Although we can never guarantee that an unbeliever will listen to us, Van Tillian apologetics always gives us something to say. If we reach an impasse over the issue of authority, we can talk about something else—history, science, psychology, or whatever. In doing so, the Christian will not abandon biblical authority, but will apply biblical authority to matters outside the Bible. And he will challenge the unbeliever so to apply *his* ultimate criteria. Let the unbeliever talk about *his* ultimate authority; then the believer and the unbeliever together can investigate the question of whether, on the basis of that authority, the unbeliever can interpret the world intelligibly. That discussion will be the subject of the following chapter.

CHAPTER TWENTY-THREE

Reasoning by Presupposition

We come now to Van Til's recommended methodology for apologetic witness. Here is, at last, his actual argument—his "absolutely certain proof" of Christian theism. Gordon Clark used to complain that Van Til claimed to have an absolutely certain proof, but never spelled it out in terms of premises and conclusion. The matter is somewhat obscure in Van Til's writings. I hope that this chapter will give us at least some idea of what he had in mind and what value it has for us.

Van Til used various names to describe his preferred form of reasoning. In his earliest syllabus, *A Survey of Christian Epistemology,* he spoke of the "method of implication," a phrase derived from idealist philosophy. That phrase suggested to Van Til a combination of induction and deduction, with a primacy of the general over the particular.[1] In this work, he argues that the phrase fits Christian theism better than it fits idealism, because in Christianity there is a true union of general and particular, unlike idealism, which tries to combine abstract generalities with irrational particulars.

Then he adds that

> from a certain point of view, the method of implication may also be called a *transcendental method*. . . . A truly transcenden-

[1]SCE, 6–10, 201–2.

> tal argument takes any fact of experience which it wishes to investigate, and tries to determine what the presuppositions of such a fact must be, in order to make it what it is.[2]

He continues:

> It is the firm conviction of every epistemologically self-conscious Christian that no human being can utter a single syllable, whether in negation or affirmation, unless it were for God's existence. Thus the transcendental argument seeks to discover what sort of foundations the house of human knowledge must have, in order to be what it is. It does not seek to find *whether* the house has a foundation, but presupposes that it has one.[3]

However, Van Til did not use the terms *implication* and *transcendental* very much after his early syllabus, perhaps fearing too close an association with Kantian, idealist, and, later, Dooyeweerdian philosophy.[4] Nevertheless, I agree with Scott Oliphint that there was no major change in Van Til's method from his earlier to his later works.[5]

In his later writings, Van Til typically calls his method "reasoning by presupposition." He defines this as follows: "To argue by presupposition is to indicate what are the epistemological and metaphysical principles that underlie and control one's method."[6] But, of course, merely telling an unbeliever what the Christian principles are does not constitute an apologetic argument. So Van Til elaborates his description of the method. The argument first seeks to establish "that

---

[2]Ibid., 10 (emphasis his).

[3]Ibid., 11. The term *transcendental* comes from Kant, who also used it to indicate an argument that seeks to establish the presuppositions of human thought. Of course, Kant's conclusions were very different from Van Til's. See my discussions in chaps. 3 and 10.

[4]See JA, 35–37, 74–77. Dooyeweerd distinguished between "transcendent" and "transcendental" criticism. He argued that a truly transcendental method of criticizing unbelieving thought would not use any concepts taken directly from Scripture, for to do that would be merely transcendent criticism. Van Til could not accept that use of *transcendental.* He insisted, contrary to Dooyeweerd, that his own approach was authentically transcendental. See HDRA and our chap. 27.

[5]See Oliphint, *The Consistency of Van Til's Methodology* (Scarsdale, N.Y.: Westminster Discount Book Service, n.d.).

[6]DF2, 99.

every method, the supposedly neutral one no less than any other, presupposes either the truth or the falsity of Christian theism."[7] And, ultimately, the argument concludes that all intelligibility in the universe is derived from Christian theism. Thus:

> The method of reasoning by presupposition may be said to be indirect rather than direct. The issue between believers and non-believers in Christian theism cannot be settled by a direct appeal to "facts" or "laws" whose nature and significance is already agreed upon by both parties to the debate. The question is rather as to what is the final reference-point required to make the "facts" and "laws" intelligible. The question is as to what the "facts" and "laws" really are. Are they what the non-Christian methodology assumes that they are? Are they what the Christian theistic methodology presupposes they are?[8]

By describing the method as "indirect," Van Til evidently wants to distinguish his method from the more traditional apologetic approaches: theistic proofs, evidential arguments, etc. As we have seen, he does endorse proofs and evidences, when they are properly formulated on Christian presuppositions. But when those proofs and arguments are properly developed, they are reducible to the transcendental or presuppositional argument:

> The theistic proofs therefore reduce to one proof, the proof which argues that unless *this* God, the God of the Bible, the ultimate being, the Creator, the controller of the universe, be presupposed as the foundation of human experience, this experience operates in a void. This one proof is absolutely convincing.[9]

How is this argument to be presented in a concrete apologetic situation? Van Til answers:

> The Christian apologist must place himself upon the position of his opponent, assuming the correctness of his method merely for argument's sake, in order to show him that on

---

[7]Ibid., 100.
[8]Ibid.
[9]CGG, 192.

> such a position the "facts" are not facts and the "laws" are not laws. He must also ask the non-Christian to place himself upon the Christian position for argument's sake in order that he may be shown that only upon such a basis do "facts" and "laws" appear intelligible.[10]

That "for argument's sake" is important. When we adopt the unbeliever's principles "for argument's sake," we do not stop reasoning analogically. We are not really adopting an unbelieving point of view, "for that would be self-destructive to the Christian apologist. Even the 'contradictions' that we demonstrate in the unbeliever's thought are contradictory as defined by a Christian view of logic."[11]

In *A Survey of Christian Epistemology,* Van Til describes the Christian's approach as that of "reducing our opponent's position to an absurdity."[12] This language is suggestive of the logical term *reductio ad absurdum,* which, together with his earlier use of the term *indirect,* suggests a model like that of the indirect argument in mathematics. In that model, one proves a proposition by assuming the opposite and deriving from that assumption a contradiction or other absurdity. Similarly:

> What we shall have to do then is to try to reduce our opponent's position to an absurdity. Nothing less will do. . . . We must point out to them that univocal reasoning itself leads to self-contradiction, not only from a theistic point of view, but from a nontheistic point of view as well. It is this that we ought to mean when we say that *we must meet our enemy on their own ground.* It is this that we ought to mean when we say that we reason *from the impossibility of the contrary.* The contrary is impossible only if it is self-contradictory when operating on the basis of its own assumptions. It is this too that we should mean when we say that we are arguing *ad hominem.*[13]

We now have before us the basic elements of Van Til's apologetic method: (1) It seeks to show that all intelligibility depends on, or

[10]DF2, 100–101.
[11]SCE, 205–6.
[12]SCE, 205.
[13]Ibid.

presupposes, Christian theism. (2) It is indirect rather than direct, negative rather than positive, *ad hominem* rather than *ad rem,* essentially a *reductio ad absurdum.* (3) It requires each member of the discussion to "place himself upon" his opponent's position "for the sake of argument" in order to show how that position affects the intelligibility of predication.

The first thing to note is that in this discussion Van Til has not presented us with an actual argument. He has presented (1) a conclusion, (2) a logical model, and (3) a practical strategy. But these give us, not a specific argument, but a set of conditions that any number of arguments might fulfill. The specific argument would, on this conception, depend upon the particular unbelieving view that the apologist confronts. The unbeliever supplies the premises of the indirect argument, the premises which the believer then reduces to absurdity.

From other things Van Til says (see especially chaps. 5 and 17 of this book), we can expand his model as follows: Once the unbeliever supplies the premise of the indirect argument, the believer reduces it to absurdity by showing that it entails the rationalist-irrationalist dialectic. He shows that the unbeliever's position involves the application of purely abstract laws to irrational facts. In this way the non-Christian's position makes rational thought impossible. Van Til is confident that this can be done with *any* non-Christian system. For, on his view, rationalism and irrationalism, so defined, necessarily follow from any denial of the biblical God (see chap. 17 for discussion of this point).

In my view, this is indeed a very powerful form of argumentation. As I have argued earlier, Van Til is right in his evaluation of the hopelessness of the unbeliever's position and in his analysis of the rationalist-irrationalist dialectic as the general structure of unbelieving thought. We shall discuss some specific examples of this argument in the following chapters.

Nevertheless, I do believe that Van Til goes too far when he seeks to *restrict* apologetic argument to this pattern. Therefore, I have a bit more to say about the three points outlined above—the conclusion, the logical model, and the practical strategy.

The Conclusion

The conclusion of Van Til's argument is that intelligible predication presupposes the biblical God. "The biblical God" includes the "what" as well as the "that"—the whole biblical teaching concerning God. Thus, it includes the biblical attributes of God, the doctrine of the Trinity, divine sovereignty, and the doctrines of foreordination, Creation, and providence.

Proving Van Til's conclusion, therefore, is a pretty tall order.[14] It requires a highly complex argument to show that *all* the elements of biblical theism are presupposed in intelligible communication. A Muslim, for example, might well agree with Van Til that the source of universal intelligibility must be personal, but would disagree with Van Til's view that that source must be Trinitarian. Therefore, a Van Tillian apologist would have to go into some detail in showing that intelligibility requires an equal ultimacy of one and many, and that such equal ultimacy in turn presupposes the ontological Trinity (cf. chap. 5).

Idealist philosophers have also claimed to have solved the problem of the one and the many by their coordination of a "concrete universal" (their pantheistic Absolute) with the particular facts of nature and history. So Van Til spends many pages trying to refute their claim and showing that only the personal, Trinitarian God of the Bible is able to coordinate universality and particularity in the way that is required for universal intelligibility.[15] Showing all of that is not easy.

Or imagine Van Til confronting a modern theistic romanticist, who agrees that intelligibility presupposes a God of love, but disagrees with the necessity of presupposing a God of justice. At that point, the Van Tillian apologist would have to show that the attribute of divine justice is necessary if the world is to be intelligible. Or, alternatively, the Van Tillian might attempt to show that unless we accept the biblical account of God (including God's justice) as comprehensively infallible, we have no basis for intelligible reasoning.

Van Til phrases his conclusion in a way that makes it look far simpler than it is. One gets the impression that all the arduous labors of past apologists, proving this or that, can now be bypassed. Now, it seems, we only have to prove one thing, that universal intelligibility presupposes God. But that one thing is so complex that it, in turn, presupposes all the other things.

Van Til seemed to give the impression, although doubtless he knew better, that he had found a "magic bullet," a simple, straightfor-

---

[14]Recall our earlier discussions of this issue in chaps. 14 and 19.

[15]SCE, 132–82; CI, 7–110.

ward argument that would destroy all unbelief in one fell swoop. Doubtless, many apologists have dreamed of hitting on such an argument—the apologetic equivalent of the "lost chord." Anselm of Canterbury prayed for such an argument in his *Proslogium* and thought he had found it in the celebrated "ontological proof." But later discussion has shown that the ontological argument, at best, requires many other arguments to make it fully cogent and to narrow its conclusion specifically to the Christian God. The same, I think, is true of Van Til's argument. It is far more complex than it appears.

I believe that Van Til's conclusion is better described as a *goal* of apologetics. To call it a conclusion is to suggest that every apologetic encounter (whether taking five minutes or five hours) must end by establishing the necessity of presupposing God for universal intelligibility. But, as I have argued before, it is unrealistic to expect that all of Christian theism can be established in a single encounter, let alone in a single argument or syllogism. The process of establishing Van Til's conclusion may be long and arduous, requiring many subsidiary arguments, definitions, replies to objections, etc. I do not doubt, of course, that by the grace of God the process may also occasionally be simple. Clearly, however, it is not always simple. The process will vary considerably, too, depending on the specific position of the non-Christian. We should not address a Muslim the same way we address an idealist or a theistic romanticist.

The Logical Model

As we have seen, Van Til insists that apologetic argument be indirect rather than direct. We prove Christianity by demonstrating "the impossibility of the contrary." Thus, in yet another respect, Van Til sets his position over against the so-called traditional method.

I confess I am not convinced that a transcendental argument for Christian theism must of necessity be indirect rather than direct. To my knowledge, Van Til never argues the point, but merely asserts it. But it is by no means obvious. We can certainly conceive of a positive argument that would lead to a transcendental conclusion. We might, for example, develop a causal argument for God's existence, prove that the ultimate cause of the world must have the attributes of the biblical God, and thus establish that all intelligibility in the universe derives from God.

Furthermore, there is no clear line between an indirect argument and a direct one. Most positive arguments can be put into negative form and vice versa, with some skill in phrasing. Consider the following negative argument, which summarizes Van Til's proposed apologetic:

> Premise 1: If God does not exist, the world is unintelligible.
> Premise 2: God does not exist.
> Conclusion: Therefore, the world is unintelligible.

But the conclusion is false; therefore, at least one premise must be false.

> Premise 1 is true.
> Therefore, premise 2 is false.

This argument, in my estimation, is equivalent to the following positive argument:

> Premise 1: If the world is intelligible, God exists.
> Premise 2: The world is intelligible.
> Conclusion: Therefore, God exists.

It is plain, at any rate, that the first argument will not work unless the second argument is sound. The first argument requires us to prove premise 1, and that requires, in effect, the second argument.

Let us imagine that we are trying to prove to a Muslim that his unitarian theism reduces to unintelligibility. If we succeed, we will still have to prove to him, positively, that Trinitarian theism does make intelligible communication possible. Indeed, we may not even be able to accomplish the former task without the latter argument.

Sometimes, other kinds of positive argument may be needed. To show that a non-Christian view of motion and rest is unintelligible, we may find it necessary to use a theistic proof from motion like that of Aquinas. We would argue that if motion is to be intelligibly explained, God must exist.

No doubt there are some rhetorical advantages in the negative formulation. Greg Bahnsen, a Van Tillian who is, in my opinion, the sharpest debater among Christian apologists today, quite bewildered atheist Gordon Stein in a debate some years ago with his "transcendental argument for the existence of God," essentially a Van Tillian *reductio*. Stein was ready to answer the traditional proofs, but not this one![16] Nevertheless, it does not seem to me that biblical epistemology restricts the apologist to negative formulations.

Why does Van Til insist so strongly on restricting apologists to negative arguments? Probably because he believes that positive arguments are universally subject to his criticisms of the traditional proofs. As we have seen, he believes that traditional proofs begin with the assumption that the world can be understood apart from God's revelation; then, they reason from their autonomous interpretation of the world to the existence of God. But, contrary to Van Til, I argued in chapter 19 that a theistic argument, say, from motion, does not necessarily begin with the assumption that motion is intelligible apart from God. The apologist offering such an argument may indeed be offering it to show that motion is *not* intelligible apart from God. Thus, his argument would have a "transcendental" thrust.

On the other hand, a negative argument may be motivated by an unbiblical assumption. An apologist might set forth a negative argument (such as the one outlined above) based on the assumption that he knows apart from revelation what constitutes an intelligible universe. That assumption might lie behind his use of premise 1 in our example. From that assumption, he may continue through his negative argument to prove the biblical God, a conclusion that, if true, would refute his initial assumption. Such an apologist makes the same error that Van Til ascribes to the traditional method.

How do we know when an apologist is assuming that the universe is intelligible apart from God? Usually, not from the form of his argument as such. Perhaps not from anything the apologist writes. That assumption may be hidden deep in his subjectivity. Indeed, it may be one perspectival way to describe original sin. As Van Til points out in his expositions of Genesis 3, that error is implicit in all sin.[17] To some extent, we all make that sinful assumption in our daily lives as well as in our intellectual arguments. For that, we all need to seek forgiveness through Christ.

Van Til is very sensitive to the spiritual side of intellectual life. He has much wisdom about the influence of sin upon intellectual

[16]The tape of the debate is available from Covenant Tape Ministry, 22005 N. Venado, Sun City West, AZ 85375.

[17]WSA, 9; DCC, 77–79.

disciplines, particularly philosophy and apologetics. But, in my view, he is too much inclined to equate these spiritual issues with formal matters of method and strategy. He wrongly assumes that positive apologetic arguments unambiguously reveal a sinful outlook, while negative arguments unambiguously reveal a righteous one. These are oversimplifications. In my view, it is not possible to make such precise equations.

Van Til calls us to faithful commitment to God as the source of intelligibility in the world, rather than to an idolatrous commitment to the world as the source of God's intelligibility. But this is an appeal to our heart condition, not directly to the formal structure of our arguments. I do not deny in principle that spiritual concerns can have specific methodological consequences. I am only saying that Van Til has not succeeded in proving that his spiritual concerns directly entail his methodological proposals. I believe that much of Van Til's presuppositionalism should be understood as an appeal to the heart rather than as a straightforward apologetic method. Thus, in *Apologetics to the Glory of God* I advocate a "presuppositionalism of the heart."[18] I reiterate that suggestion here.

The Practical Strategy

Van Til calls upon us to implement his transcendental method by the strategy of adopting the unbeliever's presuppositions for the sake of argument, in order to reduce them to absurdity. And, of course, we should also permit the unbeliever to attempt the same thing with our presuppositions.

There are some problems that arise when we seek a more precise definition of this strategy.[19] To what extent do we adopt the unbeliever's presuppositions, even for the sake of argument? Remember that unbelievers have various strategies for evading the truth. In Van Til's understanding, when the non-Christian's rationalism is attacked, he can revert to irrationalism, and vice versa. When the apologist points out the contradiction between these two, the non-Christian may revert to a deeper irrationalism and renounce logical consistency. Then what? When the believer adopts the unbeliever's presuppositions for

[18] AGG, 85–88.

[19] My thanks to Vern Poythress, who stimulated my thinking along this line.

the sake of argument, does that mean adopting all the defensive strategies too? If so, the conclusion of the argument will be that the non-Christian system is perfectly all right. Every objection is answered by an agreed-upon defensive strategy.

Clearly, that is not what Van Til means by adopting the non-Christian's presuppositions. He says:

> We would not be reasoning analogically if we really placed ourselves upon our opponent's position. Then we would, with him, have to reason univocally, and we would drown with him. We use the figure of drowning in order to suggest what it is that we really do when we say that we are placing ourselves upon someone else's position. We may then compare ourselves to a life saver who goes out to save someone from drowning. Such a life saver must be bound to the shore to which he wants to rescue the other party. He may depend upon his power to swim, but this very power to swim is an invisible cord that connects him to the shore. Similarly, if we reason when we place ourselves upon our opponent's position, we cannot for a moment do more than argue thus for "argument's sake."[20]

Here Van Til seems to be aware of the problem before us, but he does not actually answer it. His explanation tells us the *purpose* of the strategy, but it does not tell us exactly *what* we should presuppose for argument's sake.

I suspect that Van Til's strategy could be more clearly described as follows: We should address the unbeliever always from our own presuppositional commitment. From that commitment, however, we may legitimately examine the unbeliever's presuppositions and tell him our evaluations of them, how they look from our point of view. We may also evaluate their consistency (e.g., the consistency between rationalism and irrationalism) and factual adequacy from a Christian-theistic view of logic and evidence.

This criticism is "external" in the sense of being based on criteria outside the unbeliever's own system of thought. But it can become very "internal" in another sense, when we ask the unbeliever how, even from his own point of view, he is able to account for the intelligi-

---

[20]SCE, 205–6.

bility of the world. And we can try to show him that, even from his own point of view, he is unable to do so. But when we speak of "his own point of view," we are, of course, speaking of his point of view from our point of view. Our criticism will never be purely internal, purely from the unbeliever's point of view; it will always be external in the sense that it is determined by the Christian point of view. Otherwise, we would be adopting the unbeliever's defensive strategies and, as in Van Til's illustration, drowning with the one we would rescue.

In a practical situation, then, we would try to show the unbeliever that, for example, his rationalism and irrationalism separately and together destroy the intelligibility of the world and of human thought. But if this argument drives the unbeliever into a deeper irrationalism, we do not concede to him what his presuppositions permit him to concede, namely, that the world is an irrational place after all. Rather, we continue to press the claims of God's revelation. In some situations, we might point out that the non-Christian himself refutes his own irrationalism, for despite his philosophy he continues to live as if the world were a rational place. Thus, the unbeliever's own mind is part of God's revelation, witnessing against his irrationalist defense.

Van Til's strategic proposal, therefore, is a useful suggestion, although it needs clarification. But why should we be restricted to this strategy? Evidently, in Van Til's view, we are restricted to this strategy because it is the approach most conducive to indirect argumentation. However, I have given reasons in the preceding section to justify the use of positive arguments as well as negative ones. Therefore, I would not insist that Christian apologists be restricted to the method Van Til describes here.

The more I study these matters, the more I am impressed with the richness and variety that is possible within a biblical, indeed presuppositional, apologetic. Van Til offers some excellent strategies, some excellent arguments. But his are not the only ones permitted by Scripture. We should learn, with discernment, from the whole history of apologetics, and we should prayerfully employ our God-given creativity within the bounds of Scripture. Van Til has taught us that every fact reveals God. If that is so, there are vastly many apologetic arguments and strategies waiting to be formulated.

CHAPTER TWENTY-FOUR

Apologetics in Action

In this chapter we shall consider some examples of Van Til's actual apologetic presentations, seeking to understand how his methodological recommendations are worked out in practice. There are many of these presentations in his writings, dealing with non-Christian philosophy, ethics, science, and psychology, and with forms of Christian theology that have compromised with non-Christian ideas. Here we shall look at two presentations that Van Til intended as samples of his apologetic. They are fairly short, and in them his apologetic method can be discerned fairly clearly.

A Sample of Christian-Theistic Argument

The last chapter of *A Survey of Christian Epistemology* has the title I have given to this section. In this sample, Van Til says:

> We can conveniently divide the forces of the enemy into two camps. There are those who openly say that they can do without God, and there are those who covertly say they can do without God. Those who openly say that they can do without God we shall classify as Pragmatists, and those who covertly say they can do without God we shall classify as Idealists.[1]

[1]SCE, 210.

The pragmatists and the idealists were two of the leading philosophical schools of the 1930s. Van Til, however, explains that he is using these titles to designate two general tendencies, rather than to focus specifically on the philosophical schools. Therefore, although Van Til's language is somewhat dated, his discussion is not. As I shall indicate, his arguments are quite applicable to the unbelief of our own day.

Van Til's Pragmatists include "all of those who believe in the so-called open universe." They tend toward a more empiricist epistemology: "They naively take for granted that the 'facts' are there as ultimates from which we must begin our research." Some of them may speak of "God," but that will be a finite deity, not the God of Scripture.[2] The Idealists are those who "want to interpret reality in eternal instead of temporal categories."[3]

These two tendencies, broadly empiricist and rationalist, have existed in Western philosophy since its beginnings in Greece, and they are still with us as this book is being written. Today, the empirical, open-universe approach, together with the finite God, is regularly found among process philosophers and theologians, and some branches of analytical philosophy. The eternal-categories approach (together with the other!) is found among New Age monists. But the two approaches regularly cross-fertilize each other.

Van Til begins with the open-universe people, the Pragmatists. These include philosophers, but also those who seem to have no philosophy, who are not interested in intellectual issues. I gather that Van Til puts the latter on the side of the Pragmatists, because they are more opposed to the use of eternal categories than anyone else. "Epistemological loafers," he calls them, "who are not willing to take responsibility for their epistemological attitude."[4] They try to be tolerant of all viewpoints, "because nobody knows."[5] Can the apologist deal with them? Van Til answers: "Indifferentists of this sort are hard to deal with. To some extent, it is a matter of temperament. Yet where it is based upon temperament we should attempt to have them see that they may not indulge in any sort of temperament they please."[6]

---

[2]Ibid.

[3]Ibid., 218.

[4]Ibid., 211.

[5]Ibid.

[6]Ibid.

Of course, we may not be successful. In that case, "Testimony *to* such and prayer *about* such is about all that we can do. It may be that our testimony and our prayer will lead them to begin some intellectual operation of some sort, so that we may begin to reason with them."[7] I would add, "or maybe God will bring them into the kingdom by some means other than apologetic reasoning."

Van Til notes in the context that there are also people who (presumably because of a lack of intelligence or education) are not capable of apologetic debate:

> With respect to these, it is obvious that it would be useless to present the intellectual argument for Christian theism in any subtle or detailed form. Nor is this necessary. A simple presentation of the truth in positive form, and one more largely by way of testimony, may be all that is required. Christianity is not for a few elite intellectualists. Its message is to the simple and to the learned. The argument must therefore be adapted to each one's mental capacity. And it should not be forgotten that the difference between the learned and the unlearned is, after all, very small when it comes to a consideration of ultimate questions.[8]

The "refinement" of the "learned" "does not bring him very far,"[9] Van Til wisely observes.

I have quoted this section, because it is a side of Van Til's apologetic that he rarely expounds and that is not often noted. He does recognize that there are people who cannot be reached even by a presuppositional apologetic. One might get the impression from the previous chapter that Van Til would rigidly insist that any Christian witness involve "reasoning by presupposition," reducing the non-Christian's position to absurdity, etc. He does seem to maintain in those contexts that to follow any other procedure in apologetics is to engage in compromise. But in the above statements, he urges a presentation of the gospel that has little to do with *reductios* or presuppositional analysis—just the clear teaching of the Word of God. We have seen that he rejects as fideistic a view that would *limit* Chris-

[7]Ibid.

[8]Ibid., 211–12.

[9]Ibid., 212.

tian witness to testimony in this sense. Here we see that he does admit to situations in which only testimony is appropriate.

I would expand this point somewhat. Just as there are some with whom we cannot reason at all, and others to whom we can only give simple testimonies, and still others with whom we can engage in sophisticated reasoning, so there are many others along the continuum of sophistication. There is a wide variety of "sorts and conditions of men" and they are in varying degrees capable of appreciating arguments and (relatively) nonargumentative testimonies of various sorts and in various combinations. The apologist must be wise in his judgment of what is called for in a particular situation, rather than imposing a rigid model upon every encounter.

Then Van Til discusses the agnostic, another one who is not much inclined to interpret the world in eternal categories. The agnostic may be a learned person, but he claims that there is no need to make a decision concerning God. The important thing to point out to an agnostic, Van Til says, is that in fact he has made a decision:

> In trying to be agnostic, and in trying to say that they have no need of metaphysics, they have already given one of the two possible answers to every question of epistemology that may be asked. . . . [T]hey have made a universal negative statement about the most ultimate consideration that faces the mind of man.[10]

He has, in other words, denied the Christian claim that God is not only knowable, but the basis of all knowledge. Thus, agnosticism is self-contradictory. "Its claim to make no assertion about ultimate reality rests upon a most comprehensive assertion about ultimate reality."[11]

This is perhaps Van Til's simplest example of reasoning by presupposition. The *reductio* is: Granting agnosticism "for the sake of argument," a contradiction results between avoiding any metaphysical assertion and in fact making a metaphysical claim.

This argument is not altogether unique to Van Til. Plato argued against the Sophists, who were skeptical about the possibility of objective knowledge, that at least they were not skeptical in asserting their

[10]Ibid.
[11]Ibid., 213.

skepticism. This argument has been for many centuries the standard rebuttal of skepticism. But Van Til puts it into a distinctively theistic context: the problem is not merely with the rejection of objective truth in general, but specifically with the rejection of the biblical God as the presupposition of intelligibility. Essentially, the agnostic is trapped in the rationalist-irrationalist dilemma that Van Til finds distinctive of unbelief. He is irrationalist in questioning the knowability of God, yet rationalist in asserting his own rational autonomy.

Agnosticism is self-contradictory not only epistemologically, but also psychologically (the agnostic must be closed-minded and open-minded at the same time) and morally (he must be humble and arrogant at the same time).[12]

Van Til next addresses nonagnostic thinkers in the broadly Pragmatist category. Within this group, he contrasts "materialists" with "spiritualists." Materialists are those who believe that everything can be explained by matter, motion, time, and chance. Van Til here uses the example of psychological behaviorism. Spiritualists (not to be confused with occultists) believe that in addition to matter there must be some mental or spiritual factor that in psychology would explain human behavior and in the world at large would explain the process of nature. Here, Van Til warns Christians against taking sides between the two parties. There is a natural tendency for Christians to think that spiritualists, so defined, are closer to Christian theism than materialists. The materialists are, to be sure, more "crass," Van Til observes.[13] However,

> this should never blind us to the fact that any who misses the train by a step misses it just as well as he who misses it by a mile. And it is sometimes very difficult for us to make those who have a position that approaches Christianity in form see that, after all, they do not have Christianity.[14]

Note here the antithetical thrust of Van Til's apologetic. He does admit that some positions "approach" Christianity more than others. "Approach" is a rather vague metaphor; here and elsewhere I often wish that Van Til had chosen to express himself more literally. I gather,

---

[12]Ibid., 214–15.

[13]Ibid., 215.

[14]Ibid.

however, that he would credit the spiritualist with having grasped a truth that is denied by the materialist. Van Til's point, however, is that we should not put much weight on this agreement. For both materialists and spiritualists agree in rejecting Christian theism.

The relevant point is

> that they have taken for granted that the object and the subject of knowledge exist and can come into relation with one another without taking God into consideration. . . . If God is left out of the picture it is up to the human mind to furnish the unity that must bind together the diversity of factual existence. It will not do to think of laws existing somehow apart from the mind. And even if this were possible it would not help matters any, because even these laws would be thought of as independent of God and as just there somehow. In other words, the only alternative to thinking of God as the ultimate source of the unity of human experience as it is furnished by laws or universals is to think that the unity rests in a void. Every object of knowledge must, therefore, be thought of as being surrounded by ultimate irrationality.[15]

And if each object and each subject is surrounded by ultimate irrationality, "it is inconceivable that there should be any relation of any sort between them."[16]

Van Til is saying that once one abandons God as the basis of knowledge, one is forced to say that facts, laws, and subjects (thinking persons) are "just there." They are not the result of any plan or rational ordering. They are the result of chance alone. As such, the rational order of the facts, laws, and subjects is unreliable. It may be only temporary, or only apparent.

On this basis, one cannot even affirm genuine relationships between laws, facts, and subjects, according to Van Til. For relationships are part of that "rational order" which on examination turns out not to be rational after all. Van Til mentions Aristotle's problem with "the *infima species,* i.e., the relation of the individual to the lowest universal."[17] This problem may be paraphrased as follows: One can-

[15]Ibid., 216.
[16]Ibid.
[17]Ibid.

not identify individuals except by relating them to other things, classifying them by "species" and "relationships." On the other hand, one cannot define species and relations without first identifying the individuals that belong to those species and relationships.[18] Thus, it seems that the process of knowledge can never get started. Van Til's answer is that there are no "pure individuals" apart from relationships, and no "pure relationships" apart from individuals, and that the human mind receives its knowledge of individuals and relationships in a package by divine revelation. We do not need pure individuals and pure relations, because it is not our responsibility to build up the edifice of human knowledge from nothing. That is God's work alone. But without God, one cannot identify either individuals or relationships, either particulars or universals.

Here again, Van Til is seeking to reduce a non-Christian position to absurdity by means of the rationalist-irrationalist dialectic. The non-Christian position is either rationalist (making universals primary, apart from particulars) or irrationalist (making particulars primary, apart from universals). But it is always both, for the one position requires the other. Thus, the non-Christian position makes knowledge impossible.

Idealism, the view that reality is to be interpreted according to "eternal categories," also falls prey to the problem of *infima species*. For it, too, seeks to reason apart from the personal God of Scripture, and therefore its eternal categories are abstract. So it too is faced with the problem of relating abstract universals to unrelated particulars. The only solution is to base our knowledge on authoritative divine revelation. Thus disappear objections both to the biblical doctrine of God and to the doctrine of biblical inspiration.[19]

Van Til's arguments here are powerful, profound, and original. No one else has penetrated as deeply into the heart of the matter. The defects of unbelieving thought reach to its most fundamental assumptions. I have argued that apologetics should not be *restricted* to this kind of argumentation. There is also plenty of value in traditional theistic arguments, historical evidences, and the like. In his more careful formulations, Van Til himself allows for such arguments. But I have no doubt that his approach reaches more deeply than the traditional approaches.

---

[18]Compare our discussion of "ultimate laws" and "ultimate matter" in chap. 5.
[19]Ibid., 220–23.

We have seen that Van Til attempts to reduce the theistic proofs to the transcendental argument. In other words, the transcendental argument provides a *foundation* for theistic argument. For the transcendental argument eliminates the possibility of autonomous reasoning. Once autonomous reasoning is refuted, other arguments may be needed to build up positively the details of the Christian case. Those arguments can proceed freely, presupposing a Christian-theistic epistemology. The apologist will expound the data of divine revelation, including his arguments, which will be in effect the internal rationale of the revelation itself.

"Why I Believe in God"

In the previous section, we examined Van Til's apologetic interaction with several points of view, some relatively unsophisticated, others rather sophisticated. In this section, we will deal with the pamphlet with the above title. It is a remarkable piece, quite different from anything else Van Til wrote. I suspect that any somewhat educated person who began to read it would find it impossible to put down until reaching the end. I confess that this pamphlet provided my first acquaintance with Van Til's work, and it got me thoroughly hooked! It shows how his apologetic can be presented in a way that is entirely fascinating and excellently contextualized to address a modern secularist. It also summarizes concisely virtually all of Van Til's apologetic method. Significantly, this is one of his few works written on a popular level, and it is his only one directed to an unbelieving reader.

At the beginning, Van Til attracts the attention of the educated secularist by mentioning some examples of trendy modern thinkers (Jeans, Eddington, Joad, Niebuhr) who have expressed renewed interest in the concepts of God, sin, and evil. We know from Van Til's other writings that he regards such people as far from the kingdom; they have "missed the train," whether by a minute or an hour. But he is not too rigid to mention them as an attention-getting device. He reminds the inquirer that he has probably asked himself questions about God, about life after death, about the "foundation of your thought and action."[20] Therefore, he can say that "I have the feeling

[20]WIB, 2.

that you are basically interested in what I am proposing for discussion."[21]

He begins by

> comparing notes on our past. That will fit in well with our plan, for the debate concerning heredity and environment is prominent in our day. Perhaps you think that the only reason I have for believing in God is the fact that I was taught to do so in my early days. Of course I don't think that is really so. I don't deny that I was taught to believe in God when I was a child, but I do affirm that since I have grown up I have heard a pretty full statement of the argument against belief in God. And it is after having heard that argument that I am more than ever ready to believe in God. Now, in fact, I feel that the whole of history and civilization would be unintelligible to me if it were not for my belief in God. So true is this, that I propose to argue that unless God is back of everything, you cannot find meaning in anything.[22]

Thus he lays down the presuppositional gauntlet, but winsomely. Van Til was fond of the slogan *suaviter in modo, fortiter in re:* gentle in the manner of presentation, powerful in substance. As we have seen, his writings are not always *suaviter in modo,* but this one is a good example of that principle. He adds illustrations: We may argue whether air exists, but through the argument we are breathing it all the while. And "God is like the emplacement on which must stand the very guns that are supposed to shoot Him out of existence."[23]

Then he says,

> However if, after hearing my story briefly, you still think it is all a matter of heredity and environment, I shall not disagree too violently. My whole point will be that there is perfect harmony between my belief as a child and my belief as a man, simply because God is Himself the environment by which my early life was directed and my later life made intelligible to myself.[24]

---

[21]Ibid.

[22]Ibid., 2–3.

[23]Ibid., 3.

[24]Ibid.

That is to say, it is God who made Van Til's life intelligible, from childhood to maturity.

The inquirer was born in Washington, D.C., "under the shadow of the White House"; Van Til, in a thatched-roof farmhouse in Holland. Both, therefore, were born "in the midst and under the influence of 'Christian civilization,'" and therefore understand what kind of God is under discussion.[25] Since the Christian God is the Creator, coming to believe in God involves coming to accept one's own creatureliness. Van Til therefore warns his inquirer (at the same time maintaining his interest!) that "if you are to change your belief about God, you will also have to change your belief about yourself."[26] That may be hard to do, but Van Til asks the inquirer to listen just a bit longer. "You might follow my argument, just for argument's sake."[27]

Van Til then engages in some fascinating reflection on his early life. He prayed to assuage his fear of ghosts in the barn at night. His family read through the whole Bible at meals. "Ours was not in any sense a pietistic family. . . . Though there were no tropical showers of revivals, the relative humidity was always very high."[28] In short, "I was 'conditioned' in the most thorough fashion. I could not *help believing* in God—in the God of Christianity—in the God of the whole Bible."[29] Does this seem to be a damaging admission? He continues:

> Shall we say then that in my early life I was conditioned to believe in God, while you were left free to develop your own judgment as you pleased? But that will hardly do. You know as well as I that every child is conditioned by his environment. You were as thoroughly conditioned *not* to believe in God as I was to believe in God. So let us not call each other names. If you want to say that belief was poured down *my* throat, I shall retort by saying that unbelief was poured down *your* throat. That will get us set for our argument.[30]

Van Til then describes his "early schooling" in Christian schools, during which he endured the ridicule of public school children. His

[25]Ibid., 3–4.
[26]Ibid., 4.
[27]Ibid.
[28]Ibid., 5.
[29]Ibid., 6.
[30]Ibid.

inquirer, on the contrary, went to a school where he was taught to be open-minded, or neutral:

> Of course, you know better now. You realize that all that was purely imaginary. To be "without bias" is only to have a particular *kind* of bias. The idea of "neutrality" is simply a colorless suit that covers a negative attitude toward God. At least it ought to be plain that he who is not *for* the God of Christianity is *against* Him.[31]

God has clearly displayed his ownership of the universe; being "neutral" about God is like being "neutral" about the authority of the American government. Similarly, "When Eve became neutral as between God and the Devil, weighing the contentions of each as though they were inherently on the face of them of equal value, she was in reality already on the side of the devil!"[32]

"There you go again getting excited once more," Van Til continues, ever watchful to maintain his *suaviter in modo* presentation despite making strong contentions.[33] The inquirer does not think that the evidence of God is clear. However, "if the God of Christianity does exist, the evidence for Him *must* be plain. And the reason, therefore, why 'everybody' does not believe in him must be that 'everybody' is blinded by sin."[34] Van Til illustrates this with a parable about blind men who refused to believe that the sun exists.

God is plainly revealed in the world and in our individual biographies because he is sovereign. He is the *"All-Conditioner,"*[35] the controller of all things, "the emplacement on which even those who deny Him must stand."[36]

If such a God exists, the inquirer has insulted him, by failing to honor him despite clear revelation of his existence. Everything he says and does seeks to justify that insult. "You are therefore wearing colored glasses. And this determines everything you say about the

[31]Ibid., 7–8.

[32]Ibid., 8.

[33]Ibid. One recalls Ronald Reagan's gentle, but pointed, use of such language in his 1980 debate with President Jimmy Carter.

[34]Ibid.

[35]Ibid., 10 (emphasis his).

[36]Ibid., 12.

facts and reasons for not believing in Him."[37] Therefore, the disagreement between believer and unbeliever is very deep: "We really do not grant that you see any fact in any dimension of life truly."[38] We disagree on chickens and cows, as well as about eternal life.

Unbelieving philosophers object to the doctrine of Creation, because they believe that every cause must be correlative to its effects. Therefore, if God created the world, he must be dependent on it as much as vice versa.[39] They object to providence because if God controls history, "there can be nothing new and history is but a puppet dance." Thus, prophecy is also impossible.[40] Miracles cannot be affirmed, according to William Adams Brown, because human judgment decides what can happen, and it makes those judgments according to criteria that admit only natural, recurring events.[41] Therefore, when the Christian seeks to present evidence of Creation, providence, prophecy, and miracle, the unbeliever rejects that evidence on the basis of his general criteria of truth, which exclude the Christian claims from the outset.

Frustration over this situation has led some Christians to deny the clarity of revelation, to claim that the evidence "is only *probably* compelling"[42]—or even to revert to pure fideism. But this is wrong. A fideist "testimony" can easily be rejected by an unbelieving psychologist as a mere datum with a problematic cause.[43]

So Van Til says to the inquirer,

> What you have really done in your handling of the evidence for belief in God, is to set yourself up as God. You have made the reach of your intellect, [*sic*] the standard of what is possible or not possible. You have thereby virtually determined that you intend never to meet a fact that points to God.[44]

The inquirer has "colored glasses" cemented to his face, and therefore he sees the world from an unbelieving viewpoint. Only God's

---

[37]Ibid.
[38]Ibid.
[39]Ibid., 13.
[40]Ibid., 14.
[41]Ibid., 14–15.
[42]Ibid., 16.
[43]Ibid., 16–17.
[44]Ibid., 17.

grace can remove them, and he may choose to do so, using apologetic reasoning as his tool. Deep in his heart, the inquirer knows that his way of thinking is hopeless; his changeless logic cannot meet the changing facts.[45]

On the other hand, the believer does find unity in his experience: "Not of course the sort of unity that you want. Not a unity that is the result of my own autonomous determination of what is possible. But a unity that is higher than mine and prior to mine."[46]

On the basis of Christian theism, we can use the knowledge discovered by unbelieving scientists, while observing the problems into which their unbelief has led them.[47] "My unity is that of a child who walks with its father through the woods."[48] He can face difficulties in nature and Scripture, recognizing the mystery of God's ways. He concludes: "So you see when I was young I was conditioned on every side; I could not help believing in God. Now that I am older I still cannot help believing in God. I believe in God now because unless I have him as the All-Conditioner, life is Chaos."[49]

It is all there: presuppositions, divine sovereignty, rejection of neutrality, clarity of revelation, noetic effects of sin, rejection of probabilism and fideism, unbelieving views of possibility, rationalism and irrationalism, analogical reasoning, and reasoning by presupposition. But here it is stated with very little technical terminology, using wonderful illustrations (many omitted in my summary) and some memorable phrases,[50] and anticipating sensitively the thinking process of an unbelieving reader.

Van Til also mentions circularity at the end of his pamphlet:

> I shall not convert you at the end of my argument. I think the argument is sound. I hold that belief in God is not merely as reasonable as other belief, or even a little or infinitely more probably true than other belief; I hold rather that unless you believe in God you can logically believe in nothing else. But

[45]Ibid., 18–19.

[46]Ibid., 19.

[47]Ibid.

[48]Ibid., 20.

[49]Ibid.

[50]E.g., "the All-Conditioner." I wonder why he did not use that phrase elsewhere in his writings; it is remarkably evocative.

> since I believe in such a God, a God who has conditioned you as well as me, I know that you can to your own satisfaction, by the help of the biologists, the psychologists, the logicians, and the Bible critics reduce everything I have said this afternoon and evening to the circular meanderings of a hopeless authoritarian. Well, my meanderings have, to be sure, been circular; they have made everything turn on God. So now I shall leave you with Him, and with His mercy.[51]

I confess that I find this ending the weakest part of the pamphlet. Not that it is not true, but there is such a sense of pessimism about it.[52] Van Til begins by saying he shall not convert the inquirer; how does he know that? He repeats unnecessarily the material about the scientists who reject Christian teaching based on their presuppositions. And he does not explain at all adequately the sense in which his argument is (and is not) circular and authoritarian. Perhaps he wanted to avoid resembling the high-pressure fundamentalist style of evangelism, which "presses for decision." But the pamphlet could certainly have benefited, in my view, from a bit more pressure of this sort. At least it would have profited from a straightforward summary of the biblical way of salvation.

Nevertheless, I have expounded this pamphlet at such length because I believe that it is, on the whole, an admirable model for Christian apologetics, in style, intellectual depth, comprehensiveness, conciseness, rapport with the reader, and biblical soundness.

[51]Ibid., 20.

[52]I can just hear Gary North arguing that this passage is an implication of Van Til's amillennialism.

PART FIVE

Van Til as Critic

CHAPTER TWENTY-FIVE

Greek Philosophy and Scholasticism

In Part Five of our study, we shall discuss some more actual instances of Van Til's apologetic. A large amount of Van Til's writing is devoted to criticism of various non-Christian thinkers and of some forms of Christian thought compromised by their adoption of non-Christian ideas. Van Til has commented on almost all of the major thinkers in the history of philosophy and theology. I will not be able to discuss these comments in any comprehensive way, but I will address some of the areas to which he gave the most attention.

One of those areas was Scholasticism, the philosophy and theology of traditional Roman Catholicism. Van Til saw Scholasticism as an unstable compromise between Christian theism and Greek philosophy. We have already looked at Van Til's critique of the apologetic of Thomas Aquinas in chapter 19, but a broader look at his critique of Scholasticism will illumine some of his critical methods.

In our discussion of Aquinas, we noted that he was heavily influenced both by Neoplatonism and by Aristotle. Van Til finds these influences to be quite pervasive in Aquinas, although he recognizes that Aquinas does sometimes depart from these philosophers in a scriptural direction.

In *Christianity in Conflict* (2:2), Van Til discusses *The Spirit of Medieval Philosophy,* by the great twentieth-century Thomist scholar,

Etienne Gilson.[1] Gilson recognizes that the Greek philosophers did not believe in the Christian God, and he confesses freely that Aristotle's god did not create, know, or love the world.[2] At times he expresses the relation of Christianity to Greek thought very antithetically, reminding us of Van Til's own formulations: "What Aristotle lacked in order to conceive creation was precisely the essential principle and starting point."[3]

Nevertheless, Gilson believed that the Greek thinkers had made substantial progress toward a Christian concept of God: "We do not dream of disputing Aristotle's undoubted contribution to the philosophic idea of the Christian God. What is really surprising on the contrary is, that having gone so far along the right road he should have failed to follow it to the end."[4]

Thus, on Gilson's view, Aquinas and other medieval thinkers were not wrong when they saw themselves as supplementing and correcting, rather than simply negating, Greek philosophy. Often he argues that the Christian philosophers understood the ideas of the Greeks more deeply than did the Greeks themselves, so that their corrections and supplements seem like "natural growth, inevitable, almost necessary."[5]

Van Til's position, is, of course, more sharply antithetical:

> The question then is whether Aristotle can be corrected at such a basic point as creation without being corrected in his entire interpretation of all the aspects of the universe to one another.
>
> The answer would seem to be that either finding or inserting the idea of creation into Aristotle's philosophy would mean a correction of all his doctrines. In fact, there is no room at all in Aristotle's philosophy for the idea of creation. Neither can it be inserted into his system without bursting it at the seams.
>
> But this is just the point at which Romanism differs. It holds that Aristotelianism can be restricted and limited to the cre-

---

[1]New York: Scribner's, 1936.
[2]Ibid., 44–48, 65, 111, 424–25.
[3]Ibid., 68–69; cf. pp. 74, 158, 332, 446.
[4]Ibid., 45. Note similar comments on pp. 50, 81–82, 183, 200, 207, 249.
[5]Ibid., 360; cf. pp. 67, 96, 200.

> ated sphere and that in thus restricting it ample room is left for the idea of grace and its primacy over nature.[6]

Now when Van Til speaks of a "correction of all his doctrines," he evidently does not mean that every statement Aristotle made was false. That would be the extreme antithetical view that I discussed and rejected in chapter 15. But what is the alternative? "Bursting at the seams" is a picturesque phrase, but it is a metaphor, one that in this context requires explanation. Since Gilson certainly does not affirm all of Aristotle's statements, it would seem that the difference between Van Til and Gilson is, after all, a difference in degree, Gilson being relatively optimistic, and Van Til rather pessimistic, about the value of Aristotelian philosophy for Christian theology.

When Romanism tries to restrict and limit Aristotelianism to the created sphere, it has, after all, engaged in a fairly radical critique of Aristotle. Such a restriction entails major revision. It involves a rejection of Aristotle's concepts of God, analogy, and origin. It replaces Aristotle's epistemology with one in which divine revelation plays a crucial role. What is left after this criticism is a very truncated Aristotelianism indeed. But Van Til writes as if the Thomists were trying to combine Aristotle's entire philosophy with Christianity. In the context of the above quote, he says that the Thomists attempt to import into Christianity Aristotle's combination of Parmenidean unity (rationalism) and Heraclitean disunity (irrationalism). But does that dialectic remain in Aristotle's system after the Thomists have revised it?

Van Til typically thinks in terms of systems. A system is a body of teaching with a particular starting point, method, and conclusion, which are "involved in one another." Clearly, combining the Aristotelian system with the Christian system would be impossible. But is it possible to combine a truncated Aristotelianism (no longer the Aristotelian system) with Christian thought? The answer to that question is not so obvious. It may have to be answered in a more piecemeal fashion, with respect to particular doctrines, rather than the whole as a unit.

Look, for example, at Creation. According to Aquinas, God created everything *ex nihilo*, including "primary matter."[7] He created

---

[6]NRC, 5:6–7.

[7]Aquinas, in Anton C. Pegis, ed., *Introduction to St. Thomas Aquinas* (New York: Modern Library, 1948), 236.

all things by his free will, not by necessary emanation, as in Neoplatonism.[8]

Both Gilson and Aquinas do speak of God as "Being," based upon a traditional exegesis of Exodus 3:14.[9] That has a ring of Neoplatonic pantheism to it, but we should not accuse them of such an unbiblical view without more discussion. Gilson takes pains to distinguish Thomism from Greek thought at that point:

> According to Plato "the degree of divinity is proportionate to the degree of being"; but for a Christian there are no degrees of divinity; God alone is divine. . . . [P]roperly speaking there is but one God who is Being and beings, which are not God. The radical difference of the two traditions lies in the fact that, for Plato, there is no sense of the word "being" reserved exclusively for God.[10]

In this statement, Gilson is clear that "being" is not a generic substance in which God and creatures equally participate. Indeed, when we speak of God as "Being" and creatures as "beings," we are using the word *being* in two different senses: "Although therefore in our language ['being'] bears the same name as the most general and abstract of all our concepts, the idea of Being signifies something radically different."[11] When Gilson uses "Being" as a divine name, the language is awkward, but his use of the term clearly presupposes the "two-circle" metaphysic of Scripture and Van Til.

Indeed, it is because God is Being, and therefore radically distinct from beings,[12] that he is in no sense correlative to creation. Noth-

---

[8]Ibid., 199; Gilson, *Spirit of Medieval Philosophy,* 377.

[9]Gilson, *Spirit of Medieval Philosophy,* 51. On the whole, I believe this exegesis is faulty. The "I am" of Ex. 3:14 does not identify God with metaphysical being in some sense, but pledges the constant, sovereign presence of God with his people. Gilson does admit that in the text there is no "metaphysical definition of God," and he allows for various possible interpretations of the text. But he does wish to insist that the text has metaphysical implications: "If there is no metaphysic *in* Exodus there is nevertheless a metaphysic *of* Exodus" (p. 433).

[10]Ibid., 48; cf. pp. 65, 90.

[11]Ibid., 52.

[12]Gilson regularly distinguishes God as Being from creatures as beings by capitalizing the former.

ing in creation can determine his will.[13] God does not even fall within the same genus as any creature.[14]

For Aquinas, the creature is thoroughly dependent on the Creator. Everything that is and everything that happens is to be referred to God. No creature does anything independently. Aquinas's doctrine of predestination is as comprehensive as that of Calvin.[15] When Aquinas speaks of human free will, he does not define it as some kind of independence from God, but rather as the power to make one's own decisions.[16]

Therefore, it might seem as if Thomas and Gilson were philosophically fairly close to Van Til, granted that they would differ with him on many theological points. Or are they? When I was a seminary student, I took a Th.M.-level course with Van Til on Scholasticism, in which we read the text of Gilson that I have been quoting. In my term paper, I wrote a dialogue that somewhat mirrors the discussions in the seminar between those who defended Van Til's pessimistic views of Scholasticism and those who supported Gilson's optimistic view. With some revision, here it is.[17] "Antithetus" represents a disciple of Van Til (not always following Van Til precisely); "Thetus" is a Reformed student attempting to defend Gilson.

THETUS: Gilson explicitly denies that the creature has any power of resisting the Creator.

ANTITHETUS: Oh, you do not understand Scholasticism at all! Of course the Thomists speak of divine determinism of a sort, but this is the exact opposite of the Reformed view of the sovereignty of God. To the Thomist, man participates in God's Being and so is identical with and hence determined by God. On the other hand, because man also participates in nonbeing, he has a certain autonomy over against God.

THETUS: Complete determinism and complete autonomy?

ANTITHETUS: Dialectically related. Rationalism and irrationalism. The one principle must support the other, even if it must kill the other.

---

[13]Gilson, *Spirit of Medieval Philosophy*, 92; cf. pp. 102–3.

[14]Ibid., 250, 342.

[15]Ibid., 161, 210, 274, 369–70. Compare the references in chap. 19 of this book.

[16]Aquinas, in Pegis, *Introduction to St. Thomas Aquinas*, 369–70; Gilson, *Spirit of Medieval Philosophy*, 304–5; cf. pp. 339–41, 373, and his account of the Fall on p. 118–27.

[17]For those who are curious, Van Til did give me a "1" on the paper, the highest possible mark.

THETUS: But Gilson denies that we participate *ontologically* in God's Being. He holds that we are "beings," and as such are analogous to Being, but he is always careful to insist that we are not identical with Being.

ANTITHETUS: Oh, certainly. This is mystical theology. An infinite difference between God and man. God may be known only by way of remotion. Strictly speaking, the Scholastic knows nothing about God. But insofar as he knows anything about God, he must know exhaustively. Compare Barth. These are two sides of the coin. On the one hand, as nonbeing, we are infinitely far removed from Being. On the other hand, as being, we are one with God's Being. Thus, we have pure continuity and pure discontinuity correlative to each other.

THETUS: But I cannot find anything in Gilson that *says* this. And he seems, anyway, to deny it constantly.

ANTITHETUS: Well, of course, no Christian would want to state baldly that man is a part of God, so to speak. You have to be more tactful.

THETUS: I cannot imagine that any Christian would believe such a thing.

ANTITHETUS: Well, stranger things have happened in the history of Christian thought.

THETUS: But where in Gilson do you find support for such a view?

ANTITHETUS: Does Gilson not claim to be following the principles of Aristotle?

THETUS: Yes, but you know he puts a thousand limitations on that.

ANTITHETUS: Oh, certainly. He does not care for Aristotle's view of the eternity of the world. Yet he uses Aristotle's proofs for the existence of God, which for Aristotle prove the existence of a pure form with no creative power or personality.

THETUS: But surely he revises those proofs accordingly. Furthermore, how can we be so sure Aristotle was consistent? Gilson claims that Aristotle was inconsistent with his own principles in such a way that he *should have* arrived at the Christian God. Should we not at least investigate to see if this might be so?

ANTITHETUS: But both Aristotle and Aquinas are committed to the form-matter scheme. Thomas himself admitted that he could not disprove the eternity of the world on his basis, and that it required faith to believe that the world had a beginning. Thus he admits that the rational scheme he shared with Aristotle excludes Christian teaching.

THETUS: But surely he believed that the faith was not inconsistent with what could be proved by reason.

ANTITHETUS: Whatever he believed, the fact is that Thomas's Aristotelianism destroys the Christian faith. After all, none of Thomas's five proofs of God's existence in any way distinguishes his God from Aristotle's.

THETUS: But the God they prove has the attributes of the biblical God.

ANTITHETUS: But the Christian God is not merely a first mover. He is the Creator of heaven and earth.

THETUS: So is Gilson's God.

ANTITHETUS: But how can Gilson believe in biblical Creation if he thinks that man is a participant in God's Being?

THETUS: This is where we began. I do not think Gilson's "participation" is any sort of ontological union. After all, he denies it.

ANTITHETUS: He denies it by way of dialectical accommodation. He denies it to allow for human autonomy.

THETUS: But he denies human autonomy, too, and his view of free will seems to me to be no different from that of Charles Hodge.

ANTITHETUS: It is the precise opposite of Hodge's doctrine. And he denies human autonomy to allow dialectically for human participation in God's essence.

THETUS: We seem to be going around in circles. Each of us can explain everything. How are we supposed to choose?

ANTITHETUS: Do it *my* way!

Our disputants will be back a bit later. The problem is that both positions can apparently account for the data available, and each can plausibly explain away the data advanced by the other. Both are alleging inconsistency in Scholasticism, but inconsistency of different kinds. Antithetus finds in Scholasticism the contradictory but mutually supportive elements of unbelieving rationalism and irrationalism. Thetus finds in Aristotle elements of truth competing with elements of falsehood, and then he finds both also in Aquinas. From inconsistency, as we have seen, anything logically follows, and that creates problems for interpreters. If a thinker is inconsistent, anything at all can be defended as an "interpretation" of him.

Further, within the rationalist-irrationalist dialectic, there are formal parallels to Christian theism, as Van Til has pointed out. In Christianity, too, God is both above us and near us. He is sovereign, and he grants us freedom of a sort. Therefore, it is not always easy to determine which view is which. Van Til himself says,

> Of course it is not our business to look into the hearts of men. Men may be and are inconsistent *ad bonam* as well as *ad malum partem*. We deal only with systems of thought. And it is not possible even with respect to these systems of thought to be always certain that it is basically Christian or anti-Christian.[18]

Still, Van Til's critical analysis of Scholasticism seems to assume that we can judge the Scholastic system to be non-Christian.

In *Christianity in Conflict,* Van Til tends to rely on secular interpreters, such as Richard Kroner and Arthur Lovejoy, for his judgments concerning Scholasticism. It is not that he was unfamiliar with the primary sources; indeed, he knew them very well. I suspect that he quoted secular interpreters to avoid the criticism that his views were somehow idiosyncratic or extreme. Nevertheless, this use of secular sources is ironic: Van Til, the apologist of antithesis, is making common cause with secular interpreters against other Christians. In any case, it is evident that a closer scrutiny of the primary source documents is needed if we are to resolve the interpretive impasse. Van Til's critique is suggestive and cautionary, but not definitive.

Van Til's analysis of Scholasticism also deals with the "analogy of being," which he takes as a kind of Plotinian scale of being in which creatures participate by various degrees in divinity. This concept of participation, therefore, has pantheistic implications.

Gilson begins his discussion of analogy with a question: "Once Being itself is posited in its pure actuality, does it not become impossible to imagine the existence of anything that would not be Being? If God is not Being, how is the world to be explained? But if God is Being, how can there be anything other than Himself?"[19] I take this problem to be equivalent to Van Til's "full bucket difficulty": why would a God who is sufficient unto himself create a world? Van Til believes that this paradox is insoluble.

---

[18]CC, 2:1, p. iii.

[19]*Spirit of Medieval Philosophy,* 84.

Gilson should perhaps have taken the same position. He does, however, attempt a rational account of Creation, and in so doing he raises suspicions of Plotinian sympathies: "That we may have causality in the strict sense of the term means that we must have two beings and that something of the being of the cause passes into the being of that which undergoes the effect."[20]

This sounds as if God, in creating the world, produced an emanation of his own divine essence, with the result that the creation was itself a divine being. But Gilson, who, as we have seen, distinguishes radically between Being and beings, quickly adds that he has something else in mind. Basically, he argues that personal causality begins with an intention, which is part of the being of the personal cause. For example, Beethoven's symphonies began as ideas and intentions in his mind.[21] So, for God to "communicate his Being" in creation means nothing more than that in creation he expresses his intentions.

Of course, his intentions are united to his essence. A person is by nature active; he acts because of what he is. Creation is therefore "rooted in the very being of" God.[22] Does this mean that God was constrained by his nature to create the world? That would seem to imply that God had to create the world and is therefore correlative to it. Therefore, Reformed theologians have typically insisted that Creation is a "free" act of God, not a "necessary" one. Van Til himself finds mystery here:

> Here too, Christian theology does not claim to have solved the logical difficulty. The logical difficulty is this, that God's will is free, but that, when exercised in the creation of the universe, in this act of the will there is an expression of God's nature. How can an eternally active being, fully self-conscious, be free? With respect to God's own nature, the greatest necessity is the greatest freedom. With respect to the universe, we maintain that God was free in the sense that its creation was in no sense necessary as God's being is necessary. The idea of creation was present to God from all eternity, but the actual accomplishment was not. And this is as far as our finite minds

[20]Ibid., 86.
[21]Ibid., 88–89.
[22]Ibid., 89.

> can reach. At this stage, we are in danger of inserting our temporal categories into the eternal.[23]

Gilson also recognizes this difficulty, and he seeks to deal with it by distinguishing between "first act" (the "act" of Being itself) and "second act" (causing other beings).[24] The creation is "God's being" in the sense that he owns it, not in the sense that the creation is divine.[25] "In other words," Gilson summarizes, "God wills Himself necessarily but does not will anything other than Himself necessarily, and all that He does will He wills with respect to Himself."[26] That seems to me to say neither more nor less than Van Til's formulation. Clearly, at least, Gilson seeks to avoid any implication of pantheism.

But then Gilson brings up a phrase that Aquinas quotes from the Neoplatonist Pseudo-Dionysius: "Good is diffusive and communicative of itself."[27] Again, we are faced with a formula that suggests pantheistic emanationism, rather than Creation *ex nihilo.* In Pseudo-Dionysius, it most likely did mean that. But Gilson argues that Aquinas gave a different, Christian meaning to the phrase: God is good, and a good person seeks to give good things to others.[28] Of course, as we have seen already, when God creates, what he gives is something of himself, in that he executes his eternal intentions. Does God's goodness, then, constrain him to create? I presume Gilson would deal with that question as he dealt with the previous question we discussed concerning God's freedom.

Put all of this together, says Gilson, and the implication is that there is an analogy between the Creator and the creature. God is good, and therefore he gives of himself to his creatures. They therefore resemble him. I take this assertion to be virtually the same as Van Til's assertion that because God's plan controls all of nature and history, all things reveal him in some way. Although Gilson's language might suggest a more pantheizing concept, he takes pains to deny that meaning:

---

[23]IST, 249. I believe that here he makes some of the same distinctions that earlier (pp. 174–77) he criticized in J. Oliver Buswell.

[24]*Spirit of Medieval Philosophy,* 90.

[25]Ibid.

[26]Ibid., 93; cf. pp. 102–4.

[27]Ibid., 93.

[28]Ibid., 93–94.

> If then, as the idea of creation implies, the Christian universe is an effect of God, it must of necessity be an analogue of God. No more, however, than an analogue, for when we compare being *per se* with the being caused even in its very existence, we are dealing with two orders of being not to be added together or subtracted; they are, in all rigour, incommensurable.[29]

I do believe, therefore, that a case can be made for the proposition that, although Aquinas and Gilson use Neoplatonic language, their actual teaching with regard to the analogy of being is not unscriptural. As I have said earlier, I do not agree with Aquinas that theology must be limited to "analogous" language as opposed to literal. But Van Til has not persuaded me that the Thomistic view of the Creator-creature distinction is that of a Plotinian chain of being. But let us rejoin our seminar:

ANTITHETUS: Gilson says that Being is inherently diffusive of itself, and you say he means to teach the biblical doctrine of creation! You cannot be serious.

THETUS: But Gilson says that is what he means. What do you do with all the passages in his book emphasizing the distinction between Creator and creature?

ANTITHETUS: Can you not see the dialectical character of this system? Of course Gilson says that God is wholly distinct from creatures. This is the Heraclitean principle of discontinuity, wherein everything is distinct from everything else and wholly unrelated to anything else. It is the principle by which Aristotle made his God a pure form, incapable of having any meaningful relationships with the world. God is "wholly other," because the world is uncreated and uncontrolled by God. Is that the biblical distinction between Creator and creature?

THETUS: Come on, now! Is that not laying it on a little thick? You do not think poor Thomas was a Heraclitean, do you? And as for Aristotle, Thomas denies that he had the right idea about God. Thomas has a form-matter scheme, to be sure, but I cannot see that any Thomist says this scheme encompasses God.

ANTITHETUS: But he says that being is inherently diffusive!

THETUS: I explained that, did I not?

---

[29]Ibid., 97.

ANTITHETUS: Not without some wresting of perfectly clear language.

THETUS: I do not think it is perfectly clear. You have to take into account certain complicating factors. On Gilson's account, Aquinas fulfills Greek thought, to be sure, but by drastically revising it at crucial points. He believes that Aquinas often uses the Greek language with radically different meaning. Unless we want to declare a priori that Gilson's interpretation is wrong, we cannot simply take Aquinas's Greek philosophical language at face value.

ANTITHETUS: But you are the one who always wants to take Gilson in a commonsense way. I see ambiguities in his language where you do not—for example, when he speaks of Creation *ex nihilo*. It seems to me that Gilson *wants* to hold to the Christian doctrine, but his adherence to the Aristotelian form-matter scheme makes that impossible.

THETUS: And I would say that he *does* hold the Christian doctrine, but that his reliance on Aristotle and Neoplatonism produces confusing terminology. Both of us find Gilson somewhat confusing, but in what direction is the ambiguity weighted?

ANTITHETUS: I am willing to grant that Gilson is a Christian thinker. But his philosophical system is basically Aristotelian and Neoplatonist, and therefore apostate.

THETUS: How can a man be a Christian thinker if his system is apostate? I find it hard to ascribe to a man who otherwise gives evidence of Christian convictions a basically non-Christian philosophy. I believe that in this respect Christians should give other Christians the benefit of the doubt.

ANTITHETUS: Are you not being naive? Christian thinkers have often gotten confused when they have tried to mix biblical truth with philosophy. Or do you want to defend Origen and Dionysius as well?

THETUS: But Origen and Dionysius were not at all critical of the Greek philosophical scheme. Gilson radically denies it.

ANTITHETUS: Sure. Gilson wants more discontinuity, more empiricism. Less Plato, more Aristotle.

THETUS: But he denies Plato, not in the name of Aristotle, but in the name of Christ.

ANTITHETUS: That is because he thinks Christ agreed with Aristotle.

THETUS: We seem to be going around in circles again.

ANTITHETUS: Well, would you really like to see us return to Thomism? That is the bottom-line question.

Thetus: No. The language of Thomism is a confusing way in which to communicate a Christian worldview.

Antithetus: Well, then, perhaps our positions are not so far apart. I would not deny that Gilson wants to express Christian truth. I have been saying that he uses a false philosophy to express it. You say that he uses misleading language. But a philosophy is hard to separate from the language by which it is expressed. A philosophy is, to a large extent, a language ("categories") by which one may formulate a worldview. To put my position in your terms: Thomists use false language to try to express Christian truth.

Thetus: That hardly makes sense. If the language is false, it does not express truth at all.

Antithetus: That is precisely my criticism of Thomism. The system refutes itself by that kind of inconsistency. But certainly you understand what I am saying: sometimes when Christians try to express themselves philosophically, they choose such misleading language that they actually express the opposite of Scripture's teaching.

Thetus: But Gilson keeps defining what he means, and that meaning is consistently Christian. If readers are misled, is that not simply because they fail to read carefully?

Antithetus: No. A theologian must take responsibility for his language, as well as his definitions. The meaning conveyed to the reader is a function of both. The Thomists are responsible for communicating an impression of a "pure being" who spews out his essence upon lesser deities.

Thetus: I do not deny that theologians must take that responsibility. But should not our criticism take account both of the defined content and of the language in which that content is expressed?

Antithetus: Certainly.

Thetus: But then we seem to agree that the matter is not clear-cut. For once we take account of both content and language, we have to admit that there are both good and bad elements in Scholasticism. The question is, How are those to be weighted? Shall we be optimistic or pessimistic?

Antithetus: Pessimistic, I would say.

Thetus: I still believe that we should give our fellow Christians the benefit of the doubt—at least until someone rebuts that presumption by a thorough analysis of the primary sources. The analysis would have to be more thorough than what Van Til has provided.

My own response to all of this is somewhat mixed. I tend, like Antithetus, to be pessimistic in my evaluation of Thomism, yet more optimistic than Van Til. Roman Catholic thought has certainly been influenced adversely by the Plotinian chain of being and the form-matter scheme of Aristotle. I tend to find this influence in the Roman Catholic doctrine of the church, more than in the Scholastic doctrines of creation and analogy. The hierarchicalism in its government, its idea of the church as a "continuing incarnation," its often mechanical, materialistic, and indeed synergistic conceptions of grace, reflect a modification of biblical truth in the direction of Greek philosophy. Nevertheless, I believe that here, as elsewhere, Van Til exaggerates the antithesis.

But Van Til's analysis is certainly illuminating, and it warns us against using Thomistic categories uncritically. Aquinas's thought has to some extent (but not entirely) been eclipsed by other intellectual movements in the Roman Catholic church today, but it is enjoying a renaissance among evangelical apologists such as Norman Geisler and Winfried Corduan. If one is inclined to move in that direction, Van Til's analysis will point out a number of potentially dangerous pitfalls. It also warns us of some pitfalls in the very work of interpretation and critical analysis.

CHAPTER TWENTY-SIX

Immanuel Kant and Karl Barth

Toward the beginning of this book, I argued that Van Til should be understood as a theologian of "antithesis," following in the tradition of Abraham Kuyper and J. Gresham Machen. Kuyper stressed the great differences in all of life between regenerate and unregenerate people. Machen showed the antithesis between historic Christianity and modern liberal theology, these being not mere differences of emphasis within Christianity, but rather two different religions, the former Christian, the latter not.

Following in the footsteps of Kuyper and Machen, Van Til took up the burden of analyzing the "theology of the Word," otherwise called "crisis theology," "neo-orthodoxy," "dialectical theology," or "Barthianism," which had captured the imagination of the theological world following the publication of Barth's *Commentary on Romans* in 1919. Karl Barth and Emil Brunner, the main figures in this movement, were strongly critical of the old liberalism of Schleiermacher, Ritschl, Hermann, and Harnack, the liberalism that Machen had attacked so cogently in his *Christianity and Liberalism*. On the assumption that "the enemy of my enemy is my friend," some evangelicals became enthusiastic about Barth and Brunner. But were the dialectical theologians true friends of Christian orthodoxy? That was not obvious. The theologians of the Word were very critical of the "static categories" of the seventeenth-century Protestant dogmaticians. And they accepted the higher criticism of the Bible advanced by liberal scholars. How was the orthodox Reformed believer to respond to this movement?

Van Til's response was strongly negative, as can be gathered from the title of his 1946 book, *The New Modernism.* The title of his second book on the movement, *Christianity and Barthianism* (1962), reflects Machen's *Christianity and Liberalism.*

The New Modernism was thought by some to be far too extreme. G. C. Berkouwer, who had himself written a rather negative book about Barth in 1936, later wrote a more favorable, but still critical, book on Barth. In that book, he takes Van Til to task for the critical methods employed in *The New Modernism* and in the article "Has Karl Barth Become Orthodox?" He quotes some of Van Til's strongest statements: Brunner's theology is "a theology of revelation without revelation, a theology of creation without creation, a theology of Christ without Christ."[1] As to Barth, "If we substitute the word 'reality' for Barth's word 'God' we shall not be far amiss in catching his meaning."[2] And concerning Barth's theology, Van Til says that it may lead people to think

> that they are not subject to the wrath of God, that their sins need not be washed away through the blood of the Son of God and Son of Man, Jesus of Nazareth, who was born of the virgin Mary, died and rose again with the same body with which he was laid in the tomb. For men to depend upon the Jesus Christ of Barth is to depend upon themselves as inherently righteous.[3]

Berkouwer responds in some horror to these and other such statements. He notes that Hans Urs von Balthasar

> calls Van Til's presentation of Barth *"vollig grotesk"* because of the fact that Van Til deduces Barth's whole theology from the philosophical assumptions which he thinks are underlying it.

---

[1]NM, 267, quoted in Berkouwer, *The Triumph of Grace in the Theology of Karl Barth* (Grand Rapids: Eerdmans, 1956), 385.

[2]NM, 231, quoted in Berkouwer, *Triumph of Grace,* 385.

[3]Berkouwer quotes Van Til, "Has Karl Barth Become Orthodox?" *WTJ* 16 (1954): 181, in *Triumph of Grace,* 385. The article has been republished as an appendix in the 1973 edition of NM, and the quote can be found on p. 435 of that volume.

> . . . Such a rejection [by Von Balthasar and Berkouwer] . . . does not in the least imply an acceptance of Barth's theology, but constitutes only a criticism of an unsound analysis which draws conclusions which Barth himself draws least of all, conclusions, in fact, *which he himself has more than once and at great length opposed.*[4]

Berkouwer adds:

> Van Til has no eye for the fact that often in the history of dogma particular philosophical assumptions played a part in a theology, assumptions, that is, *in which* and *alongside of which* an influence of the Word of God makes itself felt in such a way that it is impossible to *deduce* the theology logically and consequentially from the particular philosophical assumptions.[5]

Therefore, he believes that "essential statements of Barth are neglected or distorted" by Van Til,[6] such as his persistent defense of the virgin birth and resurrection of Christ and of the ontological Trinity.[7] "Hence," he says, "it does not surprise me that Barth says in *amazement* that he *cannot recognize himself at all* in [*The New Modernism*]."[8]

Berkouwer also takes exception to some aspects of the "orthodoxy" that Van Til places over against Barth. He has some objections to Van Til's doctrine of (or emphasis upon?) the "self-contained God"; those objections do not come through very clearly in the text. He also appears to think that Van Til's view of the Trinity veers somewhat toward tritheism and Nestorianism, and that Van Til's view of the "equal ultimacy of election and reprobation" is not in agreement with the Canons of Dordt.[9]

I confess that I have a certain initial sympathy for Berkouwer's critique, for I have similarly criticized Van Til for "exaggerating the antithesis." Berkouwer's view that Van Til deduces Barth's theology from assumed philosophical presuppositions and does not give ad-

---

[4]*Triumph of Grace,* 386 (emphasis his).

[5]Ibid. (emphasis his).

[6]Ibid.

[7]Ibid., 386–88.

[8]Ibid., 388 (emphasis his).

[9]Ibid., 390–91. On the last point, see my discussion in chap. 6.

equate weight to statements in Barth that contradict these deductions is initially plausible to me, because I find the same kind of problem in Van Til's critiques of Aquinas, Butler, Carnell, and others. I do, of course, unlike Berkouwer, find Van Til's critiques illuminating even when they are exaggerated.

However, I think there are fewer problems of this sort in Van Til's treatment of Barth than in his treatment of Aquinas. Part of the problem with Van Til's critique of Aquinas is the rarity of his citations of primary sources. But in his critiques of Barth, his references to primary sources, especially the *Church Dogmatics* in German, are numerous and extensive. Van Til did more studying and writing on Barth than on any other thinker, over many years. For the most part, I find his interpretations and evaluations cogent and persuasive.

I am not daunted by the fact that other scholars, even Barth himself, have rejected Van Til's analysis so sharply. Interpretive differences of this magnitude are common in the scholarly world. And the history of theology is filled with examples of thinkers who, consciously or unconsciously, distorted scriptural teaching by mixing it with all manner of non-Christian philosophical ideas, all the while defending their own orthodoxy. The present climate of theological criticism has become almost too genteel, even in Reformed circles.[10] Among academically respectable theologians, it is virtually unheard of for one to charge another with heresy. Van Til looks harsh by comparison, as would anyone alleging serious error in this climate. But he is not harsh in comparison with Luther, Calvin, and other older Protestant thinkers. The present issue will turn on the question of whether Van Til has made his case from Barth's writings, not on matters of academic etiquette.

The philosophical presuppositions that Van Til attributes to Barth are essentially those of Immanuel Kant (1724–1804). Kant formulated definitively what Van Til, following Herman Dooyeweerd, describes as the nature-freedom scheme of modern thought. On Dooyeweerd's analysis, Western philosophy can be divided into three phases. The first is the form-matter scheme of the Greeks, which we have discussed. The second is the nature-grace scheme of medieval Scholasticism. Nature-grace thinkers accept the form-matter scheme as a description of nature, but then superimpose upon nature an-

[10] I am speaking here of the worldwide situation in traditionally Reformed churches. The situation is rather different in conservative American Presbyterian circles.

other level of reality, grace, in which occur the events of Creation and redemption. In the third phase, the nature-freedom scheme, the medieval realm of grace becomes secularized. Rather than a realm of sovereign divine actions, it becomes a realm in which man can act in autonomous freedom, without the restrictions of nature. None of these three motifs represents the biblical worldview, which should be described in terms of "creation, fall, and redemption."[11]

In Kant, the nature-freedom scheme received its definitive formulation.[12] Kant distinguished between the realm of "phenomena," the world as it appears to us, and the realm of "noumena," the world as it really is apart from human experience, the "thing in itself" *(Ding an sich)*. Since all knowledge comes from human experience, the noumenal world is unknowable.

The phenomenal world is a world of objective knowledge and scientific law. But since it is only phenomenal, the objective structure of that world (its forms, as Plato and Aristotle would say) derives from the structure of the human mind, rather than from the structure of the world as it really is. Nevertheless, it is a world in which determinism prevails, rather than freedom. This phenomenal world is as far as "pure" or "theoretical" human reason can reach, for pure reason cannot draw conclusions that go beyond its experience.

However, we are free to entertain ideas about the noumenal world, as long as we do not seek to proclaim them with dogmatic assurance. Indeed, through our "practical reason,"[13] we are able to evaluate what ideas about the noumenal world are most useful or profitable to believe—whether or not they are actually true. Among the beliefs about the noumenal world that Kant recommends are belief in God, the free human soul, and life after death. These beliefs, however, are "regulative, not constitutive." That is to say, their function is not to give us information about the noumenal world, which is by hypothesis unknowable, or even about the phenomenal world, which is known by empirical-logical methods. Rather, these beliefs are practical tools for regulating human life.[14]

---

[11]See CB, 240–44.

[12]Compare our previous discussions of Kant in chaps. 3, 10, 13, 17, and 23.

[13]Compare on this our discussion of Butler in chap. 20.

[14]Kant's own discussions of these matters can be found in his *Critique of Pure Reason* and *Critique of Practical Reason*. In *Religion Within the Limits of Reason Alone*, he discusses the implications of these ideas for the Christian faith.

In Van Til's view, Kant sees the world as a "pure contingency," an irrational environment upon which the mind of man autonomously imposes order. Thus, Kant's philosophy is a paradigm case of the rationalist-irrationalist dialectic. The noumenal is the irrational realm of brute fact; the phenomenal is the order rationalistically imposed upon those brute facts by the autonomous human intellect.

Van Til notes that "Kant is often called the philosopher of Protestantism. Did he not limit science in order to make room for faith?"[15] Kant limited science to the phenomenal realm, the realm of human experience. Therefore, science could not cast any doubt upon belief in God, which is a regulative idea about the noumenal sphere. Nor, of course, could belief in God place any limitations upon the autonomous methods of science, for the idea of God is not constitutive.

But what faith did Kant make room for? It was not a faith arising out of miraculous or providential historical events in the phenomenal world, for the phenomenal world is governed wholly by natural regularity. Nor can Kantian faith be governed by divine revelation, for there is no revelation in the science of phenomena. And it cannot govern our thoughts about the noumenal realm either, for that would violate the autonomous freedom we enjoy in relation to the noumenal. Kant's *Religion* is a thoroughgoing polemic against any sort of religious authority external to human reason. Still, in that book, he also argued that the various doctrines of Christianity could be reinterpreted as symbols of the triumph of the human will over the "radical evil" within.

Of what sort of Protestantism is Kant the philosopher? The liberal theologians of the nineteenth and twentieth centuries—"consciousness theologians" or "neo-Protestant theologians," as Barth called them—looked to Kant as their philosophical inspiration. The liberals saw Luther's protest as the revolt of human freedom against religious authority. Therefore, they found in Kant a profoundly "Protestant" philosopher. However, as Van Til points out, "Kant's idea of human freedom has . . . its roots, not in the Reformation, but in the Renaissance view of man."[16]

Friedrich Schleiermacher (1768–1834) therefore denied the forensic idea that salvation is purchased for us and imputed to us by the objective work of Christ in history. Rather, salvation is a subjective

[15]CB, 244.
[16]Ibid., 245–46.

process: the enhancement of religious feeling *(Gefühl)* and the consequent transformation of character through the personality of Jesus.[17]

Karl Barth's early writing was sharply critical of the neo-Protestantism of Schleiermacher and of his own teachers, disciples of Albrecht Ritschl. He said that they had made a god in their own image, and he sought to return to Scripture, to a God who really speaks from above. Doubtless he realized that in neo-Protestantism there was no biblical gospel.[18] However, he could not bring himself simply to return to an earlier period of theology. Scholasticism, he thought, was contaminated by the "analogy of being," which we have discussed elsewhere.[19] Barth does want to emulate the spirit of Luther and Calvin, but he feels the need to go "beyond" them.[20] As for the Protestant "orthodoxy" of the post-Reformation period, Barth is simply "against" it.[21]

Barth does speak well of Kant, in whom Enlightenment rationalism "understood and affirmed itself in its own limitations."[22] Although Barth disapproves of the main thrust of Kant's *Religion,* he finds suggestions in Kant of other possibilities beyond that main thrust: possible places for revelation and grace. One gets the impression that Barth thinks he can do justice to these concepts within a broadly Kantian framework, even though Kant himself did not.

In Van Til's view (and, I think, in Barth's as well), the central concept of Barth's theology is "Christ as *Geschichte.*" *Geschichte* is a German word for "history," but not the only one; the word *Historie* is translated by the same English term. Van Til explains:

> Barth himself distinguishes between *Geschichte* and *Historie.* The latter indicates the facts of the world as the neutral historian sees them. Thus the resurrection appearances of Christ deal with facts that could be seen and felt by the physical eye and hand. But the resurrection must not, says Barth, be directly identified with any such fact. To do so would be to for-

[17]Ibid., 251–53.

[18]Ibid., 2–6, 263, 415–21.

[19]Ibid., 6–7, 43–53.

[20]Ibid., 7–8, 54–66.

[21]Ibid., 8, 67–89.

[22]Ibid., 395. See discussion on pp. 395–412. Interestingly, Barth's brother Heinrich, a philosopher, was also an admirer of Kant, and Karl Barth professes to have learned about Kant from his brother (pp. 193–96).

> get that while revelation is historical nothing historical is, as such, revelational. To do so would be to deny that God in Christ is the subject of the resurrection. To do so would be to forget that God is wholly hidden even when wholly revealed and wholly revealed when revealed at all.
>
> The real resurrection must therefore be seen as *Geschichte*. That is to say it is an actual event. As such it lies at the foundation of our faith. The resurrection as *Historie* is only a subordinate aspect of the resurrection as *Geschichte*. The real relation between God and man takes place in terms of Christ as *Geschichte*. In it alone do we do justice to the idea that God is really, that is, fully man in Christ. God *is* Jesus Christ. In it alone do we do justice to the idea that man is fully man only by participation in Christ.[23]

Geschichte designates events in their totality, in their full meaning, not just those portions of events that are available to the "neutral" historian. To deal with *Geschichte* is to deal with reality. *Geschichte* has an aspect that is *historisch,* an aspect seen in events that are visible and tangible; but it is far more than any such events. In Barth's view, divine revelation is *Geschichte*. There may be events in space and time *(Historie)* that point to that revelation, but they are never identical with the revelation. That is to say, God is revealed "indirectly" rather than "directly." Or, as Barth also puts it, while revelation is historical (i.e., has a historical aspect), history as such is not revelation.[24]

To claim a direct revelation is to deny "the *hiddenness* of God in his revelation" and "the *freedom* of God."[25] God is *"wholly hidden* in his revelation to man in Christ."[26] When we claim a direct revelation, Barth says, we claim that God's revelation is our possession, in our control, available for our manipulation. Such a claim denies the transcendent sovereignty of God.

On the other hand, says Barth, we need to recognize that God is also wholly revealed in Christ. Calvin was wrong to assert a secret decree of God that elects some and reprobates others. That is to seek

[23]Ibid., 14.
[24]Ibid.
[25]Ibid., 15 (emphasis his).
[26]Ibid. (emphasis his).

a God above and beyond Jesus Christ. We should, rather, find in Christ the whole of God's revelation. Jesus Christ is God; there is no God beyond him. Thus, God's whole revelation is grace—grace to all human beings.

Jesus' being as man is his work, and that work is to save all men. His being is his *Geschichte.* In Christ as *Geschichte,* there is an "indirect identity" between God and man. In him is revealed the full being of God and man. Because of that indirect identity, God's grace is inherently universal.[27]

Christ is, therefore, both the electing God and the elect man. Indeed, he is also the reprobate man. All are reprobate in Christ, and as in Christ grace overcomes divine wrath, all are elect in him as well.[28]

In Christ as *Geschichte,* the events of redemption are freed from the limitations of calendar time. In *Geschichte,* time is taken into eternity and eternity enters time. The exaltation of Christ does not follow the humiliation; rather, as *Geschichte*, Christ's humiliation is exaltation, and vice versa. "To be sure, the resurrection is physical and historical, but this is true only in the sense that, though it is primarily *Geschichte,* it is *also* an innerworldly something."[29]

Geschichte is "primarily the divine presence which overarches and touches historical time equally in the past, the present and the future. . . . Christ's true time takes the place (*tritt an die Stelle*) of our problematic, unauthentic time. Christ's time *triumphs over* our time."[30]

Van Til summarizes:

> Thus Christ as *Geschichte* is the act of revelation whereby God is wholly revealed and wholly hidden to man. Man's faith in this act becomes participation in God's revelation. But Christ as revelation is the actual identification of his whole being of God with the man Jesus. Man's faith in Jesus thus becomes participation in his being and therewith in the being of God. Finally, God as identical with his revelation in the incarnation is the act of the reconciliation of all men. Christ as *Geschichte is* the reconciliation of all men. The

---

[27]Ibid., 16–21.
[28]Ibid., 22.
[29]Ibid., 25.
[30]Ibid., 26.

> faith of man is therefore the inevitable response to the victory of God in Christ as *Geschichte*. Through Christ as *Geschichte* all men receive the grace of God.[31]

Since man is what he truly is only in Christ, redemption is assured:

> Sin becomes therefore an impossible possibility. . . . Man is to be defined as that being who is the object of God's grace. The real man is the one who participates with Christ as the victor over Chaos. Men are men only as fellow-elect with Jesus Christ. God protects them in advance (*zum vornherein*) from the power of Chaos (*das Nichtige*). Man's being is being in the *Geschichte* as grounded by Jesus. To be man is to have experienced redemption, to be preserved by God's mercy.[32]

Barth sets his position, not only over against neo-Protestantism, but also over against Roman Catholicism, the Reformers, and post-Reformation Protestant orthodoxy. In Van Til's terminology, he wants to go "beyond" Roman Catholicism and the Reformers, but is simply "against" Protestant orthodoxy. The problem with Rome, and to a lesser extent with the Reformers, is that they did not grasp that revelation is *Geschichte* and therefore never to be "directly" identified with Scripture or tradition. Rome believes that, to some extent, man can identify himself apart from Christ, by "natural reason."[33] Thus, Rome believes that man is able to cooperate with God's grace for his salvation. Roman Catholics believe that there is an "analogy of being," that is, that one can deduce truth about God from the "objective state of affairs." Rather, says Barth, faith is not a "human possibility." In the true experience of faith, God is wholly hidden and wholly revealed.[34]

---

[31]Ibid., 29.

[32]Ibid., 41.

[33]Ibid., 44. The reader may notice that some of Barth's statements, such as this one, formally parallel Van Til's. Barth is, in terms of his own presuppositions, very much a presuppositionalist. For him, man has no knowledge of himself apart from Christ, and the very conditions of possibility are set by revelation, not by autonomous human reason. But Van Til would argue that his presuppositions and Barth's differ greatly in actual content.

[34]Ibid., 43–51.

Barth commends Calvin as a Christological thinker. Calvin avoided mechanical views of biblical inspiration and sought to attach the doctrine of inspiration closely to the content of the Bible, Jesus Christ himself. But Calvin did not understand that "it is God's nature to be active for and in all men. God is identical with his revelation in Jesus Christ. . . . Thus man exists in his indirect identity with the divine subject."[35] Calvin could not "see that sin is an ontological impossibility."[36] Unfortunately, in Barth's view, Calvin still thought of God apart from Christ, and of man apart from Christ. He still believed in direct revelation.[37]

The post-Reformation orthodoxy represents a step backwards, in Barth's estimation. Although the orthodox theologians were often formally right in their doctrine of grace,

> the followers of Calvin soon forgot to think in terms of the living Christ. They thought of saving revelation as something that had taken place in the past. For them revelation had taken place directly in history. They had no eye for the double indirectness of revelation. They believed in *Offenbartheit*. With respect to the Bible this was *Inspiriertheit*. They said that "there is revelation" and that "there is faith." They believed in the "profane 'there is.' "[38]

On the contrary, says Barth, "Revelation always takes place in the present. Scripture does not wish to be taken as identical with revelation."[39] The orthodox were mistaken to think that Scripture was true in all it contained, or that miracles were directly revelational of God.[40]

Van Til, to my knowledge, never summarized his criticisms of Barth in a succinct way. He tried to do so in the pamphlet *Christianity and Crisis Theology*, but not very successfully. In general, Van Til was scrupulous—overly scrupulous, I would say—to use Barth's own formulations. Perhaps, by this practice, he was trying to avoid the type of

---

[35]Ibid., 64–65.
[36]Ibid., 65.
[37]Ibid., 66.
[38]Ibid., 67.
[39]Ibid., 68.
[40]Ibid.

criticism made by Berkouwer, that he was merely deducing Barth's thought from alleged philosophical presuppositions. If *The New Modernism* is to some extent amenable to that type of criticism, Van Til's later writings on Barth, particularly *Christianity and Barthianism,* certainly are not. In these later writings, his account of Barth is very close to Barth's own texts, heavily footnoted. He uses Barth's own language almost to a fault. But that does not help readers who need help to understand what Barth is saying. For the most part, Van Til quotes and paraphrases Barth and expects the reader to see what is wrong.

In the absence of Van Til's own summary of his critique of Barth, I have put together this one:

1. Barth's view of the "indirect identity" between revelation and Scripture permits human beings to disagree with the teachings of Scripture, contrary to Scripture itself.

2. Barth's doctrine of God is irrationalist (or "nominalistic," as Van Til sometimes says): God, for Barth, is "wholly other," able to change into the opposite of himself. It is also rationalistic: God is wholly revealed in Christ.

3. Barth's view of the "indirect identity of all men in and with God in Christ as *Geschichte*" has pantheistic overtones, although Barth seeks to guard against them. The same is true of his doctrine of "participation," although Barth uses it to avoid the idea of a direct identity between man and God.

4. His identification of Christ with his work of saving all men has an inescapable universalistic implication, even though Barth seeks to avoid that by an (irrational) appeal to the freedom of God.

5. Salvation actually occurs, not in events of calendar time such as the crucifixion and resurrection of Jesus, but in *Geschichte,* in which temporal distinctions do not exist. Calendar-time history partakes of *Geschichte* as an aspect of it and a pointer to it, but events in that history do not themselves bring salvation.

6. To speak of God as both "hidden" and "revealed" in revelation is to deny to revelation any clear content to which human beings are unambiguously subject.

7. Contrary to Barth, Scripture does teach that God determines the final destinies of human beings through his eternal decrees. To say this is not to think of human destiny apart from Christ. Christ is both the Savior of the elect and the ultimate judge of the wicked. One cannot state a priori that grace will save all people.

8. To speak of the "ontological impossibility of sin" and "sin as chaos" (*das Nichtige*) turns ethics into metaphysics, the problem of reconciliation into the problem of overcoming finitude.

9. Barth's gospel is essentially different from that of Scripture: Barth would announce to men[41] that they are already in Christ, rather than urging them to repent and believe as God's grace removes them from the sphere of wrath to the sphere of grace.

Van Til is not alone in these criticisms of Barth. Van Til surveys the literature on Barth at considerable length, showing a wide range of agreement on his interpretations and criticisms among Reformed theologians and philosophers. Of significant interest is his account of Berkouwer, who, we recall, criticized Van Til's *The New Modernism* in the strongest terms. Berkouwer wrote *Karl Barth* in 1936 and commented on Barth in several other books. Van Til finds in these books the same criticisms that he himself has made. He finds the climax of Berkouwer's criticism in this judgment: "On Barth's view of impossibility, 'there is no transition from wrath to grace in historical reality.'"[42] Although Van Til does not say so in *Christianity and Barthianism,* he often remarked in class that this was a very serious criticism indeed—quite in line with his own critique. He said that he could not understand how Berkouwer, after making that observation, could argue that Barth was essentially orthodox.

There are, to be sure, evangelical and Reformed theologians today who seek to defend Barth, and even to emulate him. But most liberal thinkers recognized long ago that Barth was not orthodox in his view of the historicity of redemptive events. In 1957, Richard R. Niebuhr wrote *Resurrection and Historical Reason,* in which he sought to get his fellow liberal theologians to rethink their views of history. Niebuhr says of Barth:

> With this conception of revelation and history, [Barth] is forced to extrude the resurrection event from the sequence that anchors it in the New Testament, and to say of the "Easter history" that it tells us of the eternal presence of God in time, and therefore it has no eschatological significance. . . . The

---

[41]A propositional message, after all of Barth's criticisms of propositional revelation!

[42]CB, 135.

> resurrection has been construed as the summing-up, the timeless event of recognition, and so, the antithesis of the historically real.[43]

He adds, "So far as the basic problem of a positive attitude toward the biblical history is concerned, there is no indication of a 'neo-orthodox' movement."[44] Reviewing Niebuhr's book, Langdon Gilkey finds this observation "surprising but true."[45] Jürgen Moltmann, in his *Theology of Hope*,[46] agreed that there was in Barth nothing like a realistic biblical eschatology. In his view, Barth's view of revelation was "epiphany" (revelation of what is present), not "apocalyptic" (revelation of what is to come in history). This criticism of Barth has motivated the more history-centered theologies of Moltmann, Pannenberg, and the liberation theologians.

Therefore, Berkouwer to the contrary, it cannot be said that Van Til's interpretation of Barth is controversial in any major way. And his criticisms of Barth are shared not only by a large number of Reformed theologians, including Berkouwer himself, but even by some liberals. What seems to gall many readers of Van Til is not his interpretations or his criticisms, but his conclusions. We have heard some of Van Til's strong language quoted earlier by Berkouwer. The summary evaluation in *Christianity and Barthianism* reads as follows:

> The choice must therefore be made between Barth and the Reformers. On Barth's view there is no transition from wrath to grace in history. And on Barth's view grace is inherently a meaningless idea. For his Christ is composed of the interaction between a principle of continuity based on the idea of timeless being and a principle of discontinuity based on the idea of pure contingency. He has therefore no gospel of grace to present to men. He cannot challenge men by presenting them with the Christ of the Scriptures because his Christ is a mirage. It is the Christ of modern reconstruction. It is the Christ of the higher humanism.[47]

---

[43]Niebuhr, *Resurrection and Historical Reason* (New York: Scribner's, 1957), 48.
[44]Ibid., 81.
[45]Gilkey, "Biblical History and Historical Reality," *Encounter* 19 (spring 1958): 217.
[46]New York: Harper and Row, 1967.
[47]CB, 445.

Do these conclusions follow? The concepts of "indirect revelation" and *"Geschichte"* are difficult to pin down, to say nothing of the dialectic of a God "wholly hidden and wholly revealed" and the "ontological impossibility of sin." Is there a way of reading these ideas that will yield a more favorable conclusion than Van Til's?

Seeking the most sympathetic possible understanding of Barth, we might try to interpret him as follows: One sometimes gets the impression from Barth that, like Kierkegaard, his main concern is to maintain the relevance of the saving events to the believer. In Barthian circles, one frequently hears the argument that there can be no "revelation" in the strict sense until there is a response from the recipient of that revelation. Orthodox theology distinguishes between revelation (the objective content of nature and Scripture) and illumination (the work of the Spirit to impress that revelation upon the human heart). Barth and his followers have seemed to want to restrict the term "revelation" to the second concept, arguing that one cannot be said to "receive" revelation until that revelation has an effect upon him. Scripture does sometimes use the term "revelation" in that sense, in my opinion: see Matthew 11:25–27 and Ephesians 1:17. But Scripture does not warrant the denial of revelation in the former sense: see especially Romans 1:18–32, where God is clearly revealed even to those who deny him.

At any rate, Barth may be read as arguing that although God does act in calendar time (*Historie*), those calendar-time events do not actually save anybody apart from the divine act of uniting that person to Christ (*Geschichte*). Thus, the events are not saving events apart from the subjective work of the Spirit. Hence, we have the notion of the timeless, *geschichtlich* events of Creation, atonement, Resurrection, and revelation. On that interpretation, Barth would simply be employing certain orthodox concepts, using different definitions of terms: by "*geschichtlich* resurrection," for example, he would mean "the *historisch* resurrection plus the sovereign act of God in uniting the believer to Christ."

Although his language is often very abstract, Barth regularly denies that salvation is an abstract matter. He protests that by *Geschichte* he means, not an abstract principle, but the God-man, Christ Jesus. That protestation might confirm the sort of reading of Barth suggested in the preceding two paragraphs. And the fact that one can read page after page in Barth's *Dogmatics* without finding anything incompatible with orthodoxy reinforces that understanding.

His main concern in speaking of God as "wholly hidden" is often to guard God's incomprehensibility; his concern in speaking of God as "wholly revealed" is to guard the sufficiency of revelation in Christ. Both of these are legitimate orthodox concerns. "Ontological impossibility of sin" would then simply mean that God is sovereign, and that his victory over sin is a foregone conclusion. God's "becoming the opposite of himself" would simply mean God's making himself available to us by Creation, revelation, and redemption—the equivalent of Van Til's full bucket difficulty.

Continuing our attempt to read Barth more sympathetically, we might interpret him as a Christian thinker who is rather disgusted by what he perceives as the cocksureness of certain theologians: the prideful, know-it-all spirit. This would explain all the rhetoric against "possessing" and "controlling" the Word of God. Barth then supposes that he can prevent that spiritual problem, that sinful attitude, by formulating theology in a dialectical manner, as a study of a revelation one cannot "get hold of." He fails to see, on this interpretation, that spiritual problems cannot be eliminated through such formal methods. Dialectical theologians, Barthians, can also be cocksure and proud; they too can look down on others from what Helmut Thielicke called the "high horse of enlightenment." Barth's mistake here would be somewhat similar to Van Til's mistake discussed in chapter 23—the thought that one can eliminate unfaithfulness to biblical presuppositions by the mechanism of an "indirect argument."

On such understandings, Van Til's interpretation would be correct: *Geschichte* is "beyond" *Historie* in the ways Van Til describes. However, his criticisms would require some modification, and his conclusions would be wholly inappropriate. Certainly, it would still be true that Barth denies the orthodox view of biblical inspiration, that he denies the existence of pretemporal election and reprobation directed to individuals, and that he denies the movement between wrath and grace in the event of man's response to the preached word. Those are serious criticisms, but they do not, perhaps, amount to a simple denial of the biblical Christ.

Nevertheless, it is significant that Barth sees the need to place the main thrust of his own theology over against Calvin and the post-Reformation orthodoxy, not only Roman Catholicism. If he is simply trying to emphasize the subjective relevance of revelation, why does he oppose these movements, which made ample provision (in language different from Barth's, to be sure) for the subjective dimension of revelation and of redemption? Is it that he radically misunderstands the older theologians?

I am inclined to think that there is some confusion in Barth's own mind here. As we pointed out earlier in this book, contradictory formulations (like "wholly hidden and wholly revealed") can generate any number of implications. Van Til's style of criticism, as we have seen before, does not seriously consider the possibility of systematic ambiguity. In Van Til's mind, the question is simply, What system does the thinker hold to? "System," in Van Til's view, is a self-consciously consistent combination of starting point, method, and conclusion, in which all three are "involved in one another." (Or, to put it in Dooyeweerd's terms, Van Til assumes that every system of thought must be understood as "ruled" by one "ground-motif" or another, whether form-matter, nature-grace, nature-freedom, or Creation-Fall-redemption.) Van Til does grant that people are often inconsistent with their systems, although he is somewhat inclined to treat all apparent inconsistencies in Barth, for example, as "consistent" applications of the rationalist-irrationalist dialectic. But there are perhaps relatively few thinkers who have self-conscious systems in this sense. Barth himself tended to inveigh against systematic thinking of this kind, although he did defend rationality as such.

Nevertheless, in view of Van Til's analysis and critique, it would certainly be unwise for any evangelical Christian to trust Barth as a reliable guide to biblical teaching. Barth's dialectic (intensely philosophical and metaphysical, though he claims it is not) is at best speculative (Berkouwer), at worst the very antithesis of the scriptural message. In any case, the dialectic represents a sort of game with contradictory concepts that makes confident interpretation and evaluation of Barth nearly impossible. That being the case, Barth's theology does not meet the minimal criteria for sound Christian teaching.

CHAPTER TWENTY-SEVEN

Herman Dooyeweerd

Van Til followed closely the movement originated by Herman Dooyeweerd and D. Th. Vollenhoven, known as the Philosophy of the Idea of Law, the Philosophy of the Cosmonomic Idea, the Amsterdam philosophy, and sometimes Dooyeweerdianism, although Dooyeweerd was only one of many thinkers in his school of thought. Those would include S. U. Zuidema, K. Popma, J. P. A. Mekkes, Robert D. Knudsen, H. Evan Runner, H. G. Stoker, H. Van Riessen, Bob Goudzwaard, and others. In the late 1960s, the Institute for Christian Studies in Toronto was founded in Toronto, Canada, to advance this school of thought in a number of fields. Best known among the professors there have been James Olthuis, Hendrik Hart, Paul Marshall, and Calvin Seerveld.

As I mentioned earlier, Van Til claimed to have developed his basic ideas independently of the Dutch school, but when he became aware of that movement, he greeted it enthusiastically. They, in turn, listed Van Til as an editor of their journal, *Philosophia Reformata*. As we have seen, he used Dooyeweerd's analysis of philosophical "groundmotives" in his criticisms of Scholasticism, dialectical theology, and other movements. Van Til regularly advised his students who wanted to do graduate study in philosophy to work with the cosmonomic philosophers at the Free University of Amsterdam.

Over the years, however, tensions developed between Van Til

and the Dooyeweerdians, particularly Dooyeweerd himself. After H. G. Stoker described his own approach as the "philosophy of the idea of creation," Van Til told Dooyeweerd that he liked Stoker's formulation better than Dooyeweerd's "philosophy of the idea of law." "Law," Van Til believed, could be construed more "neutrally" than "creation." Dooyeweerd, however, remained steadfast.

In 1953, an English translation of Dooyeweerd's *De Wijsbegeerte der Wetsidee* was published in four volumes as *A New Critique of Theoretical Thought.*[1] The translation included some revisions to Dooyeweerd's system, revisions that Van Til believed made concessions to neutrality and autonomy. A few years later, Dooyeweerd lectured in the United States. His lectures from that tour were published in the volume *In the Twilight of Western Thought.*[2] Those lectures drew a sharp distinction between philosophy and theology, so that the conceptual contents of Scripture cannot be said to govern philosophy.

In the 1960s, there were various exchanges between the two men. In *Christianity in Conflict* (2:3), Van Til compared Dooyeweerd's critique of Scholasticism with his own, taking issue with Dooyeweerd on various matters. In *Jerusalem and Athens,* Dooyeweerd addressed Van Til's criticisms and Van Til responded. There is also an exchange in that volume between Van Til and his colleague Robert Knudsen, in which Knudsen develops criticisms of Van Til informed by the approach of the Amsterdam philosophy. Knudsen replied to Van Til in the *Westminster Theological Journal.*[3] In *Herman Dooyeweerd and Reformed Apologetics,* Van Til reflected on the exchanges to that point.

Van Til recognized, as I certainly do, that Dooyeweerd was a great Christian thinker. In my view, as in that of others, he was the greatest Dutch philosopher of all time, not excluding Spinoza. His works are voluminous, vastly knowledgeable, and brilliant in their analysis. And, on the whole, his critique of secular thought is enormously important for Christian apologists today. My booklet *The Amsterdam Philosophy: A Preliminary Critique,*[4] written in the heat of some battles, does not show sufficient respect for him. I take this opportunity to apologize for the immature tone of the booklet, although I

---

[1]Philadelphia: Presbyterian and Reformed, 1953.

[2]Philadelphia: Presbyterian and Reformed, 1958.

[3]Robert D. Knudsen, "Crosscurrents," *WTJ* 35 (spring 1973): 303–14.

[4]Phillipsburg, N.J.: Harmony Press, n.d. (probably 1972).

have not to this date received sufficient answers to many of the criticisms advanced therein. Van Til recognized, as I did not at the time, that any critique of Dooyeweerd must be combined with profound appreciation for his achievement.

Nevertheless, with some fear and trembling, I shall seek to elucidate the debate between Van Til and the Amsterdam philosophers. Dooyeweerd's philosophy distinguishes sharply between "naive" or "pretheoretical" experience, which is the experience of ordinary life, and "theoretical thought." In pretheoretical experience, we confront the world with a sense of its wholeness. In theoretical thought, we distinguish various aspects of the world in order to analyze them and their interrelations. Dooyeweerd distinguishes fifteen of these "modal aspects": numerical, spatial, kinetic, energy, biotic, feeling, logic, history, symbolism, social rules, economic, aesthetic, judicial, moral, and faith.[5] This list progresses from the "lower" aspects to the "higher" ones. Every object is "qualified by" a particular aspect: numbers by the numerical, points and lines by the spatial, molecules by the energetic, protozoa by the biotic, and so on.

These aspects are related to one another in important ways. In Dooyeweerd's view, the higher aspects presuppose the lower. For example, a being cannot have a logical capacity unless it also has numerical, spatial, kinetic, energetic, biotic, and feeling capacities. Beings qualified by a particular aspect possess the capacities of all the lower aspects as well: biotic subjects are also numerical, spatial, etc. Everything, however, participates in every sphere either as subject or object. Mere numerical objects, such as numbers, are not subjects of logic, in the sense of having the ability to think logically. But they can be analyzed logically since they are objects of the science of logic.

There are also analogies among the aspects, so that the lower spheres "anticipate" the higher ones and the higher spheres "retrocipate" the lower ones. The aesthetic sphere, for example, has various qualities analogous to the economic, so that it is possible to speak of "aesthetic economy."

Since each sphere is to some extent mirrored in all the others, it is possible to describe the entire world under each aspect. It therefore becomes tempting for philosophers and other thinkers to develop worldviews that reduce the diversity of experience to a single aspect. Marx, for example, sought to reduce everything to economic rela-

[5]*Twilight of Western Thought* (Philadelphia: Presbyterian and Reformed, 1960), 7.

tionships. Pythagoras tried to reduce everything to number, Bergson to the biotic, Schleiermacher to feeling, Heraclitus to the kinetic, Parmenides to logic, and so on. Scripturally, however, this amounts to idolatry: an "absolutization" or deification of something in the world.

Dooyeweerd attacks this kind of thinking, first, through his analysis of the various groundmotives of the history of philosophy, which we have discussed before: form-matter, nature-grace, nature-freedom, and Creation-Fall-redemption. Second, he tries to show that the absolutizations are inadequate, that the false gods cannot do the work of the true God in accounting for all reality.

God and his Word, at least the Word "in its central meaning," transcend the modal order. The center of the human self, the "heart," is also beyond the modal order. Dooyeweerd (though not all members of the Amsterdam school) refers to the human heart as supratemporal.[6] The modal aspects pertain only to the created world. Therefore, there can be no "conceptual knowledge" of God and the self.[7]

And Scripture, as the Word of God, does not address any of the specific scientific questions of theoretical thought. Theological science does deal with the Bible as a conceptual-linguistic entity. But that science is limited to a study of the faith aspect of human experience. Therefore, the theologian may not require scientists or philosophers to conform their conclusions to a theological exegesis of Scripture. In this way, Dooyeweerd is critical of traditional Reformed theology. He also criticizes its alleged reliance upon a Scholastic or nature-grace groundmotive in such areas as the traditional soul-body distinction.[8]

In my aforementioned booklet, I made many detailed criticisms of these distinctions and arguments. In general, I find Dooyeweerd's approach too schematic: the neat arrangement of modal spheres and historical groundmotives is too neat to do justice to the complexity of the world and of the history of thought. More substantively, I have many problems with Dooyeweerd's view of the Word of God, some of which will appear shortly.

One of my major concerns in 1972, however, was not specifically stated in my booklet. That was the amenability of Dooyeweerd's

[6]I agree with Van Til and others in rejecting this speculative and confusing notion.

[7]JA, 85–89.

[8]Ibid., 75, for example.

thought to a movement mentality. The development of the American Association for Christian Studies and the Institute for Christian Studies in Toronto led to a sort of Dooyeweerdian movement in the late sixties and early seventies. The young professors of the ICS rallied still younger students to the view that all traditional Reformed theology was mired in Scholastic categories and that radical reformation was needed. In the sixties, of course, it was fashionable everywhere for young radicals to insist on drastic change. In the secular world, the change was expressed as "revolution"; in the Reformed Christian world, of course, as "reformation." At Westminster Seminary, there was a club of young Dooyeweerdian students who thought that Dooyeweerd had given them much more theological wisdom than that possessed by the historic Reformed tradition, to which they placed themselves in an adversary relationship. Elsewhere, groups of radical Dooyeweerdians tried to take over various Christian schools, churches, and other institutions, causing all sorts of disunity and unnecessary grief.

This sort of youthful radicalism was far from the spirit of Dooyeweerd himself, who was, above all, a thinker and scholar. But Dooyeweerd's thought, with its sharp distinctions, its rigid exclusions, and its critique of traditional Reformed theology as well as secular thought, was the sort of thing that encouraged immature revolutionary types.

In my booklet, therefore, I tried to show that many of Dooyeweerd's most significant distinctions, e.g., between naive and theoretical thought, were inadequately defined and argued—not the sort of thing that should be dogmatically proclaimed as the unquestionable starting point for a new reformation. Typical of Dutch thinkers, including Kuyper and Van Til, Dooyeweerd rests much of his case on metaphors and illustrations, which are suggestive and intellectually fruitful, but not always defined precisely enough to do the work of close analysis and evaluation, let alone to justify condemnations of alternative formulations. Certainly, this approach is inadequate to be proclaimed dogmatically as the final truth and the basis for radical transformation of church and theology.

More seriously, I also emphasized that Dooyeweerd's view of Scripture was inadequate and that he did not clearly recognize the authority of Scripture over all areas of human life. Dooyeweerd sees the "central message" of Scripture as having no "conceptual" content; but he does not show how a message with no conceptual content can govern human thought and life. He does recognize that Scripture, as a text *with* conceptual content, is the proper object of theological science, but for him theological science is limited to the faith aspect of human life. Thus, he limits the application of Scripture to matters of ethics, science, government, and so on. Granted that he does recognize important interrelationships between the faith aspect and the other aspects, and therefore some positive applications of Scripture beyond the "narrowly religious" sphere, it is not clear to me that Dooyeweerd maintains the tradition of Kuyper, who insisted quite simply and straightforwardly that all of human life is subject to the Word of God.

Among Dooyeweerd's North American followers, that unclarity on Scripture led to a number of errors, including certain views not clearly distinguishable from situation ethics. Van Til's critique of Dooyeweerd also focuses on his view of the relevance of Scripture to theoretical thought. But to understand his approach to the question, we must first consider the issue of the "states of affairs."

States of Affairs

Like Van Til, Dooyeweerd had to explain how communication is possible among parties with radically different presuppositions. H. Robbers, a Roman Catholic philosopher, said that Dooyeweerd's philosophy eliminates all "natural knowledge" and therefore all communication between people operating under different groundmotives. Nevertheless, Dooyeweerd believed that Robbers had conceded his point that theoretical thought is grounded in something more fundamental than itself, a religious presupposition. Therefore, Dooyeweerd replies, communication is possible after all, since each thinker is bound to give an account of his own fundamental presuppositions. People of different commitments can hear one another out as they engage in this common task.[9]

So far, I gather, Van Til has no objection. But then Dooyeweerd explains the basis of this communication. As Van Til paraphrases it,

> After all, is it not true that every philosophy must give itself a theoretical account of the same reality, being bound to the

[9]CC, 2:3, pp. 34–36.

same structure of thought? Have they not all developed in one historically founded communion of thought? And must they not all submit to undeniable states of affairs in reality?[10]

Van Til agrees that there are objective states of affairs that everyone shares in common. But he wonders why Dooyeweerd is so elated over Robbers's supposed "concession":

> Dooyeweerd rejoices in the fact that Robbers is willing to allow room for religion as a principle that underlies theoretical thought. Has he not thereby shown a willingness to consider the necessity of giving up the autonomy of theoretical thought? Dooyeweerd himself says that he has not. Then what is gained? So long as he has not given up the idea of the autonomy of theoretical thought, the addition of a religious authority does not bring Robbers any closer to the position of Dooyeweerd. . . . It cannot at all fairly be said that Robbers has taken the transcendental criticism of Dooyeweerd seriously. For transcendental criticism, to be truly such, must be based upon the religious truth about God, man, and the world taken from Scripture. And that is the last thing Robbers wants to do.[11]

Van Til finds an "open inconsistency" in Dooyeweerd's second article on Robbers:

> [Dooyeweerd] argues first that it is in the light of the Scripture that the states of affairs have been discovered to be what they are. Surely then it is only he who looks through the glasses of Scripture who can see the states of affairs for what they are. Robbers is unwilling to do this. But then Dooyeweerd argues quite differently. He says that Robbers need not accept his basic cosmonomic idea in order to see the states of affairs for what they really are. And consonant with this dispensation from accepting the basic principles of his philosophy,

[10]Ibid., 36.

[11]Ibid., 40. I believe this passage is clearer if the reader strikes the "not" in the second sentence.

> Dooyeweerd further asserts that he does not at all intend to identify the actual state of affairs with his philosophical view of reality.[12]

Does Dooyeweerd mean that he is merely interested in "setting aside his framework for the sake of argument?" Van Til does not think so: "But this does not seem to be Dooyeweerd's view. He makes a definite distinction between objectively existing states of affairs and his own philosophical view. This distinction is not something that he adopts for a moment. It is rather a distinction that he says is always present."[13]

Van Til also brings up Dooyeweerd's distinction between "immanent," "transcendent," and "transcendental" criticism. Van Til paraphrases Van Riessen, a disciple of Dooyeweerd's, as explaining:

> By means of immanent criticism . . . the believer can show the unbeliever that there are important questions that he has not answered and that his position is internally contradictory. By means of transcendental criticism, we can point to the religious presuppositions which make philosophy possible. . . . With transcendent criticism, we leave the field of philosophy and place ourselves instead in the midst of religious presuppositions. By means of these, we then give witness to our faith.[14]

Dooyeweerd claims that transcendental criticism allows for dialogue, while transcendent criticism is "dogmatic" and does not. Van Til, however, notes with approval an observation by G. C. Berkouwer to the effect that the whole point of transcendental criticism is lost unless it is based on transcendent criticism. That is to say, the entire transcendental method hangs in the air except for the fact that it rests upon the fullness and unity of truth accepted on the authority of Scripture.[15]

Dooyeweerd replies in *Jerusalem and Athens* that Van Til has misunderstood his distinction: "I meant by transcendent criticism, the

[12]Ibid., 41–42.
[13]Ibid., 44.
[14]Ibid., 48.
[15]Ibid., 47.

dogmatic manner of criticizing philosophical theories from a theological or from a different philosophical viewpoint without a critical distinction between *theoretical propositions* and the *supra-theoretical presuppositions lying at their foundation.*"[16]

The purpose of a transcendental critique, he says, is

> laying bare the central influence of the different religious, basic motives upon the philosophical trends of thought. For that purpose it was necessary to show the *inner point of contact* between theoretical thought and its supra-theoretical presuppositions which relate to the central religious sphere of human existence. This is why this transcendental critique is obliged to *begin* with an inquiry into the inner nature and structure of the theoretical attitude of thought and experience *as such* and *not* with a confession of faith.[17]

He then describes the various phases of confrontation between two viewpoints. The "central religious starting point" does come up in the discussion, but not at the beginning, where it would only be rejected out of hand. Here, it seems to me, Dooyeweerd is speaking only of an argumentative strategy, an order of topics, rather than suggesting that a Christian's argument should be based at some point upon neutrality. His whole point is to show the non-Christian that neutrality is impossible, but he approaches that conclusion step-by-step.

Unfortunately, the term "starting point" can refer either to the first in an order of topics or to a substantive presupposition. Van Til sometimes falls into the same confusion when he uses the phrase "at the outset." For example:

> I believe that Christian apologetics, and in particular Reformed apologetics, is not really *transcendental* in its method unless it says *at the outset* of its dialogue with non-believers that the Christian position must be accepted on the authority of the self-identifying Christ of Scripture as the presupposition of human predication in any field.[18]

---

[16]JA, 75 (emphasis his).

[17]Ibid., 76 (emphasis his).

[18]Ibid., 98. Compare the *"ab initio"* of p. 126.

Does this mean that every apologetic confrontation must literally *begin,* temporally, with such an announcement? If that is what Van Til means, it is hard to imagine how he would defend the point. Such a pattern is certainly not followed in Scripture itself.[19] But if Van Til is using terms like "starting point" and "at the outset" in a logical sense, referring to the presuppositions actually governing the Christian's thought, whether he announces them to the unbeliever or not, then it is unclear precisely how his view differs from Dooyeweerd's at this point.

If that observation is true, then the debate between Van Til and Dooyeweerd on this particular matter would appear to result from a misunderstanding. When Van Til insists that transcendental criticism never be separated from transcendent criticism, he obviously is not referring to transcendent criticism in the sense defined by Dooyeweerd above. Van Til is not particularly concerned to affirm or deny Dooyeweerd's distinction between theoretical and supratheoretical presuppositions, which determines Dooyeweerd's definition of "transcendent." On the other hand, Dooyeweerd does not intend, by denying the need for transcendent criticism, to deny that all Christian argument must be governed by Christian presuppositions. Van Til certainly has no right to say, simply on the basis of Dooyeweerd's distinction, that he has "definitely excluded the contents of biblical teaching as having the basically determinative significance for your method of transcendental criticism."[20]

The same ambiguity between logical and temporal order confuses Van Til's discussion of Dooyeweerd's "three steps." Dooyeweerd proposes that discussion between Christian and non-Christian thinkers progress as follows: (1) Demonstrate to the unbeliever that theoretical thought is not self-sufficient, but presupposes pretheoretical experience.[21] (2) Establish that "the inter-relation of theoretical thought with cosmic time points to the need of the idea of a self which transcends time."[22] (3) Show that this supratemporal self in turn "points

---

[19]Compare our previous discussions about Van Til's assertion that Christian theism must be proved "as a unit." I have argued that this is not true if it means "all at once." It is true if it means simply that the argument must presuppose the fullness of Christian theism and must take account of the interrelationships between its various elements.

[20]Ibid., 99.

[21]Ibid.

[22]Ibid., 103.

beyond itself to its Origin."[23] Van Til objects that none of these steps can be intelligibly carried out except on Christian presuppositions—a point that is true but is not in any obvious way denied by Dooyeweerd. At any rate, Van Til does not demonstrate in this discussion that Dooyeweerd's "sharpened transcendental method is destructive of the Christian story."[24]

Nor do I accept Van Til's point that Dooyeweerd's concept of the self is "contentless" or a "pure form," simply because the Christian presupposition does not become explicit at stage two of the argument.[25]

Van Til would be making an arguable point, if he were calling on Dooyeweerd to be more explicit about the distinctively Christian content of his concepts. I suspect that the direction of Dooyeweerd's argument would be clearer—both to believers and to unbelievers—if he had been more explicit. That is a question of strategy, however. We have seen before that Van Til tends to reduce questions of strategy to questions of principle, often without adequate justification. This is one of those cases where criticism should have been confined to the level of strategy. I do not deny that strategy should be based on principle, but in this particular dispute there are no real differences of principle at stake.

Scripture and Philosophy

Some of Van Til's other criticisms of Dooyeweerd, however, are cogent. In *Christianity in Conflict,* Van Til reports an exchange between Dooyeweerd and van Peursen, who accuses Dooyeweerd of dogmatism. Van Peursen urges as a criticism that Dooyeweerd's philosophy "is entirely ruled by the central motive of the Christian religion."[26] Dooyeweerd, rather than simply pleading guilty to this charge, makes a distinction that he considers important. His philosophy, he says, is "controlled by," but not "derived from," Scripture. Evidently, "derived from" refers to logical inference from Scripture's sentences, concepts, and teachings, while "controlled by" has some nonconceptual

[23]Ibid., 107.
[24]Ibid., 121.
[25]Ibid., 104, 121.
[26]CC, 2:3, p. 55.

influence in view. In arguing for this distinction, Dooyeweerd appeals to the independence of philosophy from dogmatic theology.

Van Til asks of Dooyeweerd, however,

> how he can put an intelligible content into the phrase "Christian thinking" in terms of control (*beheersen*) rather than in terms of derivation (*afleiding*). If we are to avoid mysticism, then we must do something with the actual revelational content of Scripture. Dooyeweerd needs to borrow nothing from any theologian. But revelation is expressed in thought-content. And it is this thought-content which Dooyeweerd must be faithful to. It is this thought-content, unmixed with any interpretation by any man, which controls his own thinking. This being the case what difference remains between the idea of his thinking being controlled or being derived from Scripture? Control without derivation is an empty mystical phrase.[27]

This time, Van Til's complaint is not based on a misunderstanding. Rather, Dooyeweerd exacerbates the problem in his *Jerusalem and Athens* article. He sees Van Til's criticism as manifesting a "rationalistic scholastic tendency."[28]

In reply to Van Til's statement quoted above, he says, "I can only ask the counter question, how it would be possible to *derive* from the biblical revelation a philosophical idea of cosmic time with its diversity of modal aspects, of which it does not speak in any way."[29]

Fair enough. Van Til would doubtless agree that Scripture does not speak explicitly or in detail about such things. What Scripture does speak about is the Creator-creature distinction, the Trinity, the creation of all things through Christ, the sovereignty of God over creation, the authority of God's Word over all of human life, the fall of the human race, and the redemption of God's people by Jesus Christ. But Dooyeweerd wishes to generalize his point: "The Bible does not provide us with philosophical ideas, no more than it gives us natural scientific knowledge or an economic or legal theory."[30]

---

[27]Ibid., 56.

[28]JA, 81.

[29]Ibid., 82.

[30]Ibid.

Certainly Scripture does not provide full-blown theories in any of these fields. But granted an orthodox Reformed view of biblical authority, it does present a basic view of the world, fundamental to all of these disciplines, and authoritative for all disciplines. That worldview is of particular importance to philosophy, which purports to describe the world in its most general features. In view of this fact, it is at best highly misleading to say that the Bible does not provide (any?) philosophical ideas.

And Van Til's question still stands: How can Scripture "control" philosophy if it does not provide any philosophical ideas? Dooyeweerd explains this "control" by saying that Scripture provides "a central starting-point which transcends the modal diversity of our temporal horizon of experience and must consequently be of a supra-theoretical character."[31] This explanation uses so many Dooyeweerdian technical terms that it is probably incomprehensible to most readers.[32] It assumes all of Dooyeweerd's debatable theorizing about the temporal horizon and the relation between theory and the "supra-theoretical." Neither Van Til nor I make these assumptions, so it is hard to know what to do with this response.

Perhaps, however, we can gain some clarity as we follow Dooyeweerd's reply to Van Til a bit further. When Van Til speaks about "subordinating all our thinking to the truths of Scripture" and of the normativity of the scriptural concepts of Creation, Fall, and redemption, Dooyeweerd demurs.[33] He insists that such statements represent a strain of rationalism in Van Til's thought. First, he denies that the Bible speaks of "obeying the voice of God in terms of subjecting every human thought to divine thought."[34] One wonders here if Dooyeweerd has considered 2 Corinthians 10:5 ("bringing every thought captive to the obedience of Christ") or the biblical doctrine of human and divine wisdom.

What Dooyeweerd actually means to say, evidently, is that people receive the divine Word through the heart, rather than through

[31]Ibid.

[32]One of the major problems in the Dooyeweerdian philosophy is that it is constantly self-referential in this way. As a result, people coming from outside this system of thought, even those seeking to view it sympathetically, have a very hard time getting a handle on it. Dooyeweerd seems quite incapable of explaining his concepts in system-neutral (let alone ordinary) language.

[33]JA, 83.

[34]Ibid., 84.

thought. He has a point here—one with which Van Til, for the most part, agrees.[35] But Dooyeweerd does not define how "heart" and "thought" differ, or how they are related to one another.

In the discussion that follows, he points out that language, such as the language of Scripture, communicates

> not only conceptual thought contents, but all sorts of contents of our consciousness, such as subjective moods and emotional feelings, volitional decisions in a concrete situation, our faith in Jesus Christ, pretheoretical aesthetical and moral experiences . . . which certainly do not give expression to conceptual knowledge of the experiential modes concerned.[36]

There is much truth in this observation; theologians need to be more aware of the diversity of biblical language. However, this observation does not advance Dooyeweerd's argument concerning Van Til's "rationalism." Here again he presupposes the sharp distinction that his philosophy makes between pretheoretical and theoretical thought, aligning "conceptual thought contents" on the theoretical side. From Van Til's perspective, one can reply (1) by denying the sharpness of this distinction (Van Til is inclined to see the relation of pretheoretical to theoretical thought as a continuum, rather than as two sharply distinct categories), (2) by denying that all "concepts" are "theoretical" in Dooyeweerd's technical sense, (3) by insisting that Scripture does, among many other things, teach some "theoretical concepts," or (4) by insisting that Scripture teaches at least some ideas (into whatever category Dooyeweerd may wish to place them) that theorists must take into account.

It is certainly not obvious that, on Van Til's view, Scripture is "conceptual" in the sense of Dooyeweerd's "theoretical thought." Van Til speaks of the "simple" thought-content of Scripture. He is merely saying that Scripture controls human life, including philosophy, by what its words and sentences say, not by some mystical force that flows through it, as is suggested by some forms of modern theology. Dooyeweerd's preference for the word *dunamis* (power) to designate Scripture's relation to human life raises questions here. Is Dooyeweerd

[35]Compare our discussion of "The Primacy of the Intellect" in chap. 11.

[36]JA, 84–85.

verging on mysticism here? Does he have some third category in mind, between language on the one hand and mystical power on the other? Or is he merely saying that the language of Scripture is for the most part ordinary rather than technical? Only the latter alternative has any plausibility in the context of Reformed theology. But that alternative is one that Van Til would gladly agree with. So Van Til's "rationalism" is still unproved.

Dooyeweerd admits that there are "genuine *conceptual* contents" of God and the human ego, but he insists that these conceptual contents "do not transcend the modal dimension of our temporal horizon of experience." He then criticizes Van Til's account of the divine attributes as one presented "within the traditional framework of a metaphysical theory of being."[37] He adds, "This is why I cannot agree with your statement that God's being is exhaustively rational."[38] What Dooyeweerd seems to be saying is that if anything in Scripture is "conceptual," then it describes only the world, not God. Van Til, he thinks, is wrong to believe that Scripture teaches a metaphysic, that is to say, a general view of God in his relationship to the world. This discussion, too, is somewhat distorted by Dooyeweerd's sharp distinction between nontheoretical and theoretical thought. But perhaps we can bypass that. Let us grant that the Bible contains absolutely no "theoretical thought" in Dooyeweerd's sense. The issue still remains as to whether Scripture reveals to us any facts of which theories must take account. To deny that it does is to advocate mysticism. To affirm that it does is to justify traditional discussions of the divine attributes. For those discussions do not claim that their theory comes from Scripture in so many words, only that their assertions are *justified* by biblical exegesis. This is not to say that their exegesis has always been correct, only that they have been correct in *seeking* from Scripture a doctrine of the divine attributes.

Van Til's "metaphysic" is simply a theory derived from the factual content of divine revelation. He makes no claim that Scripture is "theoretical" in Dooyeweerd's sense, nor is it even clear that he accepts Dooyeweerd's distinction between theory and nontheory. There is certainly no basis here for Dooyeweerd to accuse him of rationalism.[39]

---

[37]Ibid., 87.

[38]Ibid., 88.

[39]There is even less basis for the similar accusations in Knudsen's article, which are easily refuted by the contexts of the quotations from Van Til that he presents. See JA, 275–305.

But the fact that Dooyeweerd accuses Van Til of rationalism suggests that there is in his own thought at least some mystical tendency not in keeping with a Reformed view of biblical inspiration and authority. He has not answered Van Til's question as to how scriptural control over human thought is possible without the derivation of human thought from Scripture. Whether he is thinking along mystical lines, or whether his view of revelation is simply unclear, he has not in this discussion laid a good foundation for truly Christian philosophy.

Dooyeweerd's vagueness on the relationship between Scripture and philosophy undoubtedly encouraged Van Til to find evidence of neutralism in his three-step transcendental argument. Legitimate questions certainly arise as to the extent to which Scripture has actually influenced Dooyeweerd's philosophy, apart from the broad, general categories of Creation, Fall, and redemption. I have myself raised questions about his strategy. Van Til, I think, goes too far in arguing that Dooyeweerd compromises the Christian faith by failing to bring explicit biblical concepts into the early steps of his reasoning. But, overall, I see in Dooyeweerd what Van Til also sees: a tendency to put his presuppositions somewhat in the background in order to achieve better communication with non-Christians. In my opinion, he does this awkwardly at best; at worst, he endangers the fundamental Reformed conviction that all of life is to be governed by the Word of God. Nevertheless, like Van Til, I honor his intention, which is to bring the scriptural vision to bear upon all human beings in every aspect of life.

PART SIX

Conclusions

CHAPTER TWENTY-EIGHT

Van Til's Successors

In these concluding chapters, I wish to give the reader some sense of the present condition of the Van Tillian movement and its prospects for the future. In this chapter, I shall focus on people; in the next, on ideas. I am interested in describing the present position of Van Til's thought in the theological world and in showing how the church can make the best use of this legacy in the future.

I sense that interest in Van Til has declined somewhat since his death in 1987. That is understandable; it frequently happens after the death of a powerful leader in any field. One thinks of the eclipse of interest in Johann Sebastian Bach after his death—an interest revived by Felix Mendelssohn and others in the early nineteenth century.

Still, many continue to labor in the spirit, and some in the letter, of Van Til's work. Readers of this volume should make their acquaintance with these men, if they have not already.

IMMEDIATE SUCCESSORS

Van Til's most immediate successor was Robert D. Knudsen, who taught in the apologetics department of Westminster Seminary for many years as Van Til's associate. Knudsen studied with Dooyeweerd in the Netherlands with Van Til's blessing. As I have indicated, however, certain disagreements between Dooyeweerd and Van Til developed over the years, and Knudsen was somewhat caught in the middle. Knudsen always remained confessionally orthodox in areas where Dooyeweerd's views were questionable: he did not join the Dooyeweerdian attack upon the Reformed confessions as "scholastic," nor did he adopt the somewhat liberal view of Scripture that emerged from Dooyeweerd's circle. Nevertheless, he was far more sympathetic to Dooyeweerd than was Van Til, and he joined in Dooyeweerd's criticism of Van Til's "rationalistic scholastic tendency." Van Til was not a man to easily accept differences among colleagues, and the relationship between Van Til and Knudsen was rather tense as I observed it. Nevertheless, Van Til supported Knudsen's continued presence in the department. Knudsen is planning to retire at the end of June 1995.

When Van Til gave up regular teaching in 1972, he passed the introductory apologetics course at the seminary to Harvie M. Conn. Conn had been a missionary to Korea, and he imparted to the course a substantial practical orientation. The students worked together on multimedia projects while they imbibed the theory of Van Til's system. Conn did not make theoretical contributions to Van Til's system, but he was a lively and exciting teacher, well informed about modern culture, with a burden to send Van Til's powerful apologetic, through the students, to the non-Christians of the world.

In 1975, Conn determined to drop his teaching in apologetics to focus on the field of missions. With Van Til's blessing, I took over Conn's introductory course. After graduating from Westminster in 1964 and spending several years at Yale, I had returned to teach at the seminary in 1968. My original teaching position was not in apologetics, but in systematic theology, under Norman Shepherd, following the retirement of John Murray. At Van Til's invitation, however, I did teach Th.M.-level courses in apologetics from the start, and I was pleased to get the opportunity to become an official member of the apologetics department in 1975. I taught both apologetics and systematics at Westminster in Philadelphia until 1980, when I took a similar position at the new Westminster campus at Escondido, California, a position I hold today.

In 1980, I was replaced at Westminster in Philadelphia by David W. Clowney, son of Edmund P. Clowney, the first president of the school. Clowney taught in the apologetics department for eight years.

He left Westminster after he became persuaded that Scripture permitted the ordination of women to church office, a position not accepted by the seminary. In 1988, he was replaced by William Edgar, formerly professor of apologetics at the Reformed seminary in Aix-en-Provence, France.

Edgar had been involved with Francis Schaeffer's ministry some years earlier. Since Van Til had been critical of Schaeffer, some members of Westminster's constituency questioned Edgar's faithfulness to the Van Til legacy. However, Edgar prepared a paper comparing Van Til and Schaeffer, and it supported Van Til's critique of Schaeffer.[1] Edgar does in the paper indicate regret that Van Til did not adequately appreciate Schaeffer's insights into modern art and general culture. Edgar himself is quite knowledgeable in those fields, particularly in music.

This succession has been very much in line with Van Til's thought, though not slavishly so. Knudsen, Conn, Clowney, Edgar, and Frame have all been enthusiastic advocates of Van Til's apologetics in its broad outlines. Of the five, I have been the most critical of Van Til. I will summarize my criticisms in the next chapter, and the reader can judge whether or not I am a "true Van Tillian." For Gary North's view that Westminster Seminary has abandoned Van Til's legacy, see below.

THE THEONOMISTS

Besides the official succession at the two Westminster seminaries, there are many others who have promoted Van Til's emphases in apologetics and theology. Most visible among them have been the members of the Christian reconstruction movement, otherwise known as "theonomy." In 1958, Rousas J. Rushdoony, the founder of that movement, published, as the first of his many books, *By What Standard?*,[2] an exposition of Van Til's thought. It is still useful as a well-organized summary of Van Til's views.

Later publications showed that Rushdoony had much on his mind besides Van Til's apologetics. He emphasized a very strong continuity between the Old and New Testaments, particularly the continuing

[1]It is still unpublished, to my knowledge.

[2]Philadelphia: Presbyterian and Reformed, 1958.

authority of Old Testament law over the New Testament believer. Distinctive to his view, among contemporary Reformed writers, was the idea that all the civil penalties of the Mosaic Law were binding upon present-day civil governments. Thus, he advocated the death penalty for adultery and homosexuality. Eventually there developed a school of thought that advocated these positions and sought to apply this approach to many areas of life. Hence, it became known as the Christian reconstruction movement.[3]

All the major writers in this movement profess allegiance to Van Til's apologetic method in its general outlines. Most, indeed, uphold Van Til's ideas in nearly "exhaustive detail." We saw in chapter 16, however, Gary North's critique of Van Til's view of common grace. North is Rushdoony's estranged son-in-law, and a leader of the Christian reconstruction movement.

The best-known apologist of the group is Greg L. Bahnsen, now director of the Southern California Center for Christian Studies. A student of Van Til's with a Ph.D. in philosophy from the University of Southern California under Dallas Willard, Bahnsen is one of the sharpest apologists working today. In my view, he is the best debater among Christian apologists of all apologetic persuasions.[4] Bahnsen is doing a valuable work in teaching people how to make practical use of Van Til's approach—"taking it to the streets," as he says.

Gary North's *Westminster's Confession: The Abandonment of Van Til's Legacy*[5] has on its cover a picture of Van Til, torn in two. As the title implies, the book argues that Westminster Seminary has abandoned its commitment to Van Til's principles. This is one of three books that were rapidly produced to answer the volume edited by Barker and Godfrey, *Theonomy: a Reformed Critique,* cited earlier. North says of his own book that it "is what some people will call a 'quickie.'"[6] He boasts about how little time he spent working on the book, evidently to suggest that the Barker-Godfrey volume was a critical pushover. Nevertheless, he attempts to argue a thesis with

[3]For my analysis of this movement (both sympathetic and critical), see my review of Rushdoony's *The Institutes of Biblical Law* in *WTJ* 38 (winter 1976): 195–217, and my article, "The One, the Many, and Theonomy," in *Theonomy: a Reformed Critique,* ed. W. Barker and W. Robert Godfrey (Grand Rapids: Zondervan, 1990), 89–99.

[4]Tapes of his apologetic encounters are available from Covenant Tape Ministry, 22005 N. Venado Dr., Sun City West, AZ 85373.

[5]Tyler, Tex.: Institute for Christian Economics, 1991.

[6]Ibid., xvii.

serious implications for the whole conservative Presbyterian community. In this case, I think he would have been better advised to take more time on the project.

In short, his argument is that Westminster abandoned Van Til's legacy by (1) failing to hire Greg Bahnsen to replace Van Til, (2) firing Norman Shepherd, and (3) producing the Barker-Godfrey critique of theonomy.

About the Shepherd firing, I have little to say at this point except that it had little if anything to do with Shepherd's adherence to Van Til's principles. The controversy leading to Shepherd's dismissal had to do with Shepherd's formulation of the doctrine of justification by faith alone. Van Til and others, including myself, believed that Shepherd's formulations were orthodox; others on Westminster's faculty and board did not. He was never declared to be unorthodox, despite many discussions and votes of faculty, board, and presbytery. Nevertheless, his contract was terminated because the debate had proved divisive to the seminary community. Beyond the fact that Van Til supported Shepherd, there was no significant connection between the controversy and Van Til's legacy.

North believes that Shepherd's postmillennialism showed a kind of natural progression from Van Tillian principles toward theonomy, and that Shepherd's dismissal aborted that development, curtailing Van Til's influence. The argument is interesting, but the fact remains that neither Van Til nor Shepherd expressed any allegiance to theonomy; indeed, both of them opposed it within my hearing. And, as North is well aware, even if Van Til should have been a postmillennialist, he was not one.

North's first and third points are answered by the fact that Van Til himself was not a theonomist and did not encourage the seminary to embrace theonomy. At one point (1978–79, to be exact), Van Til did favor inviting Greg Bahnsen to join the faculty. The faculty as a whole did not support this proposal, however, because of Bahnsen's theonomic views and some other considerations. Nobody objected that Bahnsen was too Van Tillian in his apologetic approach. In our discussions, Bahnsen's commitment to Van Til's apologetic was always considered a strength. Van Til supported Bahnsen in spite of his theonomic position, not because of it. Therefore, the faculty's opposition to theonomy, both in its refusal to hire Bahnsen and in its later book critical of theonomy, cannot be seen as in any sense an abandonment of Van Til's legacy. If Van Til was not a theonomist, how can the rejection of theonomy be considered an abandonment of Van Til's legacy?

Other Van Tillians

Many others have also sought to bring Van Tillian perspectives to bear on apologetics and theology. What I described in chapter 13 as Van Til's multiperspectivalism has been developed by me in *The Doctrine of the Knowledge of God* and especially by Vern Poythress, professor of New Testament at Westminster in Philadelphia, in many volumes. He develops especially its implications for biblical interpretation. His approach is summarized in *Symphonic Theology*.[7]

I believe that the "nouthetic counseling" of Jay Adams, which continues to be developed by the Christian Counseling and Educational Foundation, has a strongly Van Tillian thrust, particularly in its antithetical relation to secular psychology and its determination to uphold Reformed, biblical presuppositions in all counseling theory and practice.

Useful applications of Van Til's insights to many fields, including mathematics, philosophy, economics, education, and politics can be found in *Foundations of Christian Scholarship*, edited by Gary North.[8] For other literary contributions of value, see my annotated bibliography in this volume.

Others teaching apologetics today in the Van Tillian mode are Hendrik Krabbendam and William Dennison of Covenant College,[9] and Richard Pratt of Reformed Theological Seminary in Orlando, Florida. Pratt's major field is Old Testament, but he is also the author of *Every Thought Captive*, which trains young people in the use of a Van Tillian type of apologetic.[10]

Van Til's influence has been felt beyond his basic Reformed constituency. Some dispensational theologians have been attracted to his ideas. John C. Whitcomb taught Van Tillian apologetics for many years at Grace Theological Seminary. At Dallas Theological Seminary, Stephen Spencer teaches from a Van Tillian perspective

[7]Grand Rapids: Zondervan, 1987.

[8]Vallecito, Calif.: Ross House Books, 1976.

[9]Krabbendam also teaches at Greenville Presbyterian Theological Seminary.

[10]Phillipsburg, N.J.: Presbyterian and Reformed, 1979.

courses that were previously taught by Norman Geisler, an evangelical Thomist.

More General Van Tillian Influence

Van Til's influence extends somewhat to people outside his movement. For example, through Evan Runner, Peter Steen, Robert Knudsen, and others, many of Van Til's emphases have been introduced into the Dooyeweerdian movement in North America. Disciples of Dooyeweerd generally recognize a measure of kinship between themselves and Van Til, while being in various degrees aware of the differences between Van Til and the Amsterdam thinkers.

Herbert Schlossberg's *Idols for Destruction*[11] is one of the most cogent recent critiques of modern culture. It is a most impressive work of scholarship and analysis. The book does not mention Van Til, nor does it include much Van Tillian terminology. But it deals very skillfully with the rationalist and irrationalist tendencies in thought and society, and it shows the indispensibility of a Christian view of life and history. Schlossberg is influenced somewhat by the theonomic Van Tillians.

I believe that Van Til also had a profound influence upon Francis Schaeffer, and, through him, upon many others. Schaeffer studied with Van Til in 1936–37 and then left to join the student body at the newly formed Faith Theological Seminary. Schaeffer saw himself as a kind of bridge between Van Til and the more traditional apologetics, particularly that of James Oliver Buswell, and he published an article to that effect in the early 1950s.

Schaeffer conducted a remarkable ministry in Switzerland, first to children, then to adult inquirers. In time, the ministry became known as L'Abri, which is French for "the shelter." Many came to profess faith in Christ through Schaeffer's work, particularly younger intellectuals. From the late 1960s until his death, Schaeffer produced a number of books reflecting the apologetic he practiced among these inquirers.

Van Til wrote, but did not publish, a volume attacking Schaeffer's apologetic. His critique of Schaeffer was very similar to his critiques of Butler and Carnell: Schaeffer held to the traditional method; he pre-

[11]Washington: Regnery Gateway, 1990.

sented the Christian faith as a supplement to the unbeliever's knowledge; he used evidences and logical tests without first announcing their basis in scriptural revelation; he viewed the epistemology of the ancient Greeks too favorably.

I believe that Schaeffer was rather unclear on some important matters, particularly the existence of a distinctively biblical concept of truth. The epistemological basis of his reasoning is somewhat obscure. And Van Til is a far more reliable guide than Schaeffer in the history of philosophy.[12] Nevertheless, to the extent that I have defended Butler and Carnell, I would defend Schaeffer, and with roughly the same argumentation.

In any case, it is interesting that there are some elements in Schaeffer's thought that bring him closer to Van Til than are most traditional apologists. His use of the Trinity to solve the problem of the one and the many is right out of Van Til. And perhaps more significantly, Schaeffer's apologetic is transcendental in a more explicit way than either Butler's or Carnell's. Schaeffer argues that the only alternative to belief in the biblical God is matter, motion, time, and chance, in which there is no basis for rationality, moral standards, or aesthetic value.

Since his death, Schaeffer's influence has continued through the teaching and writings of his family and of disciples such as Os Guinness, Jerram Barrs, Ranald Macaulay, Udo Middelmann, and Donald Drew. Among these, one will not find much Van Tillian terminology. But, in my opinion, their writings have injected into evangelical apologetics and theology a high level of intelligence, wisdom, balance, and cultural awareness, together with an overriding concern for biblical principle. In these respects, they, like Schlossberg, are Van Til's grandchildren.

---

[12]See my remarks on Schaeffer in chap. 17.

CHAPTER TWENTY-NINE

Van Til and Our Future

In this final chapter, I would like to summarize the approach to Van Til taken in this book. I will here address the question of how we contemporary Christians can best use Van Til's ideas in our witness to the world.

In this book, I have tried to dispel the impression that Van Til's thought forms a seamless robe—that it must either be accepted or rejected in its entirety. That impression has, of course, been given both by Van Til's friends and by his enemies. Thus, the literature about Van Til tends to be either uncritical adulation or supercritical debunking.

Van Til himself tends to give that same impression. He speaks of proving Christian theism "as a unit." In teaching apologetics, he throws his whole system at the reader all at once, so to speak, rather than bit by bit. And if the reader does not grasp it all, Van Til throws it all at him a second time. Thus, the reader gets the impression that he cannot pick and choose; it is either all or nothing; Van Til must be thoroughly embraced or totally opposed. All of that, of course, is in keeping with Van Til's background in philosophical idealism, and also with his Kuyperian-Machenite antithetical mode of thought.

Yet I have dared to differ with this approach. I have tried to break down Van Til's system into its basic elements, in order to analyze and evaluate each one at a time. I do not deny that Van Til's thought is highly interrelated and systematic; I have tried to bring out those systematic interrelations as best I can. But it seems to me to make more pedagogical sense to move from the simple to the complex, from the known to the unknown.

In this process, I have concluded that Van Til's thought is not, after all, a seamless robe. There are some elements of it that are unquestionably biblical and fundamental to Christian thought and life. These constitute an indispensable basis for any future apologetic. Other aspects of Van Til's system, however, are not well grounded scripturally and can be forgotten without loss.

The strongest part of Van Til's system is what I have called the metaphysics of knowledge. This includes his teaching about the nature of God, the Trinity, the Creator-creature distinction, and the necessity of presupposing God's revelation in all human thought. In these areas I have very little criticism. Here Van Til simply reproduces the teaching of Scripture and shows its applications to human thought and life.

I do take issue with his illegitimate *application* of these principles in the Clark controversy, and his sometimes confusing statements about the use of reason, logic, and evidence. Even in these areas, however, he is essentially right. In its union with the divine essence, God's thought is different from man's "at every point." And we do need to employ the tools of reason, logic, and evidence in a properly biblical way, renouncing our own autonomy and seeking to think in subordination to God's revelation.

Van Til's view of the ethics of knowledge is an area of both strength and weakness. Certainly he is right to insist that non-Christians know, but suppress, the truth of God's revelation. In Romans 1, Scripture makes that assertion quite explicitly. But Van Til seems to search for words in order to express how the unbeliever can in one sense know, and in another sense be ignorant of, the truth of God. In certain moods, he uses the language of extreme antithesis, suggesting that the unbeliever has no knowledge at all and therefore no area of agreement with the believer. While it is true that all the unbeliever's actions and thoughts are in the service of his would-be autonomy, the language of extreme antithesis is highly misleading and confusing to the practical work of apologetics. It is better to say that the unbeliever's depravity manifests itself in many forms, and that the non-Christian can and does utter either truth or falsehood for his purposes.

Van Til's doctrine of common grace, while rightly insisting on the importance of historical process, contains the unhistorical and unbiblical notion that the free offer of the gospel is directed toward a "generality" of people, rather than toward actual persons. Then Van Til compounds the confusion by postulating, without biblical warrant, a continuous process in which unbelief becomes worse and worse over time. Nonetheless, he introduces a very helpful apologetic tool in showing that unbelief is inseparably linked to the dialectic of rationalism and irrationalism, which destroys all basis for intelligible predication.

Van Til's transcendental or presuppositional argument is correct in the goal that it sets for the apologist: to show that no meaning, intelligibility, or predication is possible apart from the God of Scripture. He is right in saying that this argument must be circular or "spiral," always resting on the presupposition of God's truth. However, it does not seem to me that we need to be bound by (1) his exclusion of direct argument, (2) his demand that we always claim absolute certainty rather than probability, (3) his occasional requirement (not observed in his own sample arguments) that we announce our entire theology at the outset of every apologetic encounter, (4) his occasional requirement that the argument conclude by proving the whole of Christian theism, or (5) his rule that we may never present Christian truth as a supplement to the unbeliever's knowledge. Nevertheless, Van Til's sample arguments, in both *A Survey of Christian Epistemology* and *Why I Believe in God,* seem to me to be excellent examples, on the whole, of the power of a presuppositional apologetic.

Van Til is at his worst in his critiques of other thinkers, but even there he provides valuable insight. His critique of the traditional apologetic method often seems to me to make unreasonable demands upon past thinkers (such as the illegitimate rules mentioned in the above paragraph). His criticisms are valuable, however, as advice on strategy and clear communication. Certainly, the apologetic tradition has obscured the gospel by failing to make clear (to unbelievers and believers alike) the radical antithesis between Christian and non-Christian thought. It has even used formulae (e.g., "Bring on your revelations! Let them make peace with the law of contradiction and the facts of experience, and they will deserve a rational man's assent") that, while true in themselves, in their context encourage unbelievers to continue thinking autonomously. Unfortunately, Van Til sometimes fails to distinguish adequately between (1) issues of communication and strategy, and (2) issues of biblical orthodoxy. He also fails to distinguish adequately between spiritual and procedural issues. For example, he suggests that direct arguments, as opposed to indirect, are unambiguous expressions of an ungodly neutralism.

There are similar problems in Van Til's critiques of Scholasticism and of the Amsterdam philosophy, but he does point out some genuine and serious errors and confusions in those systems, and even more in the system of Karl Barth. For giving the church such clear warning about these errors, he deserves the commendation of all Christians.

I believe, therefore, that we can learn much that is good and valuable from Van Til without being slavish devotees. It is not necessary for the Van Tillian movement to maintain a movement mentality. Nor is it necessary to stand in stark antithesis against all our fellow Christians who have thus far not joined that movement.

A Van Tillian apologetic for the next century should free itself from those Van Tillian restrictions which are illegitimate and then enrich itself by developing a great variety of arguments contextualized for many different sorts of apologetic encounter. Van Til has taught us that every fact of history testifies to the reality of the biblical God. But he has only begun to show us how this takes place. Our task is to further implement this vision, by showing how the presuppositions of Scripture reveal everything for what it truly is in relation to God. That is an exciting task indeed.

It is also important for us to move beyond the traditional Van Tillian preoccupation with methodology.[1] Van Tillian courses in apologetics, including mine, have focused far too much on methods, especially upon distinguishing our methods from those of other schools of thought. More time should be spent on developing actual arguments. We need to spend more time addressing unbelievers and less time arguing with one another over methods. Students of Van Tillian apologetics need to be far better informed about Christian evidences and about the current situations that the apologist must address.

My critical account of Van Til allows us to take a somewhat less apocalyptic view of methodological differences among apologists, so that we can indeed concentrate on fulfilling the Great Commission. If this book encourages believers in that work, it will have accomplished its purpose.

[1]Thanks to Greg Bahnsen, who impressed this truth upon me in recent remarks.

APPENDIX A

Van Til and the Ligonier Apologetic

(Note: I originally published this review of *Classical Apologetics,* by R. C. Sproul, John Gerstner, and Arthur Lindsley, in the Fall 1985 issue of the *Westminster Theological Journal* [vol. 47, pp. 279–99]. I reprinted it in *Apologetics to the Glory of God,* but it seems best to reprint it in this volume also, since it deals with criticisms of Van Til that are fairly widespread and not otherwise dealt with in this book. Since writing this review, I have become a bit more favorable to the use of probability in apologetics [thus differing both with Van Til and with the Ligonier version of the tradition], and I have become a bit more guarded in my defense of circularity. In general, however, the review continues to speak for me as I interact with the rival approach to apologetics.)

INTRODUCTION

Classical Apologetics, by R. C. Sproul, John Gerstner, and Arthur Lindsley (Grand Rapids: Zondervan, 1984), has been eagerly awaited. This book puts into systematic (and at least somewhat technical) form an apologetic approach of considerable interest, which up until now has been expressed primarily in popular writings and taped lectures. It is also notable for its critique of "presuppositionalism" (mainly in its

Van Tillian form). This book is one of the most extensive critiques of Van Til to date,[1] and I think of all the critiques of Van Til this one shows the most thorough research and the most accurate interpretation.[2] In saying this, I should acknowledge a possible conflict of interest: The authors express indebtedness to me for correspondence between myself and Gerstner which "significantly sharpened our understanding of Vantillian apologetics."[3] However, in commending these authors for their understanding of Van Til, I am not intending to commend myself. My contribution to their formulations was relatively small (and, as it turns out, not always understood and/or accepted). But Gerstner himself is a former student of Van Til and has (as I know from personal discussions) been mulling over Van Til's position for many years, with an intense interest and scholarly care not matched, in my view, by other critics of Van Til.[4] Thus the credit for the book's high critical standards must go to the authors themselves.

I shall not discuss the details of the book's historical studies, though these are interesting and are among the book's best features. Gerstner was a professor of church history for many years, and this is his chief area of expertise. In general, the historical sections argue that a kind of "evidentialism" similar to the Ligonier type[5] has been the common view of orthodox Christians through most of church history; hence it deserves to be called the "classical" or "traditional" view. This argument is supported by studies of Augustine, Luther, Calvin, seventeenth-century orthodoxy, Eastern and Roman ortho-

---

[1]Its only rival in this respect is James Daane, *A Theology of Grace* (Grand Rapids: Eerdmans, 1954); but that book is limited in its focus to Van Til's doctrine of common grace, and it shows much less understanding of Van Til's thought than the volume under review.

[2]I will indicate that in this book also there is much, and serious, misunderstanding of Van Til; but these authors are much closer to the truth about him than his earlier critics, such as the *Calvin Forum* group (see Van Til, *The Defense of the Faith* [Philadelphia: Presbyterian and Reformed, 1955], 4ff.) or the critics in *Jerusalem and Athens* (ed. E. Geehan; Philadelphia: Presbyterian and Reformed, 1967).

[3]P. x of the book's preface. Cf. also the slightly extravagant comment on p. 299.

[4]The book is *dedicated* to Van Til "who has taught a generation that Christ is the Alpha and Omega of thought and life" (p. v). I do not doubt the genuineness of the authors' admiration and affection for Van Til: see pp. 183f.

[5]"Ligonier" is a convenient shorthand for "Sproul-Gerstner-Lindsley," since all three authors have been associated with the Ligonier Valley Study Center in western Pennsylvania.

doxy.[6] However, the authors believe that classical apologetics today is "sick and ailing," though not dead.[7] "Presuppositionalism," they tell us, "has become the majority report today among Reformed theologians, although it cannot even be called a minority report of church history."[8] Other reviewers more historically inclined than I will doubtless seek to evaluate this thesis. Substantial arguments, I think, can be presented on either side. Of course, the issue is not terribly important in evaluating the relative validity of the two approaches. If Van Til's view is relatively new, it is not on that account false; Protestants are not traditionalists.[9] In general, it seems to me that the history of apologetics before our century is ambiguous on these questions. Orthodox Christian apologists have always believed in the supreme authority of Scripture over all human reasoning—the essence of the Van Tillian position. On the other hand, they have also spoken of various kinds of reasoning that in some sense legitimately "precede" faith.[10] The apparent contradiction here was, in general, not perceived as a problem until after Kant's "Copernican revolution," which greatly increased the epistemological sophistication of theologians and philosophers. Only after Kant could the logic of presuppositions be systematically investigated (as it was, even before Van Til, by thinkers like Hegel, Marx, Kierkegaard, Wittgenstein, and by Christian apologists like James Orr). Thus to ask whether Calvin was a "presuppositionalist" or an "evidentialist"[11] is a bit like asking whether Augustine was a Protestant or a Catholic.[12]

As to the modern situation, many of us will be surprised to hear that presuppositionalism is the "majority report" among current

---

[6]Pp. 189–211.

[7]P. 34

[8]P. 183.

[9]Van Til himself finds relatively little of value in his apologetic predecessors. See his *A Christian Theory of Knowledge* (Nutley, N.J.: Presbyterian and Reformed, 1969), and his syllabus, *Christianity in Conflict* (mimeographed, 1962).

[10]"Precede" adds to the ambiguity. Few concepts in theology are as unclear as that of "priority." More comments on this issue will follow.

[11]I use these terms to accommodate the authors under review, but really I think they are quite misleading, suggesting that Van Til is opposed to the use of evidence and/or that the traditionalists have no presuppositions to examine. On the contrary: all parties to the discussion must deal with both presuppositions and evidences, and they differ only on the *roles* to be played by these.

[12]I am not saying that such questions are unanswerable, but rather that they are subtler than often supposed, and difficult to answer in any useful way.

apologists. It all depends, of course, on how you define presuppositionalism. I suppose that a case can be made, that, in this age, following Kant, Hegel, Marx, Einstein, pragmatism, phenomenology, existentialism, Wittgenstein, Kuhn, Polanyi, Hanson, Dooyeweerd, and many others, most apologists have taken seriously the issue of presuppositions. In our time, it is exceedingly difficult to deny that human thought (whether scientific, logical, historical, philosophical, religious, or whatever) is influenced by our "pretheoretical" attitudes and commitments.[13] Perhaps this fact is what suggests to our authors that presuppositionalism is ascendant presently; they do not document their assertion, so it is hard to say. In my view, this openness to considering the influence of pretheoretical commitments on thought is a long way from a full-fledged presuppositionalism. Still, it is a positive development in the dialogue. One of my great disappointments about the current volume is its failure to deal in any serious way with these powerful philosophical currents which create, for many, considerable presumption against the Ligonier type of apologetic.

I. Ligonier and Van Til

I shall now try to analyze the authors' critique of Van Til, before discussing their positive apologetic. In the book itself this order is reversed, but I feel that in this review questions of methodology and epistemology ought to precede discussion of the authors' arguments for Christianity; and the former questions are inseparably bound up with the critique of "presuppositionalism."

Van Til's apologetics is essentially simple, however complicated its elaborations. It makes two basic assertions: (1) that human beings are obligated to presuppose God in all of their thinking, and (2) that unbelievers resist this obligation in every aspect of thought and life. The first assertion leads Van Til to criticize the notion of intellectual autonomy; the second leads him to discuss the noetic effects of sin. The Ligonier group criticizes Van Til in both areas, which we shall consider in that order.

[13]Contra Dooyeweerd, however, I maintain that the reverse is also true and that no *sharp* distinction can be drawn between "pretheoretical" and "theoretical." See J. Frame, *The Amsterdam Philosophy* (Phillipsburg, N.J.: Harmony Press, 1972).

1. Autonomy, Reason, and Circularity

The initial description of presuppositionalism shows insight in the prominent place given to Van Til's critique of autonomy:[14] this is, I think, the foundation of Van Til's system and its most persuasive principle.[15] We must not do apologetics as if we were a law unto ourselves, as if we were the measure of all things. Christian thinking, like all of the Christian life, is subject to God's lordship.

However, the book's *analysis* of the autonomy question reveals unclarity and/or misunderstanding. The authors deduce from Van Til's statements about autonomy that he wants us to "start with" God, rather than with ourselves.[16] Now "start with" is (like "precede" and "priority") an extremely slippery phrase in theology and apologetics. It can indicate a pedagogical order of topics, an emphasis, a method of study, a conviction about prominence or importance, a relation of necessary or sufficient conditionality, or a criterion of truth. I believe that Van Til almost always has the last alternative in mind, though there is occasionally some ambiguity. At any rate, one would expect the Ligonier authors to offer some analysis of this concept, to make some attempt to define it (both for Van Til and for their own system). But no such analysis is forthcoming. The authors write as if the meaning of the idea were perfectly self-evident.

So they insist that we must, in coming to know God, "begin with ourselves," and therefore reason autonomously in some sense. "One simply cannot start outside himself. To begin outside oneself, one would first have to depart from himself."[17] Now certainly in one sense this is true, and Van Til quite readily admits it. Our authors even quote him to this effect,[18] but they claim that it represents an inconsis-

---

[14]P. 185.

[15]In my view, this point is both more important and more cogent than, e.g., Van Til's view of the noetic effects of sin. The latter is often singled out as being central to Van Til's thought, but it is one doctrine which Van Til himself admitted to have difficulty formulating: see *An Introduction to Systematic Theology* (unpublished class syllabus, 1961), 26f. Autonomy is the more crucial issue, for Van Til's analysis of it indicates that *even if man had not fallen,* he would still have been obligated to reason presuppositionally.

[16]Pp. 185, 212ff.

[17]P. 212.

[18]Pp. 214f.; cf. pp. 316f.

tency in his thought, a kind of embarrassing admission.[19] Anyhow, on Van Til's view, the self is the "proximate," but not the "ultimate" starting point.[20] What this means, I think, is that it is the self which makes its decisions both in thought and practical life: every judgment we make, we make because we, ourselves, think it is right. But this fact does not entail that the self is its own ultimate criterion of truth. We are regularly faced with the decision as to whether we should trust our own unaided judgment, or rely on someone else. There is nothing odd or strange (let alone logically impossible) about such a question; it is entirely normal.

Therefore, there are two questions to be resolved: (1) the metaphysical (actually tautological!) question of whether all decisions are decisions of the self, and (2) the epistemological-ethical question of what standard the self ought to use in coming to its decisions.[21] Van Til and the Ligonier group agree, I think, on the first question, though it is not of much interest to Van Til; but that agreement does not prejudice the answer to the second question. That one still needs to be posed and resolved. And it is the second question that Van Til—and Scripture—are concerned about. Scripture regularly calls God's creatures to submit their judgment to that of their creator. If someone objects that even a choice to serve God is a choice made by the self and therefore "starting with" the self in one sense, Van Til can simply grant the point, while reminding his questioner that in another sense, in a far more important sense, this choice does *not* "start with" the self.[22]

---

[19]Unfortunately, this is rather typical of the volume. The authors make statements about Van Til which can be contradicted from his writings; but instead of reconsidering the accuracy of their interpretation in these cases, they simply accuse Van Til of inconsistency. Thus their accounts of Van Til's positions are almost always oversimplified at best.

[20]Van Til, *An Introduction to Systematic Theology*, 203.

[21]Our authors charge Van Til with confusing the order of being with the order of knowing (p. 229). At this point, however, it is they who confuse metaphysics with epistemology.

[22]If "autonomy" in the first sense necessitates autonomy in the second sense, then, of course, it necessitates autonomy for Christians and non-Christians alike. Therefore, if our authors' argument were sound, it would prove too much. It would legislate autonomy for everyone, not just for those who are "beginning" their path toward Christianity, as on the Ligonier view (pp. 231f.). Human reason, then, would be the "ultimate" criterion, not merely the "penultimate" or "provisionally ultimate" as our authors would have it (pp. 301, 331).

The same sorts of distinctions need to be made in the discussion of human reason, another topic prominent in this book. *Classical Apologetics* is rationalistic with a vengeance. The authors attack the anti-intellectual trends of our time,[23] laud signs of a "retreat from this anti-intellectual binge,"[24] show at length from Scripture our obligation to reason with unbelievers.[25] "Fideism" is the great enemy.[26] Van Til, however, they say, abandons apologetics,[27] refusing to reason with unbelievers. He doesn't believe in proofs[28] or evidences.[29] He denies that you can find God at the end of a syllogism.[30] The present reviewer, that notorious Van Tillian, cannot engage in rational argument with anyone:

> [The Arminian] can argue with Frame, but Frame will not argue with him. Frame can only tell him that he is in error and that he must change his mind because he, Frame, has been illumined by God to see otherwise.[31]

On the contrary, say our authors: Just as we cannot avoid "starting with ourselves," so we cannot avoid the use of reason (in any area of life, particularly apologetics). Any attempt to persuade an unbeliever of Christian truth requires reasoning; indeed, rational argument is necessary if we are going to show the "rational necessity of presupposing God."[32] And, in fact, presuppositionalists *do* give reasons.[33] In practice, "there is no real difference on the matter of autonomy."[34]

Buttressing all of this is the familiar argument that some basic principles of reason (such as the law of noncontradiction) must be presupposed in any intelligible discourse; indeed, *"The Law of*

---

[23]Pp. 12ff.
[24]P. 15.
[25]Pp. 18ff.
[26]Pp. 24ff.
[27]P. 188.
[28]Pp. 253ff.
[29]Pp. 276ff.
[30]P. 287.
[31]P. 301.
[32]P. 224.
[33]Pp. 238f.
[34]P. 239; cf. pp. 324ff.

Noncontradiction [is] a Universal Prerequisite for Life."[35] You can't question logic without presupposing it; you can't argue against the primacy of logic without presupposing it as primary.

So our authors support the "principle of the primacy of the intellect." This does not mean that the intellect is more excellent that the God whom the intellect discovers; rather, "primacy of intellect means that we must think about God before we can actually know him."[36] Thus, when Van Til speaks of a "primacy of the intellect based on the creator-creature distinction," he seems to be talking nonsense. If the intellect is primary, its primacy is not "based on" anything. And if God is somehow known prior to intellectual activity, then how do we know him at all?

But here, as with "starting point," some distinctions must be made. "Intellect" or "reason" can mean various things: laws of logic, the psychological faculty by which we make judgments and draw inferences, the judgments and inferences themselves, systems of thought.[37] It is certainly true that reason as a psychological faculty is involved in any rational activity. Thus putting it tautologically emphasizes the obviousness of the point. It is the same sort of obviousness we saw earlier in the proposition that one must "start with the self." But just as "starting with the self" leaves open the question of what criterion of truth the self should acknowledge, so "starting with reason" leaves open the question of what criterion of truth human reason ought to recognize. As a psychological faculty, reason has the choice of operating according to a number of different principles: different systems of logic, different philosophical schemes, different religious commitments. Van Til, therefore, may (and does!) grant that reason is involved in all human thought and life. But for him the important question is, What criteria of truth ought our reason to acknowledge?

Our authors would answer this question by saying, first of all, that reason ought to acknowledge the law of noncontradiction. (Perhaps they even define reason in terms of the laws of logic, so that for them the "primacy of reason" means, not the primacy of a psychological faculty, but the primacy of logic; that, again, isn't clear.)

---

[35]P. 80, emphasis theirs; see pp. 72–82.

[36]P. 227.

[37]Philosophers, such as Hegel, have sometimes defined rationality in terms of their systems so that, e.g., rationality = Hegelianism.

Again, however, the main point is true in a sense. The law of noncontradiction denies that p and not-p can both be true at the same time and in the same respect. That is a Christian principle, presupposed by Scripture itself. But it is, of course, also highly abstract. Nothing more concrete can be derived from the law of noncontradiction alone. To derive concrete conclusions we need additional principles, principles which are religiously, as well as philosophically, problematic.[38] Hence the tendency for various philosophers to define rationality in terms of their particular systems. It is at this point that Van Til enters the discussion and demands that God's voice be heard in the selection of rational principles. It is at this level, with this sort of concern, that he talks about "a primacy of the intellect based on the creator-creature distinction." He refers here to a reasoning process which recognizes God's standards as supreme. Perhaps for clarity's sake he would have been wiser not to speak of the "primacy of the intellect" at all;[39] but it isn't difficult to understand what he means. Reason is always involved in the human search for knowledge; but reason must always choose its standards, and that choice is fundamentally a religious one.

Our authors reply, however, that we must, after all, "think about God before we can know him."[40] And if we are trying to think about God *before* we know him, then, obviously, at that stage of our inquiry, we cannot presuppose God. We cannot make God our supreme standard until we know that he exists. Therefore we must adopt some other standard, at least "provisionally."[41] But this analysis (1) denies the clear teaching of Romans 1 that everyone knows God already (vv 20, 21), (2) posits an exception to 1 Cor 10:31: that when you are just beginning your quest for knowledge, you do not need to think "to the glory of God"; you can justifiably think to the glory of something/someone else. Such notions fall by their own weight. They are intolerable to the Bible-believer.

Our authors, therefore, have failed to show that Van Til aban-

---

[38]Cf. V. Poythress, "A Biblical View of Mathematics," *Foundations of Christian Scholarship* (ed. G. North; Vallecito, Calif.: Ross House, 1976), 159–88; J. Frame, "Rationality and Scripture," in *Rationality in the Calvinian Tradition* (ed. H. Hart, et al.; Lanham, Md.: University Press of America, 1983), 293–317.

[39]There are several other reasons why this phrase is misleading. See my *Doctrine of the Knowledge of God,* forthcoming.

[40]P. 227.

[41]Pp. 301, 331.

dons rational argument, proofs, evidences. He does abandon neutral, or autonomous reasoning; that is all. And nothing in *Classical Apologetics* shows that he is wrong in rejecting these. For the record, let me emphasize that Van Til does *not* reject proofs, arguments, evidences; on the contrary, he endorses them in the strongest terms.[42] The Ligonier authors are quite aware of this, but they dismiss it as inconsistency or insist that Van Til's arguments aren't really arguments at all.

However, it is quite impossible to argue for Christianity, or anything else for that matter, without making a presuppositional choice. One cannot reason without criteria of truth. And criteria of truth come from a wide variety of sources, ultimately religious commitment.[43] Those criteria will either be Christian or non-Christian.[44] If they are non-Christian, they will be self-defeating and subject to divine judgment.

To say this is to say that argument for Christianity will always be in one sense circular. Arguments for Christianity must be based on Christian criteria, which in turn presuppose the truth of Christianity. You can't prove God without presupposing him. This is one of the principles of Van Til's apologetics which most irritates our authors.[45] To them, circular reasoning is a logical fallacy, pure and simple.[46] But what is the alternative? Again, the alternative seems to be that an unbeliever begins his quest, either with no criterion at all or with a "provisional" criterion of a non-Christian (or perhaps "neutral") sort; then by linear, noncircular reasoning, he learns that he must adopt the Christian criterion.[47] But, as we noted earlier, this construction violates Rom 1:18ff. and 1 Cor 10:31. According to Scripture there is

[42]See *The Defense of the Faith,* 120, 196; *An Introduction to Systematic Theology*, 102ff., 114f., 196; *A Christian Theory of Knowledge,* 292; *Common Grace and the Gospel* (Nutley, N.J.: Presbyterian and Reformed, 1969), 179ff., 190ff. See also T. Notaro, *Van Til and the Use of Evidence* (Nutley, N.J.: Presbyterian and Reformed, 1980).

[43]Again, it would have been helpful if the Ligonier authors had offered some response to the rather broad range of philosophical opinion (even outside Christianity) to this effect. *Classical Apologetics* seems to be written in a curiously pre-Kantian, pre-Kuhnian context, and thus it strains our credibility. The authors have not dealt with the most serious criticisms of their position.

[44]Listen to the law of noncontradiction!

[45]See pp. 318ff.; cf. pp. 137ff., 144ff.

[46]P. 322.

[47]P. 325.

no one in this position—no one without a knowledge of God's criteria. Those who seek to adopt non-Christian standards (and there are no "neutral" ones) are simply disobedient to the revelation they have received. If one could proceed from neutrality to truth, then noncircular argument would be possible. But of course it is not possible, because Scripture condemns autonomy.[48]

Does this circularity entail the death of all reasoning, as the Ligonier authors fear? No: (1) All reasoning, Christian, non-Christian, presuppositional, "classical," is in this sense circular. There is no alternative. This is not a challenge to the validity of reason; it is simply the way in which reason works. (2) There are distinctions to be made between "narrow circles" (e.g., "The Bible is God's Word because it says it is God's Word.") and "broad circles" (e.g., "Evidence interpreted according to Christian criteria demonstrates the divine authority of Scripture. Here it is: . . ."). Not every circular argument is equally desirable. Some circular arguments, indeed, should rightly be dismissed as fallacious. (3) Reasoning on Christian criteria is persuasive because (a) it is God's approved way to reason, (b) it leads to true conclusions, (c) and everyone, at some level, *already knows* that such reasoning leads to truth (Romans 1, again).

2. The Noetic Effects of Sin

Why is it necessary to presuppose God, according to Van Til? The Ligonier authors have a theory about that. They attribute to Van Til the notion that "the fundamental fallacy of the traditional approach is in not recognizing that without knowing everything one cannot know anything."[49] (Without the double negatives: what they are saying is that for Van Til we cannot know anything unless we know everything.) This point comes up elsewhere in the book,[50] and the authors think it is important enough to embellish poetically: ". . . one cannot know the flower in the crannied wall unless he knows the world and all."[51] On this account, Van Til would be teaching that we

---

[48]Again, even many non-Christian authors (see earlier note) concede this sort of point about circularity. It simply is not responsible, in the present intellectual context, to dismiss all circularity as a mere logical fallacy.

[49]P. 186.

[50]Pp. 306, 313.

[51]P. 186.

need to presuppose God in order to have, somehow, that omniscient perspective on reality. However, they never give any references in Van Til's writings to show that he believes any such thing; and of course they cannot, for this is not his position. Van Til does sometimes argue, in terms reminiscent of idealism, that true human knowledge presupposes the existence of a comprehensive system of knowledge; but unlike the idealist, Van Til finds this comprehensive system in the God of Scripture. He explicitly denies the similar-sounding proposition that *we human beings* must have comprehensive knowledge in order to know anything:

> One of the points about which there has been much confusion when we speak of the objectivity of human knowledge is whether human knowledge of the world must be comprehensive in order to be true. . . . But we believe that just for the reason that we cannot hope to obtain comprehensive knowledge of God we cannot hope to obtain comprehensive knowledge of anything in the world.[52]

Van Til, in fact, explicitly denies the principle that we must know everything in order to know anything. He attributes this principle to "the non-Christian methodology in general, and that of modern phenomenalism in particular."[53]

On the contrary: to Van Til, our need to presuppose God has nothing to do with such idealist epistemological speculations. Rather, we presuppose God because in the nature of the case that is the right way to reason, and because, therefore, we are obligated to reason that way. The necessity is an *ethical* necessity.

Which brings us to the question of the noetic effects of sin. At this point, I find a surprising amount of agreement between the Ligonier authors and Van Til. "The pagan's problem," they say, "is not that he does not know that God is, but that he does not like the God who is."[54] The nature psalms and Romans 1 tell us that God is clearly revealed in the world, and all human beings know God through this revela-

---

[52]Van Til, *The Defense of the Faith* (1955 edition), 60.

[53]Ibid., 136 (1963 ed., p. 119). In the immediate context he discusses idealist epistemology, from which this notion comes.

[54]P. 39.

tion.[55] Thus the unbeliever is without excuse. This "natural theology," they argue, is mediated through the creation.[56] (I agree that this is the teaching of Romans 1, but I would add that this fact does not preclude other forms of revelation in addition to the mediate form described in Romans 1.) Why, then, do people need complex arguments in order to believe? The answer is that they repress the truth revealed in creation.[57] They are not morons, but foolish.[58] Their problem is not intellectual weakness, but moral refusal to accept what is clearly revealed. Or, to put it more precisely, they do have intellectual problems, but "the intellectual problem is produced by the moral problem, not the moral problem by an intellectual one."[59] They know God, but they do not know him savingly. Honestly, in all of this (and in their summary[60]) I have not found anything that I or Van Til would disagree with! The Ligonier men seem to think that Van Til holds a very different position—that he thinks sin destroyed the unbeliever's reasoning power,[61] but as usual they fail to document adequately their interpretation and they ignore statements in Van Til to the contrary.

I will surprise them even more by saying that I agree, in general, with their account of the testimony of the Holy Spirit.[62] The utterly fideistic view which they attribute to me[63] is their own creation, made up out of thin air. They present no documentation of it from my writings. Apparently they believe that my other positions necessitate such a view. I find that hard to believe! They say that for me "the internal testimony of the Holy Spirit must be utterly apart from and prior to speculative knowledge and evidence of the inspiration of the word."[64] Nonsense. I quite agree with them that the Spirit witnesses

---

[55]When our authors say that for presuppositionalists God "reveals Himself exclusively in Holy Scripture" (p. 287) (presumably in contrast with natural revelation), they are evidently getting carried away with themselves. Van Til's belief in natural revelation needs no documentation.

[56]Pp. 43ff.

[57]P. 47.

[58]P. 52.

[59]Ibid.

[60]P. 62.

[61]Pp. 241ff., esp. p. 245.

[62]Pp. 137ff., p. 162ff. See my article, "The Spirit and the Scriptures," forthcoming in *Scripture and Truth II* (ed. D. Carson and J. Woodbridge; Grand Rapids: Zondervan, 1986).

[63]Pp. 299ff.

[64]P. 299.

to the Word through witnessing to evidences (along with other ways, to be sure). As for the Spirit being "prior to speculative knowledge," I think I have expounded sufficiently the ambiguities of "priority" language in theology. In any case, I grant what I think they want me to, that people sometimes reach true conclusions about God without the witness of the Spirit.

Van Til's writings do pose some difficulty here. He does clearly recognize that unbelievers know the truth (Rom 1:21) and that they sometimes reach true conclusions "in spite of themselves," i.e. in spite of their unbelieving presuppositions. However, there are points at which he seems to say that unbelief always leads to intellectual error and that no propositional truth is possible apart from the Spirit's witness. His representations, I think, are not fully consistent. What is more, he has admitted some difficulty in this area.[65] The problems stem from Van Til's realization that even though unbelievers do know the truth, their rebellion often infests their intellectual activity. Much pagan philosophy can be explained precisely as attempts to evade the truth of God's revelation. Therefore, it is not sufficient to say (as the Ligonier writers seem to *want* to say; but see below) that the unbeliever's problems are moral rather than intellectual. Morality influences intellectual judgments.[66] At times, indeed, the authors of our volume recognize this fact: they write, "The intellectual problem is caused by the moral problem, not the moral problem by the intellectual one."[67] I agree, and I note that here they at least recognize that there *is* an intellectual problem as well as a moral one, though they don't stress that fact very much in their discussion.

The interesting net result is that *on paper* there is very little difference between the Ligonier group and Van Til on the noetic effects of sin and the testimony of the Spirit. Both maintain that depravity is total, that it causes repression of the truth, that the unbeliever has intellectual difficulties because of his moral rebellion, that he has knowledge of God but not saving knowledge. To both, the testimony of the Spirit works with and through our apologetic arguments to break down that rebellion and lead the unbeliever to acknowledge the truth which he already knows. Part of the reason for this agreement is that

[65]*An Introduction to Systematic Theology,* 26f.

[66]More than that, all intellectual judgments are morally determined. A right judgment is a judgment which we *ought* to make (the ought being a moral ought).

[67]P. 52.

the Ligonier form of the traditional apologetic (as opposed, e.g., to that of Clark Pinnock) is self-consciously Calvinistic.

But the Ligonier authors are not very consistent in their confession of total depravity. Note here what they say about people who are not yet Christians, but seeking the truth:

> [Van Til] always assumes that the person who begins to examine the universe without presupposing the existence of the divine Lawgiver necessarily presupposes his own status as a lawgiver. That is by no means a necessary assumption of the person who begins by examining the data which he has at hand. . . . They do not necessarily deny the divine being as Van Til insists that they do. People do not assert their autonomy against an initially known God as Van Til insists that they do. They simply operate according to human nature.[68]

Here, note that they deny what they earlier affirmed on the basis of Romans 1, that the unbeliever knows God. Further, they deny that all unbelievers are hostile to God, repressers of the truth. At least some unbelievers, in their opinion, are sincere seekers after truth, operating merely according to the necessities of created human nature. Seriously, now: is this a doctrine of depravity worthy of Calvinists?

So, though on paper the differences in this area are not great, there is in the Ligonier authors a lack of seriousness in the application of the doctrine of depravity to apologetics. Similarly, on the question of "common ground," our authors state a position which is precisely identical with Van Til's:

> If we consider common ground to mean a common perception and perspective of reality, then obviously no such common ground for discussion exists between believer and unbeliever. From the believer's vantage point every aspect of life, every bit of experience, every dimension of reality, is understood and interpreted from a theological perspective. . . . It would appear that both [believer and unbeliever] enjoy a

[68]Pp. 232f.

> univocal understanding of the daffodil. . . . [But] [t]he believer acknowledges the *significance* of that daffodil, not as a cosmic accident, but as something that in itself bears witness to the majesty and beauty of the Creator God. This the unbeliever does not acknowledge, positing, instead, a completely opposite and antithetical understanding of the daffodil's significance.
>
> From a different perspective, however, there is common ground, namely the whole of creation. Believer and unbeliever live in the same universe. Each sees the same phenomena. The unbeliever and the believer can agree that two and two are four, and that certain principles of deduction are valid while others are invalid. Thus a kind of common ground is established.[69]

In my opinion, Van Til himself could have written this formulation, except for the bit about a "univocal" understanding which raises a few (in my view minor) problems.[70] In fact, paragraphs nearly identical to these might be pasted together from Van Til's writings. But both Van Til and the Ligonier authors have had trouble maintaining consistency here, Van Til tending to forget the areas of agreement between believer and unbeliever ("in spite of themselves"), and the Ligoniers tending (as we have seen) to compromise their concept of "a completely opposite and antithetical understanding" between believer and unbeliever.[71]

One last comment in this area: It is unfortunate that a demonstrable misreading of Van Til at one point leads the authors to a serious misrepresentation of Van Til's position. On p. 214 they quote Van Til as saying that the Christian "has no *point of contact* with the non-Christian."[72] They take this as a statement of Van Til's own view, but in context it is actually a paraphrase of Stuart Hackett's critique of Calvinism. I could write this off as a minor mistake,

---

[69]Pp. 70f.

[70]Van Til seems to resist any positive use of the term "univocal" in regard to our knowledge of God. But if as in this context it simply means "literal," I know of no principle in Van Til's thought that would be violated by such a "univocal" knowledge of God. See my "The Problem of Theological Paradox," in *Foundations of Christian Scholarship,* 310f.

[71]Is some of this inconsistency related to the book's triple authorship?

[72]P. 214, quoting Van Til in *Jerusalem and Athens,* 16.

except that it shows, in its way, an extraordinary ignorance of Van Til's position. Van Til would *never* say that the Christian has no point of contact with the non-Christian; in fact he has said the opposite innumerable times. Mistakes like this make one wonder how seriously these authors have tried to understand Van Til. Could they have simply dismissed as inconsistencies the countless positive references in Van Til to "point of contact," focussing upon this one reference as his definitive formulation without even trying to explain the others? Or did the author of this section have such a poor knowledge of Van Til that he actually thought this was a representative formulation? It is hard to account for this sort of blunder except as a serious lapse of scholarship stemming from ignorance and intense prejudice, a desire to make Van Til say something he does not actually say, in order to make him more vulnerable to criticism.

II. The Ligonier Apologetic

I must needs be briefer in dealing with the book's positive argument for Christianity, because of the demands of time and space, and because the argument itself is not as novel or interesting (to me!) as the critique of Van Til. Still, there are a few new wrinkles.

The Ligonier authors believe, as we have seen, that traditionalist apologetics is sick and ailing, though not dead. One of the reasons for the malaise, in their view, is that other modern classicists have abandoned the traditional claim that the truth of Christianity can be demonstrated, settling for arguments which merely claim probability.[73] Here, interestingly, is another point of agreement between the Ligonier group and Van Til. Our authors here frequently sound Van Tillian notes: that if Christianity is not *certainly* true, then we have, to some extent, an excuse for unbelief.

But how can we reach the level of demonstrative certainty? On the Ligonier view, decisive appeal to special revelation is excluded; that would be "presuppositionalism." But that means the argument must be wholly based on human sensation and reason, unaided by special revelation. Everyone agrees that human reason and sensation are fallible. So whence the desired certainty? The Ligonier authors

[73]Pp. 100f., 125, 148, 276.

believe such certainty can be attained by appeal to certain "universal and necessary assumptions." These are assumptions which, though sometimes challenged, cannot be regularly and consistently denied. As such, they are prerequisites of science and, indeed, of all human life.[74] These are, the law of noncontradiction, the "law of causality," and "the basic reliability of sense perception." Since these principles cannot be regularly and consistently denied, the book argues, they must be regarded as certain, along with any of their implications. Thus the authors try to show that Christianity is one of those implications: to deny Christianity is to deny one or more of those "universal and necessary assumptions." Since we cannot deny those, Christianity also must be regarded as certain.

The argument is "transcendental,"[75] even presuppositional in a sense. The authors are asking "What are the assumptions necessary for life and knowledge to be possible?"[76] Van Til asks the same question and concludes that the whole content of God's revelation is such a necessary assumption! In one sense, the Ligonier authors are saying the same thing, but less directly. To deny Christianity, they say, is indeed to deny truths which we cannot consistently and regularly deny. Van Til, similarly, says that unbelievers cannot consistently and regularly deny Christianity, that they can exist only on "borrowed capital," inconsistently making use of Christian ideas which they wish to reject. I am tempted, therefore, to read the Ligonier argument as a kind of "indirect presuppositionalism," an attempt to show (more concretely than Van Til) the *ways* in which Christian assumptions are unavoidable. On such an approach, the authors would be asking the non-Christian to presuppose Christian concepts (concepts compatible with Scripture) of logic, cause, sense-experience, since denying these concepts leads to chaos. Van Til and the Ligonier group, on that interpretation, would again be very close. In my view, the cogency of the Ligonier argument arises from the fact that something like this is going on. But, on the other hand, we have to remember all the talk in this book about autonomy, the inconsistencies on depravity, and so on. Whatever may actually be the case, these authors at least *think* that they are reasoning on a neutral basis, with concepts of cause, etc., which are not

[74]Pp. 71f.
[75]P. 71.
[76]Ibid.

distinctively Christian, even though they imply a distinctively Christian worldview.[77]

A brief look now at the authors' theistic proofs. Their ontological argument, following Jonathan Edwards, is virtually Parmenidean: We have an idea of being; in fact, we can think of nothing else than being. Nonbeing is unthinkable. Thus being must be eternal, omnipresent, limitless in all perfections—in other words, God. There is an obvious objection to this, however, which the book doesn't even mention. However infinite being may be, our idea of being extends to finite being as well. Therefore, if "being" is divine, then finite beings are part of that divine being. In other words, without some modifications, the argument proves pantheism. And the argument fails to draw any distinction between the kind of "infinity," "eternity," "omnipresence," etc. attributable to a pantheistic god, and the very different (but similar-sounding) attributes revealed concerning the God of Scripture.[78]

The cosmological argument: Our authors state the "law of causality" first in what they admit to be tautological fashion: "Every effect has a cause."[79] Since the world is contingent, they argue, it must be an effect. What, then, is its cause? The world is not a mere illusion (nonbeing—see above), nor is it self-created, which is nonsense. If it is self-existent, then it is in effect transcendent and divine, so God's existence is proved. If it is created by a self-existent being, then again, God is proved. An infinite number of contingent beings cannot be the world-cause: if no one of them is sufficient to cause the world, then the whole series will not be sufficient either. Much could be said (and has been said) about this sort of argument. What is most notable to me is that, as in the Ligonier version of the ontological argument, the authors fail clearly to rule out the pantheistic alternative, namely that the universe is its own god. About all I can find in the book responding to this objection is one sentence: "(God) is personal because He is the pervasive cause of all things including the purpose and the personal."[80] But it is by no means obvious that a being must itself be personal in order to be the cause of personality.

---

[77]How is it possible for a concept logically to imply a Christian worldview if that concept is not itself in an important sense distinctively Christian?

[78]Pp. 93ff.

[79]Pp. 82f., 111.

[80]P. 123.

The ontological and cosmological arguments together suggest that on the Ligonier view, being is unlimited and therefore possesses all excellencies in infinite degree.[81] These excellencies include all the traditional attributes of the Christian God including personality. Therefore God exists. However, the concept of an "excellency," a perfection, is religiously problematic. What is excellent to one person is a defect in the eyes of another. Personality is a perfection to a Westerner imbued with Christian teaching. To a Buddhist, that would not necessarily be the case. Therefore, the sort of proof offered in our book presupposes a particular set of values, or else it is simply invalid. It is, in other words, either a presuppositional argument or else it is a failure.

I shall pass over the teleological argument to look at the authors' presentation of Christian evidences. Here the authors follow the pattern of other books of this kind. They begin with the premise that the Gospels are "reliable historical sources."[82] (It would not do, of course, to presuppose more than this, that these books are the Word of God. That would be circular and presuppositional.) In these reliable historical sources, we learn about Jesus: that he worked miracles and that he claimed to be God.[83] Jesus' miracles prove divine attestation of his claim; therefore he is God, and his testimony that Scripture is God's Word is to be believed. At that point, we conclude that Scripture is our ultimate standard. Thenceforth, we argue on the basis of biblical authority—i.e., like presuppositionalists![84]

A few comments on this argument: (1) The authors overestimate, I think, the current scholarly consensus on the reliability of the Gospels. They assume that almost every New Testament scholar will concede that the Gospels are "generally reliable." I doubt it. (2) Even if we grant that some very unusual events took place in the ministry

---

[81]P. 123.

[82]P. 141.

[83]Interestingly, at this point, our authors sound another Van Tillian note: miracles are of no evidential value without a theistic presupposition (pp. 146ff.). They believe that they have established the existence of God by means of theistic proof, and therefore have refuted decisively any notion that miracles are impossible. Of course, Van Til would go beyond this and say that the cogency of miracle requires, not a barely theistic, but a full-blown Christian worldview.

[84]Except, presumably, when we are doing apologetics. But why should that be an exception?

of Jesus,[85] how can we be sure that these can be explained *only* as a divine attestation to Jesus' authority? It is extremely difficult to prove (apart from Christian presuppositions) the negative proposition that no other cause could have produced these events. The authors need to prove this proposition in order to make their case, but nothing in the book amounts to such a proof. (3) Recall that these authors boasted earlier that they were offering, not just a probable argument, but a demonstration, warranting certainty. Now I can understand how they can make this claim for the earlier part of their argument: the "universal and necessary assumptions," the theistic proofs. (I do not think they succeed in making good this claim, but I can understand why they *think* they have made it good.) But when they get to the historical evidences, I do not find even the slightest plausibility in their claim to demonstration. The assumption of the Gospels' reliability is highly debatable; the argument that miracles always testify to a divinely appointed messenger is also weak. And some have questioned whether Jesus did warrant belief in the Scriptures. Of course, on these matters I think the Ligonier authors are right and the liberal critics wrong. But if they look at these questions without the full range of Christian presuppositions, I don't see how they can responsibly claim anything more for their argument than a high degree of probability.

Some Formal Matters

At the risk of losing the reader's attention, I think I should point out some editorial problems in the book which ought to be corrected in future editions. There are a great many of these, possibly in part because of the triple authorship. (1) I do not understand the need, in context, for three pages dealing with theological creativity (pp. 64ff.). (2) The excursus on probabilism in theology (pp. 125ff.) seems also to belong somewhere else. It breaks up the discussion of dysteleology. (3) On p. 185, the third point does not make much sense to me; at least it does not seem clearly distinguishable from the second point. (4) Note the typographical error on p. 187—the "poetic influence of sin" (!). (5) On p. 220, the authors give the impression that Van Til's *Survey of Christian Epistemology* is a different book from his *Metaphysics*

[85]And of course the question must be raised as to *how* unusual an event must be before we call it a miracle.

of Apologetics. Actually, the two books are one and the same, the former being a more recent printing of the latter.[86] (6) Recall our earlier point about the misreading of the Van Til reference on p. 214. (7) I agree with the authors' assessment of Runner's concept of "republication" (pp. 251f.), but it fits rather awkwardly into the context. (8) On p. 254, second paragraph, who is speaking? Van Til, Sullivan, or the Ligoniers? (9) The material on Duns Scotus (p. 260) also seems out of place.

CONCLUSIONS

There is much here to make us think. I was surprised at how close these authors were to Van Til at various places. There are, I think, some areas here for further dialogue between Van Tillian and Ligonier apologists. There is much similarity in regard to general revelation and the noetic effects of sin. There is recognition of the need for more than mere probability in grounding our faith. The authors also recognize that evidential arguments presuppose some elements of a Christian worldview. The chief difference is in the evaluation of autonomy. There is also room for further debates as to who is the most consistent with the shared Calvinistic premises.

Surely, there is plenty of room for mutual support and encouragement in the Lord. Speaking personally, I owe a great deal to John Gerstner, who for several decades was the most cogent and tireless defender of the Reformed faith in western Pennsylvania. Sproul and Lindsley, through the Ligonier Valley Study Center, continue Gerstner's ministry, sending this Reformed message all over the world by lectures and tapes: excellent communications, on the whole, of the gospel of Christ. We Van Tillians have much to learn from these valiant men; and I dare say they have much to learn from us as well.

[86] I must say that I am also somewhat disturbed by the large number of references to this title and the relatively small number of references to Van Til's more recent writings. It hardly seems fair to judge him to such a large extent on the basis of his first, relatively unnuanced, class syllabus, dating back to 1929.

APPENDIX B

Preaching the Word of the Lord: Cornelius Van Til, V.D.M., by Edmund P. Clowney

(Note: I have always thought that a comprehensive study of Van Til should include something on his preaching. That preaching was quite powerful in itself, and it was related in important ways to his apologetics. Nevertheless, I doubt if I could write a chapter on this subject that would improve on Edmund Clowney's treatment in the following article. Clowney was professor of practical theology and president of Westminster Theological Seminary for a number of years; he knew Van Til well as his student and later as his colleague. I am thankful to Dr. Clowney for giving me permission to include this study in the present volume.

This address was given as the Van Til Lecture for 1983–84 at Westminster Theological Seminary in Philadelphia on October 26, 1983. It was published in the *Westminster Theological Journal* 46 [Fall 1984]: 233–53.)

The portrait of Dr. Cornelius Van Til that hangs in Machen Hall differs from the paintings of his colleagues of Westminster's distinguished original faculty. It is the work of the same artist, DeWitt Whistler Jayne, but the pose is unique. Indeed, it is not a pose at all.

The others are painted seated, gowned in academic regalia. But Dr. Van Til is not only standing, he is teaching. I well remember when the artist made the photographs and studies from which the portrait was painted. The room in Machen Hall that is now the president's office was then a classroom. Dr. Van Til stood in front of the blackboard at the battered lectern which served him as a stage prop. In that familiar setting he did not pose; he lectured. DeWitt Jayne and I were the whole class on that occasion, but Dr. Van Til had lectured to smaller classes, and he has never despaired of advancing my education! He reviewed the history of modern philosophy, tracing the consequences of its departure from the authority of the Word of God. In his usual style he spattered the blackboard with half-written words, mostly in German: *Geist, Lebensphil, Existenzphil.* I am grateful that the artist, who was delighted with both the lecture and the lecturer's animation, also faithfully captured the blackboard graffiti. That painting well portrays the teacher to whom this lecture series is dedicated.

I am honored to be invited to lecture in this series; I welcome the opportunity to express a little of the immense personal debt that I owe to Dr. Van Til and his teaching. In particular, I am glad to attempt an important task: to show the close relation between Dr. Van Til's biblical apologetics and preaching.

One major undertaking of Dr. Van Til's scholarly work has been his analysis of the writings of Karl Barth. Barth's theology is usually characterized as kerygmatic, a theology of the Word, and particularly of the Word in preaching. Barth criticized the old liberalism for destroying the foundations of preaching. He found that as a pastor he could not preach in the mold provided by Schleiermacher. Barth's call for a return to the preaching of the Word was expressed in his commentary on Paul's Epistle to the Romans. That commentary was described as a bombshell exploding in the playground of the theologians.

Everywhere advocates of preaching rejoiced. A trumpet had sounded, calling for a return to the proclamation of the Word of God. But Cornelius Van Til did not join in the celebration. Rather he strongly criticized Barth. Van Til found in the commentary on Romans and in Barth's massive *Kirchliche Dogmatik* not a new foundation for preaching, but an undermining of the Word of God and preaching alike.

Van Til, of course, was ridiculed by some and reproved by others. His position was regarded as extreme; Barth himself may have had Van Til in mind when he described some of his critics as

Menschenfressers—cannibals! But Van Til has had significant influence on Reformed and evangelical estimates of Barthianism.

How does Van Til fare in comparison to Barth in presenting a theology of the preached Word? Has Van Til in opposing Barth overreacted? Has he measured Barth by the standards of an Old Princeton orthodoxy, standards that owe more to Scottish common-sense philosophy than to biblical kerygma? In contrast to the Barthian call for prophetic preaching, for the kind of proclamation that can confront Hitler's *Volkskirche,* does Van Til offer a retreat to a scholastic conception of Scripture, and to didactic preaching that is rabbinical rather than apostolic?

An immediate answer to such charges is that they could not be made by people who had heard Cornelius Van Til preach.[1] A *Menschenfresser* he might be to those who disagree with him, but an arid scholastic he is not. His preaching has always been proclamation; Westminster Seminary was founded in a great struggle for the defense of the gospel against the attacks of modernistic unbelief. Van Til stood with J. Gresham Machen in that struggle, and through his long career he has never ceased to contrast Christianity with liberalism. Perhaps it may be said of Van Til that he has not always given the devil his due, but at least he has recognized the voice of the Enemy when the tongue of the serpent asks, "Hath God said?"

Van Til the preacher blows the bugle reveille to awaken the people of God to stand for the truth. He is also a trumpeter of a more harmonious melody. His preaching hymns the praises of the Lord. This will be no surprise, I judge, to those who are familiar with Van Til's thought. Yet his longer writings do not convey the man's devotion in the way that his sermons did over the years. I think especially of his chapel messages at Westminster Seminary. Van Til was much influenced by Geerhardus Vos; he spoke often of days on the Princeton campus when Vos would share with him poetry that he had written in Dutch. The poetic and devotional depth of the sermons of Vos stands in a long tradition of Reformed piety in the Netherlands. Cornelius Van Til is an heir of that same tradition. Again and again in his chapel talks he would return to passages from Revelation, to Isaiah's vision of the Lord in the temple, to psalms that extolled the glory of the living God.

---

[1]See the sermons reprinted in *The God of Hope* (Phillipsburg, N.J.: Presbyterian and Reformed, 1978) 3-157.

But was Van Til's preaching more reflective of the Dutch sermons he had heard in his youth than of the apologetic system that has made his name a household word—at least in Reformed households? It is my conviction that the reverse is true. Not only is Van Til's apologetics consistent with his preaching; it is preaching that has shaped his apologetics: preaching, not the philosophy of personalistic idealism that he studied at Princeton University; preaching, not the "common sense" philosophy of James McCosh that influenced Old Princeton; preaching, not even the Calvinistic philosophy of Herman Dooyeweerd. It would be foolish to maintain that none of these philosophies influenced Van Til's thought and teaching. Of course they did, some more by the reaction they triggered than by any positive influence. But none of these, nor all of them together, provide the ground of Van Til's apologetic. The Reformed view of preaching does that.

We see the root of Van Til's approach in his rejection of Barthian theology. Van Til does not criticize Barth in the manner of an academic quibbling over footnotes, nor even of a scholastic scoring debating points. He preaches against Barth. His annotations scrawled in the margins of what may be the most worn set of the *Kirchliche Dogmatik* in the Western hemisphere are challenges, exclamations, penetrating paraphrases. Van Til is deeply disturbed by Barth's position because it strikes at the heart of his own faith. Van Til, too, would begin with the Word of God. Van Til, too, demands not only a theology that can be preached but a kerygmatic theology. His dismay is all the greater, then, when he finds Barth's view of both the Word of God and preaching to contradict the theology of Scripture itself.

The thrust of Van Til's analysis of Barth's theology of the Word is that Barth does not really begin with the speaking of the Lord but with the framework of modern post-Kantian philosophy into which any account of God's speaking must be fitted. That philosophical framework was expressed in Kant's distinction between the noumenal and the phenomenal and in the dialectic of the infinite/finite that Kierkegaard carried over from Hegel (even though S.K. sought to use it against the master of German idealism).

That dualism was Kant's strategy for defending the science of Isaac Newton from the skepticism of David Hume. In his analysis of theoretical thought, Kant argued that while we cannot know things in themselves, we can know the structures of our own thought. The structures of theoretical thought provide the ground rules for the scientific investigation of phenomena. If we are to speak of ultimate reality, of God, freedom, and immortality, we are no longer speaking in theoretical categories. Such matters are the concern of practical reason and practical reason has its own critique, its own mode of operation. To apply theoretical categories like causality to prove the existence of God, said Kant, was to confuse the forms of reason and to introduce hopeless contradiction (the "antinomies").

Karl Barth did not challenge Kant's critical philosophy. He drew from Kierkegaard the dialectical opposition of the infinite and the finite. For Barth God's revelation was on the side of the transcendent, the infinite. That meant that revelation could enter the finite only in a moment of paradox. Revelation could not become historical, it could not be identified with finite words. The Bible is not revelation, therefore, but the response in history to revelation. The Bible is not the Word of God, but the words of men responding to the ineffable Word of God. Scripture may become the Word of God only in the moment, the paradoxical moment in which God chooses to speak through it in preaching.

What is true of the Bible is also true of Christ. Barth distinguishes between the Jesus of history and the Christ event. The man Jesus is fully human and fallible just as the text of the Bible is. But the Christ of faith is the point at which the infinite becomes finite in the paradox of the God-man.

Barth therefore presents three forms of the Word: the Word Incarnate, the Word in Scripture, the Word in preaching. But the controlling rationale is the same. The infinite becomes the finite only in the moment, the event, whether the Christ-event, the event in which the Bible becomes the Word of God, or the event of preaching. This appears to exalt preaching, to lift preaching to the level of Scripture and the Incarnation. Preaching becomes the point where revelation breaks into history and creates the church again in the moment of faith.

Yet as Van Til has warned, this construction does not really exalt preaching. Rather, it reduces Christ, the Bible, and preaching to an abstraction, to a dimensionless point to be grasped by faith, a point that can be related to other such points only in a "salvation-history" that hovers above the kind of history that can be recounted by historians.

Van Til has shown the far-reaching consequences of Barth's

scheme. It has been welcomed by those who react against the liberal subjection of Christ to culture but who also want to keep faith and science distinct so that they can avoid the conflict between biblical teaching and some of the assumptions and theories of modern science. Barth's division frees them to accept, as he did, higher critical theories about the Bible, this fully human and, in their view, erroneous document. It also frees them to deny the sinlessness of Jesus, to discount the miracles and even to make the resurrection an event in "salvation-history" rather than in calendar time.

Further, it opens the way for a universalism of salvation. Barth struggles with the problem of Judas, arguing that as an elect reprobate, Judas is, like a "wooden iron," a contradiction in terms. But Judas along with all men must be at last not only reprobate in Christ's rejection but also elect in Christ's election. God's mercy must triumph over wrath even in the case of Judas.

Van Til shows that Barth's universalism is a consistent manifestation of Barth's dialectic, a fundamental approach that is grounded in modern philosophy, not in the Scriptures. Van Til takes issue with Barth because of his own commitment to the authority of the Word of God written. But Van Til never isolates the Scriptures from Christ, for the Scriptures are the Word of the Lord.

Barthian theologians accuse orthodoxy of substituting a dead book for a living Lord, of constantly speaking about the written Word and ignoring the Incarnate Word.[2] That charge certainly cannot be made against Van Til. Hear him in a sermon on Christ and Scripture: "To believe in the Scriptures as the very Word of God is dead orthodoxy unless it is that they mediate to us belief in Jesus as the Christ."[3] The whole point of the sermon is to show that the scribes and Pharisees, the opponents of Jesus, did not really hold to the authority of Scripture since they presumed to use the Scripture to con-

[2]Edward A. Dowey, Jr., an author of the "Confession of 1967" of the United Presbyterian Church, notes that "unhappily, the Westminster Confession called the Bible the Word of God about thirty times but did not use the expression even once for Christ." Dowey feels this has been set right in the Confession of 1967 since "The Confession carefully avoids saying either that Scripture 'is' God's word or that Scripture 'is' unique and authoritative as such in its own right" (*A Commentary on the Confession of 1967 and an Introduction to the Book of Confessions* [Philadelphia: Westminster Press, 1968], 100).

[3]"Christ and Scripture," in *The God of Hope* (Phillipsburg, N.J.: Presbyterian and Reformed, 1978), 11.

demn Jesus. In so doing they defined the authority of Scripture by their own tradition rather than receiving the Scripture as Christ's witness to himself. Their rejection of Jesus showed that they did not understand the *testimony* of Scripture, since Scripture bears witness to him. But more than that: their rejection of Jesus showed that they did not submit themselves to the *authority* of Scripture, for "the Scriptures are Christ's witness to himself."[4] The Bible is more than man's testimony to Christ. It is Christ's testimony to himself.

Van Til urges, "There is no appeal beyond Jesus' testimony to himself. How could there be? He is the Word that was in the beginning with God. He is the Word that was God. Before Abraham was I am: 'All things were made by him; and without him was not anything made that was made. In him was life; and the life was the light of men' (John 1:3–4)."[5] Van Til summarizes, "Thus did Jesus maintain the necessity, the authority, and the clarity of Scripture all at once by placing himself before the Jews as the one through whom their Scriptures alone received their meaning."[6]

At the heart of Van Til's apologetic is the conviction that the Christian cannot begin with an abstract framework of philosophy or logic assumed or established apart from the presence of the living God. It would be the height of folly to attempt this with, of all books, the Bible. We cannot first establish the authority of the Bible by a philosophical or theological propaedeutic that is impersonally theoretical, and then be introduced by that propaedeutic to the God of whom the Bible speaks. To the contrary, the living God made us, gave us life, and formed us in his image. We cannot think anymore than breathe apart from his provision. The Bible is the Word of God written, the inspired record of God's speaking to men and women in their sin and need. When God speaks, his creatures cannot evaluate his Word by criteria apart from God; they cannot erect or discern criteria to which he must measure up. If they attempt to do so, they actually bring God before the bar of their own reason, their own traditions, their own pride. When God speaks, it is the voice of Satan that asks, "Hath God said?" The voice of man made in God's image must be, "Speak, Lord, for thy servant heareth!"

In the lead article of *Jerusalem and Athens,* a book prepared to

[4]Ibid., 8.
[5]Ibid.
[6]Ibid., 15.

celebrate his seventy-fifth birthday, Van Til presents his "Credo."[7] He says that he writes for his friends and Christian critics so that "we may be of help to one another as together we present the name of Jesus as the only name given under heaven by which men must be saved."[8]

That purpose controls his life, his teaching, and his development of apologetics. Referring to his childhood in the Netherlands, he says, "Every minister in those days had a V.D.M. degree: *Verbum Dei Minister*. When, therefore, I became a teacher of apologetics it was natural for me to think, not only of my Th.M. and my Ph.D., but above all of my V.D.M. The former degrees were but means whereby I might be true to the latter degree."[9] To consider Van Til the apologist in relation to preaching is merely to reflect on the Van Til of the "Credo." Looking back on forty years of teaching, he would be known as Cornelius Van Til, V.D.M. He tells us this precisely so that we may understand what he has been driven to do in his apologetic labors. He begins the "Credo" with the statement, "The self-attesting Christ of Scripture has always been my starting-point for everything I have said."[10]

To show us how this is the case, Van Til describes apostolic preaching. In his address on the Areopagus Paul proclaims Christ to Gentile covenant-breakers.

> Paul does not place himself on their level in order with them to investigate the nature of being and knowledge in general, to discover *whether* the God of Abraham, Isaac, and Jacob might possibly exist. He tells them straight out that what they claim not to know, he knows. He tells them that their so-called ignorance is culpable, for God is as near to them as their own selves. He tells them, therefore, to repent of their worship of idols, to turn to the living God, lest they stand without the robes of righteousness before the resurrected Lord Christ on the day of judgment.[11]

---

[7]C. Van Til, "Credo," in *Jerusalem and Athens: Critical Discussions on the Theology and Apologetics of Cornelius Van Til* (ed. E. R. Geehan; Phillipsburg, N.J.: Presbyterian and Reformed, 1971).

[8]Ibid., 3.

[9]Ibid., 8.

[10]Ibid., 3.

[11]Ibid., 7.

In the "Credo" Van Til describes his own development in clear terms. Beginning as he did with the self-attesting Christ of Scripture, he was also Reformed in theology, for Reformed theology focuses on the Christ of Scripture; it confesses his Lordship in salvation and in revelation. Abraham Kuyper and Herman Bavinck taught him that the *idea* of Scripture must never be separated from its *message*. An inadequate view of God's sovereign grace leads to an inadequate view of God's sovereign Word. Then, "the Holy Spirit and the Word of God do not change men, men must first *agree* to be changed."[12] Reformed theology denies all autonomy of man in relation to God or the Word of God. It begins in subjection to the authority of the Word of God; God speaks in Christ and we must hear.

As John Frame has pointed out, Van Til always begins with theology; he is first of all a theologian.[13] In the "Credo" Van Til marks out a simple but critical step. If Reformed theology begins with the self-attesting Christ of Scripture, Reformed apologetics should do the same thing. His critique of the traditional apologetic, even among Reformed apologists, is that it has failed to do so. Instead, it has admitted the very view of human autonomy that is rejected in the theology it seeks to defend.

This has happened, as Van Til points out, even with the apologists of the early church. They failed to follow Paul's apologetic of proclamation. Instead they sought common ground with Greek philosophy and even reduced Christ to an emanation of the kind that Greek speculation devised.

Christian apologetics was therefore compromised from the postapostolic age on. Yet Van Til does not see a completely dark picture. If a wrong apologetic led to betraying orthodox Christology, the opposite was also true. A biblical Christology made for a biblical apologetic. Significantly, Van Til again stresses his cardinal starting point: "Since I conceived of Christian apologetics as focusing on the self-attesting Christ of Scripture, it was natural that I should learn most of [from] the development and defense of the doctrine of the person of Christ in the historical, theological development of the church."[14]

Van Til finds instruction for apologetics in the ecumenical creeds

---

[12]Ibid., 9.

[13]John Frame, *Van Til: The Theologian* (Chattanooga, Tenn.: Pilgrim Publishing, 1976).

[14]"Credo," 11.

of Nicea and Chalcedon as well as in the later Reformed confessions. In these creeds the distinction between the Creator and the creature is maintained while the Incarnation is fully acknowledged. The mysteries of God's triune deity and of Christ's divine and human "natures" are stated in ways that honor the sovereignty of God and the full deity of Jesus Christ. Van Til sees Calvin's theology as setting a capstone on Christological orthodoxy by proclaiming Christ as *autotheos*.[15] What is the significance for apologetics of Christ's sovereign and self-attesting authority? Calvin's own way of doing theology shows us. His method is exegetical rather than speculative. "Who Christ is depends on Christ's self-identification. If Christ is who he says he is, then all speculation is excluded, for God can swear only by himself. To find out what man is and who God is, one can only go to Scripture. Faith in the self-attesting Christ of the Scriptures is the beginning, not the conclusion, of wisdom!"[16]

Van Til's distinctive and crucial "Copernican revolution" in apologetics is to insist that the apologete cannot appeal to a different authority than the preacher. The apologete, too, is a minister of the Word of God. Not only does the Christian apologete stand under the Word; he insists that a creature of God can stand nowhere else. God is God; Christ is God the Son; Scripture is his testimony. No less than the preacher, the apologete declares, "Hear the Word of the Lord!"

This is not to deny to the apologete a distinctive task as a minister of the Word. He must serve his fellow preachers and the whole Christian community by reminding them of the breadth and depth of God's revelation in all his works of creation and providence. He must understand the structures of thought that men have raised, and are now raising against the authority of God's Word. He is a coach who must know the strategy of the adversary's offense so that defensive plays can be better coordinated. He must also study the defense of the world against the gospel so that he can send in signals to penetrate the gaps and confusion of the secular mind. Van Til prefers military metaphors (with scriptural precedent!). He pictures apologetics as a messenger boy, running from one divisional headquarters to another, keeping the divisions of theology in touch with the whole front. But he also compares apologetics to the artillery, laying down a barrage over the advancing troops.

---

[15]Ibid., 15.

[16]Ibid.

These metaphors may not contribute to the clarity that apologetics is in business to promote. But the main point is certainly clear. Apologetics cannot be separated from theology anymore than it can be separated from Christ or the gospel. No matter how great the philosophical expertise of the apologist, he is of necessity first of all a minister of God's Word.

Van Til, then, is not simply a philosopher with a heart for preaching. Indeed, he is not merely a theologian with a heart for preaching. He is a preacher, concerned to begin where a preacher begins, with the authority of God's own revelation, and to do what a preacher does, confront unbelief and nourish faith with "thus saith the Lord." In all his apologetic labors he continually stands with the Apostle on Mars Hill, not debating the probability of God's existence, but proclaiming the Creator God who holds all men accountable before the judgment of the risen Christ.

If indeed Van Til's apologetic is the consistent outworking of the stance of the Reformed preacher, what should the preacher learn from Van Til? Conceivably a preacher might reply: "Very little. Real preachers have always been Van Tillian. It is the theologians and philosophers that have been off base. Just as an Arminian becomes a Calvinist as soon as he starts to pray, so an evidentialist becomes a presuppositionalist as soon as he proclaims the Word of God."

While we may well admonish that preacher for arrogance, we may also concede that he has a point. Van Til has labored to bring the awareness of the *pou stō* of the preacher into apologetic reasoning. The minister of the Word who addresses men in the name of the Lord and bids them hearken to the Word of Christ, that minister will win the warm approval of Cornelius Van Til.

Yet preaching, too, needs to be reminded of its ground and its scope. Van Til calls the preacher to proclaim the Word of the Lord, and to do so in a world where Christ is Lord. At least three important consequences should be drawn for preaching. They are not novelties for Reformed homiletics, but Van Til has deepened our understanding of them. They are: first, that preaching must be God-centered; second, that God-centered preaching will be Christ-centered; and, finally, that such preaching will be rich in applied content. That is, the riches of special revelation will be grasped in the context of the general revelation of God that Scripture interprets.

First, then, Reformed preaching, like Reformed apologetics, must be God-centered. Given the form and the content of the Scriptures, we might ask how preaching can be anything else. "In the beginning God . . ." does not introduce a book that features heroes of the absurd, wizards of technology, or politicians of progress. The Bible is not only from God; it is about God. From start to finish the Bible tells us of the works of the Lord to the glory of the name of the Lord.

Today the people who still think it worthwhile to advise preachers demand preaching that is relevant and relational. The relations they are concerned about, however, are not their relations to God, but to their spouses, their children, and possibly their neighbors. When they ask for relevance they often mean sermons to support their personal goals or party prejudices.[17] Let the preacher tell them how to manage their time, or perhaps their investments; let him support unilateral disarmament or military build-up. The partisans of the political left may tolerate preaching if it "conscientizes" peasants and workers until their discontent will fuel revolution. The fascist right will support preaching that gives religious sanctions to nationalist myths and preserves the privileges of class and wealth.

The error in these demands is not necessarily in one or another of the causes the preacher is asked to espouse. It is rather a question of the starting point. If we begin with our own analysis of our situation and our needs, then assume that God is on our side, we commit the fundamental error that Van Til exposes. Preaching cannot be God-centered in the *second* place. The OT shows the sin of religion and prophecy that does not begin with God. Jeroboam was the first king of the ten tribes of Israel after the division of Solomon's kingdom. To establish political unity he decided that Israel needed its own cultus. Political loyalty might be eroded if Israelites traveled to the feasts in Jerusalem. Jeroboam therefore made two golden calves to provide a national religion. He claimed identity for this cult with the God of the exodus. He chose his own priests, his own festival "in the month which he had devised of his own heart" (1 Kgs 12:33). He built his own altar, and stood there to sacrifice as his own priest. His imaginative contextualization of worship may have seemed politically astute, but the prophet from Judah with God's Word cursed Jeroboam's altar, and the sin of Jeroboam became the very archetype of the apostasy that God judged.

The worship that responds to God's revelation is very different

[17]See "Joshua's Appeal for Covenant Consciousness," in Cornelius Van Til, *The God of Hope*, 51.

from the willful worship of our own devising. The preacher who would go in God's name must be sent from the throne-room of God's temple on high. In his ears there rings the sanctus of the angels' worship. The preacher stands before the throne of God even as he stands in the assembly of God's people. He does not merely preach to men; he praises God. Paul describes the church as those who call upon the name of the Lord (1 Cor 1:1). He describes his own ministry in the gospel as an offering of praise, bringing to God the worship of the Gentiles, who sing to his name (Rom 15:8–17). The preacher calls upon the church to hallow the name of God in adoration. But more than that, his message lifts up the name of God. No wonder Paul so easily moves from exhortation to doxology.

God-centered preaching praises God the Creator. In the language of the Psalms it proclaims, "The Mighty One, God, Jehovah, hath spoken, and called the earth from the rising of the sun unto the going down thereof" (Ps 50:1). But the Creator God reveals himself in Scripture as the Covenant God, the God of salvation. When Paul writes, "For of him, and through him, and unto him, are all things" (Rom 11:36), he has especially in view the wonder of God's saving work. God's thoughts are not our thoughts, nor his ways our ways. Saul the Pharisee had violently rejected God's plan of salvation, but now Paul the Apostle perceives that what was foolish and offensive to his Jewish pride was the wisdom of God that passes all understanding. Salvation is *of* God; he is the Author, his love is the source, his plan is the rationale. Salvation is *through* God; the Lord himself accomplishes our redemption. Our lost condition was irretrievable. Not only was doom pronounced upon the nations that knew not God; the curse fell also on guilty Israel. The name of Israel was no longer Ammi, "my people," but Lo-ammi, "not my people." Israel's hope was cut off, scattered like dry bones on the floor of the valley of death (Ezekiel 37).

Only God could remedy that condition. Only God's Spirit could bring resurrection life to the dry bones, only God's power could remove the heart of stone from disobedient Israel and give them a heart of flesh. Only God can save because only God can keep his promises. He promises not only restoration but renewal; not just a land for his people, but a new heavens and a new earth; not just deliverance from their enemies, but forgiveness of their sins (Isa 65:17; Mic 7:18–20).

Yes, God himself must come to be the Savior of his people. He puts on his breastplate of righteousness and his helmet of salvation and comes to fight for them in the battle that will set them free (Isa 59:16–19). He takes his shepherd's rod and staff and comes to seek and to save the lost sheep of his flock (Ezek 34:11–16). When he comes to gather his own, he will bring in a remnant from the nations, other sheep "not of this fold," gathered to the one Shepherd.

The God of the Bible is a sovereign Savior. Jonah, delivered from the abyss of death, lives to cry, "Salvation is of the Lord!" (Jonah 2:9). Salvation is of him, and through him, and therefore unto him. The glory and praise are his forever.

God-centered preaching is always Christ-centered. How does God come to save? Zechariah describes the glory of that day of salvation. Every pot in Jerusalem will be like a bowl at the altar. The bridles of the horses will carry the inscription of the high priest's tiara, "Holiness to the Lord" (Zech 14:20). The weakest inhabitant of Jerusalem will be like King David. And whom will the king be like? Like the angel of God: Immanuel, God with us (Zech 12:8; Isa 7:14). God comes in the incarnation. Jesus is not only the Lord's Christ (Luke 2:26); he is Christ the Lord (Luke 2:11).

Cornelius Van Til makes his starting point the fullness of God's revelation: the self-attesting Son of God, the Christ of Scripture. Van Til calls us to preach Jesus Christ from all the Scriptures. The biblical theology of Geerhardus Vos had a permanent influence on the thought and preaching of Dr. Van Til. One evidence of this is his understanding of the progressive history of redemption. He sees the war between the seed of the serpent and the Seed of the woman as it lies behind the biblical history. He sees this war, however, in the setting of the fulfillment of the promises of God. When Van Til preaches on an OT text, he stresses the faith of the OT saints, the hope that would be in vain if it were not hope in Christ. Speaking of the mound of stones erected by Joshua as a memorial of God's bringing Israel through the Jordan, Van Til describes it as a monument to sovereign grace. It therefore points to the future

> if possible even more so than to the past. Abraham believed God and it was counted unto him for righteousness. They that are of faith are the children of Abraham and are blessed with faithful Abraham. None of us can be saved by the law. For it is written, "Cursed is every one that continueth not in all things which are written in the book of the law to do them" (Gal 3:10). "Christ hath redeemed us from the curse of the

> law, being made a curse for us: for it is written, Cursed is every one that hangeth on a tree; that the blessing of Abraham might come on the Gentiles through Jesus Christ; that we might receive the promise of the Spirit through faith" (Gal 3:13).[18]

In that sermon Van Til gives eloquent expression to the sovereignty of God in redeeming his people and in fulfilling his promises. Joshua as an old man reminds the people of that sovereign grace. But then he calls upon them to choose this day whom they will serve, God or the idols. At the same time, he warns them that they cannot serve God: "Ye cannot serve the Lord: for he is an holy God; he will not forgive your trespasses and your sins" (Josh 24:19).

Van Til continues, "At the conclusion the people promised to serve the Lord even though it was, as Joshua said, *impossible* for them to do so. How else could they do it unless with Joshua they saw the Star of Jacob arising in the coming day?"[19] The covenant consciousness to which Joshua summons Israel is a consciousness of hope in Christ's coming.

For Van Til Christ is to be preached from the whole Bible. The Word of the Lord and the Lord of the Word can never be separated, far less set against each other. The Bible cannot be understood or preached without perceiving that its history of redemption and revelation focuses on Christ. Indeed, Van Til asserts with the Apostle Peter that the whole Bible comes from Christ. The OT prophets searched diligently the meaning of his salvation; they "prophesied of the grace that should come unto you: searching what time or what manner of time the Spirit of Christ which was in them did point unto, when it testified beforehand the sufferings of Christ, and the glories that should follow them" (1 Pet 1:10, 11).

Van Til would have the preacher proclaim not an imaginary Christ, but the Christ of Scripture. In so doing it will never occur to a Reformed preacher to think of the Bible as a dead book in contrast to a living Lord. The Book is living, for the words of Christ are given him of the Father, they are spirit and life (John 6:63). For Van Til the preacher, the Word he handles is always a personal message from the living Lord, his hope in life and death.

---

[18]Ibid., 43.

[19]Ibid., 46-47.

Finally, the *fullness* of revelation in Scripture is also emphasized by Van Til and has deep significance for preaching. Van Til recognizes the mystery and wonder of God's plan of redemption and of his words of revelation. He always emphasizes that God's ways are mysterious to us, but not to him. Van Til counterattacks the rationalistic skeptics who would destroy the Christian's faith by pointing out paradoxes in Christian theology. In the sermon just referred to, Van Til speaks of "the supposed contradiction between a God who must give man all, even his desire to choose for Christ, and the responsibility of man."[20] Van Til himself, in that same sermon, had made that contrast strong. God makes his saving covenant with Israel yet Joshua calls on them to choose the Lord and serve him or face destruction. But this seeming contradiction did not seem to trouble Machen, Luther, Calvin, Augustine, or Paul. Why not? Van Til answers: the "contradiction" is on the other side. They who deny the sovereignty of the living God in the name of freedom lose the freedom they seek. "They seek the freedom in a universe of chance which is supposed somehow to submit to an order imposed upon it by man whose logical powers have themselves sprung from chance."[21]

The Christian can joyfully recognize mysteries that surpass his understanding in the counsels of God. But the creature who denies his Creator finds not merely mystery but meaninglessness: contradiction and paradox unresolved and unresolvable.

The reverent acceptance of mystery must mark the preacher of God's Word. As Van Til insists, this is not a crippling handicap, but a liberating blessing. The preacher is free to present the emphases of Scripture as they are revealed by the Spirit. He does not fear to preach human responsibility as well as divine sovereignty. He will not shy away from the precious truths of the love of God because he fears that he may be qualifying the immutability of God's being.

Is God "a Spirit, infinite, eternal, and unchangeable, in his being, wisdom, power, holiness, justice, goodness, and truth"?[22] Then how can we preach that God the Father paid the price of love when he gave his only-begotten Son, his eternal Son, by sending him into the world and to the cross? How can we appreciate the fact that unlike Abraham, who was permitted to spare the beloved, the heav-

---

[20]Ibid., 56.

[21]Ibid., 50.

[22]Westminster Shorter Catechism, Q. 4.

enly Father did not spare his Beloved (Genesis 22; Rom 8:32; 5:8)?

We are tempted at once to do what Van Til refuses to do, to reduce one of the streams of biblical teaching. We may try to set aside the scriptural data summarized in the Catechism. To that end we may reinterpret the proof texts cited, arguing that God's immutability is a "Greek" concept, a philosophical abstraction. God's transcendence is then scaled down to make him more personal, more "human." On the other hand, we may find ourselves inhibited in preaching on John 3:16. Yes, Jesus loved us, and give himself for us (Gal 2:20). Yes, the heavenly Father loves us. But we draw back from saying that the Father paid the price of love. Because we cannot imagine how this could be so, we avoid proclaiming that it is so.

We must not misunderstand Van Til, or our own calling as preachers of God's Word. Van Til is not a dialectical theologian. Much as he appreciates the mysteries that remain for us, much as he would have us preach the whole counsel of God without rationalistic inhibitions, he always rejects the ultimacy of paradox and contradiction. The difficulties that we face in reconciling apparent paradoxes are difficulties due to our sin and our finitude. They are difficulties for us, not for God. When we learn to leave them with God, then they cease to be difficulties for us as well.

Since these apparent contradictions are not real and final contradictions, wisdom as well as reverence is needed in our preaching. On the one hand we must not suppress biblical revelation in order to resolve logical tensions or dilemmas. On the other hand, we must interpret Scripture by Scripture. We must understand biblical teaching in the total context of God's revelation. We dare not isolate a text, interpret it superficially, and carelessly contradict other Scriptures.

Van Til has been accused of being too traditional in theology, of taking his systematic structure too uncritically from the Reformed confessions, and from Bavinck and Warfield. Certainly Van Til's labors have been directed to showing the implications of Reformed theology for the defense of the faith rather than to developing theological formulations. But Van Til's staunch defense of Reformed orthodoxy reveals his commitment to the coherence and harmony of God's revelation. Van Til well knows that the creeds sought to express the harmony of revealed truth and to avoid reducing biblical teaching to logical absurdities. The Bible does not teach that there is one God and in the same sense three Gods. When Van Til wants us to understand that the one God is personal, he is counteracting the error of tritheism, of conceiving of God's "Being" too abstractly, as though it were a generalization, like human nature that can "exist" in three human persons. Through his teaching career he has continually repeated the Chalcedonian formula: "one and the same Christ, Son, Lord, Only-begotten, to be acknowledged in two natures, inconfusedly, unchangeably, indivisibly, inseparably."[23] He has taken particular delight in rolling the Greek adverbs off his tongue: *asynchytōs, atreptōs, adiaretōs, achōristōs.* He has never ridiculed these distinctions as logic-chopping or hair-splitting. To the contrary, he has rejoiced in the care with which they safeguard the doctrine of Christ's full deity, the very doctrine of self-attesting Christ to which he would have apologetics conform.

Van Til has heard men preach nonsense, but he has never advocated it. In practice and principle he has sought wisdom in our handling of the Word of God. The Scriptures may be abused by suppressing teachings that appear to contradict other scriptural doctrines. But the Scriptures may also be abused by preaching that makes contradiction the last word. Van Til is heart and soul a Reformed theologian. He never suggests, for example, that Arminianism and Calvinism are expressions of two streams of biblical thought, and that the Arminian emphasis on human responsibility is as necessary as the Reformed emphasis on divine sovereignty. No, he argues instead that the Arminian denial of God's sovereignty is a denial of the God of the Bible. To make divine sovereignty and human responsibility equally ultimate is to undermine both doctrines in their biblical meaning.

Human responsibility is valid and meaningful only in a universe where God has created man in his own image and holds him accountable for his life as God's image-bearer. Beginning with the Sovereign God we can understand the freedom that he grants to his creatures. But if we begin with autonomous man, our assertion of human sovereignty is already a rebellious denial of God's sovereignty and, indeed, of his existence.

We may, therefore, prize with Van Til the doctrinal guidance of the Reformed confessions and catechisms. We may rejoice in the way that our fathers use Scripture to interpret Scripture and not to set Scripture against Scripture. We may preach the whole counsel of God, not holding back anything profitable for the edification of the saints

---

[23]Philip Schaff, *The Creeds of Christendom* (3 vols.; New York: Harper, reprint 1952), 2.62.

and the conversion of sinners. But we do so with reverence and awe. Faced with the difficulties and contradictions that men may draw from our messages, we stand ready to reply with Paul, "But who are you, O man, to talk back to God? 'Shall what is formed say to him who formed it, "Why did you make me like this?"'" (Rom 9:20 *NIV*).

The wisdom of Reformed preaching is not the wisdom of the world, but "we speak God's wisdom in a mystery" (1 Cor 2:7). That wisdom has been hidden from this world, but revealed to God's apostles in the Spirit. We are not inspired as the apostles were, but the Spirit of inspiration illumines our minds and grants unction to our lips as we, too, seek to combine spiritual truths with spiritual words (1 Cor 2:13).

There is another respect in which Van Til calls us to appreciate the fullness of preaching. Van Til has always stressed God's general revelation as well as his special revelation.[24] This emphasis flows directly from the God-centered theology that is the fountain of Van Til's whole position. His objection to natural theology is not the objection of a pietism that would limit God's revelation to the Bible. Rather, Van Til objects to natural theology because it proposes to build a foundation for theology apart from the Bible. Van Til knows that it is not biblical for us to seek to interpret the works of God apart from the Word of God. Even before the fall the Word of God came to Adam and Eve in the garden. God interpreted in word the meaning of the trees he had planted in the garden. By the Word of God Adam and Eve understood their place and task in the world of God's creation.

Precisely because God does speak to us as Creator and Redeemer we do see all things in the light of his Word. Van Til has been a lifelong crusader for the Christian school movement. He has not just maintained theoretically that we are to interpret creation and history by applying God's interpretation to the world about us. He has labored tirelessly to advance the cause of Christian education in order to do just that.

Reformed preaching desperately needs Van Til's vision at this point. The preacher of the Word who would "reprove, rebuke, exhort with all long-suffering and teaching" (2 Tim 4:2), must understand the world of his hearers, the world to which the whole counsel of God must be preached. To be sure, the wisdom of the whole church

---

[24]John Frame has called attention to this in his remarkable essay cited above.

and not just of the preacher is needed to apply the Word of God to the dismaying complexity of the modern world. A little knowledge can be a dangerous thing if a preacher with a smattering of sociology, political science, or group dynamics begins to pontificate from the pulpit, proclaiming his amateurish notions or prejudices under the mantle of divine truth. The wise preacher will encourage discriminating wisdom on the part of those who daily live and struggle with the ethical issues of politics, biological research, medical procedures, and environmental stewardship. He must learn from them the nature of Christian engagement with the issues that confront us all. Yet he must learn.

Westminster Seminary requires a college or university degree of students because our Presbyterian fathers believed that ministers of the gospel should understand their culture as well as the Word that they sought to proclaim in it. We may lament the near collapse of liberal arts education or we may suspect that its demise is the consequence of the cloistered humanism that produced it. In either case preachers today need the training that only a renewal of Christian study can provide: a reformation that will be also a renaissance. One of the disappointments of Van Til's career was the failure of the Christian university movement in which he was a participant. Those who share his vision must not abandon that dream. Some have taken up the challenge, but much more must be done. Perhaps the approach should be different; certainly the resources Christ has given to his people in Asia, Europe, Africa, and Latin America are essential. The modern communications industry offers new possibilities for the structure of research; perhaps the academic format itself screens out too much to be central in producing the dialogue and work together that will fulfill the dream.

Van Til himself has applied his preaching vigorously to the tragic needs of the church. His major concern has been to confront indifferent Christians with the dreadful peril of apostasy. He preaches the antithesis between truth and error, between Christ and Antichrist. Like Paul in Galatians he warns against false teachers, and pleads with believers not to be deceived.

But while Van Til has applied the antithesis to the situation of the church, he has always taught that we must not stop there. The Reformed preacher must call on men and women to serve the Lord in every area of their lives. They must do so knowing that the battle for truth and holiness goes on in the whole of human culture and history.

Amazingly, however, for all the sweep of his vision of preaching, for all of the crusading fervor with which he storms the citadels of humanistic pride, Van Til never loses his focus on the gospel. The Christ who is Lord of all is the Christ who was crucified. I like to remember a picture in a Westminster Bulletin that showed Cornelius Van Til preaching the gospel in the open air on Wall Street, New York. At an age when most surviving Ph.D.'s would be drowsing over a novel, he was still ready to be a street preacher, a fool for Christ's sake, Cornelius Van Til, V.D.M.

Annotated Bibliography

1. Writings of Van Til

A complete bibliography of Van Til's works, including his articles and book reviews, through 1970, can be found in *Jerusalem and Athens,* pages 492–98. The following bibliography lists his books, syllabi, and more significant articles through 1978, with some comments as to their general content and importance. The abbreviations in parentheses are those used in the footnotes of this book. All books were published by Presbyterian and Reformed Publishing Company in Philadelphia, Pennsylvania; Nutley, New Jersey; or Phillipsburg, New Jersey, unless otherwise indicated.

(M) indicates a class syllabus never published except in mimeographed form. The dates are dates of publication in more or less their current form, but many of the books began as syllabi and were revised over periods of many years. Therefore, there exist versions of some titles from earlier dates than those listed.

Bavinck the Theologian. 1961. A booklet reprinted from *WTJ* 24 (November 1961): 48–64. This is a review article treating *Herman Bavinck als Dogmaticus,* by R. H. Bremmer. I consider it important because it includes Van Til's first written criticism of Dooyeweerd.

The Case for Calvinism (CFC). 1964. See chapter 21. Discusses the three "case" books of L. Harold de Wolf, William Hordern, and Edward J. Carnell.

Christ and the Jews (CJ). 1968. Treats Philo Judaeus and Martin Buber.

Christian Apologetics (CA). 1975. The basic text for Van Til's beginning course in apologetics. Five chapters cover the basics concisely. Still a very good place to begin.

Christianity and Barthianism (CB). 1962. Van Til's second book on Barth and his most impressive work of scholarship.

Christianity and Idealism (CI). 1955. Essays and reviews, some, but not all, on the subject of idealist philosophy. "God and the Absolute" reflects Van Til's doctoral project.

Christianity in Conflict (CC) (M). Issued in segments from 1962 to 1969. Van Til evidently intended this to become a broad history of apologetics. It is rather digressive, including a volume on Dooyeweerd in the midst of the discussion of Scholasticism, for example. But it represents some of his most mature thought on a number of matters.

Christianity in Modern Theology (CMT). 1955. More essays and reviews.

Christian Theistic Ethics (CTETH). 1971. The first part is Van Til's original text for his course on the goal, motive, and standard of Christian ethics. The second half was used in an elective course on modern ethical theories.

Christian-Theistic Evidences (CTEV). 1976. Van Til used this as a text for his upper-class apologetics course. It deals with Butler, Hume, Kant, William Paley, and James Orr. It also develops Van Til's own argument against modern secular science and psychology.

A Christian Theory of Knowledge (CTK). 1969. One of the "must read" books of the Van Til corpus. His best account of self-attesting Scripture. A survey of the history of apologetics, more concise than CC. Treats Scholasticism, Lutheranism, Arminianism, Kuyper, Warfield, some modern evangelical apologists, and modern theology.

Common Grace and the Gospel (CGG). 1972. Van Til's book *Common Grace* is included in this volume, along with six shorter papers on the subject. The "Letter on Common Grace" is the most interesting of the six, being probably the clearest account of Van Til's view of the theistic proofs.

The Confession of 1967 (C67). 1967. Exposes the Barthian theology underlying the new confession adopted by the Presbyterian Church, U.S.A.

The Defense of Christianity and My Credo (DCC). 1971. A brief summary of Van Til's system. If you have RP and JA, you will not need this one, because its material is also included in those volumes. But here you can get the valuable outline and summary, "The Total Picture," without buying JA. (See description of JA.)

The Defense of the Faith (DF1). 1955. This was the first exposition of Van Til's apologetics offered to the general public. It contains much of the material in CA, plus many responses by Van Til to his critics.

The Defense of the Faith (DF2). 1963. This second edition of DF was abridged by removing much of Van Til's response to critics. As a basic introduction to Van Til's thought, it is less concise and less well organized than CA, but it is more complete.

Essays on Christian Education (ECE). 1974. Collects several of Van Til's writings on this subject. Van Til was a strong advocate of Christian schools. This was a natural outcome of his view of the necessity of Christian presuppositions for all human knowledge.

The God of Hope (GH). 1978. Van Til's last book, a collection of sermons and addresses.

The Great Debate Today (GDT). 1971. Deals with a variety of modern theologians, including Pannenberg and Moltmann.

Herman Dooyeweerd and Reformed Apologetics (HDRT). 1972, 1974. This is Van Til's final word on the debate between himself, Dooyeweerd, and Knudsen (see chap. 27). I do not believe it adds much to previous exchanges.

An Introduction to Systematic Theology (IST). 1974. This was the text for Van Til's courses on the doctrine of Scripture and the doctrine of God. It deals with both subjects, plus much epistemology. It deals also with the perspectival interdependence of revelation from God, nature, and man. There is much material here that is not found anywhere else; this is one of the "must read" volumes. In its present form, the book is heavily preoccupied with the Clark controversy.

"Introduction" (IW) to *The Inspiration and Authority of the Bible,* by B. B. Warfield. 1948. Pp. 3–68. This is far more than an introduction to Warfield's great book. This is one of the better expositions of Van Til's distinctive approach, and it places Warfield's view of Scripture over against Scholasticism and neo-orthodoxy.

Is God Dead? (GD). 1966. "Christian atheism" was famous for fifteen minutes or so during the 1960s. Van Til's critique is more powerful than the movement was worth.

Jerusalem and Athens (JA). Edited by E. R. Geehan. 1971. This was a Festschrift for Van Til, including essays by many authors in his honor. Many of the essays are about him, some of them critical of him. Van Til himself presents a summary of his position and adds many replies to the authors' contributions. The opening essay includes "The Total Picture," a four-page outline and summary of his apologetic—certainly his most concise formulation. The essays are of mixed value. Those by Stoker and Dooyeweerd are mainly of interest to people who are interested in Stoker and Dooyeweerd. The essays of Gilbert Weaver, Gordon Lewis, and John W. Montgomery raise significant issues relating to Van Til, but they are, in my opinion, the only ones that do.

"Nature and Scripture" (NS). In *The Infallible Word,* edited by Ned B. Stonehouse and Paul Woolley. 1946; revised, 1967. Van Til's classic discussion of the necessity, authority, clarity, and sufficiency of natural revelation. Also his most concise survey and critique of the history of secular philosophy, Scholasticism, and modern theology.

The New Evangelicalism (M). N.d. (latest citations are dated 1960). Bernard Ramm, Billy Graham's "cooperative evangelism," Carl F. H. Henry, and *Christianity Today.*

The New Hermeneutic (NH). 1974. Ebeling, Fuchs, and others.

The New Modernism (NM). 1946. Van Til's original treatment of Barth and Brunner. Later edition contains more recent articles on Barth.

The New Synthesis Theology of the Netherlands (NST). 1975. The Reformed denomination founded by Kuyper has taken some very liberal turns in recent years. Here Van Til analyzes that development, from Kuyper and Bavinck, through Berkouwer, to the "Cahiers" group.

Notes on Roman Catholicism (NRC) (M). N.d. This is my own title for Van Til's syllabus, since I could find no other. When I was a student, only chapters 3–5 were available. I have never seen chapters 1–2, but I believe that they may have been used in developing the chapters on Küng and von Balthasar in CB. The remaining chapters deal with "Neo-scholasticism," Jacques Maritain's "True Humanism," and "Nature and Grace."

Paul at Athens. Philadelphia: Committee on Christian Education, Orthodox Presbyterian Church, n.d. A treatment of Paul's address at Athens in Acts 17.

The Protestant Doctrine of Scripture (PDS). 1967. Sometimes called "The Doctrine of Scripture." The doctrine of self-attesting Scripture developed over against Roman Catholic, neo-orthodox, and some evangelical views, including those of B. B. Warfield, Gordon Clark, Dewey Beegle, Stuart Hackett, and G. C. Berkouwer. Argues the isolation of the Reformed view.

Psychology of Religion (PR). 1971. Something of an expanded version of the material on the same subject in CTEV, or perhaps that is a condensed version of this. Another sample apologetic against one form of non-Christian thought. I find it interesting, mainly because of the surprising amount of agreement Van Til expresses with the secular psychologists.

The Reformed Pastor and Modern Thought (RP). 1971. Includes the dialogue between Mr. White, Mr. Grey, and Mr. Black, which was left out of the second edition of DF2. Deals also with Scholasticism, Kant, Tillich, other modern theologians.

A Survey of Christian Epistemology (SCE). 1969. This is Van Til's original syllabus, originally called "The Metaphysics of Apologetics," going back to his original lecture course of 1929. Although I chided the Ligonier authors for making nearly exclusive use of this document (see appendix A), I have grown fond of it recently. It is Van Til's most complete argument, one of the least digressive. It is well organized; Van Til even summarizes each chapter at the beginning of the book. More than any other book of Van Til, this gives the reader a sense of his deep understanding of the history of philosophy. The last chapter is an excellent summary of his apologetic approach.

The Theology of James Daane (TJD). 1959. Puts Daane's objections to Van Til's *Common Grace* into the context of modern theological discussion.

The Triumph of Grace: The Heidelberg Catechism (TG). Vol. 1. N.d. (my copy was made in 1958). Van Til evidently did not get beyond vol. 1 in this projected series contrasting the Heidelberg Catechism with modern theology. Includes his fullest treatments of Schleiermacher and Ritschl, and several chapters on Barth.

Who Do You Say That I Am? (WSA). 1975. One of Van Til's fuller critiques of the history of philosophy, Scholastic theology, and modern thought.

Why I Believe in God. Philadelphia: Committee on Christian Education, Orthodox Presbyterian Church, n.d. A model of Van Tillian apologetic argumentation. This is Van Til's best writing, and the only thing he wrote directed to an unbelieving reader. See my discussion in chapter 24. The booklet is not perfect, but it deserves a much wider circulation. It is a "must" for anyone interested in Van Til.

2. Writings of Other Authors

This list is rather selective, including only those titles which I consider especially significant or in some other way deserving comment.

Bahnsen, Greg. *A Biblical Introduction to Apologetics*. Sun City, Ariz.: Covenant Tape Ministry. A syllabus. Many biblical references on matters of apologetic importance. Valuable work.

_______. "Machen, Van Til, and the Apologetical Tradition of the OPC." In *Pressing Toward the Mark,* ed. Charles Dennison. Philadelphia: Committee for the Historian of the Orthodox Presbyterian Church, 1986. A very interesting essay showing that J. Gresham Machen, who had deeply imbibed the traditional apologetic of Old Princeton, moved significantly in the direction of a Van Tillian presuppositionalism. Or was Van Til moved toward his distinctive view partly by Machen's antithetical mentality? Or is it possible that Old Princeton's apologetic was not as far from presuppositionalism as Van Til believed? Much food for thought here.

Berkouwer, G. C. *The Triumph of Grace in the Theology of Karl Barth*. Grand Rapids: Eerdmans, 1956. In the appendix, "The Problem of Interpretation," Berkouwer differs sharply with Van Til's critique of Barth.

Crampton, W. Gary. "Why I Am Not a Van Tillian." *The Trinity Review* 103 (September 1993): 1–4. Just as Robbins (see below) mimics Clark, so Crampton mimics Robbins. The difference between Robbins and Crampton is that Crampton has the training to know better. This paper is not worthy of him.

Daane, J. *A Theology of Grace*. Grand Rapids: Eerdmans, 1954. See chapter 16.

Dennison, William. *Paul's Two-Age Construction and Apologetics*. Lanham, Md.: University Press of America, 1985. Outlines the Pauline understanding of the "present age" and the "age to come," and draws some inferences favorable to Van Tillian apologetics. I confess that I have not been able to follow the logic of this argument, beyond the obvious fact that the opposition of the two ages justifies antithetical thinking.

Frame, John M. *Apologetics to the Glory of God.* Phillipsburg, N.J.: Presbyterian and Reformed, 1994. Formulates an apologetic methodology; discusses the existence of God and the problem of evil.

_______. "Cornelius Van Til." In *Handbook of Evangelical Theologians,* ed. Walter Elwell. Grand Rapids: Baker, 1993.

_______. *Doctrine of the Knowledge of God.* Phillipsburg, N.J.: Presbyterian and Reformed, 1987. Attempts to develop a biblical theory of knowledge on a Van Tillian model.

_______. Letters exchanged with William White and William Dennison. In *Journey,* March–April, 1988, pp. 9–11; May–June, 1988, p. 13; July–October, 1988, pp. 45–46; January–February, 1989, pp. 14–15, 22–23. I mention these exchanges as the clearest display of the movement mentality among Van Tillians.

_______. Review of *Van Til: Defender of the Faith,* by William White. In *WTJ* 42 (Fall 1979): 198–203.

_______. *Van Til: The Theologian.* Phillipsburg, N.J.: Harmony Press, 1976. Pamphlet. See chapters 12–14.

Halsey, Jim. *For a Time Such as This.* Nutley, N.J.: Presbyterian and Reformed, 1976. When Halsey wrote this book, he was a movement Van Tillian, advocating the kind of extreme antithesis that I have criticized in chapter 15. I find the book confusing. See my references to Halsey in DKG.

_______. "A Preliminary Critique of *Van Til: The Theologian.*" *WTJ* 39 (Fall 1976): 120–36. More of the same, in critique of my VTT.

Knudsen, Robert D. "Crosscurrents." *WTJ* 35 (Spring 1973): 303–14. See chapter 27.

Lewis, Gordon R. *Testing Christianity's Truth Claims.* Chicago: Moody Press, 1976. One critical chapter on "The Biblical Authoritarianism of Cornelius Van Til"; four favorable chapters on Edward J. Carnell.

Marston, G. *The Voice of Authority.* Vallecito, Calif.: Ross House Books, 1978; first published in 1960. The simplest of the simplifications of Van Til.

North, Gary. *Dominion and Common Grace.* Tyler, Tex.: Institute for Christian Economics, 1987. See chapter 16.

_______. *Westminster's Confession: The Abandonment of Van Til's Legacy.*

Tyler, Tex.: Institute for Christian Economics, 1991. See chapter 28.

Notaro, Thom. *Van Til and the Use of Evidence*. Phillipsburg, N.J.: Presbyterian and Reformed, 1980. An excellent treatment of the issue described in the title.

Oliphint, Scott. *The Consistency of Van Til's Methodology*. Scarsdale, N.Y.: Westminster Discount Book Service, n.d. Pamphlet.

________. *Van Til and the Reformation of Apologetics*. Scarsdale, N.Y.: Westminster Discount Book Service, n.d. Oliphint's pamphlets are sound accounts of Van Til's work, well documented and well argued.

Pratt, Richard. *Every Thought Captive*. Phillipsburg, N.J.: Presbyterian and Reformed, 1979. The best popularization of Van Til's apologetics—suitable for young people.

Robbins, John. *Cornelius Van Til: The Man and the Myth*. Jefferson, Md.: Trinity Foundation, 1986. Pamphlet. I consider Robbins incompetent as an interpreter and critic of Van Til.

Rushdoony, Rousas J. *By What Standard?* Philadelphia: Presbyterian and Reformed, 1959. One of the first broad treatments of Van Til's work. Not a critical analysis, but well done. See chapter 28.

Vickers, D. *Cornelius Van Til and the Theologian's Theological Stance*. Wilmington, Del.: Cross Publishing, n.d. (probably about 1976). Vickers is a prominent Australian economist. He is fond of Van Til's work and accurate in his account of it, but not at all critical, nor particulary illuminating.

White, William. *Van Til: Defender of the Faith*. Nashville: Thomas Nelson, 1979. See my comments in chapter 1.

Index of Names

Index of Subjects

John M. Frame (A.B., Princeton University; B.D., Westminster Theological Seminary; A.M. and M.Phil., Yale University) is professor of systematic theology and philosophy at Reformed Theological Seminary, Orlando campus. He previously taught at Westminster Theological Seminary (Philadelphia) and Westminster Theological Seminary in California. He has written widely in the areas of theology, apologetics, ethics, and worship, including *The Doctrine of the Knowledge of God* and *The Doctrine of God* in the Theology of Lordship series, and *Apologetics to the Glory of God* and *No Other God: A Response to Open Theism.*